ECONOMICS OF GLOBALISATION

Economics of Globalisation

Edited by

PARTHA GANGOPADHYAY
University of Western Sydney, Australia

MANAS CHATTERJI
The State University of New York at Binghamton, USA

ASHGATE

Published by
Ashgate Publishing Limited
Gower House
Croft Road
Aldershot
Hants GU11 3HR
England

Ashgate Publishing Company
Suite 420
101 Cherry Street
Burlington, VT 05401-4405
USA

Ashgate website: http://www.ashgate.com

British Library Cataloguing in Publication Data
Economics of globalisation
    1.Globalisation - Economic aspects
    I.Gangopadhyay, Partha II.Chatterji, Manas, 1937-
    337

Library of Congress Control No: 2005931456

ISBN 0 7546 4137 6

Printed and bound in Great Britain by MPG Books Ltd, Bodmin, Cornwall.

Contents

List of Figures

List of Tables

List of Contributors

Kenneth Arrow, Stanford University, USA
Åke E. Andersson, Institute of Future Studies, Royal Institute of Technology,
    Sweden
David E. Andersson, Institute of Future Studies, Royal Institute of Technology,
    Sweden
Iwan J. Azis, Cornell University, USA
Subhayu Bandyopadhyay, West Virginia University, USA
Sudeshna C. Bandyopadhyay, West Virginia University, USA
Debasis Bandyopadhyay, University of Auckland, New Zealand
Fernando Barreiro-Pereira, National University of Distance Learning, Spain
Riccardo Cappelin, University of Rome, Italy
Manas Chatterji, Binghamton University, USA
David Colander, Middlebury College, USA
Prabal Ray Chaudhuri, Indian Statistical Institute, India
Richard Damania, University of Adelaide, Australia
Amitava Krishna Dutt, University of Notre Dame, USA
Peter Forsyth, Monash University, Australia
Partha Gangopadhyay, University of Western Sydney, Australia
Robert Grant, Georgetown University, USA
Michael Intriligator, University of California, Los Angeles, USA
Murray C. Kemp, University of New South Wales and Macquarie University,
    Australia
Tapani Köppä, University of Helsinki, Finland
Paul Krugman, Princeton University, USA
Keith Lehrer, York University, UK
Sugata Marjit, Centre for Studies in Social Sciences, Calcutta, India
Francisco Mochón, National University of Distance Learning, Spain
Arijit Mukherjee, University of Nottingham, UK
Peter Nijkamp, Free University, The Netherlands
Jeffrey Sachs, the Earth Institute, Columbia University, USA
Sarbajit Sengupta, Viswa Bharati University, India
Uday Bhanu Sinha, Indian Statistical Institute, Delhi School of Economics, India
Luc Soenen, California Polytechnic University, USA
Hadewijch van Delft, Free University, The Netherlands
Danielle van Veen-Groot, Free University, The Netherlands
Neil Warren, University of New South Wales, Australia

Foreword :

Globalisation and Its Implications for International Security

Kenneth J. Arrow

F02

F50

Everyone talks about 'globalisation' and the word has become a byword for an economic imperative on the one hand and a synonym for undermining local cultures and exploiting Third World labour on the other. In France, a man becomes a hero for burning down a McDonald's; in Seattle, Washington, and Prague, self-righteous demonstrators show true dedication by trying to shut down the workings of the institutions that implement globalism.

Let me try to present a quick overview of globalisation as I see it, with some historical background, some remarks on the growing institutional infrastructure, and some implications for the preservation of international security. It is useful, even if elementary, to classify the different aspects of globalisation.

We may distinguish at least five: the increase in international trade, capital movements, migration of people, migration of exotic biota; including pathogens, and the diffusion and possible homogenisation of culture and ideas of all kinds. At the same time, international institutions have evolved to encourage these broad movements and to the problems they create.

Why the pace of globalisation has been stepped up is hardly a mystery. Just as in the past, the fall in the costs of communication and transportation have been decisive. To be sure, some of its effects can be offset by adverse nationalistic policies, but I think it is clear that very cheap speedy information and less expensive and faster transportation have been the major factors as they have been throughout history. Only the nationalism and isolationism of the interwar period seriously retarded globalisation.

I will write briefly about the present state of the different aspects of globalisation, as outlined above; they are familiar to any informed audience. The great increase of international trade relative to world income is most well known. Specialisation has increased along the lines that economic theory would predict. There are of course disruptions as well as gains, the production of such commodities as textiles, computers and television sets has moved offshore from the United States, restraining inflation, permitting real economic growth, and stimulating economic development abroad, while imposing costs on some elements of the labour force.

Capital movements have been more troublesome in some ways. Indeed, capital markets in general, domestic as well as foreign, are always more unstable, for reasons. But it is hard to deny that foreign investment has in general been good for labour and capital in developing countries and at least for the rich, if not the poor, in developed countries.

The economic effects of increased migration are in many ways more troublesome. Economic growth and falling birthrates have created a demand for labour in developed countries. The problems faced by the European countries are in many ways greater than ours. Their birthrates are even lower, and they have higher unemployment. The proportion of immigrants in the population is higher in France and Switzerland than in the United States, and the relative tolerance for diversity derived from our history is much weaker.

Immigration is not inevitable. Japan has shown that even a virtual ban on immigration is compatible with rapid economic growth, if not with generosity towards the deprived. It would take too long to comment in detail on possible changes in United States immigration policy, but I do believe we can make life better for ourselves and particularly for the poor by suitable changes.

The migration of alien species, including pathogens, has many consequences, even apart from the spread of diseases such as AIDS. The introduction of alien species without local predators has in many cases led to a loss of biodiversity.

Finally, what can be said about the global diffusion of ideas and culture? They are indeed partly connected with foreign investment, which helps introduce both new technologies and new management styles. But most cultural diffusion is independent of investment. McDonald's spreads by franchising; its restaurants are patronised by French and Italians. It is not the only example of culinary globalisation. A visitor anywhere in Europe cannot help notice the Irish pubs. With regard to languages, English has indeed become the business norm. But languages with few speakers are headed for extinction everywhere. It is estimated that of the 6,000 languages currently spoken, only 600 will survive the next century.

I turn from the present state of globalisation to some historical remarks. It is true, though perhaps surprising to some, that all these aspects of globalisation have historical precedent. Careful studies in recent years have shown that today's trade and capital movement are no bigger in proportion to world income than they were in the thirty years preceding World War I. It is the interwar period that is exceptional. Many of today's problems also existed then. Great Britain dominated international trade, but, unlike the United States today, it was also a great exporter of capital, financing the railroads of the United States and Argentina. If anything, today's foreign investment is more directed to developing countries and less to countries.

Instability in foreign capital markets is indeed an ancient phenomenon. As early as 1300, the leading banking firm of Florence, the New York or London of its day, was forced into bankruptcy by the loan default of the ruler of a relatively backward country, King Edward I of England. This was at a time when Florence was effectively further from England than any two spots on the face of the Earth are today, further in time than the Moon. The English and the Dutch lost money in United States railroad investments and even in defaults by states. Gunboats and military intervention were powerful methods of debt collection against weaker countries, leading for example to French intervention in Mexico and, more successfully, to British control of Egypt.

International cultural globalisation has even more precedents. McDonald's is much like the omnipresent Chinese restaurant or the introduction of pizza in the United States. For even earlier episodes, try to think of Italian cuisine before the tomato or Szechuan or Indian cooking before the chilli pepper, both imports from the New World. What more remarkable cultural diffusions can we think of than the worldwide spread of an obscure Semitic religion called Christianity from a backward corner of the Roman Empire or, 650 years later, the also worldwide spread of another Semitic religion, Islam, from the impoverished deserts of Arabia, though indeed Islam remained closer to its origin?

As for disease and the spread of biota, they are also of long standing. Bubonic plague, syphilis, and smallpox are but a few of the diseases that have spread across nations and continents during periods of much less intensive globalisation.

Let me turn briefly to the development of an institutional infrastructure for globalisation. Institutions, in the sense of standing visible organisations, with headquarters and some staff, have been around for at least a century, with the International Postal Union and the international agreements on patents and copyrights. After World War I, we had the League of Nations, the International Labour Organization, and the Permanent Court of International Justice. But there was a great proliferation after World War II, the United Nations and its associated agencies, the World Bank, the International Monetary Fund, and the trade agreements which led up to the World Trade Organization. There were also many regional organisations, such as the Organization of American States, but the most remarkable of this type is certainly the European Union.

I have no time to discuss these institutions in any detail. I want to call attention to a common feature. They are all far removed from democratic control. There is of course an ultimate responsibility to the member-states, which are, for the most part democracies, but there is a good deal of autonomy. Even the European Union, which is closest to a classical state, locates its parliament far from the seat of administrative power where the important decisions are made. An extreme case is the European Central Bank, a monetary authority with no parallel political authority.

There are good reasons in terms of efficiency and practicality for this development. But I do not think the long-term implications of the growing importance of responsible agencies have been thought about.

Finally, let me turn to the implications of globalisation for international security, for the maintenance of peace and the avoidance of international conflict in ways that are compatible with justice. On the whole, one would suppose that globalisation furthers world peace. Some have held that cultural differences and misunderstanding are causes of conflict, what Samuel Huntington called, 'the clash of civilisations'. Surely, greater contact should both mitigate differences and permit greater understanding of others. The economic links should also be important. If nothing else, they create vested interests, mutually profitable relations that would suffer in case of war. One doesn't have to subscribe to a purely economic interpretation of history to believe that the interests in trade and foreign capital, either as lender or borrower, should at least weigh in the scale against war.

The history I have sketched is not kind to such optimism. What I have said may relax some fears as to the novelty of globalisation, but we also remember that the previous age of globalisation, the late nineteenth and early twentieth centuries, culminated in World War I. World War I was indeed economically destructive, breaking up long profitable ties, just as would have been and indeed was predicted at the time. But the potential destruction of economic links and those of the cultural connections at least within Europe had no force against nationalism. Even more there was in the Europe of 1914 a political movement of apparently considerable power committed against nationalism. I refer to the international socialist movement. The opposition of the individual national parties against war vanished like smoke. We lack anything corresponding today.

It may be, though, that the pressures toward globalisation already reflect an attenuation of the kind of nationalism that makes war so acceptable. Certainly, whatever may be said about the European Union, the probability that two of its members will go to war must be regarded as negligible. No one in 1914 could have made that statement, nor indeed anyone up to World War II. The world's greatest military power seems to have the greatest aversion to casualties. Its military leadership combines an insatiable demand for more weapons with an equal aversion to their use.

I offer this tentative optimism. It is not so much globalisation as the factors encouraging it that may well signal a reduction in the possibility of international armed conflict.

Book Title:

Preface :

The Asian Crisis

Jeffrey Sachs

The economic development of the Pacific region in the aftermath of the sharp crisis of 1997 is a very important and complex topic. The Asian crisis unfolded three years ago: it exploded in Thailand and then quickly spread to the region. My interpretation of what has happened in Asia and based on that interpretation how I think events will unfold there in future. Pacific Asia was the fastest growing region for two decades, with astounding performances years after years in Korea, Taiwan, East Asia and Southeast Asia. You had a region that the rest of the world was trying to emulate – a region that seemed to have figured out the elixir of rapid and steady economic growth. The region seemed to have collapsed all of a sudden and evaporated precisely on 2 July 1997 when the Thai baht was devalued and the devaluation baht initiated a generalised financial crisis that spread from Thailand to Indonesia and then engulfed Singapore, Korea, Hong Kong and Malaysia. Australia and New Zealand got caught up in this crisis as the major trading countries of this region. China and Japan, two of other giants of the region got also involved. Fortunately China did not experience the outright collapse like other developing countries. Japan has posed a question mark for much of the decade since it has not achieved significant growth since the beginning of the 1990s. The first puzzle for us is why is it that a region that was doing so well for more than a decade experienced such a sharp crisis with the devaluation of baht? Several kinds of explanations are offered since the onset of the crisis, but I would like to do my own bit of diagnosis to assess which of the explanations makes sense; which ones are really partial; how to get an overall picture about it. It is hard to understand without a clear picture: where is Asia heading in the near future?

When the Asian crisis broke out, the US government and the official international agencies located in Washington quickly jumped in with an explanation. The explanation came under the heading 'Crony capitalism of Asia'. Suddenly these economies that had been praised year in and year out for doing so very well in economic performance were attacked as really being poorly organised, seething with corruption, prone to cronyism rather than real market transactions. Washington said that Asia collapsed because it was not fit to continue to grow. The IMF was sent to Asia with the mandate to clean up these economies:

* get their banking system in order and improve corporate governance;
* get these economies oriented more like the USA and then growth will resume.

Now there was of course an element of truth in many of these assertions by the Washington community. But something was very odd about the explanation, because here are countries, which are praised year in and year out as the miracle economies and suddenly they are under heated attacks. The explanation does not make much sense to me and seemed to me like an ex post rationalisation of the crises rather than a good explanation of what happened. So my way of thinking about this is that what we saw in Asia was not a result of the sins of the Asian economies; but had a lot more to do with the structure and operations of the global economic system as a whole. In particular, when you look at the Asian countries, the thing you notice about them was that they were extremely highly regarded by the international investment community almost until the moment of collapse. They were not the pariah countries shunned for their corruption and mismanagement. These were the economies which because of their economic success attracted a considerable amount of interest from international investors. One class of international investors stands out the most, that is, international banks from Japan, Western Europe, USA that make extensive cross-border loans to emerging markets. Now if you look at the map of emerging markets of Asia, five countries, particularly, were badly hit by the crisis namely Indonesia, Korea, Malaysia, the Philippines and Thailand. These five countries were so well regarded that they had attracted $274b (US) of cross-border lending up to the crisis. These are the countries, which were so successful so that international bankers were enthusiastically lending the money till July 1997 – now here comes a core part of the explanation of the crisis. If you look at the $274b of loans, about two thirds of the total ($175b) was short-term loans with maturity less than one year, typically seven, thirty and sixty days. These countries were very successful – they could get foreign lending – not only $274b of foreign loans but also short-term lending of $175b. The big danger, it seems to me, is that a system that is based on so much short-term lending is highly volatile that is, prone to, or vulnerable to, very sharp reversals when expectation changes. In East Asia many countries were doing quite well but because of the foreign borrowing from international banks the economies were getting overheated, the real exchange rates were getting too strong causing squeeze on their export base. It does not lead to a crisis, but what happened was that these countries used pegged-exchange rates with the US dollar. Here we have countries bringing in a lot of foreign loans and that was leading to an overheating of domestic economies, rising domestic prices, exchange rate pegged for dollars, exchange rates were getting overvalued in real terms. Investors, both domestic and foreign, started to sense this by the end of 1996 and they started to withdraw some money gradually from these countries in 1997. As they did, the central banks, which were trying to keep the exchange rates pegged intervened in the foreign exchange markets, selling dollars, buying the local currency and thereby stabilising the price of foreign exchange at an overvalued level. If you keep doing that, you run down your foreign exchange reserve level and here is where the crisis unfolds. As of June 1997 those five countries – Indonesia, Malaysia, Korea, Thailand and the Philippines had short-term foreign debts to the international banks of about $175b; but their combined foreign exchange reserves was just about $100b. So, here the international banks had a lot of money exposed in the region and the banks started to realise that foreign exchange reserves in those countries going down sharply. Thailand spent lots of foreign exchange reserves defending its overvalued currency. On 2 July 1997 Thailand said it would devalue because it was running out of reserves and that was a kind of wake up call for the international banks. It told the international banks that it was a lot of short-term debts but the reserve levels in East Asia were quite low. The international banks started to look more closely at exchange rates and realised that exchange rates were pegged to the US dollar but the dollar had strengthened against the yen. So inadvertently, their countries in Asia have appreciated against the yen. The banks started to tell themselves that it was getting a bit dicey. Even though these are pretty good economies with good export base, their currencies are overvalued, their reserves are low and foreign short-term debts to international banks are very large. These bankers started to ask themselves questions: what if other banks started to withdraw their money? What will happen to my loan? It is a pretty simple calculation: the amount of liquid assets that these countries have available to repay the short-term debt is $100b and that is less than the total short-term debt of $175b. The bankers started to reason: suppose everybody tries to get out, there will not be enough assets to cover the short-term debts. So the last ones out will find that their debts are not repaid; they will get their debts into default, or scratched out over time. So the international bankers with the pressure of the devaluation, with the rising concern about overvalued currencies sensed that if other banks would move out of Asia, I would better get out of Asia in the short-run to get my money out … everybody else demands one's money. What happened after 2 July 1999 was truly amazing – the international bankers and other investors started to flee from East Asia cashing in their claims on the East Asian nations. When everybody started to do that; this was like a self-fulfilling prophecy of doom. When everybody was trying to cash in those $175b of short-term debts, there was not enough liquidity around to make the payments. So the rush for the exits raised the sense of panic that even sped up the rush to the exits and soon enough in the fall of 1997 Asia was falling into default on its short-term debts – there was an extreme crisis of illiquidity because there were not enough short-term liquid assets to cover the loans. What had happened to loans? They have been invested in long-term projects, like in downtown Bangkok – very illiquid. What we saw was a self-fulfilling financial panic. The IMF added to the sense of panic when it was sent into Asia. From August 1999 the message to the international community was 'Time to panic' as IMF's rhetoric was quite dramatic – 'The situation is much worse than you think, this is crony capitalism of the worst form'. The IMF underscored its message of doom by instructing these governments to: a) increase interest rates sharply and put the brake on credit; and b) close down insolvent banks suddenly.

All these created a tremendous sense of panic – it led investors to get their money out of Asia. When you see a financial crisis of this sort, the economic outcomes are vastly more exaggerated than what is fundamentally wrong with the real economy. So, however big were the weaknesses in Korea or Thailand that would not justify these economies going from rapid growth to extreme crisis virtually overnight. For that you have to add the concept of panic to understand how Korea went from 8 per cent positive growth to 8 per cent negative growth in one year. How Thailand did that, or how Indonesia went from 8 per cent positive growth to 13 per cent negative growth in 1998. Why was Indonesia the worst case? The panic was the most severe in Indonesia. The way the IMF handled the Indonesian banking system prompted the greatest panic in the entire Pacific Asian region – everybody fled from Indonesian banks starting in November 1997. The bad news is when you panic, exchange rates collapse and interest rates soar, business cannot get working capital and enterprises get into bankruptcy even if they are pretty well managed for the long-term. It is like being without air, being without working capital and Asia went into an extreme downward spiral in 1998. But the interesting thing and the good news is that the financial panics don't go on and on and on. They have an end and their end is kind of built into their process itself. The panic will eventually subside partly because a lot of money is taken out of the economy so that short-term debts are repaid; partly because some of the debts which are not repaid do end up getting stretched out for the long-term. That is what happened with Korea's debt. So with some combinations of repayment of loans, stretching out of loans and default, you actually will reach the end of the panic phase of the rapid withdrawal of money. Also when the exchange rate depreciates so sharply in these crisis-hit countries then the expectation comes that maybe the exchange rate has depreciated so much that it will bounce back. The combination of these two factors, the tail end of panic and the overshooting depreciation of exchange rates, sets the way for a recovery. A recovery is characterised by a strengthening of exchange rate, reduction in interest rate, return of liquidity to the region. This process took place starting in mid-1998 everywhere, Malaysia introduced capital control, yet the recovery was the same everywhere in Asia. We saw reversal of capital outflow in the latter half of 1998 and also witnessed the beginning of capital inflow into the region. The crisis was based more on panic rather than fundamental weaknesses of the region, and the recovery also came faster than that many people thought. Already in 1999 we saw a recovery in Korea and beginning of recovery in Thailand, Malaysia and Indonesia. The end of the panic is followed by a recovery of economic growth. All of this pushes us to ask about the long-term: what is Asia's long-term prospect? If you go with the view that Asia is a mass of corruption and cronyism; you might be pretty pessimistic. My own view is more optimistic than that – I think the Asian crisis was a reflection of problems of the international system. There are many challenges that the Asian countries face that are corporate governance, corruption where Asia will have to work harder. Asia will really need to put a great deal of stress on science, technology and higher education. In the end it is the knowledge economy that will be central for long-term economic development.

Introduction

Economics of Globalisation – Which Way Now?

Manas Chatterji and Partha Gangopadhyay

420

Introduction

Globalisation is a multidimensional concept having various important facets that entail economic, financial, technological and social and political processes, which continually transform the global economy, society and polity. In this book we focus on seven key aspects of globalisation: transborder trade, transborder movement of capital, emergence of a new international order, diffusion and homogenisation of economic cultures and institutions, labour market consequences, governance issues; finally prospects and problems of our global economy and society. The choice of these themes for the book is not fortuitous by any measure, these are rather carefully chosen to illuminate the complex path that globalisation has trod. In the following paragraph we explain the relevance of these themes in a coherent manner.

It is generally recognised that the process of globalisation has been significantly aided by the fall in the costs of communication and transportation that has led to an inevitable shrinkage of our globe into a quasi 'global village' – characterised by an integration typically observed in traditional village communes. We therefore view globalisation as a complex process that gradually unleashes a series of transitions: the process starts off with an increased integration of the world economy through trade and investment networks. It is well understood that the harbinger of this stage of increased integration turns on the pivot of decreasing transaction costs of transborder trade and investment. Declining transactions costs are explained in terms of technical progress that reduces the cost of communication and transport costs. Declining transaction costs have direct and positive impact on cross-border trade and portfolio and direct investment.

The economic consequence of this increased integration is twofold: first, nations become more interdependent in economic terms. Secondly, there arises a *perception* that transborder trade and investment offer tremendous and often unprecedented economic opportunities for a nation. The first transition thus results in an increased integration of the world economy – through a mesh of multinational investment, trade flows and flows of financial capital – with an equally important transition in the *perception* about the importance of transborder trade and investment as a vehicle of economic progress and prosperity for a nation. The second transition impacts on the realm of national management as national governments actively respond to this new perception that transborder trade and investment offer great benefits to those nations that entertain relevant openness to foreign trade and investment. As a number of nations vie and compete against each other to take home the spoils of the world economy, policy makers come to agree that the main barrier to the access of these spoils lies in the domestic economic structure characterised by the labyrinth of controls that has been a by-product of the Keynesian era of deglobalisation. This leads to the third transition that paves the way for homogenisation of economic ideologies, convergence of macroeconomic and trade policies and the consequent adoption of measures of domestic liberalisation. For any national government, options are pretty limited – either it chugs along with the pre-existing regime of economic control with limited global trade as pursued by China and India. Alternatively, the nation must ditch the *olden* economy and substitute it with a functional market mechanism, openness to transborder trade, liberalisation of domestic and external sectors and exchange rates, and privatisation of state-owned enterprises.

The hard fact is that the majority of nations went for the second option that represents an unprecedented *convergence* of economic ideologies during the 1980s and 1990s. This common act of nations, as though to the dictate of a common script, has further consolidated the process of integration of the global economy. The final transition typically takes place in the social and economic spheres of our globe as a direct consequence of these previous transitions. The process of globalisation can thus be reduced to this simple and uncomplicated fable. Within this simple fable highlighting various, possibly virtuous, transitions lies a plethora of terribly complicated subplots without which it is impossible to understand the process and consequences and ramifications of globalisation. This book offers a collection of papers from accomplished scholars to examine these subplots in greater detail. These subplots and their analysis arise in the following schema and thus the plot of this book thickens.

Part A: Economics and Globalisation

First and foremost, we attempt to understand the *potential* and *perceived* gains from transborder trade that seemingly initiates the very first transition towards a global economy. In the common parlance, it is widely held that such benefits are significant and can easily be explained by models of transborder trade. We invited one of the greatest trade theorists to share his research findings. Kemp's short chapter shows how difficult it is to sustain the simplistic notion that all participating nations gain from transborder trade. To put it boldly, the frontier of trade theory does not necessarily endorse the view that free trade is inevitably welfare enhancing even when markets are characterised by atomistic competition. One may thus raise a peevishly simple question of whether the propelling motive of globalisation, that is gains from transborder trade, was an ever-shifting mirage!

Let us not lock our horns over the above question, and move forward. Let us, instead, look at the immediate consequence of these perceived gains from trade: nations after nations have adopted series of liberalisation measures to jockey for a significant positioning in the global economy. We now refer to the second and the third transition paths/processes. How has the world shaped up with these transitions? Krugman forcefully argues that the world has become more *dangerous* and precariously *vulnerable* with these transitions. Financial, economic and currency crises are the price that all of us must pay for the vulnerability of these nations today.

He also suggests necessary policy reforms to redress this vulnerability. In the preface of this book Sachs, on the contrary, argues that the global economy is resilient enough to tide over crises like the Asian crises. He analyses the factors responsible for the Asian crises to examine the robustness of the new world order as driven by these two transitions. Azis, on the other hand, raises a poignant question about the role of international agencies in making the new world order more fragile.

It is anticipated that the above issue is going to raise many more thorny debates in future years about the precise architecture of the world economy and the global financial system. It is beyond doubt that the current global order is influenced, and possibly propelled by, the homogenisation of and the convergence on an economic and social model that citizens of the world have come to treat as a shared and common model. The third over-riding theme of this book, therefore, examines the dynamic process of convergence of ideas, ideologies and policies. Colander highlights the importance of viewing globalisation as a dynamic process. Intriligator examines the costs and benefits of the globalisation process and highlights an ever-increasing role of national and international cooperation to spread the benefits of globalisation. Anderssen and Anderssen argue that the notion of economic and social integration as highlighted by the literature of globalisation is mis-founded whilst they offer an alternative index of integration to shed light on the future prospect of world economy.

The most contentious aspect of globalisation stems from its perceived and actual effects on labour markets that partly emanate from the lack of mobility of labour across borders. Future years will witness more and more debates and a sharpening of discussion, especially, on immigration policy in the context of the lightning pace of capital mobility. To many perceptible observers, this lack of mobility is not only *unjust* but also a major impediment to the future path of globalisation. In this context, we have three challenging contributions: Nijkamp et al. argue that globalisation and mobility of people are intricately interconnected phenomena; globalisation without mobility does not have much significance. The success of globalisation will therefore depend critically on the mobility of labour. The chapter by Dutt examines the labour flows to understand the impact of labour flows on growth and inequality in the global economy. Lehrer argues that the failure to attain equity in the global economy has to be understood in the context of international agencies and their incentives, constraints and failures.

Globalisation is neither the manna from heaven nor does it take place in a vacuum. Globalisation is a product of conscious decision of internationalisation by multinational firms. Once a multinational firm enters a country, the regulatory regime responds to its entry by creating appropriate regulations to minimise social costs and maximise social benefits of multinationalisation in order to avoid crises, instability and over-exploitation of non-renewable resources. In order to entice the entry, or enhance its investment, the nation goes through a series of reforms that makes the nation more market-friendly and less authoritative and the multinational investment become more productive – privately and socially. Globalisation thus entails a detailed process of governance at various levels by MNCs, governments and regulatory agencies that engenders a gradual integration of the global economy. Lehrer in his chapter attempts to analyse the extent to which underlying forces, other than economic ones, need to be addressed in order to explain the duress of low-paid workers in low technology industries worldwide. A value of life approach is used as a start-off point, and is widened into a discussion of the impact of an attenuation of social values, which would otherwise provide social cohesion – as social distance is increased. Cappellin looks at the process of international integration of a multinational firm and, thereby, highlights some of these governance issues. Köppä argues cooperation is the only way to moderate costs of globalisation and balance costs and benefits of globalisation.

Part B: Economic Issues of Globalisation

In this segment we unravel various economic consequences of globalisation, that is, the end game of the aforementioned transitions as outlined in the previous section. In the light of the end game we attempt to take stock of the problems and prospects of globalisation. Forsyth examines the economic ramification of aviation as a globalising force. He puts forward the notion that the aviation industry has failed to be global due to rampant regulations and state-owned airlines. The future path of globalisation will hence be propelled by the liberalisation of the aviation industry. Neil Warren examines the prospects of internet revolution that has further reduced the distance between nations and cultures.

There is no gainsaying the fact that financial markets, capital and stock markets are the transmitter of globalisation and globalisation, in turn, profoundly influences these markets in transitional economies. How does globalisation impinge on these markets that, in turn, drive the economic progress of a nation? Bandyopadhyay contests the conventional wisdom that the pre-condition for economic progress in the current global order is a low share of government in the financial sector of an economy. Grant and Soenen examine the exposure to exchange risks for global business and offer policy prescriptions for such firms. Chapters by Mukherjee, Marjit and Sengupta; Ray Choudhuri and Sinha; Bandyopadhyay and Bandyopadhyay cast a hard look at various aspects of globalisation in the light of models of transborder trade being characterised by market imperfections. They thus attempt to understand the welfare implications of cross-border trade. Damania examines the optimal response of a regulator to enforce a desirable regulatory regime in a globalised economy. In the final chapter Barreiro-Pereira and Mochón argue that a key element of globalisation is increased integration of the international commodity market. Globalisation can therefore be tested by considering some stylised facts of the international commodity markets. These authors utilise the ratio of exports plus imports divided by GDP as a proxy for globalisation. They offer interesting results by looking at the positive effects and the negative disparities coming from globalisation in Spain for twenty-two years.

PART A
ECONOMICS AND
GLOBALISATION

Chapter 1

Economic Development and the Gains from International Trade and Investment

Murray C. Kemp

F10, F02 F21,
F10 F30 F41
O19

Introduction

Among development economists it is commonly believed that, as a general rule, development proceeds at a faster pace and/or at a higher level in open economies than in closed economies. Typically, partial support for this view is derived from the classical gains-from-trade proposition. Any version of proposition must include a clear statement of the sense in which a country as a whole may be said to be 'better off' in one situation (free trade) than in another situation (autarky), and it must include a detailed specification of each trading country. Concerning the first of these requirements, most economists have been prepared to follow Vilfredo Pareto who in 1894 formulated the (non-hypothetical) compensation principle. According to this principle, a country may be said to be better off in a new situation if and only if there is put in place a scheme of domestic lumpsum compensatory transfers such that, after compensation, no individual is worse off and at least one individual is better off. Any demonstration that free trade is beneficial to a particular country must consist of (i) the complete specification of the trading economies and of their schemes of lumpsum compensation and (ii) a proof that the world economy thus specified has an equilibrium defined in terms of market clearance.

In the present chapter I shall focus on (i), devoting very little space to the technical details of proofs; the latter may be found in Kemp (1995, 2001) and in Kemp and Wan (1993). Instead, I shall offer a mildly idiosyncratic history of doctrine, beginning with Montesquieu, pausing briefly to consider the contributions of Smith and Ricardo, then jumping over an arid century and a half to the last thirty years, which have yielded several propositions which collectively have greatly widened the scope of the classical gains-from-trade result. Therefore they are of special interest to development economists.

A Brief History of Doctrine up to 1972

In his *Lettre a un Anglais* Montesquieu discussed what would now be called the welfare implications of international trade. The novelty of the essay laid in its focus on the wellbeing not of the Prince but of the People, that is, the population at large. The central questions concern the sense in which a country may be said to benefit from the opportunity to trade with other countries and the variety of circumstances under which trade is indeed beneficial. As we have noted before, the first of Montesquieu's questions was answered by Pareto only at the end of the nineteenth century, and substantial progress in answering the second question had to wait for eighty years. The best known and most influential contributor, David Ricardo, simply evaded the first of Montesquieu's questions by confining attention to trading countries with homogeneous populations. Other nineteenth century economists (Mill,[1] Edgeworth and Marshall) acknowledged that individuals differ in preferences, endowments and information but failed to come to grips with the implied problem of evaluating a change in trading arrangements. The nineteenth century economists were all influenced by Bentham, but no attempt was made to formulate a gains-from-trade proposition based on utilitarian principles. Nor could such a proposition have been established.

Eventually, in the 1930s, Pareto's message was received in England. Unfortunately, the leading English economists misinterpreted the message as advocating what would now be called the hypothetical compensation principle; see especially the contributions of Hicks (1939) and Kaldor (1939). The same mistake was made on the other side of the Atlantic; see Schumpeter (1949). This misunderstanding gave rise to a decade of confused controversy which was blown away only by the appearance in 1950 of Paul Samuelson's 'Evaluation of real national income'.

Thus, finally, two and a half centuries after Montesquieu's *Lettre*, English-speaking economists knew what had to be established by any acceptable gains-from-trade proposition. Such a proposition had to provide detailed specifications of the trading economies, including their schemes of lumpsum compensation, and a demonstration that the compensated world economy has a market-clearing equilibrium. By most fortunate coincidence, Samuelson's paper was closely followed by the well-known papers of Arrow and Debreu (1954) and McKenzie (1954) on the existence of a competitive equilibrium. It was only a matter of time before the Arrow-Debreu-McKenzie tools would be successfully applied to the gains-from-trade problem and Montesquieu's agenda discharged.

The Post-1972 Period

The first completely satisfactory gains-from-trade propositions appeared about thirty years ago; see Grandmont and McFadden (1972) and Kemp and Wan (1972). Not surprisingly, they were based on specifications of the trading economies borrowed from Arrow, Debreu and McKenzie. In particular it was specified that, in each economy,

(a) markets are complete (for each commodity there is a market) and freely accessible,
(b) all agents coexist,
(c) preferences and production sets are convex,
(d) exchange is by barter (there is no money), and
(e) there are no market distortions (externalities, public goods, commodity taxes or other artificial restraints on the freedom of agents to purchase, sell or produce).

Since 1972 the list of specifications has been substantially shortened. Even before 1972 there was an undercurrent of dissatisfaction with the complete-markets specification of the post-Arrow-Debreu-McKenzie models of general equilibrium. And, soon after, it was shown by Hart (1975) that, in a context of incomplete markets, competitive equilibria may be constrained suboptimal. This finding suggested that it might not be always possible to find a scheme of compensation such that free trade is beneficial in the sense of Pareto. Following the appearance of Hart's paper there came to light an example of Pareto-inferior free trade; see Newbery and Stiglitz (1984). The example incorporated incomplete markets. Its appearance therefore reinforced the earlier Hart-induced doubts about the robustness of the 1972 propositions. Indeed Newbery and Stiglitz expressed the view that their example established the general invalidity of the 1972 conclusions in a context of incomplete markets. Nevertheless, it was later shown that the 1972 conclusions remain valid even when markets are incomplete; see Kemp and Wong (1995a). In examples of the type unearthed by Newbery and Stiglitz, the locus of individual utilities is upward sloping over the relevant ranges.

The specification that all agents coexist is quite unrealistic. Members of different generations either overlap only partially or fail to overlap altogether. If possible, the specification should be relaxed. However it is known from the earlier work of Malinvaud (1953, 1962) and Samuelson (1958) that economies with overlapping generations and an infinite horizon may have Pareto-inefficient equilibrium paths; and, more recently, Kemp and Long (1979) and Binh Tran-Nam (1985, 1986) have produced examples of Pareto-harmful free trade. Nevertheless it has been possible to show that, provided international borrowing and lending are unhindered, the 1972 conclusions are preserved for such economies; see Kemp and Wong (1995b) and Kemp and Wolik (1995).

The specification that all production sets are convex is debatable. Nevertheless, it has been traditionally viewed as essential to any demonstration that free trade is potentially (after compensation) beneficial. Indeed trade textbooks still carry diagrammatic demonstrations that, without convexity, there may be no scheme of compensation which will ensure that under free trade every agent is better off than in autarky. The virtual unanimity of professional opinion rests on the perception that (i) increasing returns to scale give rise to non-marginal-cost pricing and production inefficiencies which vary from industry to industry and that (ii) the opening of trade might promote those industries in which inefficiency is greatest. Nevertheless, attempts to formally demonstrate that if individuals' production sets are non-convex then the 1972 conclusions are invalid have all been shown to be defective. Indeed we now have a formal demonstration that, potentially, any trading equilibrium is beneficial to each trading partner. If the production sets are not convex, an equilibrium may not exist; but if an equilibrium does exist, as the authors of textbooks explicitly assume when drawing their diagrams, then free trade is necessarily potentially beneficial (see Kemp and Shimomura 2001).

Looking Ahead

It must be apparent that considerable progress has been made in broadening the context in which international trade is known to be potentially beneficial. Further progress may be expected. Already it is known that for symmetrical cash-in-advance monetary economies, with possibly incomplete markets, free trade is potentially beneficial; and even those assumptions may prove to be unnecessarily severe.

Moreover, the neglect of inter-generational bequests and other gifts in existing treatments of trade gains in a context of overlapping generations may yet be shown to be unnecessary. Finally, it might prove possible to relax the assumption that markets are costlessly accessible to individual traders. Indeed some progress has already been reported (see Kemp 2001, Chapter 5). The agenda for further research is an attractive one.

Note

[1] In a youthful article in the *Westminster Review*, J.S. Mill argued for the repeal of the Corn Laws even if political necessity implied compensation of rural land owners; see Mill (1825). However Mill does not appear to have made use of Paretian arguments in his later work.

References

Arrow, K.J. and G. Debreu (1954), 'Existence of an Equilibrium for a Competitive Economy', *Econometrica*, Vol. 22, pp. 265–92.

Binh, T. N. (1985), 'A Neo-Ricardian Model with Overlapping Generations', *Economic Record*, Vol. 61, pp. 707–18.

Binh, T.N. (1986), 'Welfare Implications of International Trade without Compensation', University of New South Wales.

Grandmont, J.M. and D. McFadden (1972), 'A Technical Note on Classical Gains from Trade', *Journal of International Economics*, Vol. 2, pp. 109–25.

Hart, O.D. (1975), 'On the Optimality of Equilibrium when the Market Structure is Incomplete', *Journal of Economic Theory*, Vol. 11, pp. 418–43.

Hicks, J.R. (1939), 'The Foundations of Welfare Economics', *Economic Journal*, Vol. 49, pp. 696–712.

Kaldor, N. (1939), 'Welfare Propositions in Economics and Interpersonal Comparisons of Utility', *Economic Journal*, Vol. 49, pp. 549–52.

Kemp, M.C. (ed.) (1995), *The Gains from Trade and the Gains from Aid*, Routledge, London.

Kemp, M.C. (2001), *International Trade and National Welfare*, Routledge, London.

Kemp, M.C. and N.V. Long (1979), 'The Under-exploitation of Natural Resources: A Model with Overlapping Generations', *Economic Record*, Vol. 55, pp. 214–21.

Kemp, M.C. and K. Shimomura (2004), 'Gains from Trade in a Cournot-Nash Equilibrium', *Japanese Economic Review*, Vol. 51, to be published.

Kemp, M.C. and H.Y. Wan (1972), 'The gains from free trade', *International Economic Review*, Vol. 13, pp. 509–22.

Kemp, M.C and H.Y. Wan (1993), *The Welfare Economics of International Trade*, Harwood Academic Press, London.

Kemp, M.C. and K.-Y. Wong (1995a), 'The Gains from Trade when Markets are Possibly Incomplete', in M.C. Kemp (ed.), *The Gains from Trade and the Gains from Aid*, Routledge, London, ch. 10.

Kemp, M.C and K.-Y. Wong (1995b), 'Gains from Trade with Overlapping Generations', *Economic Theory*, Vol. 6, pp. 283–303.

Kemp, M.C. and N. Wolik (1995), 'The Gains from Trade in a Context of Overlapping Generations', in M.C. Kemp (ed.), *The Gains from Trade and the Gains from Aid*, Routledge, London, ch. 10.

Malinvaud, E. (1953, 1962), 'Capital Accumulation and Efficient Allocation of Resources', *Econometrica*, Vol. 21, pp. 233–68 and Vol. 30, pp. 570–73.

McKenzie, L.W. (1954), 'On Equilibrium in Graham's Model of World Trade and Other Competitive Systems', *Econometrica*, Vol. 22, pp. 147–61.

Montesquieu (Charles de Secondat, Baron de La Brede et Montesquieu).

Newbery, D.M.G and J.E. Stiglitz (1984), 'Pareto Inferior Trade', *Review of Economic Studies*, Vol. 51, pp. 1–12.

Pareto, V. (1894), 'Il Massimo di utilita dato dalla libera concorrenza', *Giornale degli Economisti*, Vol. 9, pp. 48–66.

Samuelson, P.A (1950), 'Evaluation of Real National Income', *Oxford Economic Papers*, New Series, Vol. 2, pp. 1–29.

Samuelson, P.A. (1958), 'An Exact Consumption Loan Model of Interest, With or Without the Social Contrivance of Money', *Journal of Political Economy*, Vol. 66, pp. 467–82.

Schumpeter, J.A. (1949), 'Vilfredo Pareto (1848–1923)', *Quarterly Journal of Economics*, Vol. 63, pp. 147–73.

Chapter 2

Crises: The Price of Globalisation?

Paul Krugman

Introduction

The good old days probably weren't better, but they were certainly calmer. It is true that the recovery from the international financial crisis that began in Thailand in July 1997 was faster than most observers (myself very much included) had imagined possible. The crisis, however, was terrifying while it lasted, and the after effects are still being felt. Indeed, while South Korea and Malaysia have staged rapid recoveries, the recovery of Thailand itself has been more hesitant. And Indonesia, whose population is larger than that of all the other Asian crisis countries combined, seems to have suffered a political and economic setback whose end is not yet in sight.

Moreover, even optimists about the world economy now suffer from persistent, if low-grade anxiety. Before the Mexican crisis began in late 1994, many observers viewed the post-Cold-War process of globalisation with unequivocal optimism. Even after the PCSD's plunge, it was possible to regard the 'tequila' crisis as something uniquely Mexican, not as a warning of broader vulnerability. But now, even those who regard the growing integration of world markets as very much a good thing – a group that includes the author – cannot avoid wondering whether repeated financial crises are an inevitable by-product of growing trade in goods and services.

The purpose of this chapter is to shed some light on this question. The answer I will suggest is that growing integration *does* predispose the world economy toward more crises, mainly because it creates pressures on governments to relax financial restrictions that in earlier decades, made 1990s-style financial crisis much less likely. However, the link between integration and crisis vulnerability is not a rigid one. Policies to limit financial vulnerability, including controls on both capital inflows and capital outflows, remain an option – albeit a more costly option as trade increases. On the other hand, there is a reasonable case to be made that countries can protect themselves against financial crises by dollarising or euroising – albeit only by paying a price in flexibility that may expose them to other difficulties, even other kinds of crisis. And there is also some hope of light at the end of the tunnel. In the long run, integration may solve the problems it initially creates.

In order to reach these conclusions, however, I must first develop a conceptual framework. The chapter has four parts. The first tries to put current problems in perspective by taking the 'view from 1983' – that is, the view from an earlier crisis, one in which increased integration seemed likely to help, not hurt crisis management. The second part attempts to provide a framework for understanding modern financial crises – not an easy task given the fragmentation of the crisis-modelling literature. Such models lead naturally to the question of what might be done to reduce the risk of crisis, and the reasons why no single proposed solution (other than 'motherhood' issues like transparency) has commanded general agreement. The final part of the chapter then tries to ask how growing world trade affects the trade-offs among those possible solutions.

The View from 1983

Anyone who has followed international financial affairs over an extended period of time knows the feeling: call it 'conventional wisdom deja vu'. You are listening to or reading about some current debate in which there are certain propositions that everyone takes as given, and suddenly you get a dizzy feeling because YOU remember the propositions everyone took as given, five, or ten, or fifteen years previously – and they weren't the same propositions. Many of today's most prominent international macroeconomists spent their formative years as policy analysts working on the Latin American debt crisis of 1982–1989, a crisis that is sometimes seen as a forerunner of the crises of the 1990s. Like the 1990s crises, the debt crisis followed a period of large-scale private capital inflows in the crisis countries. There are other parallels: regional 'contagion' concerns about spillovers to the financial stability of Western nations, direct and politically touchy IMF involvement in the affairs of the troubled nations. Indeed, the fall of 1997 felt to some of us weirdly similar to the fall of 1982. The same sense of embarrassment so that many supposed experts had so recently been enthusiastic about the prospects of the countries now under financial siege. It was the same feeling of dread as, one after another, countries that were supposed to be different and less vulnerable – Brazil in 1982, Indonesia and Korea in 1887 – fell victim to the crisis.

The major difference was, of course, that in the runup to 1982 capital flows to developing countries mainly took the form of sovereign borrowing. Even where governments or state-owned enterprises were not the borrowers, private borrowing mainly took place with government guarantees. And the case of Chile – where the borrowing was not *de jure* official, but where the government felt compelled ex post to take responsibility for the debts for private banks – only emphasised that this was in the main a crisis of *sovereign* debt. Some analyses of the Asian financial crisis, notably the moral-hazard models of Dooley (1997) and Corsetti et al. (1998) – and, yes, Krugman (1998) – do argue that the debts taken on by Asian banks were implicitly guaranteed by governments. More broadly, some discussion of the Asian crisis seems to be based on concepts drawn – often without sufficient realisation that private and sovereign debt pose different issues – from earlier experiences of problems with sovereign debt. But one widely held view from the 1980s – one that was based partly on empirical evidence, but also grounded to some extent in the theory of sovereign debt – seems to have disappeared in the current debate. In the 1980s it was widely believed that *openness to trade reduced the likelihood of financial crisis*.

The empirical evidence was fairly straightforward. Suppose that one had ranked developing countries in 1982 by the share of external debt in GDP. It soon became apparent that only some of the high-debt countries were actually caught up in the debt crisis: others (for example, South Korea – which *Institutional Investor*, in its famous April 1982 risk assessment, ranked below Mexico) retained access to world capital markets. In other words, the debt/GDP ratio was a poor predictor of crisis. But then what distinguished the countries that did find themselves in crisis from those that did not? One answer is that, in general, Latin nations were shut out of capital markets while Asian nations were not, with the Philippines – the most Latin of Asian nations, in several respects – the exception that proves the rule. But it was also true that countries with a given debt/GDP ratio were less likely to get caught up in the crisis, the higher the ratio of exports was to GDP. Indeed, the debt/export ratio turned out to be a much better predictor of crisis vulnerability than the debt/GDP ratio.

Why was openness apparently good for crisis prevention? There was, at the time, a widespread interpretation that an open economy was more credible in its promises: The more important trade was, the greater the cost of trade disruption if a country with exports equal to 7 per cent of GDP might decide that the legal snarls those exports might face if it refused to pay its debt were less important than getting debt relief. This very possibility deterred banks from lending it any more money. A country with exports equal to 35 per cent of GDP would not face a comparable temptation. In effect, by opening to trade, a country gave hostages to the financial markets – hostages that ensured its own credibility and, therefore, acted as a protection against crisis.

A secondary benefit of openness, which some of us noted at the time, was that it made the adjustment to reduced capital inflows easier. For a country with initial exports of 7 per cent of GDP, switching from a current account deficit of 4 per cent of GDP to a surplus of 2 per cent of GDP would represent a very difficult adjustment, requiring either massive depreciation or a huge contraction in output. For a country with initial exports of 35 per cent of GDP, a much smaller depreciation and/or fall in output would do the trick. And again, for prospective lenders, the belief that the country could adjust to a cut-off of funds relatively painlessly would, in itself, make that cutoff less likely.

The view from 1983 or so, then suggested that in a way the Latin debt crisis was the result of an opening of capital markets that got ahead of the integration of good markets. And it seemed possible, even probable, and, as a result, increased the share of trade in GDP – becoming, in effect, more like Asian developing countries rises along the lines of 1982 would become obsolete. Instead, of course, both Latin and Asian economies have since experienced crises that were if anything more severe, at least in their first year, than those of 1982. High ratios of exports to GDP have offered little protection, and now there is a widespread sense that trade openness actually makes it harder, not easier, to avoid crises. However, we need some framework for thinking about why and how these more recent crises happened.

Modelling Modern Crisis

Although the Asian financial crisis has led to a torrent of both academic and policy papers, no canonical model of that crisis has emerged. Economists are still divided over whether the crisis should be viewed as the inevitable and predictable end of a process of excessive borrowing and investment (e.g. Corsetti et al. 1998), or as a temporary jump to a bad equilibrium in an inherently fragile system – and, if so, what features of the affected economies made them fragile in that sense. This lack of agreement over the nature of 'modern' economic crises makes assessing the effects of other factors on vulnerability to crisis difficult, to say the least: If we can't agree on what happened, how can we say whether increasing trade or whatever makes it more or less likely to happen again? Nonetheless, there has been a definite drift in the post-crisis literature away from models that emphasise excessive overall debt to those that emphasise some kind of self-fulfilling panic. The vulnerability of economies to such a panic, in turn, is increasingly ascribed to some form of mismatch – between the maturity of debts and that of real investments, or between the currency denomination of debts and that of assets, or (probably) both. Let us briefly review each approach.

Maturity Mismatch

The idea that financial crises can arise out of a mismatch between the maturity of investments and that of debts is the core of the classic Diamond and Dybvig (1982) model of bank runs.

The best-known applications of this idea to recent international crises are the series of papers by Chang and Velasco (1998, 1999). The basic idea is this: Imagine an economy in which the rate of return on investments is considerably higher if resources are committed to projects that take a considerable length of time to mature – and which yield much less if terminated prematurely. If such projects had to be financed directly by individuals, investors could only finance them by surrendering liquidity: Their funds would be tied up in the projects and would not be available if unpredictable personal demands created a need for funds before the projects come to fruition.

Financial intermediaries can resolve this problem. Assuming that the personal emergencies that create demands for early liquidation are more or less uncorrelated, a financial intermediary can pool the funds of many individual investors, giving each of them the right to withdraw funds or demand out of a small reserve of liquid assets, allowing most of the funds to be invested in high-return illiquid projects. The perceived liquidity of individual investors is retained, yet the necessary long-term commitment of resources is also achieved.

Unfortunately, such liquidity-creating financial intermediation also creates the possibility of a self-fulfilling panic – a bank run. If a large fraction of the holders of claims on the intermediary were all to demand payment at the same time, there would not be enough liquid assets to satisfy their demands, and because the long-term investments are worth little if terminated prematurely, they would offer little help. And this means that if, for whatever reason, many of those who hold claims come to believe that other holders of claims are about to cash out, they will rationally try to cash out too. So, a fundamentally sound intermediary can be destroyed by a self-fulfilling run; if this happens to an economy as a whole, there can be a crisis that reflects not the unsustainability of the previous prosperity but merely the economy's 'fragility,' its vulnerability to bank runs.

On the face of it, the general story has considerable relevance to the Asian crisis. Plain old-fashioned bank runs played an important role in some countries, notably Indonesia in November 1997. Other aspects of the crisis, while not fitting the model so literally, share some of its flavour – for example, the way that refusal of foreign banks to rollover short-term loans pushed South Korea into financial crisis late in 1999. And yet, there are some problems with this traditional maturity mismatch story. One problem is that the way the story explains the real cost of financial panics is unsatisfying. In an earlier paper (Krugman 1999a) I summarised this problem as follows. In the Diamond-Dybvig model the costs of premature liquidation are *physical* – a bank run literally leads to investments being cannibalised before completion, with the output cost to the economy the result of a literal destruction of physical capital. There are a few real examples of this process in Asia – half-completed structures left to disintegrate for lack of funding, or dismantled for scrap metal. There are also some more complex stories that can be viewed metaphorically as examples of physical liquidation – for example, potentially profitable export opportunities not to be taken because working capital has been sold to pay off bank loans. But surely the main channels through which financial panic has turned good assets into bad, involve not so much physical liquidation of unfinished projects as macroeconomic crisis. Companies that looked solvent before the crisis have gone under because collapsing investment has produced a severe recession, or because capital flight has led to currency depreciation that makes their dollar debts balloon. Or to put it another way, Diamond and Dybvig used a physical metaphor for the costs of premature liquidation as a way to focus on the problem of multiple equilibria on the part of depositors – fair enough. But to make sense of the Asian crisis, it is probably important to have a better metaphor, once that comes closer to matching the stylised facts *of* actual experience (Krugman 1999a).

But if the nature of the costs is macroeconomic – and if, as this passage suggests, the crucial point is not just a flight *to liquidity* but a flight *from the country* – we need an approach that somehow recognises the role of both the *trade balance and the exchange rate.* These concerns led me – and, independently, a number of others, including Aghion et al. (1999) and Calvo (1999, 2000) – to emphasise a different mismatch, involving not maturity but currency.

Currency Mismatch

The basic idea behind currency mismatch stories is that for whatever reason (and the reason is, as we all see, important), firms in many developing countries have substantial debts in foreign currency. This, in turn, means that any currency depreciation will, other things being the same, worsen the balance sheets of these firms. If their investment is constrained by their net wealth – which is more likely if they are also highly leveraged with domestic-currency debt – there is the potential for a self-fulfilling logic of crisis that is similar in spirit to the maturity mismatch story but considerably different in detail.

The story runs as follows: Suppose that for whatever reason there is a flight of capital from a developing country. This will depreciate the currency, producing balance-sheet problems for domestic firms. If these problems are sufficiently severe, they will outweigh any expansionary effect of depreciation on demand, creating an economic contraction that feeds further capital flight and so on. The key linkage is not physical destruction of investment projects in process, but the transfer problem – the need to effect an outflow of capital through a real depreciation.

The end result of this process is an abrupt switch of the current account from the deficit to surplus: a large real depreciation of the currency; financial devastation for the corporate sector; and presumably, though this depends on the specifics of the model, a decline in output. (Realistically, one would also expect the crisis to be reinforced by banking panics along the lines described above.) The most striking thing about the Asian crisis is not the decline in output, though this was severe enough; it was the sheer, probably unprecedented size of the current account reversal, with the crisis countries as a group shifting from a current account *deficit* of 5 per cent of GDP in 1996 to a current account *surplus* of 9 per cent in GDP in 1998. This reversal is why the transfer problem surely belongs at the centre of the story.

But, more generally, the overall picture certainly fits this balance-sheet version of the crisis. A fully-fledged model of balance-sheet-driven crises is necessarily fairly complex; even the rather cumbersome analysis in Krugman (1999a) is only a partial job. The recent effort by Cespedes, Chang, and Velasco (2000), while much more complete, also seems to lose some of the message along the way. I am still digesting their model. However, it appears that by assuming both rational expectations and an assured long-run return of the economy to its original steady-state, they end up ruling out the sort of self-fulfilling crisis that was the original point of the story. However, it may be helpful to sketch out a simplified version of the story derived from Aghion et al. (1999), and originally presented in Krugman (1999b).

In this simplified model, we think of a Mundell-Fleming-type economy that produces a single good sold both domestically and on foreign markets; and we assume that arbitrage keeps the domestic interest rate equal to the foreign rate plus some fixed risk premium (ignoring expectations of the future depreciation, changes, in the risk premium, and so on.

With a fixed money supply, there would be a unique level of GDP at which the domestic interest rate equals the foreign rate plus the risk premium; more generally, if the monetary authority leans against exchange rate movement, we might represent asset-market clearing with a backward-learning curve like AA in Figures 2.1 and 2.2. In the goods market, a depreciation of the currency – a rise in the price of foreign exchange – will make domestic goods more competitive, increasing net exports. If this is the only effect, the goods market curve GG will be upward-sloping, as in Figure 1, and there will be a unique equilibrium. If, however, there are sufficiently strong balance sheet effects, they can outweigh this competitiveness effect, causing the goods-market curve to bend backward over some range. In Figure 2.2, GG is shown as an S-shaped curve. Loosely, the idea is that when the domestic currency is sufficiently strong, most firms are not wealth-constrained, and so the balance-sheet effect is weak. When the domestic currency is very weak most domestic firms with foreign-currency debt are already bankrupt, so that things can't get any worse, and the pro-competitive effect of depreciation is contractionary for intermediate levels of the exchange rate.

In Figure 2.2 there are two locally stable equilibria. What might cause the country to hop from the normal equilibrium to the crisis equilibrium via a process of self-fulfilling capital flight? The answer is anything – a political crisis, an economic crisis in a neighbouring country (hence 'contagion'), whatever causes the hyperdepreciated equilibrium with many firms bankrupt to become the new focus of expectations. Such a hop to a bad equilibrium will certainly be a source of dismay and even outrage in the affected countries. Policy makers will feel that the economy's sins do not deserve such severe punishment, and if schooled in post-Keynesian macroeconomics, they will feel that there must be something they can do to avoid it. Yet, in theory and practice, the policy options, once a crisis is under way, seem very limited. Ordinarily,

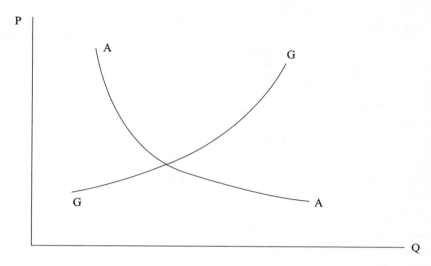

P: price of foreign exchange
Q: output

Figure 2.1   Equilibrium in foreign exchange markets

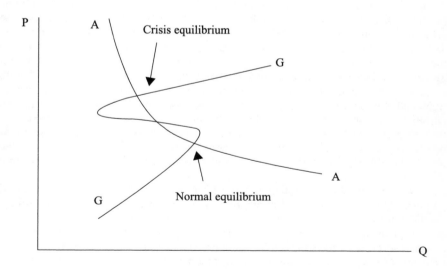

P: price of foreign exchange
Q: output

Figure 2.2   Foreign exchange markets and multiple equilibria

we expect countries to be able to use monetary policy to fight recession. What is so disturbing about the crisis of recent years is that the logic of these crises seems to rule out such monetary reactions – indeed, to force countries to meet an economic slump with monetary tightening. The point is fairly clear from Figure 2.2. If the economy is, for whatever reason, at risk of hopping to the crisis equilibrium, the last thing the central bank wants to do is to loosen monetary policy, which, other things being the same, will tend to weaken the currency and, therefore, all but ensure that the bad equilibrium does, in fact, materialise. Indeed, even a reasonable central bank might well try a draconian tightening instead, hoping to persuade the market that the currency will stay strong and, hence, shepherd it back into the normal equilibrium. But this will be an expensive policy (not only in monetary terms) but in its social impact. One could argue that the cost is only a short-run setback to the economy so this cost, even if it is temporary, is not at all minor. But the example of Indonesia suggests, again, that a sufficiently severe short-run shock can produce lasting effects by shattering political stability. Are there other policies that could help mitigate the crisis?

One answer is for the IMF or (other sources) to serve as a lender of last resort. However, this term is often used much too loosely in the context of international rescue packages. In the classic lender-of-last-resort role, the central bank (or J.P. Morgan, or someone) provides funds to an *individual* debtor that cannot meet its payment demands. A country, however, is not an individual. Admittedly, in 1982, when the crisis was basically one of sovereign debt, one could, to some extent, think of national governments as the troubled debtors; and even in Mexico 1995, the particular problem of *tesobono* debt still fit the sovereign-debt picture. But in the Asian crisis, the problem was not the ability of the government to meet its obligations, but the desire of private agents, both foreign and domestic, to pull funds out of the afflicted economy. So, if the IMF is the lender of last resort, to whom is it lending? The answer – which is not often stated clearly – is that the IMF is providing funds to the domestic government that will, in turn, be used to support the currency through a *sterilised intervention.* Short-term loans from abroad provide the central bank with dollars, which are then thrown into the market; but unless monetary policy is further tightened, this is ultimately only a swap of dollars for domestic debt, not for domestic currency. Such interventions would have the effect, other things equal, of reducing the risk premium. Schematically, we can think of intervention as shifting the goods market curve in Figure 2.2 to the right, while shifting the asset market curve to the left. If the effect is large enough, these shifts will *eliminate* the crisis equilibrium, and, therefore, prevent a crisis from occurring.

But will the intervention be that effective? The conventional wisdom for advanced countries is now that sterilised intervention is largely ineffective – that any official capital inflow in a crisis will simply generate a matching increase in the private outflow. This makes the focus of much developing-country discussion on the lender-of-last resort role a little strange. The same objection applies to arguments like that of Feldstein (1998) – that countries can protect themselves against crisis by maintaining very large reserves.

However, one can offer a few justifications for believing that large-scale liquidity provision might work. The easiest justification – though one you wouldn't want to count on too much – involves the multiple-equilibrium nature of the crisis. A big loan from the IMF, announced with much fanfare, might not be enough to literally rule out the crisis equilibrium. But it might, nonetheless, create a focal point for expectations, tipping a country threatened with crisis back into the normal, calm equilibrium. On the other hand, one has to doubt whether a policy that cannot succeed unless it somehow manages to change expectations can consistently manage to change expectations in the first place,

More concretely, it is arguable that the conditions under which sterilised intervention is ineffective do not exist in developing countries (or more to the point, do not exist *yet* – as we will see, this is one of the reason to worry about whether increasing integration will further increase the risk of crisis). Sterilised intervention is ineffective when there is high private capital mobility, to the extent that domestic and foreign securities are viewed by a sufficiently large group of investors as very close substitutes. If that was the case, one might expect capital flight in a crisis to occur in a wide variety of ways; in particular, one would expect to see domestic residents buying foreign assets on a large scale, using the proceeds from sales of domestic assets. Some of that happened in 1997–1998; but the bulk of capital flight took only one form, refusal by foreign banks to rollover short-term credit. This suggests that the channels of short-term capital mobility remain more limited than sceptics about sterilised intervention would have supposed.

Econometric evidence lends additional weight to this conclusion. As shown by a number of studies (e.g. Frankel and Rose 1997, Rodrik and Velasco 1999), short-term external debt – and, in particular, the ratio of such short-term debt to reserves – is by far the best leading indicator of recent crisis. If assets were broadly fungible, this would not be the case.

Unfortunately, while the limited extent of capital mobility in developing countries probably means that the size of international loans needed to forestall a crisis is less than the most pessimistic estimator – which tend to suppose that only a loan equal in value to M2 or even M3 is really enough to forestall a crisis – that does not mean that the numbers involved are small. In practice, international institutions have not been willing or able to provide enough rapid deployment of funds to prevent very severe crises. And the situation does not seem likely to improve.

If a country cannot use conventional macroeconomic policy to fight a crisis and cannot get enough external resources to offset private capital flight, what is left? The logically obvious answer is to cut the Gordian knot directly, by simply preventing the capital flight. The convivial form of such action is negotiated standstill with foreign banks, as was done in Korea and Brazil; the unconvivial form is *de jure* imposition of capital controls, as in Malaysia. Needless to say, Korea and Malaysia did not escape the crisis (though Brazil's devaluation was benign – which was a great relief at the time, and also has important implications for future policy); but both have staged rapid and impressive recoveries, though, as always, it is very hard to establish any causal link.

What is the difference between the Korean and the Malaysian answer (leaving aside the very different political context)? The advantage of a standstill negotiated with banks is that it is a milder policy, one that does not pose as great a risk of alienating potential future investors. Also, capital controls require an elaborate administrative mechanism that both creates red tape for current-account transactions and, over time, exposes officials to dangerous temptations. The disadvantage of a bank-centred policy for relief is that it takes on only one channel of potential capital flight.

In any case, many observers suspect that while the attempts by Korea and Malaysia to curb capital flight and, thus, end a crisis may have worked this time – or, if you think these policies did not play an important role, you can say that the countries at least got away with them – the scope for such policies will be less in the future than now. If this is true, the reason is that globalisation will make such policies either ineffective or too costly. To understand (and possibly challenge) the logic of this concern, however, we need first to look at another set of issues: not policy during crises, but policy aimed at preventing crises.

Crisis Prevention

Suppose we agree that the best working story we now have about crisis is that they involve a self-fulfilling process of capital flight and balance-sheet collapse, one that is very difficult to stop once it starts. There are at least three key factors in this story: the vulnerability of countries to capital flight, because there is a large pool of potentially mobile funds; the vulnerability of firms to balance-sheet calamity, because they have large foreign-currency denominated debts; and the psychology of investors themselves, who can be caught up in individually rational but collectively disastrous panic. All serious proposals for reducing the risk of crisis involve doing something that will diminish the force of one or more of these factors. Let us consider four types of policy proposal in turn: those that involve discouraging foreign-currency debt by letting exchange rates float; those that, on the contrary, attempt to eliminate the risk of currency crisis by permanently fixing the exchange rate or, better yet, dollarising; those that involve some form of limits on capital *inflows*; and those that involve some form of capital outflows.

Floating Exchange Rates

Can there be a consensus nobody agrees with? Most people involved in discussion of international financial 'architecture' seem to believe that such discussions have reached a consensus about 'bipolarity', defined to mean that countries should have either floating exchange rates or rigidly fixed rate and currency boards or even dollarisation. And it's true that there are a few advocates of compromise systems these days. However, many individual analysts don't really seem to believe that the important thing is to make a choice one way or another; on the contrary, they seem to be firmly attached to one of the poles. In particular, reports from international financial institutions seem mainly to favour floating rates, while a considerable number of academics (such as Barry Eichengreen and Guillermo Calvo) have been increasingly strong advocates of dollarisation.

The currently popular argument for floating exchange rates for developing countries, which one often hears from officials and can find in such writings as Goldstein (1999), is *not* the traditional macroeconomic one – that is, it is not the argument that floating rates give nations monetary autonomy, insulating the economy to some extent from external shocks, and allowing active policy in response to declining demand. Instead, the argument is that fixed exchange rates encourage domestic firms to borrow in foreign currency, and thereby set the stage for the kind of crisis described above.

Why should a fixed but adjustable exchange rate encourage borrowing in foreign currency? It's not all that obvious: If there is a risk of a currency crisis that will cause the domestic-currency value of foreign-currency debt to explode, forward-looking firms should take that risk into account when borrowing. And in any case, why should domestic firms for whom adverse shocks on the exchange rate would normally be correlated with other adverse shocks – take on that risk? Wouldn't the normal logic of risk-sharing suggest that *foreigners* would take on the risk, therefore lending in *domestic* currency?

Nonetheless, as an empirical matter, firms in countries with fixed rates *do* seem to be unusually willing to borrow in foreign currency. Perhaps this reflects 'disaster myopia': The clear and present benefits of borrowing at a lower interest rate prevail, while insufficient weight is given to the catastrophic cost if the domestic currency is devalued. Or possibly, as Calvo (1999) has argued, there is an element of asymmetrical information: Domestic firms have more information than foreign lenders about when a devaluation is likely, so that an offer on their part to borrow a domestic currency is inherently suspect.

However, if one grants that whatever the reason, fixed rates foster dollar-or euro-denominated debt, there is then a case to be made that a floating-rate regime offers some insurance against financial crises.

Eichengreen and Haussman (1999) call this the 'moral hazard' argument regarding the exchange regime, because they regard it as part of the general – and, in their view, incorrect – argument that developing countries borrow too much because such borrowing receives implicit guarantees. It is actually a somewhat problematic use of the term. There may be a sense in which the implicit commitment to use reserves to defend the currency constitutes a form of moral hazard, but I doubt that anyone thinks that this implicit guarantee is the main reason why fixed rates encourage foreign-currency debt, if they do.

The objection that they *don't* raise is that if the problem is excessive foreign currency debt, discouraging that debt with a fluctuating exchange rate seems a strangely indirect policy. The only way it makes sense to prefer this to a more direct form of capital inflow control is if you think that there really is some form of disaster myopia, so that borrowers won't think about the risks of depression unless they are confronted with daily evidence that the exchange rate isn't permanently fixed.

The ultimate appeal of floating exchange rates is the hope that they can turn Brazil into Australia. The Australian example shows that it is possible for a country to attract large inflows of capital without, apparently, becoming vulnerable to Asian-type financial crises. A key ingredient in Australia's stability seems to be the fact that its firms do not rely heavily on foreign-currency-denominated debt (indeed, as ordinary risk-sharing would suggest, they actually sell substantial amounts of *domestic* currency debt abroad). And because a currency depreciation does not wreak balance-sheet havoc with Australian firms, the country was actually able to use exchange rate flexibility as a stabilising device, with a drop in the Australian dollar largely insulating the country from the crisis afflicting its neighbours.

The question is how important the exchange rate regime was in creating this happy flexibility? If Australia had had a fixed exchange rate since 1983, would its US-dollar debts have been so large to make devaluation too dangerous? Conversely, if Brazil or Mexico maintain their floating rates for another decade, will they develop deep domestic-currency financial markets that will allow firms to finance themselves without creating currency mismatch?

The basic belief of the dollarisation is that the answer to at least the last question is no – that the 'original sin' of developing countries is too deeply embedded to be washed clean by a floating-rate regime! And that is what pushes them to the opposite regime.

Dollarisation

It is a truism that can defend any exchange rate with a sufficiently large reduction in the supply of money. So, the crisis process, described above, in which expectations of weaker currency cause a depreciation whose balance-sheet effects ratify those expectations, can always be short-circuited by sufficient monetary tightening would, in fact, take place if a crisis was to 'try' to happen? Then the tightening would not be necessary in the first place. If a central bank can credibly declare its willingness to defend an exchange rate at all costs, the actual cost of that defence would be relatively small. (Multiple equilibria are strange things.) How could a country make such an ironclad (gold-plated?) commitment to defend the currency credible? The obvious answer is to institutionalise the commitment in some way. And hence, one has the case for currency boards, or, better yet, dollarisation (which we should now think of as a generic term that implies adoption of any major-country currency, although either the dollar or the euro are the only current candidates).

Some readers may notice that even if such an institutionalised commitment to a fixed exchange rate succeeds in eliminating the risk of crisis due to currency mismatch, it does not eliminate the risk due to maturity mismatch. This limiting of the ability of the national government to serve as a lender of last resort, arguably increases that risk. Advocates of dollarisation respond by saying that a dollarised market will involve longer-term lending, and will therefore, in fact, be less at risk even of maturity crises. I will return to this debate briefly in the next section of the chapter.

The new advocates of dollarisation for developing countries, such as Guillenno Calvo and Barry Eichengreen, differ in important ways from more traditional advocates of currency boards and currency unions. The traditional case was essentially based on faith in markets: give people a stable currency, and the free market will take care of the rest. In particular, the traditional arguments for hard pegs dismissed concerns about inflexible prices and wages. By contrast, the new dollarisation advocates are motivated mainly by *distrust* of markets. When Eichengreen and Haussman make the case that reliance on foreign currency debt is dangerous but deeply rooted in the failures of developing-country financial markets, and unlikely to be reduced by a floating exchange rate, they call this doctrine of 'original sin': it is the imperfection of markets, not their reliability, that motivates these economists to advocate a permanent commitment foreign currency.

Like the advocates of floating rates for developing countries, advocates of dollarisation believe that by selecting the appropriate exchange rate regime countries can greatly reduce the risk of crisis. So, in that sense, they are saying that crises are *not* an inevitable by-product of the changed nature of the world economy. But they are, nonetheless, saying that a price must be paid to avert the threat of crises, because the old stick-price logic still remains. In permanently fixing its exchange rate, a country obliges itself to adjust to real shocks via deflation or inflation. And all evidence suggests that this is as difficult as ever – that the old arguments in favour of exchange rate flexibility remain relevant.

Consider, in particular, the case of Argentina. The country's currency board has been widely praised and retains immense popularity within the country. And it probably has given Argentina some immunity to speculative attack. On the other hand, it is a straitjacket for macroeconomic policy. The current situation in Argentina bears a clear family resemblance to that of Britain following the return to gold, with financial credibility strong but the real economy persistently weak,

Notice that I am not calling for an abandonment of the Argentine peg. Given the extensive dollarisation that has already taken place, with not only external debt but also much internal debt denominated in dollars, there is every reason to believe that a devaluation would be contractionary – not to mention the entailed severe loss of credibility.

On the other hand, when neighbouring Brazil devalued in early 1999, the results were clearly expansionary – even thought the failure to defend the *real* was humiliating for the government, the effects were benign, more like what happened to the UK in 1992, than what happened to Thailand or Indonesia in 1997. The most likely explanation is that Brazilian firms did not have large dollar-denominated debt. So the self-reinforcing balance-sheet effects that were so devastating in other developing countries did not materialise.

But why is Argentine private debt largely dollar-denominated, while Brazilian debt is not? One answer surely is the exchange rate regime, bringing us back to the bipolarity issue. Because Argentina's fixed rate has led to large dollar-denominated debt, abandoning the peg would probably be catastrophic; so one might as well go all the way to dollarisation.

But there is also the issue of regulation: Governments can actively discourage foreign-currency borrowing. (My understanding is that Brazilian regulations have, in fact, had the effect of discouraging such borrowing, though I am happy to be challenged.)

Capital Inflow Controls

As already pointed out, there are two lines of evidence that put short-term foreign-currency debt at the core of modem crisis: econometric evidence that says that such debt is the best predictor of crisis risk, and the raw fact that failure to rollover this kind of debt was the main component of the capital-account reversal in Asia from 1996 to 1998.

When one adds to these empirical concerns the growing belief among theorists that foreign-currency debt (although not necessarily *short-term* foreign-currency debt) plays a key role in the mechanics of crisis, it would seem to be a natural conclusion that prudential limits on such debt would be a key part in any package of measures to limit the risk of failure crisis. And, indeed, proposals to emulate Chilean controls were a very active topic of discussion a year or two ago.

More recently, however, the popularity of such measures has evidently faded away. Aside from the general decline in interest in reform now that the crisis is past, there seems to be three main reasons for this loss of momentum.

The first is that those who worry about short-term external debt have started to emphasise the exchange rate regime rather than direct controls or taxes. It seems rather peculiar, again, to rely on currency volatility to provide an implicit tax on foreign-currency borrowing; but the other doubts about limits on borrowing seem to have created a preference for such indirect measures.

Second, there have long been questions about whether limits on borrowing are Really enforceable – whether, in particular, domestic borrowers can evade Chilean-type taxes by making more complication transactions. I would argue that the evidence suggests that such scepticism is excessive. There will be some evasion, but perfection is not required in this case. More fundamentally, the very imperfections in developing country financial markets that are so much emphasised in recent writing – their 'original sin', as Eichengreen and Hassman phrase it – will limit the ability of domestic firms to make the other side arrangements that replicate short-term dollar debt through untaxed or uncontrolled transactions. To characterise this argument slightly: you can't assert that firms must borrow abroad in dollars because they lack the credibility or institutional means either to borrow in local currency or to hedge their dollar debts, and then at the same time assert that if dollar borrowing is discouraged those firms will borrow in domestic currency and hedge it back to a *de facto* dollar debt.

Finally, with the crisis past, most analysts have returned to a general concern that any form of regulatory intervention that imposes considerable red tape on firms will damage the ability of countries to participate in the broader gains from globalisation. This brings us, finally, to the central topic of this chapter. But before moving on we need to turn briefly to the question of capital *outflow* controls.

Capital Outflow Controls

Another initiative that has rapidly fallen out of favour as the crisis has receded is the proposal for 'private sector involvement' – basically, some set of ground rules or understandings that would regularise standstill agreements on short-term debt when a crisis strikes. Again, both the logic and empirical evidence behind such proposals is clear. If crisis are self-fulfilling panics, investors are in a prisoners' dilemma, in which it is not only in the country's interest but their own to impose a sort of curfew that gives the market a chance to calm down. And in 1997–1998, it was overwhelmingly a reversal in the direction of short-term bank flows that made up the reversal in the overall capital account of the crisis countries.

Nonetheless, the vociferous objections of banks have largely shut down discussion of private sector involvement. The main objection, as I understand it, is the belief that in future crises there will be many other channels of capital flight; so singling out the banks will be ineffective and will simply penalise them. Furthermore, the prospect that they will be so singled out if another crisis should materialise, will deter banks from lending in the first place.

Even if these objections are accurate, one answer would be not to give up on private sector involvement but to widen it – to propose that broad capital export controls be imposed as a crisis measure. Needless to say, this idea – however directly it may follow from the theory of the case – is anathema to almost all respectable commentators. The main reason seems to be both belief that such controls will be ineffective and fears that the threat of such controls will undermine the broader gains from globalisation – again bringing us to the main point of this chapter.

Also, and again in parallel with the discussion of capital import controls, some of the doubts about private sector involvement appear to be inconsistent with the doctrine of 'original sin' that is supposed to explain why countries are vulnerable in the first place. If domestic financial markets are so underdeveloped that firms must borrow in foreign currency, the ability of capital flight to do an end run around a standstill on the resulting foreign-currency debt is a source of vulnerability, having the prospect of private sector involvement later deter foreign lending now might not be such a bad thing.

But leaving such scepticism aside, what one finds in this case, as in the case of capital inflow controls, is that the ultimate source of unwillingness to take measures that might reduce the risk of crisis is concern that doing so might undermine the benefits of globalisation.

Globalisation and Crises

Consider a typical middle-income developing country twenty-five years ago. (Which country are we talking about? Never mind.) It would have had many problems, but it would not have been at any risk of a 1990s-style crisis. For one thing, the currency would not have been fully convertible: One would have needed a licence to buy foreign exchange, and this would not have prevented *rapid* flight in a crisis. Secondly, there would have been relatively little external debt, mainly sovereign and mainly long-term. Balance-of-payments problems could and would occur; indeed, adverse shocks to the current account would be all the harder to deal with because offsetting capital inflows would not be easy to obtain. But devaluation would be a very much available option – indeed, probably a required part of any IMF package.

Now, consider the corresponding country today. It has liberalised its exchange market along with many other parts of the economy and has achieved encouraging success in raising productivity, developing non-traditional exports, and so on. This success has attracted considerable foreign investment. Some of this investment is direct, but there have also been large financial inflows, mainly dollar, euro, or yen-denominated loans to domestic firms. There may also be considerable internal lending denominated in foreign currency.

The result is an economy that is doing much better in good times, but is also far more vulnerable to sudden crises. When bad news, or even a rumour of bad news arrives, rapid capital flight is now all too possible. And devaluation is now risky at best, disastrous at worst, because of this foreign-currency debt.

Why did countries make themselves vulnerable in this way? Can they reduce that vulnerability while retaining the good things about their transformation? Why have countries become vulnerable?

Why couldn't countries have retained the controls that limited both foreign-currency debt and potential capital flight? The answer is that some have – indeed, the biggest developing countries, China and India, still operate under extensive capital controls, and do not have large private-sector foreign currency debt. And surely it is because the two Asian giants had not yet liberalised their capital account to the same extent as other Asian nations that both (thank God) rode out the world financial crisis with little turbulence.

But neither is, to say the least, an economy without troubles. And at least some of these troubles are connected to the very aspects of the economic system that protected them against financial crisis. Exchange controls probably make it more difficult to export: they necessarily require exporters to turn in their foreign exchange receipts (even when they are given the right to retain some portion, they require approval for imported inputs, and so on). Such controls also presumably deter direct investment because potential investors cannot be sure about what the rules will be for importing inputs, repatriating earnings, etc. And, last but least, a pervasive system of controls creates incentives for corruption – something that has become partly quantifiable in China, as the deficit in errors and omissions has become startlingly large.

These costs are not new. However, concerns over the costs of a controlled system is much greater now than it was twenty-five years ago, not because the old system works worse now than it did then, but because the opportunity cost of that system seems larger. Export opportunities for developing countries are much more diversified than they were in the 1970s. Potential foreign direct investment, especially investment that uses countries as export platforms, appears to be much larger. And there is now a widespread belief (which I share) that growth led by exports and a general opening to the world is the last best hope of developing countries for real development. So, the cost of a regime that crimps globalisation appears much higher now than it did a generation ago.

This, then, is the main sense in which the growing integration of the world economy had increased the risk of financial crises. Basically, growing potential gains from trade and foreign investment make it increasingly expensive for countries to maintain controls that might interfere with flows of goods and services or deter multinational enterprise. But removing these controls makes it more likely that countries will develop the financial vulnerabilities that make financial crises possible.

We might note that even the now-preferred method of limiting financial vulnerability – a floating exchange rate, which deters domestic firms from taking on large foreign-currency debt – is certain to come under increasing pressure as globalisation proceeds. There has been a gradual drift in the academic literature toward the proposition that floating rates do, in fact, diminish trade (see, for example, Rose (2000)). Anyone who has followed the bitter debates over UK entry into the euro also knows that many private-sector participants claim that floating rates are a deterrent to direct investment. In a way, it does not matter whether these arguments are true, as long as they remain widely believed. They will add to the pressure to keep the exchange rate stable. Again, the prospect of gains from integration will push countries away from policies that might have made crises less probable.

Is Dollarisation the Answer?

The growing support for dollarisation among serious economists not usually associated with doctrinaire free-market views is a new and surprising development. The movement has a powerful case. It argues, in effect, that private-sector dollarisation, in the form of large-scale foreign-currency-denominated debts, can only be prevented with measures that will undermine the gains from participating in a global economy. And if there is extensive private-sector dollarisation, retaining a distinct national currency becomes a liability rather than an advantage. So, the best thing is to go all the way. Leaving aside for a moment the question of whether this strong view is truly correct, one then needs to ask whether dollarisation will itself eliminate the risk of crisis.

This is usually posed as a question about the ability of the central bank to serve as lender of last resort in domestic financial difficulties. That is, will the risk of crisis driven by currency mismatch simply be traded for an equal risk of crisis driven by maturity mismatch? Opinions remain sharply divided about whether this is a real problem. Clearly, once there is no longer a national currency, one cannot print money to rush to troubled institutions. It does not seem politically realistic to suppose that the Fed or the ECB will be willing to grant an unconditional guarantee to provide such funds. On the other hand, if the national government remains able to borrow, or maintains large reserves of liquid assets, there will still be ready funds. An unsatisfying answer is that if it is cautious, the government of a dollarising country ought to be able to prepare itself to deal with many potential financial crises but not all.

The greater risk seems to me to be that dollarisation will set the stage for *non-financial* crises. Consider, again, the current difficulties of Argentina. It is an economy that is depressed by inadequate demand, facing sustained deflationary pressure, and also facing budget deficits largely because of that depressed economy. The picture is worsened by growing social unrest. Yet, there seems to be little if anything that the government can do – monetary policy does not exist, expansionary fiscal policy is ruled out (indeed, fiscal moves have been contractually in order to calm creditors). I would not predict that this will turn into a sustained political and economic downward spiral, but others, including former President Menem, have made just such a prediction.

Of course, Argentina is not yet officially dollarised – it only has a currency board. And the answer of dollarisation advocates is, therefore, that it should finish the job. But why, exactly, would that help? (It would probably lower interest rates, but that would be a one-shot gain, and probably not enough of one to generate an economic recovery.) And even a fully dollarised economy would clearly be vulnerable to the sort of overvaluation/budget difficulties now facing Argentina.

The point is not that Argentina is lost – the country is very far from being at that point. It is, rather there were reasons why countries went off the gold standard in the first place, and those reasons are just as relevant today. To steal a line the *Economist* once used about Britain and the EMS: If developing countries were to dollarise they would not have their current problems – they would have other problems instead.

Partial Measures?

It is probably true that given the potential gains from integration, the opportunity cost of old-fashioned currency control regime, which were both extensive and permanent, is simply too high. But can more limited measures still have a role? At this point I know that I am very much out of step with the way the discussion has gone over the past year. However, let me argue that the major arguments against limited measures have not held up well in the light of recent events.

First, the main argument against regulations designed to limit short-term foreign-currency debt is that such regulations cannot be made effective – that capital flight can still take place through other channels and that firms can roll their own foreign-currency debt in indirect ways. Such views are sometimes linked to Friedman-like (that's Tom, not Milton) depictions of the 'electronic herd' – of capital movements that have become unstoppable thanks to modem technology. But the capital flight in this last crisis was remarkably prosaic; it really was mainly a matter of short-term foreign-currency debt.

It is probably also worth pointing out that everyone is in favour of prudential regulation in other areas – limits on bank exposure, requirements for transparency and reform of corporate governance, and so on. There does not seem to be any good reason why prudential regulation of foreign-currency exposure should be regarded as either less legitimate or less feasible than any other regulation.

Second, the same prosaic nature of the capital flight in the recent crisis suggests that private-sector involvement is not as infeasible as its opponents have made it seem. The time may come when such measures will address so small a part of the problem that they are completely ineffective; but that time does not appear to be now.

Finally, it is interesting to go back and read the early pronouncements of financial officials and the investment community about the prospects for Malaysia's capital controls – pronouncements that explicitly warned that such controls were entirely unworkable, that the result would be a severe economic contraction. Even if you are sceptical about the role of the controls in Malaysia's recovery – the evidence is indeed far from decisive – at least one can say that such measures are not as disastrous or impossible to implement as many people claimed, even in an economy with both a high share of trade in GDP and large foreign direct investment. As a last resort, in times of very severe crisis, emergency capital outflow controls remain an option.

In short, it would be wrong to paint the picture too starkly. The enhanced gains from trade and investment mean that countries cannot now justify the extensive controls that once made them immune to financial crisis of the kind now common. But more limited protective measures, both as protection against crisis and as ways to contain crisis when they happen, remain vital options.

Will Globalisation Solve its Own Problems?

Despite the possibility that the link from globalisation to risk of crisis can be weakened, it's still a more shadowed picture than we would like to see. I believe that these shadows are real. Despite our best efforts, the closer integration of the world economy is also likely to mean an increased risk of crisis in the years ahead. But is this only a transition problem? Can we expect that in the long run a more integrated world will again become one relatively free from financial crises? There are two channels through which this might happen.

The first is that growing integration of markets for goods and services could make financial crises less likely. I am not talking about the argument, commonly offered in the context of European monetary union, that growing integration will eliminate asymmetric shocks to national economies. This argument seems to me wrong both in theory and practice. (Growing trade leads to growing specialisation, which, if anything, makes shocks less symmetric than before.) Instead, it's a question of macroeconomic response. Going back to the loose model of financial crisis illustrated by Figure 2.2, the key element in that figure is the perversely sloped region of the goods market curve – corresponding to the possibility that contractionary balance-sheet effects of currency depreciation will outweigh the expansionary pro-competitive effects of such depreciation. But suppose that the traded share of output increases.

This will mean that the pro-competitive effect of depreciation operates on a larger share of the economy (and also that the adverse balance-sheet effects of depreciation on spending fall more on imports, less on domestic goods). In the limit, a country that exported everything it produced could not have that backward-sloping curve: Depreciation would be unambiguously expansionary. No country is at that limit, or likely to get anywhere close. But growing integration of goods markets will, nonetheless, help reduce the possibility of perverse effects of depreciation.

The second channel through which globalisation might reduce the risk of crisis is via direct investment. Local subsidiaries of multinational firms will not be subject to the same adverse balance-sheet effects of depreciation as domestic firms. Indeed, it is very difficult to see how an economy consisting mainly of local operations of international firms could manage to have a financial crisis of any kind, except as part of a global crisis.

Again, there is no economy – not even Singapore – that has reached this limiting case, or is likely to any time soon. Even regional economies within the United States have local firms that can get into mutually reinforcing financial difficulties. But movement in that direction will, again, make crises a bit harder to create. The effect of increasing economic integration on the risk of crisis, then, will arguably be an inverted U. After some decades of growing risk, things will start to get calmer again. But remember that China and India haven't yet opened up to the extent that they can have modern financial crises – and yet the pressure for them to do so is steadily growing. A best guess is surely that the ride will continue to be very bumpy for many years to come.

References

Aghion, P., P. Bacchetta and A. Banerjee (1999), 'A Simple Model of Monetary Policy and Currency Crises', mimeo.

Calvo, G. (1999), 'Fixed Versus Flexible Exchange Rates: Preliminaries of a Turn-of-Millennium Rematch?', mimeo.

Calvo, G. (2000) 'Capital Markets and the Exchange Rate (with special reference to the dollarization debate in Latin America)', mimeo.

Cespedes, L., R. Chang and A. Velasco (2000), 'Balance Sheets and Exchange Rate Policy', NBER working paper, No. 7840.

Chang, R. and A. Velasco (1999), 'Liquidity Crisis in Emerging Markets: Theory and Policy.' NBER working paper, No. 7272.

Corsetti, G., P. Pesenti and N. Roubini (1998), 'What Caused the Asian Currency and Financial Crisis?' NBER working paper, No. 6843.

Diamond, Douglas and Philip Dybvig (1983), 'Bank Runs, Deposit Insurance, and Liquidity', *Journal of Political Economy*, Vol. 91, pp. 401–19.

Dooley, M. (1997), 'A Model of Crises in Emerging Markets', NBER working paper, No. 6300.

Eichengreen, B. and R. Haussman (1999), 'Exchange Rates and Financial Fragility', presented at Jackson Hole conference 1999.

Feldstein, M. (1999), 'A Self-Help Guide for Emerging Markets', *Foreign Affairs*, March–April.

Frankel, J. and A. Rose (1997), 'Currency Crashes in Emerging Markets: An Empirical Treatment', *Journal of International Economics*, Vol. 41, pp. 351–66.

Goldstein, M. (1999), *Safeguarding Prosperity in a Global Financial System* (Report of Council on Foreign Relations task force).

Krugman, P. (1998), 'What Happened to Asia?', mimeo.

Krugman, P. (1999a), 'Balance Sheets, the Transfer Problem, and Financial Crises', in P. Isard, A. Razin and A. Rose (eds), *International Finance and Financial Crises*, Kluwer, Norwell, MA.

Krugman, P. (1999b), 'Analytical Afterthoughts on the Asian Crisis', mimeo.

Rodrik, D. and Velasco, A. (1999), 'Short-term Capital Flows', NBER Working Paper, No. 7634.

Chapter 3

IMF Perspectives and Alternative Views on the Asian Crisis

Iwan J. Azis

F33

F30, Ō19 Ō11

Ō16,

Introduction

[LDCs]

Let us compare the analyses of East Asian economies prior to the 1997 crisis and those after the crisis broke out. We are likely to find that the two would demonstrate an overwhelmingly sharp contrast. Praises toward the region's economic performance before summer 1997 appeared in many pages of articles, books, and reports, including those published by the International Financial Institutions (IFIs), especially the IMF and the World Bank. The latter's piece on 'East Asian Miracle' was probably the culminating point. As soon as the crisis broke out, these institutions began to propagate a sharply different analysis. The very same countries previously praised for their policies and remarkable performances were swiftly placed into the category of those with misplaced development strategies. All of a sudden, nothing was right with these countries.

When confronted with such an embarrassing contradiction, the international institutions are quick to claim that they actually *saw* the faults, and *already reminded* the governments in East Asia about these flaws (e.g., weak banking system, unsustainable exchange rate system, and widespread corruption). To strengthen their arguments further, institutions such as the IMF quickly moved to bolster its surveillance of national policies and international markets, among others through the establishment of the *Contingent Credit Line* facility (the CCL), designed to enable the Fund to deploy financial resources more effectively to help prevent financial crises, rather than to deal with the problems after the damage has been done. This was part of the increasingly demanded reforms of the institution. Yet, all these efforts were put in place *only after* the crisis broke out. While the debates between those who demand swift reforms in the IFIs and those who are more in favour of moderate and gradual reforms, are very timely and fascinating to follow, this is not what this manuscript is intended to analyse. Rather, the current study attempts to examine the policy perspectives of the IFIs (more particularly of the IMF) and the alternative policies presumably favoured by the crisis-affected countries. When the two differ, efforts are made to explore the possibility of a joint policy acceptable to both parties. It is expected from this approach that we could enhance our knowledge about the background of policy responses to a crisis, and it would help us to understand why in some cases those policies have only a small degree of effectiveness.

This is unmistakably a very broad topic. Any analysis of this type could risk making an erroneous generalisation, unless one uses a specific case study. In this chapter, I use the episode of the Asian crisis as a specific example. It is in this context the causes of vulnerability that led to the Asian crisis. A specific method known as the *Analytic Hierarchy Process* (AHP) is used to quantify the perceptions of both parties in order to generate the payoff values on certain policies or joint policies. A brief mathematical exposition of the method is presented

Finding the Usual Suspects

The standard framework of analysis often used to examine whether or not a country is prone to a crisis, rests upon certain measures to evaluate a country's vulnerability. When economic indicators point to a high vulnerability in the system, it is more likely that the respected economy will fall into a crisis. Sometimes, it only requires one triggering factor to precipitate the actual crisis. However, other countries may share a similar degree of vulnerability, yet they do not suffer from a crisis. Hence, explaining the causes of vulnerability is not the same as explaining the causes of the crisis, although the two could be closely related.

The terms 'fundamentals' are often used to indicate the state of macroeconomic affairs. There are several ways to measure fundamentals. When high inflation, budget deficit and looming current account deficits are detected, along with a relatively low economic growth, it is said that the (macroeconomic) fundamentals are weak. However, a more refined definition of 'fundamentals' is warranted. In exploring such a definition, the Asian crisis is used as the reference case. Let us first look at some of the background developments in the region prior to the crisis. Up to 1996, countries throughout East Asia produced a strong economic growth (Azis 1999). The region's inflation rate was low, consistently at one-digit level. During the period, there was even a deflation in some countries. One of the important factors behind the low inflation has been the management of the government budget. Practically all countries had a surplus budget, a very different situation than in Latin America during the 1980s. Export performance was also strong until 1995. However, beginning in 1996 the growth of exports declined, and the current account deficit (CAD) widened, i.e., from 8.1 to 8.2 per cent of GDP in Thailand, from 3.6 to 3.9 per cent in Indonesia, and from 2.7 to 4.3 per cent in the Philippines during 1995–1996 (Table 3.1). Korea's CAD also increased from 1.7 to 4.7 per cent in the same period, but it quickly reduced to 2.5 per cent by mid-1997. With the exception of Thailand, these ratios are lower than a typical deficit in most Latin American countries. Thailand was the only country in the region that failed to reverse the increasing trend of CAD. The export growth became slower because there was a downturn in the semiconductor cycle, affecting exports particularly from Korea, Malaysia and Thailand.

Other factors at work include the devaluation of Chinese Yuan in 1994 (more than 40 per cent), a stronger US dollar (practically all countries in the region pegged their currencies to the US dollar), and massive capital inflows that put pressure on the exchange rates to appreciate. Increased competition from other countries, including those from new emerging markets, fuelled more difficulties.

Even with slower export growth, all countries managed to maintain relatively large foreign reserves. Before July 1997, the recorded reserves in terms of months of imports were 5.5 for Indonesia (May), 6.3 for Thailand (April), 3.9 for Malaysia (last quarter of 1996), and 3.1 for the Philippines (May). There was also a suspicion

Table 3.1 **Selected indicators of Southeast Asian economies prior to the crisis**

	GDP Gr %	Export Gr %	Import Gr %	FDI Gr %	I/GDP US$Bill	%GDP	Current account
Indonesia							
1991	7.0	13.5	18.5	35.5	35.5	−4.3	−3.7
1992	6.5	16.6	5.5	19.9	35.9	−2.8	−2.2
1993	6.5	8.4	3.8	12.8	29.5	−2.1	−1.3
1994	7.5	8.8	12.9	5.2	31.1	−2.8	−1.6
1995	8.2	13.4	27.0	106.2	31.9	−7.0	−3.6
1996	7.9	9.7	5.7	44.2	32.1	−8.7	−3.9
Thailand							
1991	8.4	23.8	15.8	−17.6	44.1	−7.6	−7.6
1992	7.8	13.7	6.0	4.9	40.0	−6.3	−5.7
1993	8.3	13.4	12.2	−14.6	39.9	−6.4	−5.1
1994	8.9	22.2	18.5	−24.3	40.4	−8.1	−5.6
1995	8.7	24.7	31.6	51.4	42.3	−13.6	−8.1
1996	6.7	−1.9	0.8	13.0	41.0	−14.7	−8.2
Malaysia							
1991	8.4	18.6	27.4	71.4	35.5	−4.2	−8.8
1992	7.8	9.7	0.6	29.6	35.9	−2.2	−3.9
1993	8.3	17.0	15.8	−3.4	29.5	−3.0	−5.0
1994	9.2	26.8	32.7	−13.3	31.1	−4.5	−6.2
1995	9.6	20.3	24.8	−4.8	31.9	−7.4	−8.8
1996	8.2	6.5	1.4	14.6	32.1	−5.2	−5.3
Philippines							
1991	−0.5	14.5	11.1	2.6	20.0	−1.0	−2.2
1992	0.3	2.8	11.5	−58.1	20.9	−1.0	−1.9
1993	2.1	22.0	29.9	443.0	23.8	−3.0	−5.7
1994	4.4	15.5	16.7	28.5	23.6	−3.0	−4.3
1995	4.8	28.7	22.4	−7.1	22.2	−2.0	−2.7
1996	5.7	18.7	24.0	−6.7	23.2	−7.7	−4.3

*) Exports are f.o.b, imports are c.i.f, except for Thailand, Gr: growth.

Source: IMF, *International Financial Statistics*, various volumes, UNCTAD, FDI/TNC database.

that the slower growth of exports was due to currency overvaluation. Was the region currencies really overvalued before the crisis? With low inflation, the proposition is disputable. By using two approaches, a monetary model and a simple *purchasing power parity* (PPP), Chinn (1998) found that even when the resulting overvaluation is detected, the size of the overvaluation in crisis-stricken countries was smaller than that in the crisis-free countries. From the PPP-based approach, the Singapore dollar is found overvalued by 13 per cent, on a par with the Thai baht and Malaysian ringgit. Even when a modified model that incorporates monetary and real sectors is used, the Singapore dollar is found to be overvalued by 45 per cent, whereas in Thailand, Malaysia and Indonesia the size of the currency overvaluation is much smaller, i.e., 3.7, 0.4, and 4.7 per cent, respectively. This is obviously inconsistent with the actual fall of the respected currencies after July 1997. Data suggest that the widening CAD in the region was caused more by increased imports, particularly of the capital and intermediate goods category. Strong investment, domestic and foreign, was the prime reason. The investment-GDP ratio ranged from 23 per cent in the Philippines to a high 43 per cent in Thailand.

In sum, based on standard macroeconomic variables, it is hard to claim that East Asia's economic fundamentals were weak, causing the region to be highly vulnerable. Thailand was perhaps the only exception. Would a more refined definition of 'fundamentals' alter the claim? What other indicators should be included in the measure? One important indicator needs to be added is the quality of the banking sector. This could be evaluated, among others, by examining whether or not there was a credit boom prior to the crisis. If lending increases rapidly, banks will not be able to screen out higher risk loans as easily. This could weaken the bank's portfolios. If banks are weak, the government may be less likely to endure a period of overvaluation and recession due to increased bankruptcies.

By 1980s, most East Asian countries had liberalised their industrial sector, albeit with different degrees of extensiveness (Korea is a latecomer in this respect). Despite the region's high saving rate – over 30 per cent of GDP – huge inflows of capital were still required to finance even higher rates of investment (an indication of over investment). This raises a question about the investment *quality*. It may suggest that the investment surge is a sign of weakness rather than strength. Capital flows could take the form of either increased share in the stock market, surging deposits in home country's banks, and private foreign debts. Whichever the form, when the inflows occur, pressures for the exchange rates to appreciate are built up. This is the reason why monetary authorities throughout the region often conduct the *impossible trinity*, i.e., defending the exchange rates, while simultaneously maintaining the inflation target and keeping the independence of monetary policy. These objectives cannot be met simultaneously. Either the goal to control inflation needs to be moderated, or some degrees of currency appreciation should be allowed.

Like anything else, the 'Asian way' was to opt for a middle ground, i.e., using the exchange rate band. This happened in Indonesia, the Philippines, Malaysia, and Thailand. The Korean won had been gradually adjusted to maintain Korea's competitiveness. At the same time, domestic credit also surged, either to complement or substitute capital inflows. Hence, early indications show that there was a significant increase in the growth of credits prior to the crisis. However, whether or not such an increase represents a credit boom, one must look at it more carefully by comparing the trend with that in other countries experiencing a crisis. In this manuscript, I make the comparison with the Latin American situation prior to the crisis in Mexico in 1994. In addition to weak banking system, two additional indicators of 'fundamentals' are proposed. The first usual suspect is the appreciation of real exchange rate (RER). The more appreciated the RER, the more depreciation (read: collapsed exchange rate) required to reach an equilibrium, should capital flows reverse. Another additional indicator is the size of foreign reserves, measured in terms of its ratio to M2, in which the latter represents the potential amount of liquid monetary assets that could be converted to foreign exchange in the event of a crisis. The higher the ratio of M2/foreign reserves, the less able the government is to defend the currency against devaluation.

To recapitulate, consider the following,

Scenario 1) $(e/Eo) f(LB) -1 < \theta$ then $D = 0$
Scenario 2) $(e/Eo) f(LB) -1 > \theta$ and $R > N.k$ then $D = 0$
Scenario 3) $(e/Eo) f(LB) -1 > \theta$ and $R < N.k$ then $D = 0$ or $D = (e/E0)$

where (e/Eo) is a measure of real exchange rate appreciation, $f(LB)$ is a measure of lending boom, 0 is an expected devaluation threshold for investors to move out of the country, R is foreign exchange reserves, N.k is potential capital outflows (number of investors times the amount of capital they will move out), and D is the extent of a devaluation.

In scenario 1, the fundamentals are healthy and there is no devaluation. In scenario 2 the fundamentals are not healthy, but the country has enough foreign exchange to defend the currency. In scenario 3 the fundamentals are unhealthy and the foreign reserves are low. Whether there is a devaluation or not, it would depend on investors' expectations. If investors expect a stability, there will be no devaluation since k = O, but if they expect a devaluation, N.k > R and D > 0 (a speculative crisis). By using this framework, Sachs et al. (1996) showed that for Latin America, the 'financial crises occurred only in countries with weak fundamentals and low foreign exchange reserves relative to M2'. The contagion from the 1994/95 Mexico crisis did not spread to countries with strong fundamentals or high reserve ratios. Thus, some countries with weak fundamentals may have escaped from a crisis, but no country with large reserves or strong fundamentals fell victim. At most, countries that were healthy experienced a 'temporary decline in asset prices which would soon be reversed leaving little or no trace behind'.

Let us look at the episode of Asian crisis by using the same approach. In the Indonesian case, there were weak signs of a lending boom prior to the crisis. The recorded growth of credits was only 18 per cent, much lower than 116 per cent in Mexico prior to the 1994/95 crisis (compare Table 3.2 and Table 3.3). The M2/ Reserves ratio was highest among the Asian countries; yet, it was considerably smaller than in Mexico (6.3 versus 9.1).

Like Indonesia, Korea's RER also depreciated, not appreciated, before 1997. Korea's lending grew at a modest rate (13 per cent), and the M2/Reserve ratio was comparable to the Indonesian ratio. Being able to weather the financial crisis, Malaysia's economy contracted but not at the rate experienced by Indonesia and Thailand. Lending was up by 26 per cent before the crisis, but its M2/reserve ratio

Table 3.2   Indicators of pre-1994 Mexican crisis

	RER (% change av. 1986–89 to av. 1990–94)	Bank Credits (% change 1990–94)	M2/Reserves (Nov. 1994)
Latin America			
Argentine	−48	57.12	3.56
Brazil	−9.59	68.33	3.62
Mexico	−28.51	116.24	9.06
Asia			
Indonesia	11.75	0.66	4.56
Korea	−10.35	8.4	6.54
Malaysia	9.82	4.1	2.1
Philippines	−0.07	50	4.1
Thailand	0.002	39.2	3.65

Source: Summarised from Sachs et al. (1996).

Table 3.3   Indicators prior to the 1997 Asian crisis

	RER (% change av. 1989–93 to av. 1994–96)	Bank Credits (% change 1992–96) (1997)	M2/Reserves
Indonesia	2.46	17.8	6.28
Korea	8.75	12.7	6.35
Malaysia	8.97	25.9	3.82
Philippines	−6.89	212	4.93
Singapore	6.88	6.2	1.03
Thailand	7.58	36.7	4.95

Source: Author's calculation.

was much smaller than in Indonesia and Korea. The Philippines was the only country with appreciating RER before the crisis.

Bank's lending increased substantially (212 per cent), and the M2/reserve ratio reached close to 5 (Table 3.3). Although the Philippines' fundamentals before 1997 were actually worse than before the Latin American crisis, the country was considered among the least affected by the Asian crisis. As expected, Singapore exhibited the strongest position among the countries observed. It had the M2/reserve ratio close to one, implying that it had the ability to defend its currency in the event of capital outflows. At the same time, the RER depreciated, and no signs of credit boom was detected. It is no surprise that Singapore was able to weather the crisis. Although Thailand's growth of credit was higher than in other crisis countries, except the

Philippines, the other two indicators did not suggest strongly that the country was heading for a crisis.

Hence, even when additional measures of 'fundamentals' are considered, one still could not claim that East Asia's macroeconomic fundamentals were *raison d'etre* for the region's vulnerability. When the fundamentals in Thailand, Indonesia and Korea, are compared with those of the three countries heavily affected by the Latin American crisis, i.e., Mexico, Argentina and Brazil, the results are highly inconsistent. While the three Latin American countries had large appreciations in their RER, nearly 30 per cent and above, such a level of appreciation did not happen in Asia before summer 1997. None of the Asian countries approached 30 to 60 per cent rate of appreciation. Furthermore, Thailand, Indonesia and Korea did not have a lending boom on the scale that Latin American countries had. Yet, capital inflows in East Asia were higher than in Latin America. In the Asian case, private foreign debts are much more serious than domestic credits. The size of total private debts, especially those of the short-term category, was quite alarming.

These debts alone can explain why pressures on the local currencies had been so persistent (Yoshitomi and Ohno 1999). During 1995–1996, in all countries private foreign borrowing increased dramatically. By the end of 1996, it was recorded more than US$70 billion in Thailand, US$50 billion in Indonesia, and US$22 and US$13 billion in Malaysia and the Philippines, respectively. Unlike in Korea, most of these private debts were made by the corporate (non-bank) sector, making the negotiation of debt restructuring more difficult to conduct (Table 3.4). With the exception of the Philippines, the Japanese banks had the largest exposures in the region. The fact that by June 1997 the US banks had 'only' US$4.6, US$4, US$2.8, US$2.4, and US$10 billion exposures in, respectively, Indonesia, Thailand, the Philippines, Malaysia and Korea, may suggest why the U.S government did not put its fullest capacity in helping the region, despite the prevailing robust state of its economy.

More seriously, the proportion of short-term debts (STD) was high. In all countries, STD was larger than the long-term borrowings. By June 1997, the size of STD was US$46 and US$35 billion in Thailand and Indonesia, respectively. When contrasted with the size of foreign reserves, countries hit hardest by the crisis were precisely those that had their STD greater than foreign reserves (Forex), i.e., Korea (more than 2.0), Indonesia (1.7) and Thailand (1.5).

Thanks to a widespread optimism about the region's future growth and the celebrated label of 'East Asian Miracle', many private investors – local and foreign alike – were poised to expand their activities in the region. This was the second wave of foreign capital flows to ASEAN, coming mostly from the US, Europe and Japan (the first wave occurred during the second half of 1980s, when the Japanese investment in the region surged, following the *Yendaka* phenomenon). The high domestic interest rate did not dampen their enthusiasm, largely because foreign loans were obtained easily at a relatively low rate, and stable pegged exchange rates were perceived as a guarantee for earning stability. The label 'miracle' swayed lenders and the international financial community, making them lend recklessly.

The fast growing number of banks and multi-finance corporations, following deregulation in the banking sector, also produced considerable effects. Many big companies (conglomerates) set up new banks primarily to serve their own often-risky projects. Despite regulatory measures formally imposed by the monetary

Table 3.4   Foreign debts (US$ billion, except for the last row)

	Indonesia			Korea			Malaysia			Philippines			Thailand		
	End 1995	End 1996	Joo-97	End 1995	End 1996	Joo-97	End 1995	End 1996	Joo-97	End 1995	End 1996	Joo-97	End 1995	End 1996	Joo-97
Borrowers															
Banks	8.9	11.7	12.4	50	65.9	67.3	4.4	6.5	10.5	2.2	5.2	5.5	25.8	25.9	26.1
Public sector	6.7	6.9	6.5	6.2	5.7	4.4	2.1	2	1.9	2.7	2.7	1.9	2.3	2.3	2
Non-bank	28.8	36.8	39.7	21.4	28.3	31.7	10.1	13.7	16.5	3.4	5.3	6.8	34.7	41.9	41.3
Total	44.4	55.4	58.6	77.6	99.9	103.4	16.6	22.2	28.9	8.3	13.2	14.2	62.8	70.1	69.4
Lending banks															
Japan	21	22	23.2	21.5	24.3	23.7	7.3	8.2	10.5	1	1.6	2.1	36.9	37.5	37.7
USA	2.8	5.3	4.6	7.6	9.4	10	1.5	2.3	2.4	2.9	3.9	2.8	4.1	5	4
Germany	3.9	5.5	5.6	7.3	10	10.8	2.2	3.9	5.7	0.7	1.8	2	5	6.9	7.6
Others	16.8	22.7	25.3	41.1	56.3	58.9	5.8	7.8	10.2	3.7	6	7.2	16.8	20.8	20.1
Maturity															
Short-term debt (SID)	27.6	34.2	34.7	54.3	67.5	70.2	7.9	11.2	16.3	4.1	7.7	8.3	43.6	45.7	45.6
Long-term debt (LID)	16.8	21.2	23.9	23.3	32.4	33.2	8.7	11	12.6	4.2	5.5	5.9	19.2	24.4	23.8
SID and Forex															
Foreign reserves (Forex)	14.7	19.3	20.3	32.7	34.1	34.1	23.9	27.1	26.6	7.8	11.7	9.8	37	38.7	31.4
SID)/Forex	1.88	1.77	1.71	1.66	1.98	2.06	0.33	0.41	0.61	.53	0.66	0.85	1.18	1.18	1.45

Source: Compiled from BIS.

authority (e.g., legal lending limit, capital adequacy ratio), weak enforcement has discouraged the development of a healthy banking sector. Many governments in the region also played favouritism. A few selected private sectors with high leverage and well-connected groups were given special-non-transparent-facilities. These private businesses could obtain credits from the state banks with a rate that was much lower than the prevailing market rate, and under far more lenient conditions. This obviously spells trouble for the state banks since the probability of default of such loans is very high. Hence, there was an irony: privatisation *increases* – instead of decreases – the public sector's burden.

The combination of corruption, cronyism and nepotism, popularised as CCN, resulted in misdirected credits, many of which went into projects with the best connection rather than those with the best economic or financial prospect. Indeed, returns on capital fell sharply in the region during the 1990s, most dramatically in Korea. Loans were advanced on the basis of inadequate project appraisals, much of which went to the real estate related sectors. When the latter crashed, many banks and finance companies suffered from a serious liquidity problem. The above story may have been told and read in various occasions. Yet, it is a kind of a story with a limited sense of priority. Anything suspected to have caused the system to be vulnerable are thrown in, without assigning any degree of importance to different factors. The main focus of the current study is precisely to assign priorities to those factors mentioned above.

Exploring Sources of Vulnerability and Policy Responses

In the process of assigning priorities, one must first determine whose perspectives a particular set of priorities represent. In this context, there are two sets of perspectives to be considered. First are those of the IMF who has been involved in the policy-design in many countries after the crisis, and the second set reflects the alternative views. In many instances, the latter belong to the crisis-affected countries that eventually succumbed to the IMF rescue programme, hereafter the 'recipient countries'.

Let us examine the perceptions of the two parties in terms of what are the sources of vulnerability that led to the crisis, and what should be the corresponding policy prescriptions. From the IMF perspectives, a weak banking system (labelled WEAKBANK in the first column of Table 3.5 was among the most serious sources of economic vulnerability in the Asian crisis countries. Among others, this was reflected through the high growth of bank credits (yet, as indicated earlier, it was far from what is called a credit boom). Like in most standard analyses of financial crisis, the IMF was also of the opinion that the fixed exchange rate system prior to the crisis, labelled FIXEDER, had put the region in a susceptible position. However, such an opinion only emerged after the crisis broke out. In many instances during the 1990s, the IMF tends to praise the system for its ability to propel a robust economic growth with stability. It is common to concentrate the analysis of a financial crisis on the fixed exchange rate system. When things went wrong, the exchange rate tends to be overvalued. While the nominal rates maybe fixed, under such circumstances the real exchange rate would likely appreciate, hurting exports and the overall balance of payment.

Table 3.5   **Sources of vulnerability and policy response: IMF's vis-à-vis alternative perspectives**

X	IMF views Y	Z	Unintended outcomes	Alternative views Sources	Policy
	Y	Z		Sources	Policy
WEAKBANK	CLM	BLENDING	ECCOST	CORPDEBT	LBDH
FIXEDER	TMP	CPFLOWS	NOBS	CGION	MPBC
GOVANCE	LIQ	RERAF	SAVERS	PRUDEBANK	
		GOVT	SOCCOST		

X:	Source
Y:	Policy
Z:	Expected outcomes
WEAKBANK:	Weak banking system
FIXEDER:	Fixed exchange rate system and exchange rate appreciation
GOVANCE:	Poor governance
CLM:	Budget, bank restructuring and fundamental reforms
TMP:	Tight monetary policy
LIQ:	Liquidity support and open capital
BLENDING:	Resume bank lending
CPFLOWS:	Positive net capital flows
RERAF:	Low inflation to avoid appreciation of currency
GOVT:	Improved governance and BOP
ECCOST:	High cost and ineffective restructuring
NOBS:	No real improvement in the balance sheet
SAVERS:	No capital inflows and big windfall to savers
SOCCOST:	High social cost
CORPDEBT:	Massive inflows and corporate debts
CGION:	Contagion
PRUDBANK:	Weak prudential enforcement
LBDH:	Debt rescheduling and capital control
MPBC:	Moderately tight financial policy and gradual bank and corporate restructuring

The poor governance in the corporate, banking and government sectors (labelled GOVANCE) is another source of vulnerability. The IMF believes that this featured heavily throughout the Asian crisis countries, exacerbating the vulnerability of the country's financial system. It is no surprise that the IMF tend to assign a relatively high degree of importance on this factor. With the above assessments, the prescribed policies were designed to overcome those sources of vulnerability. The weak banking system needs to be resolved by a systematic banking reform. When necessary, it should also include the closure of non-viable banks. At the same time, the problems of poor governance have to be resolved by major reforms that allow drastic and fundamental changes in microeconomic and institutional structures. To the extent that a real appreciation of the exchange rate and the overall market confidence are determined by the inflation rate and government signals to the market (its seriousness to respond to the shock), at the early stage the IMF also requested the recipient countries to tighten its budget. This policy is fairly standard in the IMF conditionality.

A tighter budget would help reduce the inflation rate that could simultaneously assure the market that the government is dealing seriously with the problem.

The bank restructuring, fundamental changes and microeconomic reforms, and the tightening of government budget, are all combined in a policy item labelled CLM. But a more important – yet also most controversial – medicine prescribed by the IMF is the policy to tighten the monetary sector by raising the interest rate (labelled TMP). In addition to curbing the inflation caused by the currency depreciation, such a policy is also expected to prevent further capital outflows and/or to attract new capital inflows, both of which would help strengthen the local currency. Only with CLM and TMP in place the IMF's role as a lender of last resort in providing liquidity supports given a fairly open capital account (labelled LIQ), can be expected to function. Yet, according to the mandate given to the IMF, such a financial help should be directed only for supporting the country's balance of payment. Despite the IMF's frequent requests for budget consolidation and bank restructuring, no IMF resources can be used for these purposes.

Each of the policy described above has its specific rationale and objective. Bank restructuring and fundamental micro economic reforms are meant to clean up the financial and real sector, and to enhance the quality of governance (labelled GOVT)). The corresponding improvements in the banks' balance sheet would allow banks to resume their intermediation function by extending loans (BLENDING). A strict government budget together with tight monetary policy could help remove any inflationary pressure that might be fuelled by the exchange rate depreciation. If successful, the RER could be prevented from appreciating (labelled RERAP). In turn, this would help increase the country's exports, and improve the balance of payment position. As indicated earlier, the tightening of monetary policy by raising the interest rate is also expected to generate positive net capital flows (CPFLOWS). So much is for the IMF's basic arguments. As far as the 1997 Asian crisis is concerned, some of the intended outcomes did not really materialise. Even worse, several unintended outcomes emerged. In some instances, the latter even overwhelmed the positive results coming out from the prescribed policies. The following is a list of such unintended outcomes. In restructuring the banking sector, a huge amount of resources, mostly public money, had to be spent for the main component of the program, i.e., bank recapitalisation. Indeed, as discussed in the preceding section, a most notable sign of vulnerability prior to the crisis was the sheer size of private sector debts, largely short-term and un-hedged. As the exchange rate began to collapse, the local currency value of these debts surged, hurting the balance sheet position of most corporate and banking sectors throughout the region. Hence, a bank recapitalisation programme was inevitable.

However, in practice, the programme often absorbed a resource amount beyond what the country could actually afford, given other programmes that need to be financed during the crisis (the costs of bank recapitalisation could range from 30 to 60 per cent of GDP). Yet, by 1999, almost two years after the programme was implemented, the intended objective of resuming banks' intermediation function has been practically unmet, implying that the programme is cost ineffective (labelled ECCOST in Table 3.5). In all Asian crisis countries, bank recapitalisation had been conducted practically by using public money. While each country has different format and mechanism, they all used some sort of government bonds. The value of bonds would appear in the asset side of the bank's balance sheet, removing the prevailing bank's negative net worth. However, actually the real financial position of the banks did not improve. With a considerable amount of bonds in their assets, most banks still have liquidity problems, since most of their assets are non-liquid. The only fresh money comes from the payments for the interest of the bonds. As a result, many recapitalised banks are not in a position to lend.

In this sense, the item representing no real improvements in bank's balance sheet (NOBS) listed in Table 3.5 is one of the unintended outcomes. In most Asian crisis countries, the expected capital inflows after the interest rate was raised did not occur. From this point alone, one could have expected that the costs of setting a high interest rate (e.g., credit crunch, exacerbating firms' balance sheet) are likely to exceed the benefits. Yet, there is still another kind of cost for the economy. The high interest rate has provided huge windfalls to savers, who are generally of the medium and high-income category, while a large number of population did not have bank savings. Hence, the high interest rate policy could potentially worsen the income disparity. In Table 3.5, this unintended outcome is labelled SAVERS.

Another unintended outcome is related to the tightening of government budget. It is often the case that this would mean massive expenditure cuts, including in those items related to social overhead capital. In the Thailand and Indonesian case, many subsidies (e.g., fuel, food, etc.) would have to be either slashed drastically or removed completely from the budget, causing prices of some basic necessities to increase. This could potentially deteriorate the general social conditions of the country (SOCCOST). One could always argue that, generally, the IMF did not have a sufficient time to analyse the costs and the benefits of each of the policy choices. Yet, they were expected to produce a policy package after the crisis arrived, or, at the height of the crisis. Hence, it would not be fair to put the blame on the IMF. What I intend to argue in this manuscript is not really to criticise the IMF. Rather, looking back at what happened after evaluating the working and repercussions of the IMF-style policies, I am ready to claim that a number of those policies were ineffective. In some cases, they even aggravated the situation by creating undesirable outcomes. Never mind who initiated the policies, the fact is, the effectiveness of some policies has been low. From various discussions I had with policy makers, analysts, and observers throughout the Asian crisis countries, I found that most had their own opinion – not necessarily in line with the IMF's – with regards to what caused the country's vulnerability and the crisis, and what should be the appropriate policy response. Obviously, the views may not be the same in all countries, and even in one country I also found different opinions among analysts and policy makers. But what is more interesting is that, in most cases the differences are more on the priority (ranking of importance) of the listed sources and policies, rather than on the substance and types of arguments. The list of what I perceived as the recipient countries' alternative views is shown in the last two columns of Table 3.5. In line with the discussions in the preceding section, the recipient countries tend to view massive inflows of private debts to be a major source of vulnerability (CORPDEBT). In some countries, policy makers had already detected the surge of such debts as early as in 1992. But at the time the trend was viewed as normal, as a consequence of the increased role of private sector in the economy.

For right or wrong reasons, many believed that things could have been different (a continuing 'miracle') had Thailand not fallen into a crisis. If there would be a slowdown, they argued, it would not have caused a recession at a proportion that Asian countries outside Thailand had actually suffered. In essence, they believed that a contagion (labelled CGION) played an important role in precipitating the crisis and escalating its depth. On the banking sector, many agreed with the IMF assessments that this sector has been weak. But most people are also of the opinion that financial sector's weaknesses actually began to build up immediately after the financial liberalisation was implemented. The latter, of course, has been persistently promoted, if not insisted, by the international organisations including the IMF since 1980s. The key problem rests on the lack of enforcement of prudential regulations (PRUDBANK), not the lack of regulation itself. With the above assessments, the recipient countries tend to believe that any restructuring policy, be it for the banking or corporate sector, have to be done in a gradual manner, in order for these economic unitsto be able to adjust with the new environment. A drastic measure would destabilise the system that needs to be rescued in the first place. Since deteriorating market confidence precipitated capital outflows, some control measures in financial policies (monetary and budgetary) are needed. However, unlike that is usually proposed by the IMF, the tightening of the financial policy should be moderate, so that it will not aggravate the already damaged balance sheets of many banks and corporate firms throughout the region. The combination of gradual restructuring and moderate financial policy is denoted by MPBC in Table 3.5.

Similarly, budget retrenchments ought to be done moderately. Some even argued that under the distress situation, the budget should have been made more expansionary, in order to avoid the so-called 'bad' equilibrium (see Krugman 1999a, Azis 2000a). Notwithstanding the question whether a gradual and moderate measure is more effective than drastic one, the above policies alone will not likely help to strengthen the exchange rate. As long as indebted banks and corporate sector could not resolve the mismatch in their foreign debts, it would be difficult to avoid pressures on the exchange rate. Hence, the opinion expressed tends to opt for some sort of a debt haircut. In Table 3.5, this policy measure is labelled LBDR. Although from the perspectives of the IMF and the recipient countries each policy can be considered as a stand-alone proposal, realistically speaking, attempts must be made to find some combined policies that would be acceptable to both parties. A non-zero sum game matrix could be used to identify those joint policies. Yet, like in most conflict situations, there is no guarantee that agreeable joint policies (equilibrium points) do exist. If they don't, a series of compromises ought to be made.

Before proceeding with the standard game theoretic approach, however, the most critical question would be how we can come up with proper payoff values for each party. Unlike most game theoretic exercises, here I would adopt a particular method known as *Analytic Hierarchy Process* (AHP), from which the payoff values are determined based on the perceptions of the two parties involved.

Analytic Hierarchy Process

By combining the theory of scaling and the theory of hierarchy, AHP provides an effective and powerful means to capture and systemise perceptions based on a pre-designed hierarchy. From the hierarchical framework, some sort of payoff values can be generated. The basic essence of AHP is to rank elements according to their importance by comparing them in a *pairwise* manner, such that, ratio scales rather than ordinal scales, are obtained. The original ranking based on 'experts' perceptions does not have to be perfectly consistent (*transitivity* assumption is not strictly required). For clarity purposes, a brief mathematical exposition of AHP is shown below (for more detailed expositions, see Saaty 1994a and Saaty 1994b, and for an explanation of AHP's non-mathematical procedure, see Azis and Isard 1999). The critical early step is to arrange the problem (state of affairs) into a hierarchical framework.

When there are three elements (policies) in the hierarchy, such as in the earlier cited example, only three input judgements are required. But in general case, the precise value is hardly given, simply because the input judgement is only an estimate. It suggests that there are some perturbations. While the reciprocal property still holds, it is no longer so for the consistency property. When more than two elements are compared, the notion of consistency can be associated with the assumption of *transitivity*. In words, the inputted judgements do not have to reflect a full consistency (in fact, in addition to permitting some degrees of inconsistency, another strong point of AHP is its allowance for a rank reversal to occur (Saaty 1994b)). Yet, as shown earlier, the resulting matrix and the corresponding vector remain consistent. It is the consistent vector w that reflects the priority ranking of the elements in each level of the hierarchy. The resulting priority ranking in each level, are derived from computation.

The Analysis

Let me first discuss the policy evaluation related to whether or not the IMF-inspired policies are effective. Like most policy evaluations, there are always positive and negative consequences of a particular policy. Only after weighing each of these consequences can one better understand the nature and intensity of the overall implications of the policy. Furthermore, in evaluating the effectiveness of a policy, one also needs to consider the time frame used in the analysis. The efficacy question could be approached by either analysing counterfactual policies, or, by evaluating the performance after the policy is implemented. Using a specific country case, I have done some counterfactual scenarios based on an economy-wide model (Azis 2000a, 2000b). Here, I am taking another approach by repeating the perception evaluation after the set of policies have been implemented. For such a purpose, a two-stage analysis was conducted. First, I evaluated the expected outcomes of the policies put forth prior to the actual policy implementation. This was done based on what I perceived as the IMF's arguments for selecting such policies. These expected outcomes were weighed in terms of their importance. On the other hand, the unintended outcomes also need to be considered. The importance of each of them will have to be scrutinised. Subsequently, 'yes' and 'no' types of questions are explored.

Under the expected outcomes of the policies, the relevant question would be: 'Is the IMF policy *effective*?' While the answer may likely lean towards 'yes,' what is more important in this analysis is the intensity of the answer. That could be obtained only after weighing the importance of all the expected outcomes. Only then can the 'yes' and 'no' questions be raised, and they are posed with respect to each of those outcomes. After performing a series of pairwise comparisons and matrix multiplications, the derived weights for 'yes' and 'no' are, respectively, .63 and .37 (as explained in the preceding section, these are the elements of a normalised eigen vector of a pairwise comparison matrix).

A similar approach was taken for the unintended outcomes. The relevant question would be: 'Is the IMF policy *ineffective*?' The question is raised with respect to each of the unintended outcomes. For example, consider the following question: 'Given the possibility that there will be no real improvements in banks' balance sheet, labelled NaBS, can we infer that the IMF policy is ineffective?' The answer may be 'yes'. But as before, it is the intensity of such answers that matters most. After constructing a series of pairwise comparisons, the resulting weighs for 'yes' and 'no' are .627 and .373, respectively, suggesting that after considering all the potential unintended outcomes, the intensity of perceptions that the IMF policy is ineffective is roughly 1.7 times more than the perceptions that the policy is effective.

Combining the scale priority of 'yes' from the 'benefit' hierarchy and the scale priority of 'yes' under the 'cost' hierarchy would give the relevant 'benefit/cost' ratio, based upon which the analysis can be made. In the above case, the benefit/cost ratio is .630/.627 = 1.005. Hence, the perceptions that the IMF policy is effective are more favoured, albeit by only a very small intensity, than the views that it is ineffective. Notice that the priority ranking in both hierarchies is examined *prior* to the actual policy implementation (the first stage). Hence, all of the listed outcomes, expected and unintended, are only potential in nature. In the second stage, a similar approach is applied to the two hierarchies, but this time the evaluation is done *after* considering the factual outcomes and the repercussions of the policy. With the exception of Korea towards the end of 1998, new capital inflows in the region could hardly be detected. On the contrary, even with a high interest rate policy, capital still fled the countries. The usual adverse repercussions of a high interest rate policy (e.g., credit crunch, output collapse), strongly undermine the merits of the policy. More importantly, it exacerbated the loss of market confidence, fuelling further capital outflows. Having realised these facts, the weight assigned to the expected capital inflows (CPFLOWS) needs to be adjusted downward, e.g., from .526 to .299.

Despite the seemingly improved balance sheets of many banks after the restructuring programme, most of them remain unable to resume their intermediation function. The amount of bank lending (BLENDING) continued to be negligible. Thus, the corresponding priority has to be reduced, i.e., from .107 to .104. Given the fact that these priority weights are derived from a normalised eigen vector, the weights for the remaining two elements, i.e., RER and GOV, are automatically adjusted upward. With the new priority ranking of the expected outcomes, the resulting 'yes' and 'no' pertaining to the question whether the IMF policy is effective, is also changed. This time, the weight for 'yes' is .624 and the weight for 'no' is .376.13 The resulting outcome indicate that, the benefit/cost ratio for 'yes' is .624/.627 = .995, reversing the conclusions obtained earlier. This suggests that, after looking at what happened since the implementation of the IMF policy, *ceteris paribus*, the perceptions are leaning towards a conclusion that the policy is ineffective.

An important conjecture drawn from the analysis is that, perceptions over a particular issue could alter when circumstances change (e.g., after evaluating the actual facts). Yet, the ranking in each hierarchy itself may not necessarily change, although in the above example it does, i.e., the predominant position of CPFLOWS is taken over by RER. In general, whether or not the ranking changes (a rank reversal being one extreme possibility), the resulting benefit/cost ratio may alter, although the overall conclusion could remain the same (e.g., the benefit/cost ratio may decline from 1.005 to 1.001, in which case the conclusion about the efficacy of the IMF policy is unchanged). In our case, both the ranking of elements (expected outcomes of the IMF policy) and the overall conclusions based on the altered benefit/cost ratio, change. By all means, however, this is not a rule.

While useful for understanding the nature and the extent of different, or sometimes conflicting, perceptions about the crisis, the above analysis leaves any potential 'conflict' of opinion (prescriptions) unresolved. To dwell with various elements in order to uncover the intensity of what causes the vulnerability and what would be the proper policies, is my next task.

Recall that a hierarchy for each party has been constructed. To introduce some elements of reality, in which give-and-take elements are usually involved in the process, it is important to take account of each party's understanding on the other's position. This implies that combining the policies at the bottom level of each hierarchy, would be a proper step to take. The new hierarchy that combines the two sets of policies. Note that at the bottom of the hierarchy the listed policies are now joint policies.

Once the new hierarchy is set, a priority ranking of the sources of vulnerability based on each player's perspectives is established. For example, it is perceived that the IMF tends to put the weakness of the banking sector (WEAKBANK) as the most important source of vulnerability (.648), followed by the poor governance (GOVANCE, .23) and the fixed exchange rate system (FIXEDER, .122). Under each of these sources, alternative joint policies are evaluated (there are 6 joint policies, since the IMF and the alternative views came up with, respectively, 3 and 2 prescribed policies, see again Table 3.5). In this way, the IMF is provided with information about what would be the recipient countries' alternative preferences for each of the IMF's proposed policy. Indeed, in practice, before a formal agreement ('letter of intent') is signed, both parties usually shared their views and opinions. Such information has to be disclosed and made known.

Let me first provide an example that is not necessarily reflecting the real case in terms of what each party actually perceives (the example is only intended to show a particular type of outcome, i.e., non-equilibrium solution). After conducting a series of pairwise comparisons, suppose that the priority ranking points to a joint policy CLM-MPBC being the most preferred from the IMF's point of view (i.e., .232)). Note that such a preference is derived after taking into account the predominance of weak banking system as the cause of vulnerability, and the possible reaction from the recipient countries to each of the IMF policies. Suppose that after considering the utmost importance of the corporate debts as a source of vulnerability, the recipient countries are strongly in favour of a joint policy LIQ-MPBC (.439), which is a combination of IMF's provision of liquidity supports providing an open capital account (LIQ) and the recipient countries' adoption of moderately tight financial policy plus restructuring of the banking and corporate sector that will be done gradually (MPBC). It should not be too difficult to judge why these countries strongly prefer such an option. Putting together all the weights from the combined hierarchy into a non zero-sum matrix in Table 3.6 results in constant shifts (moves) from one joint strategy to another, without the possibility for the system to settle down at a particular solution. A failed negotiation or unreachable agreement could be a situation that such an example represents. Yet, in all cases during the Asian crisis, some sort of agreements have actually been reached. Hence, a more realistic case needs to be developed.

Table 3.6   Non-equilibrium case

	f- IMF-7 TMP	f- IMF-7 CLM	f- IMF-7 LIQ
Recipient LBDH	(.220; .067)	(.179; .108)	(.130; .093)
Recipient MPBC	(.165; .259)	(.232; .034)	(.073; .439)

In a standard game theoretic approach, one could transform the non-equilibrium state in Table 3.6 into an equilibrium case by adopting particular techniques under certain assumptions. Here, I refrain from doing so, primarily because what I intend to emphasise is the transparency of the process, not merely finding the solution. It should be clear that all numbers (payoff values) that appear in Table 3.6 are generated from the perceptions expressed by each party. There was a clear procedure and transparent mechanism involved in the process. Hence, instead of using a mechanical game theoretic approach to arrive at an equilibrium state, I re-simulated the perceptions of both parties. Two attempts were made, i.e, re-simulate the system by imposing an IMF-led adjustment, and re-simulate a scenario in which the recipient countries initiated the move. One could clearly see from Table 3.6 that should the IMF make the adjustment first, the weight of the joint policy CLM-MPBC is reduced to .191, dismissing it as the IMF's most preferred choice. Instead, the newly favoured joint strategy is TMP-MPBC (receiving .256). Indeed, judging from the actual developments, a tight money policy (TMP) appears to be non negotiable from the IMF standpoint. In contrast to CLM-MPBC, under TMP-MPBC the budget retrenchment is no longer too strict, but the tight monetary policy has to be sternly implemented. Judging from the payoff values of the recipient countries, however, the most preferred joint policy is LIQ-MPBC (.439), that is, they will adopt a moderately tight financial policy and a gradual restructuring in the banking and corporate sector, while the IMF extends its liquidity supports to help improve the balance of payment position and strengthen the exchange rate without rendering to a restricted capital account. With these different preferences, an equilibrium state is still achievable, since the recipient countries will have the policy that they actually prefer, i.e., MPBC, although the IMF could not extend financial supports without imposing conditionality, particularly on the monetary policy. Hence, instead of LIQ-MPBC that would yield .080 for the IMF and for the recipient countries, the agreeable joint policy is TMP-MPBC (yielding .256 and .259 for the IMF and the crisis countries, respectively, see Table 3.7).

Table 3.7   Equilibrium case 1: IMF made the initial move

	IMF-7 TMP	IMF-7 CLM	IMF-7 LIQ
Recipient LBDH	(.180–; .067)	(.169–; .108)	(.125–; .093)
Recipient MPBC	(.256+; .259)	(.191–; .034)	(.080+; .439)

Under some circumstances, the IMF could either be forced or prefer to let the recipient countries to initiate the policy adjustment. In this scenario, in which the recipient countries raise the intensity of their preference towards CLM MPBC (the weight is increased from .034 to .149), but not enough to overtake their preference for LIQ-MPBC (.397) and TMP-MPBC (.246). This is despite the fact that the weights for the latter two have been reduced. This adjustment alone is sufficient to transform the system from a non-equilibrium to an equilibrium state. As shown in the non-zero sum matrix in Table 3.8, such an adjustment could lead to an equilibrium solution, in which the IMF would get its original first-best choice (.232) based on Table 3.6, and the recipient countries would obtain their newly high prioritised choice (.149). As indicated earlier, the joint policy CLM-MPBC implies that the budget is firmly curtailed, but the monetary policy is not too tight.

Table 3.8   Equilibrium case 2: recipient countries initiated the adjustment

	IMF TMP	IMF CLM	IMF LIQ
Recipient LBDH	(.220; .070+)	(.179; .057–)	(.130; .081–)
Recipient MPBC	(.165; .246–)	(.232; .149+)	(.073; .397–)

Based on the three cases described above, the scenario that is closest to the real policy episode during the Asian crisis is the equilibrium case 1, in which the implemented policy was a combination of a tight money policy with the government budget being slightly slashed, and the restructuring of the banking and corporate sector is conducted only in a gradual manner. In reality, however, the IMF often pushed for more drastic restructuring, especially that the progress in improving the governance in practically all crisis countries has been too slow, far from originally expected.

Debates about Conditionality

Many analysts have reviewed critically the role of the IFIs, especially of the IMF, in reducing the risk of financial crises. Their policy response to a crisis is also often criticised. The arrival of the 1997 Asian crisis, followed subsequently by the crises in Brazil and Russia, made the debate on the issue even more intense.

One of the contentious points relates to the question whether or not the IMF should continue intruding with deep structural reforms as part of its programme conditionality. As described earlier, one of the major differences between the IMF perspectives and the alternative views is precisely on the subject of bank/corporate restructuring and other microeconomic reforms. During the Asian crisis, the IMF has been persistently pressing for sweeping and fundamental reforms not only in the financial sector but also in various microeconomic fronts (CLM). The nature and extent of the requested reforms were so wide-ranging (even in Korea, the IMF requested that eight structural problems need to be resolved), that some analysts doubted whether industrial economies of Europe could implement, let alone accept, such a sweeping conditionality, despite their far more developed institutions than what the Asian crisis countries had. The alternative views clearly prefer to undertake reforms in a gradual fashion (MPBC). No less seriously is the question whether the IMF's conditionality has not gone beyond its IMF's basic mandate. Shouldn't the IMF go back to the basic, i.e., dealing only with short-term balance of payment liquidity problems, and let other IFIs such as the World Bank and the Asian Development Bank deal with longer-term issues of structural adjustment and micro economic reforms? On this subject, there has been a series of debates, and several reports have also been produced. One of such debates occurred in the US, the most influential shareholder of the IMF.

Under the legislation authorising US participation in the quota increase of the IMF and the establishment of New Arrangement to Borrow, a congressionally appointed bipartisan group named the *International Financial Institution Advisory Commission* (IFIAC) was established. The group, headed by Carnegie Melon University Professor Allan Meltzer, a long time IMF foe, was asked to report on the future role and responsibilities of international institutions including the IMF. It needs no further explanation to realise the importance of this Commission's work in determining the IMF role to prevent and respond to a crisis. Among other things, the Commission's proposal is to limit the IMF lending to only short-term credits (four to eight-month maturity) with a very high interest rate, but essentially without conditionality, to only solvent countries. The idea is, the recipient country should be given incentives to repay the debt quickly.

But the major essence of the Commission's recommendation is to scale back the IMF's roles significantly. This has become a major target of disagreements among several analysts, including, most importantly, those at the US Department of Treasury. In response to the IFIAC's report, more known as the *Meltzer Commission*, the US Treasury issued its own recommendations, in which it basically rejected the main thrust of the Meltzer Commission, arguing that reducing the capacity of the IMF would undermine the promotion of proper macroeconomic policy reforms in many (non eligible) countries. Furthermore, restricting lending to only short-term credits with high interest rate would render the programme ineffective in promoting recovery in the prequalified countries. In turn, it could substantially harm the D.S economy (e.g., farmers, workers and businesses), hence the broader D.S national strategic interests.

While the issue of conditionality may not appear as critical (at least it has not been the main thrust of the IFIAC report), it has actually taken a centre stage in the more general debate. During the Asian crisis, it has sparked the most critical differences between the IMF and the recipient countries in seeing what kind of policy deemed appropriate in responding to the crisis. Recall from the non-equilibrium case in Table 3.6 that the highest payoff value for the IMF, should it be given an exclusive choice (without confronted with other party's possible reaction), is the implementation of CLM (.232), which is essentially a sweeping micro economic reform in various sectors. This is the kind of conditionality most recipient countries are neither willing to accept nor having the capacity to implement, even if officially they may agree to do so. The unanimous first choice for these countries, as far as restructuring and other micro economic reforms are concerned, is to implement them in a gradual manner (the highest payoff, .439, is MPBC, see again Tables 3.5 and 3.6).

It is interesting to note that Japan, considered to be the last and most important 'defender' of the Asian crisis countries, had also expressed its disagreement with the idea of imposing sweeping structural reforms as part of the IMF's conditionality during the Asian crisis. Indeed, since the publication of the World Bank's 'East Asian Miracle,' Japan has been always taking a cautious stand with respect to the 'Washington Consensus' type of market mechanism. It repeatedly emphasised the importance of each government to decide itself what, how and at what pace to reform (state intervention), instead of forcing the agenda through various means of influence from outside.

The non-equilibrium case in Tables 3.5 and 3.6 reflects a situation whereby the two parties insist on their policy preferences. If the IMF is willing to adjust, i.e., making the payoff value for CLM-MPBC smaller than that under TMP-MPBC (e.g., from .232 versus .165 to .191 versus .256), an equilibrium solution can be reached. Alternatively, if the IMF is firm with its stand, the only other equilibrium alternative is for the recipient countries to accept, reluctantly, or, only formally, the required sweeping reforms. In return, they are neither obliged to implement a tight monetary policy nor compelled to retrench the government budget (CLM-MPBC).

Earlier, I have explained the policy interpretation of CLM-MPBC from the financial standpoint. What does it stand for, in terms of fundamental micro economic reforms? Most policy makers in the recipient countries acknowledged that many sectors still need to be reformed. They agreed with the premise, and accepted the prescription by co-signing (along with the IMF) the official letters of intent (LOI). However, they are also fully aware that, realistically, such comprehensive and fundamental reforms are hard to implement. Not even GECD countries could execute the sweeping programmes with such great details and comprehensiveness. It is more likely that the actual implementation would be gradual. Because of this different opinion, wrangles and disputes between the two parties over the programme implementation are often resulted. It is also worth noting that, increasingly the free market preachers have to face widespread popular discontent. From Seattle, Chiang Mai, Washington, to Prague, the message of those who demonstrated during the IMF's meetings was fairly compelling: a significant number of people represented by progressive citizens, ranging from labour unions, environmental groups, and farmer organisations, in both developed and developing countries alike, are ready to battle over an alternative framework of development. Clearly, opponents and critical groups are not dead, they are only quiescent. On issues pertaining to financial crises, these groups have come up with specific proposals. For example, in December 1998, *Friends of the Earth,* the *Third World Network* and the *International Forum on Globalisation* jointly asserted through their 'Call to Action: A Citizens Agenda for Reform of Global Economic System', that the rules and institutions of global finance should seek to reduce instability in global financial markets. More interestingly, they specifically pointed out the need to create maximum space for national governments to set policies that could best prevent any financial instability from transforming into a crisis, among others through regulating capital movements. This is essentially in contrast with 'the idea of imposing rules from outside, such as the case with the IMF conditionality. Hence, the discussions about policy choices such as CLM and MPBC are highly relevant for the current development debate.

Conclusion

The episode of Asian crisis revived the debates about the appropriateness of a standard policy response to a crisis. This study attempts to explicate them by comparing the IMF perspectives and the alternative views presumably held by the recipients of the IMF programme over the questions of what caused the vulnerability in the East Asian economies that led to the 1997 crisis. A traditional policy mix of credit tightening and fiscal restraints had been imposed as part of the IMF funding condition. It appears that its fairly successful experiences with the handling of the Latin American crisis convinced the IMF that such a policy mix was appropriate. Nobel laureate James Tobin believes that the IMF's Asian packages are also based on its experiences with Mexico in 1994. But the pre-crisis conditions in East Asia were very different from those in Latin America (on inflation, budget, balance of payment, the nature and borrowers of foreign debts). Beyond that standard policy, the IMF also insisted on rather drastic and fundamental changes in economic and institutional structures (labelled CLM in the text). Their experiences with policy adjustments of this kind in Eastern Europe and the former Soviet Union (to shift from communism to a market economy) had inspired the IMF to do the same thing with the crisis-affected countries in East Asia.

By using a particular method to generate ratio scales to reflect the degree of importance of the intended and unintended outcomes of the IMF-inspired policies, a benefit/costs analysis reveals that the claims on the effectiveness of those policies could be reversed after the actual outcomes are evaluated. The initial analysis supports the claim that the policies are effective, but the post-factual analysis suggests the opposite. This has an extremely important interpretation with respect to the IMF's role. At a relatively short period of time, it was difficult for the IMF to design carefully, and prescribe systematically, a set of policies for the crisis-affected countries. Indeed, when a country approaches the Fund, usually its economy is already in a rather bad shape. Yet, the IMF is expected to act quickly in order to contain the progression of the crisis. Not enough time is available for the IMF to weigh the costs and the benefits – or to predict the effectiveness – of the policies.

Having said that, however, the arguments contained in the critical evaluation of those policies remain valid. This study attempts to distil the unintended outcomes of those policies, with the expectation that it would help us to understand better, why in reality some policies with a fairly strong theoretical ground provide only a small degree of effectiveness.

While the IMF arguments for insisting fairly drastic and fundamental microeconomic adjustments in the recipient countries appear to have strong rationales (who would not agree with ending corruption, curtailing the special business privileges, and imposing the practice of good governance), such adjustments could severely undermine the sources of East Asia's strength and stability. Worse, they are not really needed for the return of capital, nor are they required to restore market confidence. For the crisis-affected countries, to make drastic changes in the midst of a currency crisis would be more disastrous than helpful (poor timing). According to the alternative views, changes would be better conducted in an evolutionary and gradual fashion (labelled MPBC in the main text), such that only few shocks will be created in the system.

From several experiments to capture the IMF perceptions and those of the alternative views, a joint-policy of CLM and MPBC is found to be a possible equilibrium solution (equilibrium case 2). This implies that the monetary policy should be only moderately tight, and, while fundamental changes in the economic and institutional structures are formally accepted, the actual implementation is likely to be gradual. Under such a scenario, one could consequently expect continued wrangles between the IMF and the recipient countries over the issues of programme implementation. If the IMF could be more flexible with its conditionality on structural changes, disputes could be avoided (equilibrium case 1). It is a matter of empirical test to find out whether or not such an equilibrium joint-policy is optimal.

References

Azis, I. and W. Isard (1996), 'The Use of the Analytic Hierarchy Process in Conflict Analysis and an Extension', *Peace Economics, Peace Science and Public Policy*, Vol. 3, no. 3, pp. 120–30.

Azis, I. (1999). 'Do We Know the Real Causes of the Asian Crisis?', in Barry Herman (ed.), *Global Financial Turmoil and Reform: A United Nations Perspective*, The United Nations University Press, New York.

Azis, I. (2000a), 'Modeling the Transition from Financial Crisis to Social Crisis', *Asian Economic Journal*, Vol. 14, no. 4, December, pp. 66–81.

Azis, I. (2000b), 'East Asian Crisis and Poverty: A Modeling Approach', High Level Symposium on Alternative Development Paradigms and Poverty Reduction, December, ADB Institute, Tokyo.

Azis, I. (2001), 'Modeling Crisis Evolution and Counterfactual Policy Simulations: A Country Case Study', *ADB Institute Working Paper*, No. 23, Tokyo.

Azis, I. (2005). 'What Would Have Happened in Indonesia if Different Economic Policies had been Implemented When the Crisis Started?' *The Asian Economic Papers*, MIT Press.

Blustein, Paul (2001), 'The Chastening: Inside the Crisis that Rocked the Global Financial System and Humbled the IMF', *Public Affairs*.

Chinn, Menzie D. (1998), 'On the Won and Other East Asian Currencies', NBER Working Paper, No. 6671, August.

Claessens, S. and S. Djankov (2000), 'Publicly Listed East Asian Corporates: Growth, Financing, and Risks', in Dominique Dwor-Frecaut, F. Colaco and M. Hallward-Driemeier (eds), *Asian Corporate Recovery: Findings From Firm-Level Surveys in Five Countries*, The World Bank, Washington DC.

Feldstein, Martin (1998), 'Refocusing the IMF', *Foreign Affair*, March/April.

Fischer, Stanley (2000a), 'Managing the International Monetary System', presented at International Law Association Biennial Conference, London, 26 July.

Fischer, S. (2000b), 'Strengthening Crisis Prevention: The Role of Contingent Credit Lines', presented at the Banco de Mexico 75th Anniversary Conference.

Fischer, S. (2000c), 'Stabilization and Monetary Policy: The International Experience', Mexico City, Mexico, 15 November.

Greenspan, Alan (2000), 'Globalisation', remarks made at the Banco de Mexico 75th Anniversary Conference, 'Stabilization and Monetary Policy: The International Experience', Mexico City, Mexico, 14 November.

Klein, L.R. (1998), 'The Asian Economic Crisis', paper delivered to the Second Committee of the UN General Assembly, 7 October.

Kohler, Horst (2000), 'In Search of Stability and Broadly-Shared Prosperity: Reform ofthe International Monetary System', presented at the Meeting with ED Parliamentary Committees, Brussels, 7 November.

Krueger, Anne (2000), 'Conflicting Demands on the International Monetary Fund', *American Economic Review*, Vol. 90, No. 2, May, pp. 112–34.

Krugman, P. (1999), 'Balance Sheets, the Transfer Problems, and Financial Crises', in P. Isard, A. Razin and A. Rose (eds), *International Finance and Financial Crises*, Kluwer, MA.

Lane, T., A. Gosh., J. Hamman, S. Phillips, M. Schulze-Ghattas and Tsidi Tsikata (1999), *IMF-Supported Programmes in Indonesia. Korea and Thailand: A Preliminary Assessment*, IMF, Washington DC.

Sachs, J.D., A. Tornell and A. Velasco (1996), 'Financial Crises in Emerging Markets: The Lessons From 1995', *Brookings Papers on Economic Activity*, No. 1.

Saaty, Thomas (1994a), *Decision Making in Economic, Social and Technological Environments with the Analytic Hierarchy Process*, Vol. 7, RWS Publications.

Saaty, Thomas L. (1994b), *Fundamentals of Decision Making and Priority Theory*, Vol. 6, RWS Publications.

Tobin, James and Gustav Ranis (1998), 'The IMF's Misplaced Priorities. Flawed Funds', *The New Republic*, available online at the following address: http://www.thenewrepublic.com/archive/03 9 8/03 0998/tobin03 0998.html.

US Treasury News (2000), 'From the Office of Public Affairs: Strengthening the International Financial Architecture', LS–758, released on 8 July.

World Bank (1993), *The East Asian Miracle: Economic Growth and Public Policy*, Oxford University Press, Oxford.

Yoshitomi, M. and K. Ohno (1999) 'Capital Account Crisis and Credit Contraction', *ADB Institute Working Paper*, No. 2.

Chapter 4

Globalisation and Economics

David Colander

Globalisation: What is it? What does economics have to say about it? What does it imply for the prospects for the US economy? And what does it imply for the economics profession?

What is Globalisation?

You hear the term globalisation all the time. There are demonstrations against it, speeches in favour of it, and incessant talk about it. If you do an Alta Vista search for globalisation you get over 300,000 hits; if you mention a book with globalisation in the title to publishers you can see the saliva; and if you put globalisation in the title of your course, you increase enrolment by 40 per cent. Globalisation is hot.

But what is it? Clearly, globalisation has something to do with increased integration of the world society, with an emphasis on increased economic integration. It also has something to do with businesses changing their reference point – thinking globally rather than locally. Finally, it has something to do with technological change. But, although the term is new, none of these elements, nor academic discussions of them, are. They have existed since at least World War II. For example, the economic integration of world economies has been ongoing over the last fifty years, as countries have worked through GATT and the WTO to reduce trade restrictions. In the 1960s and 1970s there was major discussion of the growth of the multinational corporation as businesses changed their reference point from domestic to international. Similarly, technology has been continually bringing the economies of the world closer together. For example, throughout this period improved transportation, such as air transport, made the world smaller, and improved communication, such as the international expansion of telephone service, made it possible for individuals around the world to talk as if they were neighbours. All these changes were chronicled in the academic discussion.

So what's new is not the process, but the name; globalisation is simply a new name that has been given to the process of the latest cycle of internationalisation. Perhaps the most significant development leading to the use of the new term is the political breakdown of the former Soviet Union. That breakdown ended the Cold War as we knew it and created a true world market place in which discussions of intergovernmental relations began to focus more on economic than political considerations. Businesses could start thinking of all countries as potential consumers and producers rather than as potential allies or enemies. This changed the focus of thinking from politics to economics, and changed the term to characterise it from internationalisation to globalisation.

What Does Economics Have to Say about Globalisation?

While economics cannot provide answers about the effects of globalisation, it can provide insight by putting issues into perspective, and that is what I will briefly try to do here. My first point is that globalisation is part of a process of specialisation and expanding trade – a process that has been ongoing since the 1600s. The nature of that expanding trade has been significantly influenced by the international political environment, so it is not a smooth expansion. Generally, however, the movement has been toward increased trade. Consider the colonisation that occurred in the 1700s. That colonisation established trade among continents and close political and economic integration among areas all over the world. It globalised our dealing with the world as much or more than recent events. The gold standard provided an international monetary standard that made trade among various countries financially feasible. Then the development of corporations and the protection of insurance allowed global trade to proceed, and are as important to the globalisation of the world as the Internet. In short, trade, led by technology, drives the economy toward a globalised economy.

Trade, in turn, is part of a broader set of developments in specialisation and the division of labour. The gains from this specialisation have driven the economy forward, and, when combined with the institutional development of markets that foster that trade, have morphed into the dynamic process of growth. It is a dynamic process that takes different forms at different times, but the process is one that Adam Smith discussed back in 1776. Consider the following passage from Smith's *Wealth of Nations*.

> This division of labour, from which so many advantages are derived, is not originally the effect of any human wisdom, which foresees and intends that general opulence to which it gives occasion. It is the necessary, though very slow and gradual consequence of a certain propensity in human nature which has in view no such extensive utility; the propensity to truck, barter, and exchange one thing for another ... (This Propensity) is common to all men, and to be found in no other race of animals, which seem to know neither this nor any other species of contracts. Nobody ever saw a dog make a fair and deliberate exchange of one bone for another with another dog. Nobody ever saw one animal by its gestures and natural cries signify to another, this is mine, that yours; I am willing to give this for that.

Smith explains how trade leads to specialisation and division of labour, which leads to technological growth, which leads to economic growth, which leads to more specialisation and more division of labour, which leads to more trade. You end up with a virtuous circle that drives economies forward and creates the wealth of nations.

Angus Madison (1995) shows the close correlation between the development of markets in the late 1700s as the primary organising factor of the economy and the world growth rate. It makes clear the fact that markets have been associated with growth. Now correlation does not mean causation, but the close correlation between the introduction of markets and the increase in the growth rate puts the onus on those who would argue that markets are not conducive to growth.

My reason for dwelling on this discussion of specialisation and trade is to emphasise that globalisation is part of a broader evolutionary process in economics that has been going on for centuries and will likely continue to go on for centuries. Sometimes the dynamics of trade operate within the arbitrary confines of a nation state; at other times the dynamics of trade and specialisation operate outside the confines of a state, but the dynamics of trade and specialisation lie at the foundation of globalisation.

Economic Texts and Globalisation

When you read the economics textbooks of the 1990s, you did not read much about the growth process. In fact the textbooks of that decade seldom mentioned division of labour, specialisation, and technology. Instead they talked about Pareto optimality and static efficiency in micro, and business cycles in macro.

One of the positive feedback effects of globalisation on economic texts is that it is changing them. The initial change has occurred in macro where growth is now given equal billing with business cycles, albeit in a somewhat sterile Solow growth model. In micro, the change was much harder to make and is still coming together. The reason is that the textbook presentation of micro is intricately entwined with ideas of static efficiency and allocation theory. Dynamic elements, such as increasing return, learning by doing, and path dependencies are not to be found in the texts because they are hard to integrate with their static discussions of efficiency; they muddy the efficiency story.

One cannot blame the texts for their content; they simply reflect the profession. Globalisation is changing the profession's focus, albeit slowly, from static efficiency to dynamic issues of growth, and in twenty years, I hope, the micro presentation in the texts will include significantly more discussion of the division of labour, specialisation, and dynamic efficiency than it now does.

The shift in focus away from the dynamic efficiency and toward static efficiency occurred in the work of David Ricardo. Adam Smith was writing before the Industrial Revolution took place. Thus when he gave examples of specialisation, such as the famous pin factory, they were internal to a firm. But the dynamic argument was there. Ricardo was writing when the Industrial Revolution was in full swing, and he could have expanded the dynamic elements of Smith's discussion. But he did not; instead he focused on the static dimensions of comparative advantage and efficiency. This allowed him to make a wonderfully complete formal presentation of the advantages of trade and the role that comparative advantage plays in trade. But his formal proof came at a significant cost; he had to give up many of Smith's dynamic arguments – learning by doing, the role of the extent of the market, increasing returns, and path dependencies.

The profession followed Ricardo, and the static model that evolved from Ricardo's work emphasised the law of one price – the law describing the process through which prices of both factors and goods are driven toward their end state: equality across geographic areas. But in focusing on that law, the texts missed another important law of economics – the law of dynamic growth, the law that states that trade will drive economies to grow through specialisation, learning by doing, and economies of scale. It is this law that globalisation is causing texts to rediscover.

Globalisation and the Two Economic Laws

The key element of the globalisation story that the textbooks lack involves the interplay between the law of dynamic growth and the law of one price. The story told by the law of one price is one of diffusion of growth. If the benefits of globalisation were diffuse, there would be little interest in globalisation. But while globalisation does make society as a whole richer in an economic sense (notice I said richer, not better off – that's a much harder question) and increases the wealth of nations, globalisation does not mean growth for everyone; it can lead to enormous disparities in income. To understand that part of the story one must understand the law of dynamic growth.

The key element of the dynamic law of growth for globalisation is that it pushes the economy toward disequilibrium. Whereas the law of one price diffuses the benefits of trade, the law of dynamic growth tends to be place specific. The cumulative process that drives it affects certain areas significantly more than other areas. There are two reasons for this.

The first has to do with the spread of ideas. The growth process begins with an idea in an industry. That idea spreads to other individuals communicating with friends in a different industry. These friends are then stimulated to integrate that idea into their industry and the growth process continues. Since the close communication necessary for this process to work often has a geographic component, the cumulative growth process generally has a geographic component. For example, a firm might figure out a better way of coordinating its labour through flexitime. Workers and managers talk and other firms who see that it works adopt it. Making new ideas work involves many aspects where one needs specific advice as to what works and what doesn't. Thus, continual consultation is needed. This need for continuous consultation tends to make the dynamic growth occur unevenly geographically throughout the economy.

The second reason involves investment. Growth generates income, which creates an investment fund that allows more experimentation and more learning by doing. So successful firms have funds to invest, which tends to make them even more successful. Since financial markets for new ideas, such as the venture capital market, generally have a significant geographic component, they too tend to make the dynamic growth occur unevenly geographically throughout the economy. The result is Kaldor's virtuous circle.

The above argument is that there are relative winners in the growth process. But if there are relative winners, there must be relative losers; the other side of the law of dynamic growth is the areas that do not grow, or grow much slower than average. They end up with a vicious circle of no growth and fall further and further behind. The dynamic law of growth creates enormous income inequalities that put strains on the social and political systems.

What stops this place-specific cumulative process of growth is the law of one price. When differences among regions get too great, the law of one price starts working. That law of one price can operate in a number of ways. Workers and firms may move into the growing area. This in migration holds profits and wages down from what they would have otherwise been. Alternatively, successful people and firms, who have internalised the new idea, can move from successful to unsuccessful, cheaper, locales to hold their costs down and improve the quality of all their lives. For example, the high rents and shortages of workers in Silicon Valley drive firms to other places – Sacramento, Utah, Vermont, India and Costa Rica. But this diffusion process is slow, and is often overwhelmed by the ongoing place specific growth. Full diffusion takes place only in those industries where significant growth has ended. For major technological changes that can be twenty or thirty years.

There are many institutional arrangements that can influence the diffusion. The friendship network, the regulatory structure, the communications network, and the financial network are examples. The study of growth, and hence the study of globalisation, requires a study of these networks and information flows in an information poor contextual setting.

At the end of the story of growth, the law of one price always wins out. It is that ending that the textbooks and the profession have focused on. But society has little interest in that long run ending. It is interested in the interim period, which can be decades or even centuries. In that interim period we can get the enormously large differentials in wages and prices of goods. The fact that the law of one price will eliminate these 'eventually' is not particularly relevant to policy makers. When 'eventually' actually arrives, most policy makers are out of office. Policy makers tend to be interested in the now and the near future – the intermediate run is their long run. It is for that reason that policy discussions tend to focus on how countries or regions can get on the right side of the law of dynamic growth.

Economics does not have much specific to say about these policy issues other than the general platitudes. Trade and specialisation require a regulatory structure – agreements about property rights and enforceable contracts. Inevitably, as technology changes, the ideal regulatory structure changes, and as it does political pressure is brought to bear on nation states and existing regulation. As international trade expands, to deal with global externalities, and to provide a more efficient regulatory structure, the nature of governmental regulation must change. More international cooperation is required; new institutions must develop, and new agreements must be reached. Standards must be developed. A language of communication must be chosen. The nature of these standards makes a big difference in how various areas will fare within the global economy.

If history is any guide, the regulatory structures will lag the economic developments, and will be forever playing catch-up, but the pressures will be there. Thus, while I do not see an international government, I do see an increased set of international agencies charged with coordinating regulation and dealing with the political side effects of globalised production and trade.

What Does Globalisation Have to Say about Prospects for the US Economy?

In the 1990s the US was on the right side of the place-specific growth. Part of the reason for this was that it had the right institutions for growth – relatively low personal taxes, a well developed venture capital market, firm property rights for ideas, and significant government support of research that private individuals were allowed to appropriate. These attributes, combined with a large amount of dumb luck, started a dynamic virtuous circle of growth, and led, to calls of the US economy having reinvented itself and become a new economy. I believe these calls are overblown. Much of the US success is simply 'right place, right time'.

The answer to the question of how long the 'new economy' will continue reduces to the question of how long it will take the law of one price to diffuse the benefits of growth and how much place-specific growth will occur in the US. The answer to these questions depends on a number of issues. Probably the most important is US immigration policy. The US has an enormous shortage of skilled workers. If major immigration of skilled foreign workers is allowed, in the immediate run high tech wages will be held down and firms will be more likely to stay in the US. In the intermediate run, the advantage of this policy for the US is less clear. These skilled workers will provide the seeds for ideas to spread to other countries. If they return to their home countries, taking their earnings and their knowledge with them, in the intermediate run that immigration can hasten the workings of the law of one price. However, if little immigration is allowed, firms are more likely to move activities outside US borders, increasing the probability that the cumulative growth process will take off elsewhere. So regardless of US policy, the pressure of the law of one price will be there.

The development of the Internet and e-commerce will work to increase the speed of the diffusion by making geographic place less important, but not by as much as globalisation zealots claim. The reality is that the Internet has significant limitations as a market place. To emphasise this point I suggest to my students that they think of the Internet as simply a fancy catalogue with speed ordering. There are clearly limits to what one will buy through a catalogue (at least until virtual reality becomes a reality). Thus the expansion of the Internet's influence will be limited.

Goods that fit the catalogue Internet sales model have certain characteristics. They must be goods that one does not need to test out, or try on before buying. They must be goods that one does not care who is selling. They must be goods that have a significant standardisation and generic quality. That limits the range of retail goods significantly, making b2c (business to customer) expansion limited.

Consider Priceline's 'name your own price' business model – it is useful in rationing off time-dimensional goods such as hotel rooms and airline seats, but it is less likely to be successful at selling storable goods, where, because of inventory, net marginal costs fluctuate little. C2c (customer to customer) sales are essentially flea markets, and are more a hobby for people than a significant economic event. So the goods that best fit into the e-commerce model are b2b (business to business) sales, and that is where most of the growth of Internet sales will likely be. Increases in b2b Internet sales will slightly speed up the law of one price, but they will leave geographic elements highly important.

Probably the biggest advantage the US has in continuing its lead in the latest round of technological improvements is that the standard language of business communication has become English. This gives an enormous comparative advantage to English speaking countries, and is worth trillions of dollars in wealth to them. Had Spanish developed as the de facto language, the recent US growth would not have occurred. Imagine the cost of training the 200 million people in the US who do not speak Spanish to speak Spanish to a level where they can communicate effectively. At $10,000 per person, that would be $2 trillion dollars. And even then many individuals would not be facile at Spanish communication. But it is precisely such cost that is being presented to developing countries as an entry cost to take part in the Internet revolution. Interestingly, the smaller countries, which have adopted English as their primary second language, are in a better position than larger countries that have not. Thus, Finland may be in a better position than France to take a lead role in the global economy.

When one thinks of global equity, a case can be made for a transfer from English-speaking nations to non-English speaking nations to partially compensate them for adapting to the English standard. I don't expect such a transfer to occur. But at some point pressure will come for such transfers.

The second advantage the US has is the seeming acceptance by the world of its liberal property rights approach to ideas. Currently US patents and copyrights are being given for broad conceptual business methods, such as one-click shopping, name-your-own-price auctions, and supplying movies over the Internet, along with the more traditional technologies and ideas that have been allowed to be patented. These patents are being given out for a relatively long time relative to the changing technology. Some of these methods and technologies will become the standards, and if accepted by world economies, they will involve trillions of dollars flowing into the US long into the future. US policy recognises this and has made acceptance of US intellectual property rights a requirement for countries entering the world-trading environment. I expect these property rights to be a hot issue of contention in the future. Despite these two advantages, eventually I see the law of one price as overwhelming the law of dynamic growth for the US, and as that happens, the end of the US new economy. That end will come suddenly. In manufacturing, the law of one price has already overwhelmed the law of dynamic growth. Manufacturing is now global. But, luckily for the US manufacturing makes up only a small fraction of the cost of a product. Thus, as US manufacturing is transferred abroad, the process actually creates jobs in the US. Consider Nike shoes. A subcontracting company produces all Nike shoes, primarily in China. But when one buys Nike shoes, the actual shoes make up only a small percentage of their costs. What one is actually buying is a collection of activities that goes into the value added of shoes – the advertising, distribution, and legal services – and much of that has remained in the US. Countries will be looking for ways to maintain the value-added stream within their individual borders, but in each aspect they must fight the law of dynamic growth.

What Does Globalisation Imply for the Economics Profession?

Let me now turn to my final question: How will globalisation be affecting the economics profession? This question has more general relevance than it seems since the discussion can be seen as a case study for how globalisation might proceed in other industries in the future. The heart of my story is that at some point in the next fifty years the law of one price will exert itself and remove the US domination of the academic economics market. When that happens; US-centred structure of the profession will change. Virtual universities, collections of scholars from around the world who have combined into an accredited programme of study in a particular field, will increase enormously, and will significantly displace many geographically-based programmes.

Growth of these virtual universities will put pressure on existing universities to develop and expand their brands. This will most likely be done by newly developed accrediting agencies, which will be created by an international consortium of universities. How fast these virtual universities take off depends on technological growth. True virtual universities will only develop when in-person classes are replaced by complete virtual classes, where each student, regardless of where they are, is virtually recreated in an interactive classroom setting. When one can enter a virtual connection port and it is almost impossible to distinguish 'being there' and 'virtually being there', place specific dynamic growth will be undermined and the law of one price will rule. But that is decades away.

In the interim quality US programmes will remain, but weaker programmes will either die or enter into virtual partnerships that increase course options for their students. Most will merge into consortiums and the degrees they give will be consortium degrees. The best of the current campuses will remain as places where students can live if they choose, but a graduate student accepted into a 'virtual university' will be able to reside at any of the twenty or so locations that comprise the physical 'university' – or can reside at none of them, as long as he or she is close to a virtual communication port. I would expect that students attending these virtual universities will be generally geographic nomads, residing at two or three individual schools during their studies to work personally with specific mentors.

A Change in the Geographic Centre of Gravity of Economics

This rise of virtual universities will mean a de-Americanisation of graduate schools in general and of graduate economics programmes in specific. Of course, the geographic centre of the economics profession will be harder to measure since most foreign programmes will have US components and vice versa. As the law of one price takes hold the economics profession will likely have three competing geographic centres: one in Europe, one in the United States, and one in Asia. The seeds of the end of American dominance of the economics profession are already being sown; today foreign students heavily dominate the student body of top economics programmes. Currently, the majority of these top foreign-born economists are staying in the United States. At some point this will change and geographic units of virtual universities in their countries of origin will make lucrative offers to these economists to return home. As they move back home, they will take the top journals, reputations, and the core of the profession with them.

A second change that will occur because of globalisation is increased specialisation in economics training. Today 'graduate work in economics' is rather uni-dimensional. Becoming 'an economist' means studying economics at a graduate programme in economics, and the majority of graduate programmes, and all the top-ranked programmes, are quite homogeneous. In the first years of graduate school, in particular, everyone learns essentially the same set of models, and the same approaches. Globalisation will bring about division of labour and need for specialisation. The majority of consortiums granting economics-related degrees will have multiple tracks. People no longer will become generic economists; instead they will become clearly designated specialists in public finance, health care, macro forecasting, forensic economics, industrial relations, and other areas. Graduate study in economics will still start with one semester of general core courses: one in micro, one in complex systems analysis, and one in statistics, but these courses will not be the technical courses they are now; they will be survey courses given to acquaint students with the broad field of economics. Immediately after these courses, students will begin specialised study in one, or sometimes two, areas of specialty. Each of these areas of specialties, or tracks, will have its own set of required courses and knowledge.

The track that will be most equivalent to the programme students follow today will be the economic theory track. But this track will become a specialty track for those few going on in theory; it will be very small; its requirements will be very difficult; and since few jobs will be available for its graduates, most of its graduates will have to spend some years in low-paid postdoctoral work hoping to find one of the few theoretical research positions available. One of the new tracks will be a 'general economics' track, which will primarily serve to prepare individuals to teach economics principles to undergraduates. That, as it is today, will be one of economists' most important jobs. This track will primarily give an overview of various subfields rather than going deeply into the technical aspects.

Redefinition of Boundaries

This increased specialisation will be accompanied by a redefinition of boundaries of graduate economics programmes within institutions. Currently, firm institutional boundaries exist between public policy schools, arts and sciences schools, engineering schools, business schools, law schools, and medical schools. In the future, these boundaries will break down. New specialties will evolve out of a combination of schools or programmes within schools. For example, a person studying health economics in the future will go to a health economics programme that will evolve out of a combination of economics programmes, medical school programmes, and public policy school programmes. A person studying macroeconomics will study jointly with engineering complex systems schools and an economics programme. In the future there will no longer 'economists', but, instead, health economists, statistical specialists, simulations experts who focus on economic issues, public finance specialists, and so on.

The changing of the boundaries will not come easily and will involve much infighting. Initially, as these programmes grow they will hire their professors from existing graduate economics programmes. But as they become more specialised and rigorous, these schools will become self-replicating. They will hire their own PhD graduates to teach in their programmes, develop their own journals, and split off from economics *per se*. As they do, the demand for economists from traditional programmes will fall.

Conclusion

This has been a far-ranging chapter, but one that I hope has added some insight into the globalisation concept. The arguments it made were the following. First, globalisation is not new, but simply the latest incarnation of Adam Smith's story of specialisation, division of labour, and trade. Its emergence on the scene has had a positive effect on the economics profession by forcing it to start to come to grips with the dynamics of growth, and reduce its concentration on static efficiency and the law of one price. The texts are beginning to introduce these changes. Second, once one brings back Smith's dynamic story, economic reality can be portrayed as a key determinant by two major forces – the static law of one price – driving the economy toward an equilibrium, and a dynamic law of growth, with its thermodynamic turbulence creating place specific growth and pockets of no growth. Third, the US economy in the early 2000s was on the right side of this virtuous circle, but that new economy will not continue forever. While the US has a number of advantages going for it – the English language standard and the world acceptance of US property rights of ideas – eventually the law of one price will diffuse those benefits, and the US economy will falter. Finally, a predicted loss of the US dominance of the economics profession was presented as a case study for how the law of one price will eventually overtake the geographic specific growth that led to US domination.

References

Madison, Angus (1995), *Monitoring the World Economy*, OECD, Paris.
Smith, Adam (1937 [1776]), *An Inquiry into the Nature and Causes of The Wealth of Nations*, Modern Library, New York.

Chapter 5

Globalisation of the World Economy: Potential Benefits and Costs and a Net Assessment

Michael Intriligator

F₀₂ /
F₅₀

Introduction

Globalisation is a powerfully real aspect of the new world system, and it represents one of the most influential forces in determining the future course of the planet. It has many dimensions: economic, political, social, cultural, environmental, security and others. The focus here will be on the concept of globalisation as applied to the world economy. Of course, this concept is interpreted differently by different people. Partly as a result of these different interpretations, there are very different reactions to globalisation, some see it as a danger to the world economic system while others see it as a means of advancing the world economy.

There are three purposes of this chapter. First, it will clarify the notion of globalisation as it is generally applied to the world economy. Second, it will evaluate both the potential benefits and the potential costs stemming from globalisation. Third, it will consider how the costs or dangers stemming from globalisation could be offset through wider international cooperation and the development of new global institutions.

This chapter argues there are both positive and negative aspects of globalisation. Some of its positive features stem from the effects of competition that it entails, and some of its negative aspects (that could potentially lead to conflicts) could be offset by international or global cooperation through agreements on policy or through the development of new international institutions. Thus, while globalisation can cause international conflicts, it can also contribute to their containment through the beneficial effects of competition and the potential of global cooperation to ameliorate economic and various other threats facing the planet.

Globalisation of the World Economy: An Interpretation

Globalisation will be understood here to mean major increase in worldwide trade and exchanges in an increasingly open, integrated and borderless international economy. There has been remarkable growth in such trade and exchanges, not only in traditional international trade in goods and services, but also in the exchange of currencies, capital movements, in technology transfer, in people moving through international travel and migration and in international flows of information and ideas.

One measure of the extent of globalisation is the volume of international financial transactions, with some $1.2 trillion flowing through New York currency markets each day, and with the volume of daily international stock market transactions exceeding this enormous amount.

Globalisation has involved greater openness in the international economy, an integration of markets on a worldwide basis, and a movement toward a borderless world, all of which have led to increases in global flows. There are several sources of globalisation over the last several decades. Technological advances have significantly lowered the costs of transportation and communication and dramatically lowered the costs of data processing and information storage and retrieval. The latter stems from developments over the last few decades in electronics, especially the microchip revolution. Electronic mail, the Internet, and the World Wide Web are some of the manifestations of this new technology. A $2,000 laptop computer is many times more powerful than a $10 million mainframe computer of twenty years ago.

A second source of globalisation has been trade liberalisation and other forms of economic liberalisation that have led to reduced trade protection and to a more liberal world trading system. This process started in the last century, but two World Wars and the Great Depression interrupted it. It resumed after World War II through the most-favoured-nation approach to trade liberalisation, as embodied in the 1946 General Agreement on Tariffs and Trade (GATT) and now in the World Trade Organisation (WTO). As a result, there have been significant reductions in tariffs and other barriers to trade in goods and services. Other aspects of liberalisation have led to increases in the movement of capital and other factors of production. Some have suggested that globalisation is little more than a return to the world economy of the late nineteenth century and early twentieth century, when borders were relatively open, when there were substantial international capital flows and migrations of people, and when the major nations of Europe depended critically on international trade. This is particularly the view of some British scholars, looking back to the period of British imperial dominance of the world economy. While there are some similarities in terms of trade and capital movements, the period of a century ago did not have some of the major technological innovations that have led to a globalised world economy today that is qualitatively different from the international economy of the last century.

A third source of globalisation has been changes in institutions, organisations with a wider reach, due, in part, to technological changes and to the more wide-ranging horizons of their managers, who have been empowered by advances in communications. Thus, corporations that had been mainly focused on a local market have extended their range in terms of markets and production facilities to a national, multinational, international, or even global reach. These changes in industrial structure have led to increases in the power, profits, and productivity of those firms that can choose among many nations for their sources of materials, production facilities, and markets, quickly adjusting to changing market conditions. Virtually every major national or international enterprise has such a structure or relies on subsidiaries or strategic alliances to obtain a comparable degree of influence and flexibility. As one measure of their scale, almost a third of total international trade now occurs solely within these multinational enterprises. With the advent of such global firms, international conflict has, to some extent, moved from nations to these firms, with the battle no longer among nations over territory but rather among firms over their share of world markets. These global firms are seen by some as a threat to the scope and autonomy of the state, but, while these firms are powerful, the nation state still retains its traditional and dominant role in the world economic and political system.

Non-governmental organisations, the NGOs, have also taken a much broader perspective that, as in the case of the global firms, is often multinational or global. Even international organisations, such as the United Nations, the International Monetary Fund and World Bank, and the new World Trade Organisation have new global roles. Overall, multinational enterprises and other such organisations, both private and public, have become the *central* agents of the new international globalised economy.

A fourth reason for globalisation has been the global agreement on ideology. with a convergence of beliefs in the value of a market economy and a free trade system. This process started with the political and economic changes that started the 1978 reforms in China a 'falling dominoes' series of revolutions in Eastern and Central Europe starting in 1989 that ended with the dissolution of the Soviet Union in December 1991. This process led to a convergence of ideology, with the former division between market economies in the West and socialist economies in the East having been replaced by a near universal reliance on the market system. This convergence of beliefs in the value of a market economy has led to a world that is no longer divided into market-oriented and socialist economies. A major aspect of this convergence of beliefs is the attempt of the former socialist states to make the transition to a market economy. These attempted transitions, especially those in the former Soviet Union and in Eastern and Central Europe have, however, been only partially successful. The nations involved and their supporters in international organisations and advanced western market economies have tended to focus on a three-part agenda for transition, involving: 1) stabilisation of the macroeconomy; 2) liberalisation of prices; and 3) privatisation of state-owned enterprise. Unfortunately, this 'SLP' agenda fails to appreciate the importance of building market institutions and providing for an appropriate role for the government in a modern mixed economy.

A fifth reason for globalisation has been cultural developments, with a move to a globalised and homogenised media, the arts, and popular culture and with the widespread use of the English language for global communication. Partly as a result of these cultural developments, some, especially the French and other continental Europeans, see globalisation as an attempt at US cultural as well as economic and political hegemony. In effect, they see globalisation as a new form of imperialism or as a new stage of capitalism in the age of electronics.

Some have even interpreted globalisation as a new form of colonialism, with the US as the new metropole power and with most of the rest of the world as its colonies, supplying it not only with raw materials, as in earlier forms of European colonialisation, but also with technology production facilities labour, capital, other inputs to the production process and markets on a global basis. Whether one sees globalisation as a negative or as a positive development, it must be understood that it has clearly changed the world system and that it poses both opportunities and challenges. It is also clear that these technological, policy, institutional, ideological and cultural developments that have lead to globalisation are still very active.

Thus, barring a radical move in a different direction, these trends toward greater globalisation will likely continue or even accelerate in the future. One important aspect of these trends will be the growth in international trade in services that has already substantially increased, but promises even greater growth in the future, especially in such areas as telecommunications and financial services. The result will be continued moves toward a more open and more integrated world as it moves closer and closer to a planet without borders and to a more integrated, open and interdependent world economy. The result will be an even greater worldwide flow of goods, services, money, capital, technology, people, information and ideas.

Impacts of Globalisation on National Economies

Globalisation has had a significant impact on all economies of the world. It affects their production of goods and services. It also affects the employment of labour and other inputs in the production process. In addition, it affects investment, both in physical capital and in human capital. It affects technology and results in the diffusion of technology from initiating nations to other nations. It also has major effects on efficiency, productivity and competitiveness.

Several impacts of globalisation on national economies deserve particular mention. One is the prodigious growth of foreign direct investment (FDI), which is much greater than the growth in world trade. Such investment plays a key role in technology transfer, in industrial restructuring, and in the formation of global enterprises, all of which have major impact at the national level. A second is the impact of globalisation on technological innovation. New technologies, as already noted, have been a factor in globalisation, but globalisation and the spur of competition have also stimulated further advances in technology and speeded up its diffusion within nations through foreign direct investment. A third is the growth of trade in services, including financial, legal, managerial, and information services and intangibles of all types that have become mainstays of international commerce. In 1970, less than a third of foreign direct investment related to the export of services, but today that has risen to half and it is expected to rise even further, making intellectual capital the most important commodity on world markets. As a result of the growth of services both nationally and internationally, some have called this 'the age of competence', underscoring the importance of lifelong education and training and the investment in human capital in every national economy.

The Benefits of Globalisation Stemming from Competition

It has already been noted that globalisation has both positive and negative effects. This first part of this chapter will focus on the positive effects of globalisation, stemming from competition, while the next will focus on its negative effects, which could lead to potential conflicts. Finally, the last part will consider the potential for international cooperation to diminish or to offset the negative effects of globalisation.

Globalisation has led to growing competition on a global basis. While some fear competition, there are many beneficial effects of competition that can increase production or efficiency. Competition and the widening of markets can lead to specialisation and the division of labour, as by Adam Smith and other early economists writing on the benefits of a market system. Specialisation and the division of labour, with their implications for increases in production, now exist not just in a nation but on a worldwide basis. Other beneficial effects include the economies of scale and scope that can potentially lead to reductions in costs and prices and are conducive to continuing economic growth. Other benefits from globalisation include the gains from trade in which both parties gain in a mutually beneficial exchange, where the 'parties' can be individuals, firms and other organisations, nations, trading blocs, continents, or other entities.

Globalisation can also result in increased productivity as a result of the rationalisation of production on a global scale and the spread of technology and competitive pressures for continual innovation on a worldwide basis. Overall, these beneficial effects of competition stemming from globalisation show its potential value in improving the position of all parties, with the potential for increased output and higher real wage levels and living standards. The result is a potential for greater human well being throughout the world. Of course, there is the distributional or equity issue of who does, in fact, gain from these potential benefits of globalisation.

The Costs of Globalisation and Potential Conflicts

Globalisation involves not only benefits, but also has costs or potential problems that some critics see as great perils. These costs could lead to conflicts of various types, whether at the regional, national, or international level. One such cost or problem is that of who gains from its potential benefits. There can be substantial equity problems in the distribution of the gains from globalisation among individuals, organisations, nations, and regions. Indeed, many of the gains have been going to the rich nations or individuals, creating greater inequalities and leading to potential conflicts nationally and internationally. Some have suggested the possibility of convergence of incomes globally based on the observation that the poor nations are growing at a faster rate than the rich nations. The reality, however, is that a small group of nations, the 'tiger economies' of East Asia, have been growing at rapid rates, while the least developed nations of Africa, Asia, and South and Central America have been growing at a slower rate than the rich nations. These poor nations are thus becoming increasingly marginalised. The result has been not a *convergence* but rather a *divergence* or polarisation of incomes worldwide, with the rapid-growth economies joining the rich nations, but with the poor nations slipping even further behind. This growing disparity leads to disaffection and possibly even international conflicts as nations seek to join the club of rich nations. This issue of distribution is a major challenge in the process of the globalisation of the world economy.

A second cost or problem stemming from globalisation is that of major potential regional or global instabilities stemming from the interdependencies of economies on a worldwide basis. There is the possibility that local economic fluctuations or crises in one nation could have regional or even global impact This is not just a theoretical possibility as seen in the exchange rate and financial crisis in Asia, in Thailand in 1998 and then spread to other Southeast Asian economies and even to South Korea. These linkages and potential instabilities imply great potential mutual vulnerability of interconnected economies. A worldwide recession or depression could lead to calls to break the interdependencies that have been realised through the globalisation process, as happened in the Great Depression of the 1930s, with competitive devaluations, beggar-my-neighbour policies, escalating tariffs, other forms of protectionism, etc. The result could be economic conflict, gravitating to economic warfare and possibly to military conflict, repeating the history of the interwar period leading to the largest war in human history.

A third type of problem stemming from globalisation is that the control of national economies is seen by some as possibly shifting from sovereign governments to other entities, including the most powerful nation states, multinational or global firms, and international organisations. The result is that some perceive national sovereignty as being undermined by the forces of globalisation: Thus globalisation could lead to a belief among national leaders that they are helplessly in the grip of global forces and an attitude of disaffection among the electorate. The result could be extreme nationalism and xenophobia, of Europe, including both former enemies and devastated allies, into this new world system and in promoting reconstruction and growth.

The present Cold War period has some similarities to the one after World War II in that a new world system must be created. Such a system will have to take account of the new situation of a world not divided by ideology, rather one that is increasingly more integrated. The sequence of revolutions that began in Europe in 1989 led directly or indirectly to the end of the Cold War, the demise of the Warsaw pact, the unification of Germany, the dissolution of the Soviet Union, and the attempted transition of the former socialist states to democracy and a market economy, with only mixed success. The West for its part, has largely failed to establish structures such as those developed after World War II to bring Russia other former Soviet States and Central and Eastern Europe into the world economic and political system.

In some respects, the current treatment of Russia is similar to the treatment of Germany after World War I, rather than its treatment after World War II. NATO expansion is perhaps the most serious error made in the post Cold War period, in that it isolated Russia and added little to European security but at an enormous expense. The total cost of NATO expansion will, in fact, be of the same order of magnitude as the current value of the Marshall Plan, some 490 billion. A new Marshall Plan for the former socialist nations of Europe could have promoted their transition and growth through institution building, industrial restructuring, investment and capital inflows, their integration into the world economy and their cooperation. These measures would have contributed more to European security than the acquisition of globalisation could lead again to catastrophic outcomes, such as those stemming from global environmental impacts, such as global warming, and pandemics.

Role of Global Cooperation in Dealing with Global Threats and in Creating a New Post Cold War System

The last two parts have highlighted both the benefits and the costs stemming from globalisation. Some could see globalisation as a very dangerous negative development by focusing on the costs and the potential for conflict while others could see it as a positive development offering unprecedented opportunities. Both of these views contain some elements of truth, but each should be offset by the other in order to gain a full understanding of the impacts of globalisation. There are twin myths here, the optimistic one that globalisation leads to only positive outcomes and the pessimistic one that globalisation leads only to negative outcomes. Any objective treatment or net assessment, however, would have to recognise both the benefits and costs of globalisation.

What is the net result of globalisation, when taking both benefits and costs into account? The answer depends crucially on the nature of the world system. In a world beset by conflicts, globalisation would probably have a net negative impact. Conversely, in a cooperative world, globalisation would probably have a net positive impact. Thus, globalisation represents a major challenge and at the same time an unprecedented opportunity in terms of the possibilities for conflict or cooperation. The challenge is to create a new world system in the aftermath of the Cold War and a movement toward globalisation that would enhance its generally beneficial effects and would minimise its actual or potential costs. The key to such a world system will be cooperation among the nations of the world and dynamic innovation, including the establishment of new institutions The challenge of the present globalised and post cold war economy is comparable to the challenge facing the winning nations in World War II. The old world had been destroyed and a new world had to be created. Not one, but two world systems were created, one in the West and the other in the East. Both involved the creation of new institutions that would replace the ones that had been destroyed in the war. Each side had its own ideology and organisation, that in the West being market-oriented and that in the East being socialist. Now, of course, the ideological divide has dissolved, where there is a convergence of ideology on the value of a market economy. A small group of Americans helped create a new world system for the West during the period from 1945 to 1955. One of the major participants was Dean Acheson, the US Secretary of State during part of this period. His memoirs are aptly named *Present at the Creation* given his role in creating this new world system. Another was Will Clayton, who developed the blueprints for both the Marshall Plan and the General Agreement on Tariffs and Trade. These people, together with President Truman, George Marshall, and others created the institutions that brought the devastated nations of Europe into the world community. These institutions included GATT, which evolved into the WTO; the United Nations; the World Bank and the IMF; the Marshall Plan and OEEC (later to evolve into the OECD); NATO; and others. These institutions and the new world system that they helped create were most successful in bringing the nations along with calls for protectionism and the growth of extremist political movements, ultimately leading to potentially grave conflicts.

It is sometimes alleged that one cost of globalisation is unemployment in the high wage industrialised economies. The low unemployment rate in many high wage nations and their high rates in many low wage nations disprove this allegation. National policy and technological trends are much more important determinants of employment than global factors. A related myth is that globalisation is threatening the social welfare provisions of some states, but other factors are much more important, including domestic fiscal policy and demographic trends. In both cases, globalisation is a convenient scapegoat for the failures of national policy.

It is also important to appreciate that the economic aspects of globalisation are only one component of its effects. There are potential non-economic impacts of globalisation involving greater risks and potential costs, even the possibility for catastrophe. One is that of security, where the negative effects of globalisation could lead to conflicts. The very process of globalisation may lead to the integration of markets which could make conflicts escalate beyond a particular region or to raise the stakes of conflict, for example from conventional to weapons of mass destruction. A second non-economic area in which globalisation could lead to catastrophic outcomes is that of political crises, which could escalate from local to large-scale challenges and, if unresolved, to a catastrophic outcome. A third such area is that of the environment and health, with the greater interconnectedness stemming from advanced fighter jets and other military equipment by some of these nations that have been admitted into NATO.

Overall, the challenge of globalisation will require truly cooperative efforts of the more powerful nations, especially among the new greater powers of the European Union, the United States, Canada, Japan, Russia, China, India, Brazil and others. Their joint activity in establishing new political arrangements and institutions could go a long way to solving global problems, including economic and other problems stemming from globalisation. Just as it was true in the earlier period of the creation of a new world, it will be necessary to revamp existing institutions or to create new ones so as to deal with economic challenges, such as the problems of distribution and mutual vulnerability stemming from globalisation. These institutions must have global perspectives and responses and they will require substantial resources and enforcement mechanisms, including some elements of supranational decision making and authority, along with appropriate transparency and accountability.

Consider how global cooperation and new international institutions can treat several of the previously identified problems, costs of globalisation. The first of these problems was that of the distribution of income and specifically the gains from globalisation both within and between nations. A supranational institution based on global cooperation could address this problem. It would, in effect, tax the nations gaining from globalisation and use the proceeds to provide technical assistance to those losing from globalisation. This is already being done in a somewhat haphazard way through the World Bank and in particular, its soft lending arm, the International Development Association provides subsidised loans to poor nations on more favourable terms than the World Bank could give. It should be done, however, on a more systematic basis, which would require either a new international institution or an expansion and change in the nature of the World Bank. The rich nations should be expected to support the establishment of such an institution as an investment in global stability, if they recognise the dangers of serious disparities in the worldwide distribution of income. The second of the problems identified earlier as stemming from globalisation is the fragility of the international economic system, leading to mutual vulnerability. Again, international cooperation and the development of new institutions or the expansion of existing institutions could address this problem. The International Monetary Fund could be instrumental in dealing with this problem. The IMF has played a key role in providing support to nations that have experienced instabilities, as in its support for Mexico during the peso crisis and its agreement to support South Korea during the East Asia financial crisis. A more credible insurance against these risks would require a substantial augmentation of the resources of the IMF, the assets of which have not grown at the same rate as international financial exchanges. International cooperation could also lead to the implementation of the Tobin tax, a small tax on foreign exchange transactions that could play a valuable role in limiting destabilising currency speculation and at the same time, provide funding for international organisations.

The third previously identified problem stemming from globalisation is that of the perceived loss of sovereignty of national governments and political leaders. This development could lead to the fear of the loss of ability of nations to determine their economic policies, political disaffection, and the rise of extremist politicians and political movements. The process of globalisation however, need not lead to a loss of sovereignty of national governments. It can also establish the proper role of political leaders, drawing a firm line between what is in the province of these governments and their leaders on one side, and what is in the province of international organisations and multinational or global enterprise on the other.

Participation in the establishment of the necessary institutions to deal with these and other problems stemming from globalisation, will, in themselves, help political leaders to regain a sense of control over their futures and positions in the global community. For example, the regulatory regimes of nations and even international organisations have become more porous and more easily overcome through advances in technology. Examples include the lack of regulation of the global integrated capital market, of trade in information services that is widely expected to grow enormously, and of labour and environmental safeguards. Cooperation among nations and international organisations could offset these developments by themselves, taking advantage of recent technological advances and using them to reassert control through cooperative activities.

Overall, there are several possible vehicles for cooperation as a way of responding to the challenges of globalisation. One is the strengthening of existing international institutions. Another is the establishment of new institutions, as in the case of the World Trade Organisation, which has a binding dispute settlement mechanism of a supranational character. A third is the establishment of larger entities, such as the European Union; or loose combinations of nations to treat certain economic issues, such as the G8 or the Asian Pacific Economic Cooperation (APEC). Global cooperation through formal or informal institutions provides an increasingly important mechanism to ensure the proper treatment of global problems, including those stemming from globalisation. Through such global cooperation it should be possible to ensure equity and stability in a globalised world, leading to economic growth for all, the transition to a market economic for former socialist states and economic development for the poorer nations. Such cooperation is also the way to treat the economic problems of globalisation including those of environmental and wealth protection on a world-wide basis, freedom from political crises or instability, and global peace and security for the planet.

References

Agnew, John A. and Stuart Corbridge (1995), *Mastering Space: Hegemony, Territory and International Political Economy*, Routledge, New York.

Archibugi, Daniele and Michie, Jonathan (eds) (1997), *Technology and Economic Performance*, Cambridge University Press, Cambridge.

Bhagwati, Jagdish N. (2000), *The Wind of the Hundred Days: How Washington Mismanaged Globalisation*, MIT Press, Cambridge, MA.

Brittan, Sir Leon (1997), 'Globalisation vs. Sovereignty? The European Response', the Rede Lecture, Cambridge University, 20 February 1997.

Clark, Ian (1997), *Globalisation and Fragmentation: International Relations in the Twentieth Century*, Oxford University Press, New York.

Feenstra, Robert C. and Gordon H. Hanson (1996), 'Globalisation, Outsourcing, and Wage Inequality', *American Economic Review*, Vol. 86, pp. 240–51.

Friedman, Thomas L. (2000), *The Lexus and the Olive Tree: Understanding Globalisation*, 1st Anchor Books Edition, Anchor Books, New York.

Giddens, Anthony (2000), *Runaway World: How Globalisation is Reshaping Our Lives*, Routledge, London.

Greider, William (1997), *One World, Ready or Not: The Manic Logic of Global Capitalism*, Simon and Schuster, New York.

Griffin, Keith (1996), *Studies in Globalisation and Economic Transitions*, ICS, London.

Hirst, Paul Q. and Graham Thompson (1996), *Globalisation in Question: The International Economy and the Possibilities of Governance*, Blackwell Publishers, Oxford.

Hutton, Will and Anthony Giddens (eds) (2000), *Global Capitalism*, New Press.

Kofman, Eleonore and Gillian Youngs (eds) (1996), *Globalisation: Theory Practice*, Pinter, New York.

Krugman, Paul R. and Anthony J. Venables (1995), 'Globalisation and the Inequality of Nations', Working chapter series, No. 5098, National Bureau of Economic Research, Cambridge, MA.

McBride, Stephen and John Wiseman (eds) (2000), *Globalisation and its Discontents*, St Martin's Press, New York.

McGrew, Anthony G., Paul G. Lewis, et al. (1992), *Global Politics: Globalisation and the Nation-State*, Blackwell Publishers, Oxford.

Micklethwait, John and Adrian Wooldridge (2000), *A Future Perfect: The Challenge and Hidden Promise of Globalisation*, Crown Publishing, New York.

Mittelman, James H. (2000), *The Globalisation Syndrome: Transformation and Resistance*, Princeton University Press, Princeton.

Mittelman, James H. (ed.) (1996), *Globalisation: Critical Reflections*, Lynne Rienner Publishers, Boulder, CO.

Nye, Joseph S. and John D. Donahue (eds) (2000), *Governance in a Globalising World*, Brookings Institution Press, Washington.

Robertson, Roland (1992), *Globalisation: Social Theory and Global Culture*, Sage, London.

Rodrik, Dani (1997), *Has Globalisation Gone too Far?*, Institute for International Economics, Washington, DC.

Spybey, Tony (1996), *Globalisation and World Society*, Polity Press, Cambridge, MA.

Thurow, Lester (1995), *The Future of Capitalism*, William Morrow, New York.

Toffler, Alvin and Heidi (eds) (1995), *Creating a New Civilization: The Politics of the Third Wave*, Turner Publishing, Inc., Atlanta.

United Nations Conference on Trade and Development (1997), *World Investment Report, 1997: Transnational Corporations, Market Structure and Competition Policy*, United Nations, New York; Geneva.

Waters, Malcolm (2001), *Globalisation*, 2nd edn, Routledge, London; New York.

White, Randall (1995), *Global Spin: Probing the Globalisation Debate: Where in the World Are We Going?*, Dundurn Press, Toronto.

Chapter 6

Globalisation in Stages

David E. Andersson and Åke E. Andersson

Introduction

Globalisation is a somewhat complex concept. It is both dynamic and multi-dimensional. It is tempting to view it simply as a process of increasing reliance on foreign trade. Such a one-dimensional approach is not reasonable, because it does not reflect the spatial dimension. An increasing reliance on trade of all countries could just be an expansion of each country's trade relation with the nearest neighbour without any expansion of the spatial coverage. The analysis of globalisation should thus be reflected in measures that ideally would measure quantitative as well as spatial degree of expansion.

Furthermore, globalisation has implied increasing interdependency between increasingly distant nations and regions in many respects. It is also clear from the historical evidence that globalisation has been progressing in overlapping stages with an acceleration during the 1980s and 1990s.

Trading Capitalism

Certain aspects of globalisation can be traced back to the era of European trade capitalism. While powerful empires had controlled distant territories in earlier periods, economic activities remained local and the relationship between the political centre and outlying territories was one of unidirectional domination. Our understanding of globalisation requires substantial reciprocity, competition, and decentralisation of economic power. Only then is a self-reinforcing accumulation of interdependent networking feasible. These preconditions were not present in the Roman Empire, nor were they present in the early Asian civilisations.

In medieval Europe, political fragmentation was the rule. Not only was there a separation between ecclesiastical and secular power, but secular power was further divided between local feudal lords with jurisdiction over relatively small territories. It thus became possible for small and comparatively independent towns to form in the cracks between the fiefdoms, often in conjunction with the building of a cathedral or monastery. The resulting system of towns became the driving force for the early development of trade and the division of labour between rural agriculture and the economic functions of towns, mainly small-scale manufacturing and the exchange of goods.

Political fragmentation has however always been viewed as a destructive threat to prosperity by the empire-builders of the world. This was as true of Julius Caesar as it is of Jiang Zemin. But it was exactly the political fragmentation of medieval

Europe that engendered the economic takeoff of the continent. This takeoff was not planned in some European court or diocese, but was the result of the efficiency-inducing tendencies of inter-jurisdictional competition. More specifically, the feudal lords and bishops were constrained by the possibility that their subjects might escape to more attractive jurisdictions. Self-interested rulers therefore had an incentive to supply a reasonably attractive environment for their subjects. While heavier policing of the border and stiffer punishments for desertion may have been equally effective at reducing the risk of emigration, these measures could neither lure prospective immigrants nor increase the agricultural surplus.

Only the protection of certain individual freedoms – especially the freedom to trade and to retain some of the profits – could simultaneously increase aggregate rents and the subjects' loyalty. Medieval Italian history provides an illustration of the long-term effects of political decentralisation. While northern Italy was divided among competing city states and other small jurisdictions, southern Italy was controlled by the Norman kingdoms of Sicily and Naples. The southern kingdoms practised a form of centralised feudal absolutism, which prevented the spontaneous development of capitalist institutions. Regional differences in the evolution of one such institution – impersonal trust – have been studied by political scientists such as Robert Putnam (1993) and Ronald Inglehart (1997). Their conclusion is that impersonal trust is still much lower in the south than in the north and centre of Italy. Moreover, Putnam argues that the centralisation of medieval southern Italy has affected the contemporary economic structure: the lack of impersonal trust has hampered the development of voluntary associations between individuals such as (indigenous) corporations, partnerships, and professional associations. In this respect, southern Italy resembles other 'lagging civilisations', for example Russia and China.

The incentives that fragmentation provided were however not unambiguous enough to compel an instantaneous conversion from feudal to capitalist institutions. Most feudal lords were loath to give up their inherited privileges. But these privileges placed them at an economic disadvantage vis-à-vis those jurisdictions that had adopted some of the institutions of capitalism. The first non-feudal jurisdictions were small towns which had the economic function of coordinating trade between different fiefdoms. The simultaneous dependence on several jurisdictions made it possible for the towns to be exempted from the rigid hierarchical relationships of a single fiefdom. Instead, they could develop new institutions that were more conducive to trade. Over time, some trading centres, such as Venice and Florence, developed institutions that were clearly superior in economic terms. A virtuous circle was set in motion in places like these, where more efficient institutions attracted new immigrants, while at the same time enriching and empowering the political rulers and established residents of the jurisdiction. It is essentially such virtuous circles that have given birth to all the main gateway regions of the world, for example medieval Venice, seventeeth-century Amsterdam and twentieth-century Hong Kong.

Over time, the economic superiority of urban capitalism over rural feudalism became increasingly obvious. That capitalistic towns would provide more opportunities for industrial serfs than feudal demesnes is unsurprising. The attendant risk of rural flight was one reason why many lords gradually improved the living conditions of serfs and provided them with a degree of economic independence. What is more surprising is that the economic inefficiencies of feudalism at a later stage made many feudal lords eschew the manor for a more exciting life in the city (Rosenberg and Birdzell 1986). There were in sum two forces that contributed to the growth of the network of cities and towns between the thirteenth and the eighteenth centuries. The combined effect of institutional innovation within the cities, improvements to transportation networks and technology, and the resulting extension of markets, was one such force. The other force was the slow but protracted migration of feudal lords and former serfs to established towns and the creeping conversion of feudal communities to the institutions of capitalism.

The growth of the early European towns led to a gradual expansion of trade, and also to a slow accumulation of new roads and ports. Initially, almost all trade was local or regional. But as a result of innovations in shipbuilding and the linking of Southern and Northern Europe, long-distance trade became a much more profitable option in the thirteenth century (Pirenne 1936). The resulting extension of the market greatly increased the economic opportunities associated with trade, and accelerated Europe's urbanisation. In the following one hundred years, thousands of new towns appeared, thereby superimposing an urban network economy on what had now become backward still feudal hinterlands.

The early centres of the European trading system were the independent city states of northern Italy, such as Venice, Florence, and Genoa, and the system of cooperating Baltic towns known as the Hanseatic League. The Hanseatic League included towns such as Bruges, Lübeck, Hamburg, and Riga. These medieval towns were the first examples of regional economies devoted to the pursuit of profit through trade. They were later joined by most towns in the Low Countries, which gained in importance as a consequence of their central position between the Mediterranean and the Baltic regions. The first continental network economy consisted of a system of capitalist trading centres, comprising Northern Italy, Germany, the Low Countries, and a few outlying towns near the Atlantic, Baltic, or Mediterranean in other parts of Europe.

The first globalisation stage – in a literal sense – occurred in conjunction with the invention of the *caravelle*. This new type of ocean-going ship for the first time made intercontinental trade and colonisation possible. It also initially shifted Europe's centre of trade from Bruges to Lisbon. While the centrality of Lisbon was short-lived, the technological breakthrough irreversibly extended the trading network to new nodes in the Americas, Africa, and Asia. An early example is the network of Portuguese trading ports in Asia, which included Goa, Melacca, Macau, and Nagasaki. On a small scale, these ports introduced capitalist institutions to Asia and attracted adventurous Indian and Chinese entrepreneurs. They were the precursors of the two lasting nodes that Europe exported to Asia; Hong Kong and Singapore.

Although the British government or East India Company created those nodes when the Industrial Revolution was already well under way, the causes for Europe's advantage over Asia were already present much earlier. While China had a technological edge over Europe as late as the twelfth or thirteenth century, it lacked the decentralisation, competition, and diversity that had evolved in Europe. Taken together, these factors caused a process of European institutional evolution that facilitated the widening (globalisation) and deepening (complexity) of economic interdependencies. The effects of the institutional evolution of pre-industrial European capitalism were diverse and substantial. Examples include the appearance of financial markets in Venice and Florence, rapid economic innovation of new inventions (as opposed to the inventions themselves), the establishment of a stock exchange and a central bank in Amsterdam, and, ultimately, the Industrial Revolution in Britain.

The Innovation and Diffusion of the Industrial Economy

The industrial revolution did not occur in all parts of the world at the same time. Rather, industrialisation had been occurring in four overlapping waves, starting in Great Britain, Belgium and the eastern parts of the United States of America in the late eighteenth and early nineteenth century. The second wave involved the nearest neighbours of Great Britain, France and Germany and occurred during the mid-decades of the nineteenth century. During the third wave the periphery of Europe, and Japan was industrialised starting in the last decades of the nineteenth century. The fourth wave was characterised by a spread of the industrial system of production to the newly industrialised countries in East Asia and Latin America. The international innovation-diffusion pattern has been called 'the flying geese phenomenon' by some economists, studying the industrialisation of East Asia (Fujita 1989).

One of the basic ideas of the industrial system is that each region should concentrate the production system on such goods and services employing resources, available in relatively large amounts in the region and abstain from producing goods and services needing comparatively scarce resources. The consequence of such a specialisation, based on the comparative factor abundance, leads to a large dependence on trade with other regions.

The economic history of the nineteenth century gives ample statistical evidence both of the growth of productivity and real income per capita during this period as well as of an even faster growth of trade-dependence among the industrialising countries – e.g. the share of imports of Swedish GNP increased from approximately 15 per cent in the 1860s to a level of 23 per cent shortly before World War I (Jörberg 1974).

Table 6.1 indicates the consequences for the income development of populations involved in the global spread of the industrial system at the end of the eighteenth century till the end of the twentieth century. The table indicates that each wave of industrialisation has been characterised by successively higher average growth rates of real product and income per capita. The willingness to adopt the industrial economic model is certainly related to these experiences. However, the question is why each wave is associated with a higher growth rate. Two explanations seem to be of the greatest causal importance:

1   the technological and economic efficiency of infrastructure has been steadily increasing
2   there has been an increasing advantage of being late, e.g. an increasing advantage of technological, organisational and institutional *benchmarking*.

There is no reason to assume that these advantages of being backward will be lost in the future. The flying geese formation will spread to other parts of the global economic periphery with increasing opportunities of growth for the newly industrialised regions.

Table 6.1 Growth rates for representative national economies during the four waves of industrialisation

	Period	Annual growth rates of GDP per capita
First wave		
Great Britain	1785–1967	1.0%
USA	1834–1967	1.7%
Second wave		
France	1840–1966	1.8%
Germany	1860–1967	1.8%
Third wave		
Sweden	1870–1967	2.9%
Italy	1899–1967	2.3%
Japan	1879–1967	3.2%
Fourth wave		
South Korea	1950–1992	5.8%
Taiwan	1950–1992	6.0%

Sources: Maddison 1988; UN and World Bank Statistics.

Migration

Until the middle of the nineteenth century, trade and the European colonisation of other continents had been the main globalising forces. Although some European civilians migrated to explore economic opportunities in the Americas, the migration flows amounted to a mere trickle. Most of these early European migrants worked as traders or shopkeepers in isolated European outposts such as New York (formerly known as New Amsterdam), Philadelphia, and Rio de Janeiro.

In the nineteenth century, two factors caused the long-distance migration flows to increase dramatically. The introduction of steam-powered ships and the attendant fall in transport costs was one such factor. The other factor was the industrialisation of Europe, which led to structural unemployment among the European peasantry. Consequently, long-distance migration for the first time became an attractive option for large masses of the population in European countries.

The first wave of emigrants mainly consisted of people from the early industrialising countries, such as England, Holland, Germany, and France. These were later joined by emigrants from Scandinavia, Ireland, Italy, and Spain. The main destinations were temperate regions under European cultural domination, primarily the United States, but also Canada, southern Brazil, Argentina, and Australia. Mass long-distance migration involving non-Europeans was also initiated in the nineteenth century. These flows included the coercive resettlement of African slaves in both North and South America. It also included the voluntary emigration of Chinese and Indians, especially to European colonies with large indigenous populations such as the

Straits Settlements (in present-day Malaysia and Singapore), the Dutch East Indies (Indonesia), and British Eastern and Southern Africa.

From the nineteenth century onward, we may also distinguish between two distinct types of migration. On the one hand, there was a small but economically significant elite group of professionals, financiers, and moneyed entrepreneurs. These migrants sought influential positions by meeting the new demands for specialists, which was conditioned by the increasing division of labour in the emerging gateways to the New World. New York City stands out as an attractor of elite immigrants. Especially important among these new immigrants were continental European Jews, who had an added emigration incentive in the form of religious persecution in many parts of Europe. But there are also many other examples of elite emigration flow, such as Indian lawyers and doctors emigrating to various British colonies, and Chinese (especially Hokkien and Teochew) merchants establishing business concerns in many parts of Southeast Asia (Turnbull 1989).

Of greater demographic importance for the receiving countries was the mass migration of Europe's poor. These people were often smallholders or labourers from lagging and economically stagnant regions such as rural Germany, southern Italy, or Ireland. They were generally less educated and more conservative than the average for their native countries. Many were attracted by the greater opportunities for preserving their traditional way of life in the New World, in which a low population density and abundant natural resources made agriculture and the life of the village economically viable. They tended to favour environments that were as familiar as possible, both in terms of nature and culture. Of course, nature was a given factor, whereas culture could be improved upon through the accumulation of immigrants from a single source within a small area. Together, this created the mosaic of immigrant communities that characterised the great immigration countries of the world. Examples of location preferences in the nineteenth and early twentieth centuries were Minnesota and Maine for Swedes, Illinois for Poles, central Midwestern states for Germans, and New York and Argentina for Italians. Although much diluted over time, these early settlement patterns can still be detected in the frequency distributions of last names in the respective settlement regions.

While elite migration has increased and become increasingly diverse in its origin-destination linkages over time, the mass migration flows have not only increased but also shifted dramatically in the course of the twentieth century. With the post-war prosperity of Western Europe, this region has become a destination rather than a source of mass migration. But the spontaneous ethnic segregation of poor immigrants has persisted, with Turks moving to Germany while Algerians move to France and Koreans move to California or New York.

The shift in mass migration patterns points to the question of the causes for elite and mass migration. Our view is that there are several contributing factors which can be divided into push and pull factors, while the difference between the two groups is influenced by transaction cost levels. Important push factors include, most dramatically, political upheavals in the country of origin, but also institutional shortcomings such as lawlessness, corruption, and insecure property rights. Groups suffering religious or political persecution are 'pushed' even more strongly than the population in general. Pull factors, on the other hand, include favourable conditions for entrepreneurship, an impartial legal system, secure property rights, and a generally law-abiding citizenry. These institutional attractors are in some cases enhanced by various agglomeration economies, such as knowledge externalities or accessibility to specialised services. Agglomeration economies explain the greater attractiveness to immigrants of New York City or London relative to other parts of the United States or Britain.

The greater relative frequency of elite migration can be explained by the transaction costs faced by these migrants. Prospective elite migrants are typically fluent in the language of the destination country, the relocation costs amount to a low share of total income or assets, and they often have a great deal of experience of interacting with people of different cultural backgrounds. Moreover, they can afford to visit their home countries regularly and normally have the skills and money to keep in touch with their relations by various forms of communication.

Mass migrants, on the other hand, often face enormous transaction costs. Many of them have never interacted with people outside the home village and are not familiar with the language or culture of their destination. The clustering of such migrants in ethnic minority areas is an attempt to reduce these transaction costs. Indeed, local ethnic churches and community organisations often play an important role in familiarising poor migrants with their new environments (Lakshmanan et al. 2000). Given the much higher transaction costs, the combined push and pull effects have to be that much stronger. These combined effects may for example be strong enough for both a Dutch software engineer and an Ethiopian refugee, while at the same time being too weak for a Malay policeman or an unemployed German assembly-line worker.

A cultural qualification to the foregoing reasoning is that cultures differ in their general attitudes to migration. The high migration propensities among Jews, Gypsies, and Hakkas are legendary. But the willingness to migrate also differs between larger ethnic groups. Opinion surveys have repeatedly shown that a much higher proportion of Britons than French or Germans have a desire to live in other countries. This higher propensity is also substantiated by the much higher number of Britons (compared with the number of French or German residents) who reside in Japan, which unlike America or Australia is culturally unrelated to Britain. Likewise, Chinese from Guangdong or Fujian have proved to be more migration-prone than Chinese from Shandong or Tianjin, which is also true of Filipinos as compared with Indonesians.

The Globalisation of Science

Agglomeration economies (i.e., local spillover effects) are crucial to the production of knowledge. While manufacturing networks and retailers, have likewise been shown to benefit from local accessibility to supporting economic activities, scientific research stands out in terms of spatial concentration. Local access to other scientists, laboratories, and knowledge-intensive firms are important for explaining the productivity of individual scientists (Andersson and Wichmann Matthiessen 1993).

Most scientific production in the nineteenth and early twentieth centuries took place in a small number of cities and specialised university towns such as London, Paris, Oxford, or Cambridge. The feasibility of scientific creativity – especially in the natural sciences, medicine, and engineering – depended upon daily access to other scientists and university resources. For a creative scientist wishing to bring her/his ideas to fruition, it was necessary to move to one of a handful of regions with a sufficient agglomeration of specialised knowledge. While the 'market area' of each knowledge centre was in some sense global, the actual production was very much a local affair. The scientists in a particular region mainly worked in isolation from what happened in other regions.

Interactions between scientists from different regions increased in the three decades following World War II. Globally distributed academic journals and specialised international conferences became increasingly influential in this period. For the individual scientist, this meant that it was possible to keep abreast of the latest findings in other parts of the world. A substantial reduction in long-distance transportation costs additionally allowed scientists to visit other regions more frequently and academic exchanges therefore became more common. This was also the period when co-authorships involving scientists living in different countries became a regular occurrence. Even so, long-distance interactions remained infrequent exceptions to the established scientific networks within each urban region.

A thoroughgoing globalisation of science production, as opposed to what could be called the ancillary globalisation of the preceding period, occurred between about 1975 and 1995. While the number of published scientific papers in refereed journals grew by 7 per cent per year from the mid-1970s to the mid-1990s, the yearly growth of international co-authorships amounted to 14 per cent (Andersson and Persson 1993). The growth of international scientific linkages as a proportion of total linkages thus underwent a phase transition that mirrored the concurrent transitions in international trade and international capital flows.

One can approximate the pre-transition world of science as a number of mutually exclusive geographical 'science production regions'. In each region, there is a centre of knowledge production. Scientists originating in one area flock to the centre (e.g., the regional university), after which their scientific results flow to the world community of scientists. This, then, represents a globalisation of outputs. After the transition, not only the outputs, but also the inputs become globalised, in that scientists working in two or more different science production regions jointly produce knowledge that is consumed globally.

As in the case of the world's financial flows, communication technology has been the decisive factor for the globalisation of scientific research. The instantaneous transfer of information through communication networks is a prerequisite for long-distance collaborative research. The development of networks for the transmission of information was primarily the result of research undertaken by the Army Research Programs Administration in the United States (Stough 2000) from the late 1960s onward. A succession of computer networks beginning with the Arpanet was developed there. The early networks were designed for use by the military and various research groups. Eventually, however, they evolved into the contemporary general-access Internet. Other technological advances such as facsimile transmission and satellite communications as well as further reductions in the cost of air travel supported the globalisation of science.

In this model we explicitly assume that the value of a research product of knowledge-firm i (located in region i) is determined by the information and the knowledge received from region j; ($j = 1, ..., n$). We further assume that knowledge is of importance to research quality, only. The P and Q functions are both assumed to be concave and differentiable, everywhere.

$$\text{Maximise } G_i = P_i\left(I_{1i},\ldots,I_{ni};K_{1i},\ldots,K_{ni}\right) \cdot Q\left(L_i,I_{ii}\right)$$
$$\underset{\{I,K,L\}}{}$$

$$- \sum_j \tau_{ji} I_{ji} - \sum w_{ji} K_{ji} - w_i L_i - \tau_{ii} I_{ii}$$

$$\left.\begin{array}{l} \dfrac{\partial G_i}{\partial L_i} = P_i \dfrac{\partial Q}{\partial L_i} - w_i = 0 \\[4mm] \dfrac{\partial G_i}{\partial I_{ii}} = P_i \dfrac{\partial Q}{\partial I_{ii}} - \tau_{ii} = 0 \end{array}\right\} \begin{array}{l}\text{Marginal}\\ \text{productivity}\\ \text{conditions}\end{array}$$

$$\left.\begin{array}{l} \dfrac{\partial G}{\partial I_{ji}} = P_i \dfrac{\partial P_i}{\partial I_{ji}} \cdot Q - \tau_{ji} = 0 \\[4mm] \dfrac{\partial G}{\partial K_{ji}} = P_i \dfrac{\partial P_i}{\partial K_{ji}} \cdot Q - w_{ji} = 0 \end{array}\right\} \begin{array}{l}\text{Marginal}\\ \text{interactivity}\\ \text{conditions}\end{array}$$

Let us further assume that

$$\tau_{ji} = \alpha_i + \beta d_{ji};$$

$$w_{ji} = w_i + b d_{ji}; \text{ and}$$

$$\frac{\partial P_i}{\partial I_{ji}} = Q_j^{\gamma} I_{ij}^{-\lambda}; \frac{\partial P_i}{\partial K_{ji}} = Q_j^{g} K_{ji}^{-\ell}$$

Then

$$Q_j^{\gamma} I_{ij}^{-\lambda} Q_i = \alpha_i + \beta d_{ji}; \text{ and}$$

$$Q_j^{g} K_{ij}^{-\ell} Q_i = w_i + b d_{ji}$$

Thus:

$$I_{ji} = \frac{Q_i^{\lambda} Q_j^{\gamma/\lambda}}{\left(\alpha_i + \beta d_{ij}\right)_j^{1/\lambda}}; \quad \left(j = 1,\ldots,n\right)$$

$$K_{ji} = \frac{Q_i^{\ell} Q_j^{g/\ell}}{\left(w_i + b_{ji}\right)^{1/\ell}}; \quad \left(j = 1,\ldots,n\right)$$

In the new theory of the firm there is not only the marginal productivity condition for each one of the inputs influencing the optimal inputs of resources, regulating the scale of operations. There are also the quality oriented *marginal interactivity conditions* to be observed in the search for an optimal management strategy. The extent to which interaction ought to be by direct contacts or by transmission of information by communication links is an empirical issue determined by the degree of substitutability between knowledge and information in the creation of product quality and consumer willingness to pay.

It should also be observed that the marginal interactivity conditions will tend to generate gravity-like interaction behaviour in space. Such behaviour has been recorded statistically in recent studies of research interaction (Andersson, Persson, 1993).

Empirical analyses of international co-authorship patterns (Andersson and Persson, 1993; Andersson, 2001) reveal that although co-authorship frequencies are a decreasing function of distance, it is becoming a much flatter function (i.e., distance is becoming less important). Cultural distances, which can be measured by characteristics such as a common language or historical political ties, now explain much more of the variation in interregional scientific cooperation. The widespread use of the English language is one example of a characteristic that makes international co-authorships more numerous than what would otherwise be expected (Andersson 2001).

Although the world of science is becoming more interconnected, spatial considerations have by no means vanished. What we have witnessed is rather the emergence of an interdependent network of nodes. The agglomeration economies associated with each node are still important in providing scientists with opportunities for regular knowledge-exchange and other productivity-enhancing resources. There are now more nodes than ever before with a sizable production of knowledge, but certain countries as well as regions within countries have a disproportionate share of the global output. Most of the leading regions in terms of published scientific papers are located in north-western Europe or the United States, and a very low share of the papers originate from areas outside of Europe, North America, and Japan (Matthiessen et al. 2000). Science is global, but the effective access of a node to the global network varies according to a number of social characteristics. Apart from the urban volume and 'density' of knowledge, which makes Southeast England the world's leading node, certain other factors influence the per capita production of knowledge. Apart from the general economic development level, these factors include a generally internationalised economy and a high proportion of creativity-oriented 'post-materialists' (see Inglehart 1977, 1997). Consequently, Scandinavia, Holland, Switzerland and Britain have the highest per capita outputs in the world, while East Asian countries, including Japan, have much lower outputs of scientific papers than living standards alone would predict. Measured as citations or co-authorships, the knowledge production gap becomes even wider.

The Dynamics of Clustering and Globalisation

Integration of different regions or nodes into spatial clusters of increasingly large dimensions is an intriguing theoretical issue in the study of globalisation. The easiest way to see this expansion is by pair-wise integration of regions (or nodes) by a link. Historically, some of these links have been formed by military plans. In other cases they have been evolving in an interaction with increasing flows of trade between nodes. However, the probability of establishing such a link decreases with the distance between nodes. The mathematical biologist Stuart Kauffman (1995) has proposed a stochastic network expansion model that can be used not only for his own analysis of molecular expansion but also to create an understanding of the evolution of economic networks. The expansion of a network from a disconnected set of nodes can be illustrated with the following figure.

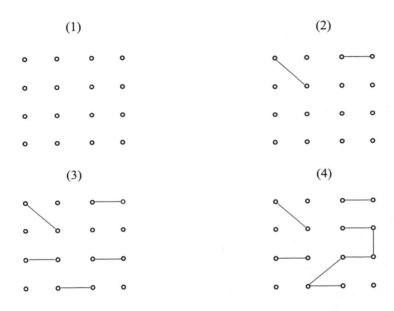

and so on ...

Figure 6.1   Expanding regional networks

The probability of a formation of successively larger interaction clusters increases with the number of links in relation to the number of (fixed) nodes. Simulation studies of these processes show that there is a remarkable phase transition when the number of links exceeds the number of nodes. This is illustrated with the following computer-based figure (Figure 6.2) for a system, consisting of 400 evenly distributed nodes on a square surface.

While the link investments can only give rise to benefits associated with interaction between pairs of nodes, at later stages successively larger clusters of interaction are being formed until *almost* all of the nodes are integrated into a global network of interaction possibilities.

According to this model of dynamic network evolution, globalisation becomes inevitable as long as infrastructural investments into networks are progressing in

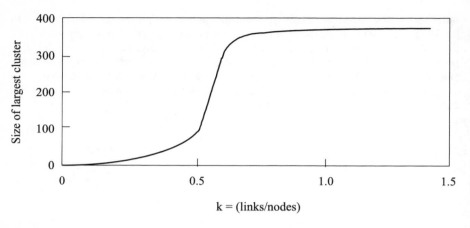

Figure 6.2   Cluster formation and phase transition

a spatially, reasonably balanced process. The dual picture of this process would
be reduction in transport and other spatial transaction cost with a mirror image
in phase transition at some stage of a global cluster formation. The integration of
world telecommunications fits nicely into this theoretical explanation of the global
integration process.

Global Financial Integration

During the 1970s the post-war regulation of the financial markets began to be
questioned and the deregulation process was initiated. For administrators of private
and public funds the possibilities of international diversification of the portfolios of
stocks and bonds turned out to be extremely advantageous compared to intra-national
diversification. By 1980 it had become clear that an international diversification of a
portfolio could lead to an increase in the yearly returns from 7 to 12 per cent without
any need to increase the exposure to financial risk. Similar calculations for European
countries showed equal or larger returns, especially for portfolio managers in small
economies. However, it took around fifteen years thereafter before the financial
markets could be claimed to be truly globalised, as can be illustrated by Table 6.2.

  In the case of Sweden by 1990 less than 10 per cent of the value of stocks on
the Swedish stock exchange was in foreign hands. By the year 2000 this share is
estimated to have grown to approximately 50 per cent.

The Phase Transition of Global Trade in the 1980s

During the 1980s it became popular among economists and businessmen/women
to discuss international and interregional trade in terms of 'global outsourcing'.
Especially American companies had begun a search for providers of inputs delivered
from increasingly long-distance sources. A classical large scale factory with their

Table 6.2   Transactions of bonds and securities across country borders as a percentage of gross national product

	1980	1985	1990	1996
USA	9	35	89	152
Japan	8	63	120	83
Germany	8	33	57	197
France	8	21	54	229
Italy	1	4	27	435
Canada	10	27	64	235

Source: IMF (1997).

own local production of all types of inputs was giving way to smaller production units based on just-in-time deliveries of inputs from all over the world. At the same time newly industrialised countries and regions had reached a production capacity large enough for a penetration of consumer goods markets in Europe, North America and Japan.

The following table illustrates the growth of production and trade during the period 1979–1997.

Table 6.3   The development of production and trade 1979–1997 (real annual growth rates)

	1979–86	1987–94	1995–97
Global gross disposable product	3.1	3.3	4.0
World trade volume	3.5	6.2	7.4
Exports from OECD	4.4	7.4	10.0
Exports from Asia	6.4	12.8	10.0

Source: IMF–WEO (1997–1998), Washington, DC.

Obviously there was a jump or a phase transition in the connection between the growth of total production capacity and world trade between the first period of the table and the period 1987–94.

There are many explanations to this phase transition. One important fact is the dramatic reduction in the pricing of telecommunication services. The IMF has estimated the international telephone price per minute to have been reduced by almost 90 per cent between 1960 and 1990. And with the emergence of possibilities of internet trading, combined with the greatly simplified procedures for international payments much of this globalisation of trade can be explained. If the internet-telecommunications explanation is the most important, then we should expect business-to-business interaction in the future by the internet to give rise to even greater rates of expansion of world trade.

The Growth of Business Networking

In recent years the world has witnessed a number of formations of global networking corporations by mergers and acquisitions. Not only in the financial markets where the advantages of global network corporations are obvious but also in the manufacturing sector global network corporations have become dominant entities.

A number of examples can be found in the automobile industries such as Daimler-Chrysler, GM-Saab-Opel, and Ford-Jaguar-Volvo. In the pharmaceutical industry the merger process started early and some of the more recent network corporations are Astra-Zeneca and Pharmacia-Upjohn. Similar processes can be seen in the communications and computation industries as well as in the entertainment sector.

In all these cases there is one common denominator – economies of scale in creative activities, e.g. research and development, design and marketing. If the costs of a new idea can be shared globally a much larger research and development, design and marketing budget can be made profitable. On the other hand there is also a strong tendency towards decreasing scale of operations in the production and distribution units. The global network corporations tend to become creativity and logistical systems driven networks with an increasing number of small and spatially dispersed production and distribution units. A Swedish company – Ikea – is a typical example of this stage of globalisation.

The New Role of Policy Making and Planning

Integration of the global financial markets is leading towards equalised risk compensated real rates of interest. This forces decision-makers in all regions to equalise marginal efficiencies of investment.

All regional as well as national policy makers are consequently forced to take actions, leading to reduction of the risks, as these are perceived by financial investors, often located in distant regions and nations.

Such regional risk reducing actions include reformation of political institutions, privatisation and deregulation but also re-regulation of the financial institutions, ensuring transparency, fairness and low transaction costs for foreign investors.

The speed of structural economic transformation will increase as a consequence of the formation of new global network corporations, simultaneously exploiting the advantages of a global scale of operations and regional and local presence to the consumers. The loss of national and regional fiscal, monetary and regulatory political control will force all regional policy makers to develop long-term attraction of their regions for the increasingly mobile firms and their qualified labour.

The Changing Nature of Gateways

The long process of globalisation has manifested itself as successive superimpositions of new networks on existing networks. A parallel process has been the creation of forms of interaction (networking) that have been dependent on the new networks. These networks have been structured as links between geographical nodes, with the nodes commonly referred to as gateway cities or regions (Andersson and Andersson 2000). Thus, networks amount to the transportation and communication infrastructures that link various nodes to one another, whereas networking refers to the flows of exchange or cooperation on these networks.

The first networks that were global in the sense of serving long-distance economic interaction were created in medieval Europe for trade in goods that had a high value per unit of weight, such as spices, gems, and small items made by artists or artisans. These early networks consisted of waterways and unpaved cross-country roads. The nodes were at first centres of exchange and later also of banking, an example being fourteenth and fifteenth century Florence, where the Medici family specialised in funding trading expeditions (Andersson 2000). The pre-industrial gateways were also centres of learning, retailing and specialised production of tools and ornaments. The financial functions of nodes became more sophisticated over time, so that by the seventeenth century it was possible for Amsterdam to become the main European gateway by virtue of having a central bank with public guarantees and a stock exchange.

The Industrial Revolution triggered a phase transition in the interconnectivity of the world economy. Railways and steam-powered ships led to an increase in the volume of mobile tradable goods, while factory production raised outputs and lowered production costs. It became profitable to trade in ordinary consumer goods as well as in bulky raw materials. The new industrial gateways combined new functions with the new infrastructure: raw materials came to be transported by rail to manufacturing cities, after which they were exported by sea to other parts of the world. The gateway regions of the nineteenth century thus combined rail and sea accessibility with manufacturing and financial service capabilities. Cities such as New York, Philadelphia, Manchester and Antwerp were well placed as nodes in the industrial network economy.

The Industrial Revolution also supplied the infrastructural and technological means for mass migration. The new gateway cities not only attracted migrants from their immediate hinterlands, but also immigrants from much further afield. These were not only attracted by the demand for labour in the new factories, but also by pervasive agglomeration economies such as an increasing demand for specialised services that the growth in population and productivity made possible. Enterprising individuals had every incentive to leave rural areas for more rewarding activities in cities. In America, this urbanising flow was complemented by the flow of European immigrants taking advantage of continued opportunities for profitable agriculture, which a low population density, fertile lands, and homesteading laws made possible.

Industrial society also hosted a second trade-inducing infrastructural and technological transformation in the twentieth century. The second transformation consisted of infrastructural investments in freeways and airports and innovations in motor vehicle and air transportation technology. By the third quarter of the twentieth century, these two modes of transportation had made it possible for gateway cities to be located away from rail and sea networks, while at the same time facilitating the formation of large, multinational, corporations. These corporations integrated the production of a good vertically, out-sourcing the production of labour-intensive low-value-added components to regions with low labour costs, while keeping high-value-added activities in the centres of the industrialised world. High-value-added activities within multinational corporations include research and development, precision engineering, and quality control. New networking comprising intra-firm trade was added to the conventional trade networks of cross-border inter-firm transactions.

By 1975, the elaborate network infrastructure and networking linkages of industrial society had been put in place. Trade comprised the full range of consumer durables and intermediate goods. But in one sense the world economy had remained constant since before the Industrial Revolution: networks concerned the transportation of goods. Other networking activities than the trade in goods were exceptional and mostly limited to tourism and migration. Cities were nodes in international trading networks, but the production of financial and consumer services, science, and culture remained intranodal.

The digitalisation and computerisation of communication networks, which was started in the 1970s, has revolutionised the scope of globalisation. In the post-industrial economy, globalisation is not limited to trade and migration. Stock and currency markets, consumer services, and the production of culture and scientific research have all benefited from the integration of computer and communication networks and thereby attained global catchment areas. This has increased the competitive pressures on a host of formerly sheltered firms as well as regional governments. Firms now have to compete globally among firms when raising capital, but at the same time the sources of capital have also globalised. Established retailers now have to compete with online retailers, while governments have become constrained by global currency markets and the judgements of overseas investors in the local stock market. An illustration of this globalisation is the volume of international transactions of bonds and securities as a share of the gross domestic product. From 1980 to 1996, this share rose from nine to 152 per cent in America and from one to 435 per cent in Italy (Andersson 2000).

A consequence of these developments is that the gateways to the new network economy can assume one or more of an increasing number of functions. Gateways have become more diverse, with some acting as access points to a whole range of networks, while others have developed a single gateway niche. The networks of earlier periods can be pictured as one single, multilayered trading network where the number of layers differed between links, but where the denser networks essentially filled the gaps between the rigid and sparse air and rail networks. By contrast, the post-industrial networks consist of layers, which only partially overlap, a characteristic that is even more evident for the interactive networking that takes place on the networks.

Some established gateways such as London have complemented its traditional nodal roles with new coordinating functions, such as in the post-industrial financial, science, film, and music networks. Other previously peripheral locations have managed to establish gateway niches, for example Basle as a science node and Stockholm as a Northern European financial and science gateway. Central to all the new gateways is that they at least for one economic activity have an attractive combination of agglomeration economies, inter-regional accessibility, and favourable institutions.

Economies of scale in production interact with decreasing transport and other spatial transaction costs in the determination of a spatial competitive equilibrium. In the long run, the prices of goods and factors tend to be established at the minimum of the sum of average production, transport and transaction costs. This implies that there will always be unexploited increasing returns to scale in a competitive spatial equilibrium. Any improvement of the network capacity and the corresponding decrease of transport and transaction costs will thus lead to a further exploitation of increasing returns to scale. This means that a phase transition of a network as modelled above will also trigger a corresponding phase transition of the competitive spatial equilibrium of production.

References

Andersson, Å.E. (2000), 'Financial Gateways', in Å.E. Andersson and D.E. Andersson (eds), *Gateways to the Global Economy*, Edward Elgar, Cheltenham.

Andersson, Å.E. and D.E. Andersson (eds) (2000), *Gateways to the Global Economy*, Edward Elgar, Cheltenham.

Andersson, Å.E. and O. Persson (1993), 'Networking Scientists', *Annals of Regional Science*, Vol. 27, pp. 11–21.

Andersson, Å.E. and C. Wichmann Matthiessen (1993), *Øresundsregionen – Kreativitet, Integration, Vækst*, Copenhagen, Munksgaard.

Andersson, D.E. (2001), 'Science Cooperation Networks in Eastern Asia', in D.E. Andersson and J.P.H. Poon (eds), *Asia-Pacific Transitions*, Macmillan, London.

Fujita, M. (1989), *Urban Economic Theory*, Cambridge University Press, New York.

IMF (1997) World Economic Outlook (May), Washington, DC.

Inglehart, R. (1977), *The Silent Revolution*, Princeton University Press, Princeton.

Inglehart, R. (1997), *Modernization and Postmodernization – Cultural, Economic and Political Change in 43 Societies*, Princeton University Press, Princeton.

Jörberg, L. (1974) 'Svensk ekonomi under 100 år', in B. Södersten (ed), *Svensk ekonomi*, Raben and Sjögren, Stockholm.

Kauffman, S. (1995), *At Home in the Universe; The Search for Laws of Complexity*, Penguin, London.

Kobayashi, K. and Takebayashi, M. (2000), 'Exploiting Gateway Externalities: the Future of Kansai', in Å.E. Andersson and D.E. Andersson (eds), *Gateways to the Global Economy*, Edward Elgar, Cheltenham.

Lakshmanan, T.R., D.E. Andersson, L. Chatterjee and K. Sasaki (2000), 'Three Global Cities: New York, London and Tokyo', in A.E. Andersson and D.E. Andersson (eds), *Gateways to the Global Economy*, Edward Elgar, Cheltenham.

Maddison, A. (1988), *Phases of Capitalist Development*, Oxford University Press, Oxford and New York.

Matthiessen, C.W., Schwarz, A.W and Find, S. (2000), 'Research Gateways of the World: an Analysis of Networks Based on Bibliometric Indicators', in Å.E. Andersson and D.E. Andersson (eds), *Gateways to the Global Economy*, Edward Elgar, Cheltenham, pp. 17–30.

Pirenne, H. (1936), *Economic and Social History of Medieval Europe*, London.

Putnam, R.D. (1993), *Making Democracy Work: Civic Traditions in Modern Italy*, Princeton University Press, Princeton.

Rosenberg, N. and L.E. Birdzell (1986), *How the West Grew Rich*, Basic Books, New York

Stough, R.R. (2000), 'The Greater Washington Region: A Global Gateway Region', in Å.E. Andersson and D.E. Andersson (eds), *Gateways to the Global Economy*, Edward Elgar, Cheltenham.

Turnbull, C.M. (1989), *A History of Malaysia, Singapore, and Brunei*, Allen & Unwin, North Sydney.

Chapter 7

Sustainable Mobility and Globalisation: New Challenges for Policy Research

Peter Nijkamp, Hadewijch van Delft and Danielle van Veen-Groot

F22 R40
J61 F02

Introduction

The Greek philosopher Heraclitos once summarised his view on the world concisely in two words: 'panta rei', which means: everything is in motion. This statement seems to apply very well to our modern world, where mobility, interaction and communication have become a leading characteristic; motion is the driving force of progress. The increasing mobility (persons, goods) is also a worldwide source of much concern. Clearly, mobility is a 'normal' – and even positive – phenomenon in a growing economy; it may increase economic efficiency through the gains of trade and labour mobility and it also offers more social opportunities to all members of society through a better access to a wide variety of amenities. But there is a growing awareness that the positive effects of mobility are offset by negative externalities, such as environmental pollution, congestion or lack of accessibility, and high accident rates.

There have been numerous studies on the positive impacts of transportation on the development of regions and cities (see for an overview Buinsma and Rietveld 1998). Also the social costs of mobility have been studied quite extensively (see for in-depth survey Verhoef 1996). An important question is, of course, whether the current trends in mobility growth will come to a standstill. Governments all over the world witness serious concerns on the impact of CO_2. Many policy documents express a curbing of the mobility growth curve as a major target, but it is questionable whether this reversal of trends is to be regarded as a realistic or plausible option. Experts predict that the chances for a drastic change in mobility behaviour are extremely low (see Nijkamp et al. 1998). Also the recent Kyoto agreements are extremely modest in light of the expected rise in welfare and population growth.

There are many forces at work which induce even more mobility. Of course, there are changes in behavioural patterns (e.g., a high expenditure pattern for mobility, a higher willingness to migrate, a rise in leisure activities, an increase in female labour force participation, a tendency towards an ageing society, and so forth). But there are also many structural developments in the world economy and in a modern production system which induce high mobility modes of living. The focus here will mainly be on the latter type of driving forces, which are hard to change. These key forces will be mapped out in a compact manner. We will then try to trace the consequences of various types of possible scenarios at the interface of the society and its mobility for a distinct set of relevant welfare indicators in our economies.

A Changing Perspective

The transformation from a stable development to structural dynamics is a marked and noteworthy feature of our modern economy. The external environment of business life has drastically changed in recent years; new markets, new international policy arrangements, new technologies, new tastes of consumers, etc. Business life is faced with a great variety of new challenges and opportunities. In this part we will address four major driving forces impacting on mobility behaviour and the expected consequences for economic activities (see Figure 7.1). These four drivers are: the emergence of global markets, the developments of industrial networks reflected in particular in various forms of outsourcing, the rise in flexibility in working arrangements leading to a twenty-four-hour economy, and the trend towards economic and political power concentration in large-scale agglomerations.

Emergence of Global Markets

Although it is definitely exaggerated to call our world a global village, it cannot be denied that the action radius of economic activities has increased to unprecedented degree. The rise of global markets and global players is especially noteworthy. The globalisation trend does not only lead to more spatial flows of goods, services, persons and information, but is also accompanied by new foreign investments, not only in the industrialised heartland of our world, but in all regions where new opportunities are likely to emerge. This means that there is a trend towards a Schumpeterian economy with a strict competition for new market opportunities.

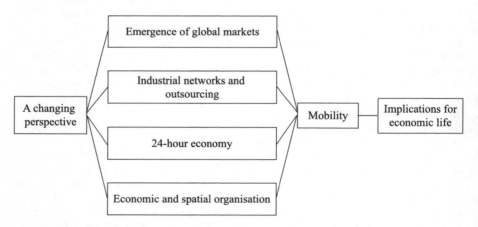

Figure 7.1   Driving forces of mobility

In the same vein we observe also the development towards globally operating commercial companies (Pizza Hut, Marks & Spencer, etc.). The globalisation trend is also reflected in worldwide integrated product markets, access to a global stock of knowledge and technology, and the emergence of global capital markets.

The improvement in transportation technology and the extension of transportation networks causes also a geographical spread of commodity markets.

Since our world is getting smaller all the time, business enterprises are inclined to shift their operation towards locations with the most favourable cost-efficiency or productivity. New competitive factors seem to become important drivers of location and investment decisions of entrepreneurs. This does not only hold for globally operating, multinational companies, but also – and increasingly – for firms with a local or regional sales market, which are faced with strong competition from outside.

In a competitive global market we do observe monopolistic competition elements with distinct market niches, a phenomenon sometimes called the 'hamburger economy'. This type of economic organisation is based on rationalised and standardised products (Coca-Cola, McDonalds, etc.), which have a worldwide image, so that marketing activities may have a high penetration rate. Thus, it seems that the trend towards global markets will be accompanied by a trend towards worldwide market niches.

A phenomenon that is accompanying the current globalisation is the trend towards a network economy at all levels: local, regional, national, global. Industrial interdependencies are emerging in an attempt to minimise costs in a mature industrial economy, in particular through outsourcing. The fierce competition in mature markets leads to a trend towards a concentration of core activities, with a strong emphasis on a logistic organisation of production. Physical production may then become more fragmented with a loss of integrated chain production within the firm, while assembling and distribution gain in importance. The emerging component industry is based on worldwide trading and transport (cf. Lagendijk 1994).

The new information and communication technology (ICT) sector allows for a sufficient and efficient co-ordination of dispersed production patterns. Production tends also to become more footloose, due to the integrating potential of the ICT sector. Global networks are supporting this phenomenon, not only in terms of industrial linkages, but also in terms of infrastructure networks. Such networks which are based on high mobility are thus becoming the vehicles for intensive global competition.

Flexible Labour Organisation and the Twenty-four-hour Economy

From a socioeconomic perspective, we witness a clear break with the past. Instead of a standard working week of forty hours with a fixed working hours during five days a week, we observe at present a tendency to totally different types of labour organisation and working arrangements. More labour force participation of traditionally non-active population segments, more part-time jobs, more flexible wage contracts and more shifts towards work at other times of the day are the signs of a rise in flexibility on the labour market. This flexible behaviour is also accompanied by shifts in consumer behaviour (e.g., shopping behaviour in the evenings or on Sundays). Thus, the daily time span of economic activities is extending towards a twenty-four-hour operation of the economy. This is also reflected in the industrial sector which tends to move towards multiple shifts in order to make the most efficient use of the capital stock. In a globalising economy this flexibility is also important, as it allows for direct worldwide contacts despite the existence of time zones. The emergence of call centres is a good illustration of this phenomenon.

This flexibility in working arrangements leads also to a rise in personally-tuned modes of transport. Mass transit may then become problematic, as the mass flows which make public transport profitable are only compatible with the traditional labour model. On the other hand, the existing infrastructure may be used more efficiently in case of flexible working arrangements, thus leading to a decline in congestion growth.

Economic and Spatial Concentration

In a networked economy, nodal centres play a strategic role. Hubs are then able to acquire a dominant position. Such nodal centres refer to industrial power concentration in the form of global oligopolies controlling a significant part of the world market, but they refer also to main ports and gateways in international infrastructure networks. It is without any doubt that proximity effects – through their intense communication possibilities – offer many scale advantages. Although the ICT sector may suggest a 'death of distance', fact is that geographical agglomeration forces are becoming increasingly important for the complex ramification of an industrial network economy. Thus scale economies of all kind seem to favour concentration and agglomeration, while at the same time the ICT sector allows for a spatial spread of production. Clearly, the economies of density and scale may be affected by congestion and accessibility problems, thus causing an outflow from central city areas (CBDs) to suburban areas and new extra-urban locations (such as the city edge), but the main orientation still remains to the city as the pole of innovation, incubation and communication (see Capello et al. 1998). The resulting patterns are then diverse: mass flows between major metropolitan areas and diffuse flows within the metropolitan area.

Implications for Business Life

There are clearly changing perspectives for modern business life, which will impact on mobility patterns. There seems to be an overriding trend towards higher mobility rate, although the resulting patterns are not always unambiguous. For example, globalisation may be reflected in more trade and transport, but it may also be that globalisation leads to more regional outsourcing and concentrated regional foreign investment. In the latter case new systems of regional markets may emerge, which include a lower mobility rate than a uniform globalisation development. Thus, the geographical scale at which a phenomenon takes place may be decisive for the change patterns in mobility rates.

Another phenomenon is the emerging specialisation and market niche orientation which prompt logistic and storage capacity challenges. These tendencies are also reflected in changing consuming behaviour (such as homeshopping, information provision via the Internet etc.). This may also have complex mobility consequences, which may however differ per region or economic sector. It seems plausible that overall the above described changes in external environments of modern business life are facilitated by and in turn lead to high mobility transport systems, but the relationship between these two phenomena is not a rectilinear one. As a consequence, it will also be hard to infer unambiguous ramifications of our society. Clearly, the predictive power of our analytical apparatus is insufficient to infer unambiguous mappings of the future mobile society. This issue will be taken up again, but first we will focus on the new playing field for business life.

New Playing Field

The current transformation processes are of a pervasive nature. It is no surprise in light of the changing perspectives that infrastructure – in combination with transport systems – is increasingly regarded as the carrier of new spatial-economic developments. Consequently, due attention is increasingly given to free access, capacity, efficiency, convenience and price of infrastructure, especially in a European setting where the unification process is critically dependent on transborder infrastructure networks. In this part we will pay particular attention to the enlargement of the action radius of goods, persons and information, their implications for urban development and for economic developments in general. The structure of this part of the chapter is depicted in Figure 7.2.

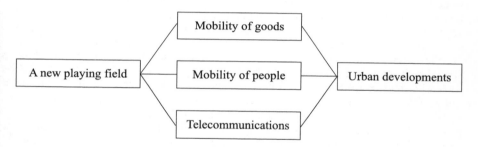

Figure 7.2   Mobility in a new context

Mobility of Goods

The volume of goods transported has shown a steady rise in the past decade. For example, the growth in road freight transport in the Netherlands in the past years has been about 3.5 per cent. Clearly, this growth figure is related to the internationalisation of our economies. In this context, the OECD (1997) has made a distinction of four categories of effects of the globalising activity patterns on the economy:

- scale effects: efficiency effects due to economies of scale and density;
- structure effects: changes in the composition and location of production and consumption centres;
- technological effects: emergence of new patterns of development and dispersion of technologies;
- product effects: changes in the product-mix.

These effects will have both quantitative and qualitative impacts on mobility patterns. As mentioned above, the volume impacts are dependent on the qualitative composition of commodity flows, but also on the volume of these flows. Furthermore, there may be far reaching consequences from the current regionalisation tendencies. And finally, new transportation systems (such as subterranean transport) may have drastic consequences for the costs and benefits of current surface transport modes. In conclusion, globalisation may manifest itself in a trend toward regionalisation or even to mixed spatial modes such as 'globalisation', which is a blend in regional self-reliance and global orientation.

Mobility of People

The closed economic communities from the past with fixed social and cultural structures and characteristics have largely vanished and been replaced by open, emancipatory and outward-looking individuals with a focus on urban or international life. This has had significant consequences for mobility behaviour, as the increased action radius (reflected *inter alia* in suburbanisation and long-distance tourism) has allowed modern people to be part of a widely-ranging network society. In addition to traditional journeys from home to work, we also witness a sharp rise in social and leisure mobility, in which the car is the dominant travel mode.

Government policy in many countries has even favoured the above sketched development, due to a support for new towns, growth centres, population dispersion etc. Only recently, we observe countervailing policy strategies oriented towards more spatial concentration (e.g., compact cities).

Clearly, the rise in mobility has been favoured by the general rise in welfare in the past decades. This is mainly reflected in high car ownership and numbers of kilometres driven. The transportation sector is one of the few sectors where the growth of CO_2 emissions has not yet come to a standstill, so that the environmental consequences of the modern mobile society are certainly a source of much concern.

Telecommunication

Besides the mobility increase of people and goods, we can also observe the trend towards a modern information society dominated by the ICT sector. The information of a modern economy is accompanied by a high throughput of material flows. To a large extent, telecommunication is a supporting carrier for the modern transport sector (and sometimes it even stimulates more physical flows), and to a minor extent it may act as a substitute (e.g., in case of teleshopping, telecommuting, distance learning, etc.). But even in cases where the ICT sector would replace physical movements, we observe a tendency of people to use the additional discretionary time for other types of mobility patterns, so that the net effect may be negligible (or sometimes even negative).

In any case, the general observation is that for the time being there is a great need for face-to-face contacts in modern network society. Since the social reference group is no longer the local village, but sometimes the so-called global village, it seems plausible to expect a continued rise in mobility, if no further counter-actions are undertaken.

Urban Developments

In most western societies, some 65 to 70 per cent of the population lives in cities. Thus, the mobile society is large accompanied by an urban society. And clearly, the mobility patterns have an influence on the way of modern living. In general, major cities have become the socioeconomic and cultural focal point of most inhabitants, even if they live at quite some distance from the city. Such a long-distance orientation is also facilitated by the ICT sector. Also modern business life witnesses a tendency towards spatial deconcentration, even though the contact, communication and management patterns are still oriented towards large urban agglomerations. Thus, a modern city is exhibiting a combination of positive and negative scale economies, which are directly connected with a transportation and land use sector.

The negative extremalities of geographical mobility have prompted a series of policy measures at both the supply side (e.g., infrastructure, modal split) and the demand side (e.g., parking policy, gasoline taxes, etc.). Clearly, the spatial lay-out of local, regional, national and international economies lies at the heart of the mobility issue. Consequently, there is also much interest in physical planning measures (e.g., compact city design, bundled deconcentration etc.). Despite the wide range of policy strategies available and implemented, the actual success of policy in reducing mobility growth has been very modest. Apparently, there are so many barriers, resistances and uncertainties in sustainable transport planning that immediate success is not likely to occur. But what will the future bring us? This question will now be investigated by the use of the scenario methods.

The Future of Mobility in Scenarios: The Spider Model

Mobility shows up in a force field of two contrasting developments. Economic growth and global networking provoke a continued rise in mobility. For example, van Doren (1991) in his 'opus' on 'A History of Knowledge' expects a further exponential growth of the action radius of people in the future up to a level of 3,000 miles in one century from now, which can be travelled comfortably. Others, on the other hand, claim that the mission of sustainable development would require a trend towards slow motion and a lower action radius (see for an overview Nijkamp and Baaijens 1998). The main question in our chapter is not: what is the most probable future option? Rather we address the question: which future patterns can be imagined and how can policies cope with them? In order to study these questions, we will focus in the sequel of this chapter on a chain of three analytical steps (see Figure 7.3).

A Force Field Analysis

It is generally accepted that transport is normally a derived demand and hence dependent on decisions taken elsewhere or based on different purposes than cost minimisation. However, in taking decisions on how to bridge distance, individuals cause a great many externalities which show up as uncompensated costs for others. Sustainable mobility would then require an incorporation of such external costs in transport decisions, which are in turn caused by key forces taking place elsewhere. The

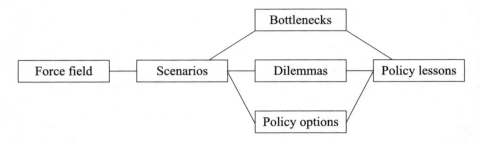

Figure 7.3   Analysis framework

following key forces – presented by way of a contrast analysis – can be distinguished (see van Geenhuizen en Nijkamp 1997).

- **internalisation**. On the one hand, the expansion of entrepreneurial activities towards world markets may imply totally different transport systems or movements, but on the other hand there is a tendency towards regional and local production systems, which would require a regional focus in the transport system. In this context, global competition and regional self-reliance may be seen as contrasting forces.
- **environmental protection**. Clearly, on the one hand, we may witness a tendency towards continued economic growth, with the environment acting at best as a constraint, whereas on the other hand an ecological orientation may be favoured which would presuppose a change in life styles and human behaviour and also a diminishing 'growthmania'.
- **social cohesion**. In a modern society we observe a trend towards individualisation with a strong emphasis on freedom and self-determination, in contrast to other or previous societies where collective care and solidarity were the preponderant social values.
- **spatial dispersion**. Also here we observe contrasting developments: a de-urbanisation trend leading to long-distance community based on private cars and high mobility rates versus a compact urban pattern of living in which collective modes of transport are dominant.
- **spatial equity**. Modern economic and technological developments are increasingly focused on metropolitan areas, whereas at the same time there is a broad recognition of the need to favour less central areas or to exploit the potential of such areas (e.g., in case of outsourcing).
- **accessibility**. Since the plans to give priority to Trans European Networks (TENs) there has been much debate on the distributional aspects of new infrastructure policy. TENs may favour economic progress in well connected urban areas, but may cause a backwardness of regions not connected to the TENs.
- **economic policy**. In the past decade we have witnessed a drastic change in economic policy in many countries. On the one hand, we have seen a clear change towards more deregulation and privatisation, whereas on the other hand we also hear signals on the need for re-regulation and a coordinating role of governments.

- **decoupling**. In recent years the idea of decoupling has become very popular (reflected inter alia in notions like de-materialisation, informatisation, industrial transformation, Factor 4 etc; see also Von Weizsacker et al. 1997, van Veen-Groot and Nijkamp 1997). The background of this concept is that there is a need to have a continued economic growth without eroding at the same time the environmental and resource base of the economy. This provokes the question whether economic growth would have to be favoured for its own sake, or whether part of the economic growth would have to be used for social change and technological conversion.

The previous force fields can be summarised as follows:

Driving forces	Development
• internationalisation	global competition vs. regional cooperation
• environmental protection	efficient growth vs. ecological life styles
• social cohesion	individualisation vs. solidarity
• spatial dispersion	de-urbanisation vs. compact city design
• spatial equity	metropolitan focus vs. regional outsourcing
• accessibility	European networks vs. regional networks
• economic policy	market orientation vs. a social market model
• decoupling	economic growth vs. environmental sustainability

The previous forces and developments can be mapped out in various ways. For example, one may depict the contrasting forces of integration-fragmentation versus regionalisation-globalisation. This results in the following two-by-two configuration (see Figure 7.4).

Clearly, Figure 7.4 is merely illustrative and other, related force fields can be depicted as well. These driving forces will now be used as the building blocks of our scenarios to be described in the following pages.

Spatial and Transportation Scenarios

Many regions of the world (Europe, the Pacific, Latin-America, etc.) go through a state of drastic restructuring, as pointed out above. To obtain a reliable long-term view on the most likely development patterns of these economies is a challenge, but in practice almost an impossibility. The time horizon of most models does usually not extend towards a period of more than a decade. For long-term forecasts we often resort to simulation models, chaos models, bio-computing models and the present. Against this background we nowadays observe great popularity of scenarios.

Scenarios are visions and images of the future, put together in a consistent way but without claiming necessarily a high degree of realism. A scenario is a decision support tool which is meant to act as a tool for communication and reflection, with a view on generating policy debate and action on an uncertain future (see e.g. Nijkamp et al. 1998). There is a great variety of scenarios: backcasting vs forecasting scenarios, extrapolation vs contrast scenarios, and so forth. In the light of the previous observation, we will describe four illustrative scenarios.

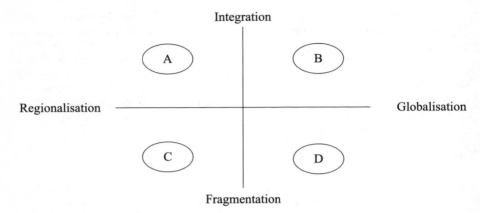

A: Market competition with many small players
B: Market competition with super-blocks
C: Global incoherence
D: Protectionism with small players

Figure 7.4   An illustrative mapping of some global forces

Source: GBN Scenario Book (1991).

   These four scenarios will next be mapped out and interpreted by of the recently developed SPIDER-model (see for full details Nijkamp et al. 1998). This model is a qualitative representation of the major substantive components of a future spatial-transportation image. It incorporates four axes which aim to map out a qualitative rank order the strategic features of these future options. The meaning and interpretation of each of the axes in the four quadrants originate from the driving forces described above. First, the substance of the four scenarios will be outlined, while next we will visualise their characteristics in the SPIDER-model.

a.   Growthmania

In the 'growthmania' scenario all policies and actions serve to stimulate economic growth and wealth. This means an emphasis on economic and technical efficiency, individual ambition and a liberal land use policy (including inter alia a deconcentration of cities). There is of course a shift to a drastic privatisation of the transport sector (e.g. privatisation; of public transport, liberalisation of transport regulations). The consequence will be a low share of public transport and a high ownership and use rate of private cars. High income groups are mainly found in spacious green areas at the edge of cities; low income groups live in older urban areas, while medium income groups tend to live in suburban areas at some distance from the city centre. Thus, there is a clear socioeconomic and spatial segmentation of society. In general, this scenario is based on high mobility rates whose social costs can at best redressed by road charges. But, in general, there is not a high priority attached to environmental sustainability issues, so that the geographical patterns of living and working more or less mirror socioeconomic welfare positions of citizens.

b.   Technomania

The 'technomania' scenario takes for granted that the problems inherent in scarcity of land, transportation externalities and environmental decay can be mitigated and solved by the introduction and adoption of modern technology. This pertains to the ICT sector (encouraging electronic road-pricing, tele-working, tele-shopping etc.), but also to energy, environmental and vehicle technology (e.g. fuel cells). The flexibility in labour organisation (e.g., multiple shifts, flexible office and shopping hours etc.) helps to create also new adjustments to changing conditions. The road transport sector may experience efficiency gains as a result of the introduction of electronic control devices. Also new infrastructure options (e.g., subterranean facilities) will be constructed in order to reduce the social costs of transport. In general, the scarce space is used in the technically most efficient way. This scenario places much emphasis on R&D, education and mobility, so the access to 'technomania' is mainly reserved for citizens well trained in the use of modern technology. This technology is able to curb the exponential growth curve of mobility increase.

c.   Sociomania

The 'sociomania' scenario is based on collective interest and action, with an emphasis on social security, social housing and employment. Likewise, public transport is strongly supported and abundantly subsidised. The spatial lay-out of cities reflect a mix of living, working and recreation. Urban planning aims to create high densities, which also means subterranean planning solutions (e.g., underground parking garages, partly underground shopping malls and multilayer department stores). Cities are meant to be socially integrated, while long-distance commuting is an exception. There is much interest in buying and consuming locally (or regionally) produced goods. Thus, this spatial-transportation model is based on socioeconomic solidarity and a geographical distribution characterised by social cohesion. There is a strong role for the government, while the fiscal burden is high. Clearly, the decline in action radius means a low mobility level, while the extensive use of public transport stimulates also environmental sustainability at the local level.

d.   Ecomania

Finally, the 'ecomania' scenario is a clear break with the past. The preponderant objective is to save the environment through a reduction of mobility. This means first of all a large-scale introduction of polluter pays' principles (e.g., parking fees, user charges, congestion levies) but also the establishment of strict standards, land use and saving regulations (including compact city design) etc. As far as possible, this eco-scenario also uses the potential offered by modern technology (e.g., traffic management). Furthermore, a modal split is strived for, mainly in favour of railways and other modes of public transport. This also means that the accessibility of cities improves. It is clear that decoupling is a major strategy in the 'ecomania' scenario, accompanied by new vehicle technology (e.g., electric cars). This scenario presupposes also a strong international coordination of environmental and transportation policies, and in general a strong involvement of governments.

After the description of these four scenarios, it is important to interpret some of the underlying developments and to draw some policy lessons. This is particularly important as scenarios may be helpful in identifying contingencies and bottlenecks in development, so that also policy strategies can be envisaged. This issue will be further taken up in the next part.

Contingencies in Scenarios

The four 'mania' scenarios described can also be visualised in an overview diagram that is based on the SPIDER-concept (see Figure 7.5). This figure is more or less self-explanatory. It should be noted that the scores on the attributes of each scenario are based on qualitative rank orders, so that the results can only be interpreted in a qualitative sense. The size of the area within the envelope curve of each scenario has of course no absolute meaning.

A closer investigation of the results of the scenario mappings clarifies that in 'growthmania' accessibility will likely be the most severe bottleneck. The drastic mobility rise leads to an intensive use of infrastructure and parking facilities, this holds for both people and goods, only information-intensive enterprises may face less problems. Without large-scale infrastructure investments, this scenario will meet strong capacity constraints, leaving aside environmental quality constraints.

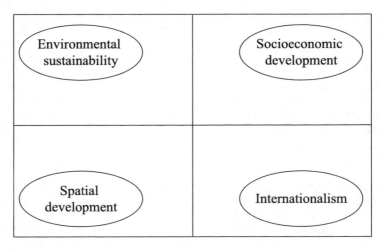

a. Growthmania   c. Sociomania
b. Technomania   d. Ecomania

Figure 7.5   The Spider model

Next, the 'technomania' scenario exploits the fruits of modern telecommunication and of the ICT sector in general. Also sophisticated forms of new vehicle technology are to be expected and used. Inner cities will however, face a problematic accessibility by private car. The use of the 'third' dimension' (or 'vertical' solutions) plays also a dominant role in mitigating land use and transportation problems. In the 'sociomania' world the dynamics in economic life are less dominant; there is much emphasis on the maintenance of stable local or regional markets. Public transport serves thus as a connecting network activity. This requires high density flows and spatial concentration. The high taxes in this scenario lead to a relatively low discretionary income, so that by definition the expenditures on luxury mobility will be lower. Finally, we will briefly look at the 'ecomania' image, where the environment is regarded as the most precious and privileged sector. Pollution costs are then fully internalised, be it via gasoline taxes, road taxes, or parking fees. Mobility is not forbidden, but strongly discouraged. Furthermore, governments are supposed to invest heavily in environment-benign transport systems. Consequently, there will be a tendency toward geographical concentration. The high costs of transport will discourage peripheral or isolated firms and amenities.The previous observations and findings can concisely be summarised in the following survey table (see Table 7.1).

Table 7.1   A survey table of bottlenecks and solution directions of the four 'mania' scenarios

Scenario	Bottlenecks	Solution strategies
A	Parking facilities Poor public transportation Urban quality of life	Market-based parking fees New forms of distribution Flexible work organisation
B	Technological inertia Knowledge acquisition/ transfer	Encouragement of innovativeness Subterranean infrastructure Telematics and ICT
C	Fiscal burden Spatial concentration	Local/regional production Strong public transport
D	High costs of transport Spatial density	Railway and public transport investments Local/regional policy focus New forms of distribution/logistics

Contradictions in Transport

The above ideas may also be helpful to understand paradoxes in scientific statements on the transport sector. European countries and regions are gradually moving towards an integrated network economy, where important nodes of economic, cultural and technological progress are linked together by a well-connected infrastructure network (cf. also Bannister and Berchman 1993). Since the approval of the Maastricht Treaty the notions of interconnectivity, interoperability and intermodality have gained much popularity, as it is recognised that a network is more than the sum of nodes and modes. In particular, the synergy offered by networks offer a decisive advantage, but the intensified use of European networks has also many shadow sides.

The role of transport in a modern society is a source of much scientific research and policy concern, surrounded by much uncertainty and hence diverging views. Transport is one of the most dynamic sectors in the European economy and reflects at present the transition from a fragmented and protected space-economy and integrated and open European market. But at the same time, the access and benefits from the European network are unequally distributed, among different socioeconomic groups and among different regions in Europe, so that serious equity problems emerge. And finally, the large-scale mobility resulting from the European free market is a cause of many environmental externalities and hence of serious criticism.

Against this background, European policies also have an ambivalent character. On the one hand, there is a dedicated policy to exploit the benefits of the integrated European market by constructing Trans European Networks (e.g. the rapid train system). On the other hand, there is the need to offer to all European citizens free access to well-developed infrastructure networks at all geographical levels. And finally, there is the target to keep the environmental consequences of the transport sector within sustainable limits.

In the light of these observations, European transport policy is faced with many challenges. More people express their right to be more mobile; more European countries and regions want to be connected to European networks; and more people express their concern about environment quality in Europe. This provokes a series of fascinating policy research issues. Can the justified needs of all Europeans be met within the existing infrastructure capacity? Are different forms of mobility patterns and life styles necessary? May telecommunication technology offer a promising solution (e.g. tele-working)? Or is a different geographical organisation of the European space-economy needed?

It seems that the severity of these problems call for direct and immediate action. In this context, several European countries are designing a number of regulatory and economic counter-incentives (Austria, Germany, France, etc.). In addition, the inevitable problem of road congestion on important European corridors deteriorates efficient transportation conditions. All of these issues call for a concrete and coherent European transport policy. In this respect, the Transport White Book of the European Commission (1993) states: 'The activities of the European Community in the field of research and development regarding transport must supply the new tools for the attainment of sustainable mobility: efficient, safe transport, in the best possible social and environmental circumstances'.

Despite all policy ambitions, the road towards a uniform policy is not straightforward. Many dilemmas have to be faced and overcome. We will discuss here a few of such illustrative contradictory developments by means of concise statements and key explanations:

- **double causality**
  a. Infrastructure is a necessary but not sufficient condition for economic growth

b. Economic growth is a necessary, but not sufficient condition for new infrastructure investments

key: the main question is one of financing and distribution of public funds; in case of a mismatch there is the phenomenon of missing links and missing networks which may hamper a balanced development

- **flying carpet**
  a. The historically low prices of international travel mean that mobility growth will not be stopped
  b. The growth in mobility will have to come to a standstill because of environmental constraints

  key: the absence of market-based regulatory regimes (including unpriced externalities) causes a major disturbance in mobility which favours free ridership

- **infrastructure capacity**
  a. On average there is sufficient infrastructure capacity
  b. In the margin there is insufficient infrastructure capacity

  key: a major problem arises from the absence of a properly functioning price system, in particular peak load pricing.

- **telematics**
  a. Telematics is necessary to ensure efficient transport
  b. Telematics will cause additional congestion

  key: telematics in itself is just a technological mechanism and ought to be complemented with a system of 'carrots and sticks' on human behaviour to ensure a balanced solution.

- **sustainable mobility and capacity expansion**
  a. Sufficient infrastructure capacity increases the chances on sustainable transport
  b. Excess infrastructure capacity decreases the chances on sustainable transport.

  key: the validity of the law of Say ('each supply creates its own demand') can only effectively be coped with if there is a fully operating user charge system

- **infrastructure costs**
  a. Infrastructure costs are normally underestimated
  b. Excess infrastructure capacity decreases the chances on sustainable transport

  key: there is a problem of missing effective and consistent policy-making institutions, so that at present in a democratic society there will be a natural tendency towards overspent budgets

- **competitiveness and peripherality**
  a. An improvement of transport is a necessary condition for integration of Central-and East-European countries
  b. Infrastructure expansion towards the East is not necessarily favourable for the economics of Central- and East-European countries

  key: there is insufficient recognition of the market potential of remote areas, and there are insufficient added value strategies.

- **Trans-European networks**
  a. Trans-European Networks are good for Europe

b.   Trans-European Networks are better for nodal centres in Western Europe and worse for the hinterland.

key: the main problem with the TENs is formed by the difference in spatial accessibility of these networks, so that equity issues are aggravated.

This list of dilemmas and paradoxes is not exhaustive, but offers a good illustration of the great many challenges faced by the transport sector. The need for proper policy responses is high; we will offer a few of them in the final part.

Policy Opportunities and Lessons

In this final part we will examine some possible policy consequences from the perspective of the above scenario analysis. Sustainable transport policy presupposes a multi-faceted and also multilayer policy ramification. Two broad levels of policy making may be distinguished, viz. national/international and local/regional. These two levels have also different opportunities for developing and implementing strategies to favour sustainable mobility. This is briefly summarised in Figure 7.6.

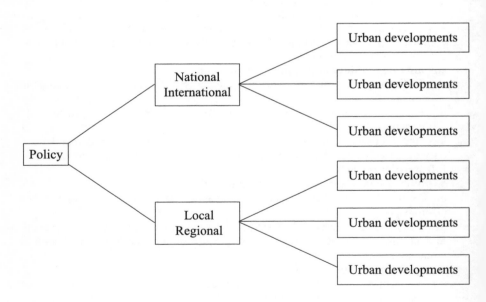

Figure 7.6   Policy fields

Some concise remarks on the possibilities and flexibilities of various policy strategies will now be made.

National/international policy

The following important (but certainly not exclusive) areas of policy intervention aiming at sustainable transport from a national/international perspective may be envisaged.

Infrastructure

Infrastructure is not only a matter of supply (how much, which kind, where), but it also has to be offered at a reasonable market price. Thus, financing and pricing are critical success factors for an infrastructure policy aiming at favouring a sustainable transport systems.

Standards

An important policy tool is the formulation and enforcement of standards on sustainable mobility, e.g., on maximum emissions per car, on vehicle design and technology (e.g. catalytic converters), on speed limits, on safety regulation, on traffic management etc. Such common agreements are also needed in order to avoid the emergence of different environmental and transport policy regimes which might violate the principle of equal competitive conditions between regions or countries.

Price regulations

Market-based price interventions are usually regarded as efficient means to achieve a fair balance in case of social costs. Such price measures may incorporate taxes, charges, fees, but also subsidies. The main problem here is not the economic underpinning, but the social acceptance and feasibility (see Verhoef 1996).

Local/regional policy

It is clear that local and regional policy addresses more specifically sustainability questions at the meso/micro level. Three fields stand out here.

Land use

Physical planning has become an important policy vehicle for influencing the size, the mode and the environmental impact of transport. This applies to infrastructure, but also training programmes, industrial location, facility locations and so forth. In general, land use intervention will have a decisive impact on the future activity pattern of our modern, mobile society.

Parking

A very effective – though usually not very popular – measure to control traffic movements in cities is through a strict system of parking policy, especially for private cars. Parking policy can adopt two forms: reduction of parking facilities or a rationing via a price regime (parking fees). A price system may be able to discriminate between different periods of the day or between different time spans of parking. Clearly, a strict parking policy in cities is usually also meeting fierce resistance from local shopkeepers. It seems – given the spatial distributional impacts of parking policy – plausible to develop a more strict parking strategy at a regional level, while being accompanied by a support for local and regional public transport policy.

Logistics

Distribution of goods and people has become a very complicated task. Modern logistics aims to solve many of such complicated questions, based on cost minimisation (or other performance criteria). Transport is increasingly faced with the question of how to organise physical movements in the most efficient way. Therefore, there is a great policy task in offering the best possible logistic facilities, as the value added of modern logistics is usually higher than that of physical transport per se. This situation also explains the current interest in gateways and mainports.

There are also new policy opportunities whose relevance can be clarified by means of the above described scenarios. These opportunities are:

- **Telematics**. Telematics may significantly increase the efficiency of existing transport networks (see also Nijkamp et al. 1996).
- **Modern technology**. The use of advanced technology may pertain to different transport policy fields, such as vehicle design, road maintenance, noise reduction, safety equipment, automatic goods identification, and so forth.
- **Alternative infrastructure design**. In this contact, much may be expected from new forms of construction, such as subterranean solutions, like parking garages, underground warehouses and department stores, transport terminals, but also underground roads or even vacuum tunneling. The use of the 'third dimension' may also gain importance by constructing office building or other facilities as a new layer above existing motorways or railways.

Conclusion

The start of the new millennium heralds an era of global interaction. Our world is in a continuous state of flux. Modern transport systems have created the conditions for an unprecedented rise in mobility, both regionally and worldwide. The action radius of the 'homo mobilis' is still on the rising trend to a halt. The ever rising mobility pattern applies to all types of trips: work, business, shopping and leisure. The same tendency can also be observed in a freight transport, at both the metropolitan/regional and the international level, a clear rise in freight movement can be observed.

Greater freight movement and personal mobility put a higher claim on the capacity use of transport infrastructure. In the past, public authorities have often responded to the rise in demand by offering an expansion in the supply of infrastructure. But for both economic and ecological reasons this traditional option is gradually diminishing. As a result we witness nowadays a new policy trend that attempts to optimise the use of existing transport systems. Indeed, there is a great challenge in this new view on transport policy. Not only is there the potential offered by advanced means of communications, in particular, the New Information Technology sector (NIT) – as reflected in transport Telematics and just-in-time (JIT) deliveries of inputs and outputs – but also we recognise the great many opportunities created by a better integration of existing – usually disjointed – transport system.

References

Banister, D. and J. Berechman (eds) (1993), *Transport in a Unified Europe*, Elsevier, Amsterdam.

Bruinsma, F. and P. Rietveld (1998), *Is Transport Infrastructure Effective? Transport Infrastructure Accessibility and the Space Economy*, Springer-Verlag, Berlin.

Capello, R., P. Nijkamp and G. Pepping (1998), *Sustainable City and Energy Policy*, Springer-Verlag, Berlin.

Doren, Ch. Van (1991), *The History of Knowledge*, Ballantine Books, New York.

Lagendijk, K. (1994), 'Internationalization of the Automobile Industry in Spain', Thesis Publishers, Amsterdam.

Nijkamp, P. and S. Baaijens (1998), 'Slow Motion', discussion paper, Tinbergen Institute, Amsterdam.

Nijkamp, P. and M. van Geenhuizen (1997), 'European Transport: Challenges and Opportunities', *Journal of Transport Geography*, Vol. 5, No. 1, pp. 3–11.

Nijkamp, P. and G. Pepping (1996), *Telematics and Transport Behaviour*, Springer-Verlag, Berlin.

Nijkamp, P., S. Rienstra and J. Vleugel (1998), *Transportation Planning and the Future*, John Wiley, Chichester and New York.

OECD (1997), *Economic Globalisation and the Environment*, OECD, Paris.

Veen-Groot, D.B. van, and P. Nijkamp (1997), 'Sustainable Transport and "Factor Four"', paper presented at conference *Managing Sustainability – The European Perspective and Experiences*, University of Rostock, Germany.

Verhoef, E. (1996), T*he Economics of Regulating Road Transport*, Edward Elgar, Cheltenham.

Weizsacker, E. von, A.B. Lovins and L.H. Lovins (1997), *Factor Four: Doubling Wealth, Halving Resource Use*, Earthscan, London.

Chapter 8

Globalisation, South-North Migration, and Uneven Development

Amitava Krishna Dutt

Introduction

Globalisation is a term that is now commonplace in discussions on the world economy, both in academic circles and in the popular press. Attention is being drawn to the large increases in international trade and direct foreign investment (FDI), and the phenomenal increases in international financial flows of capital, as a result of lower costs of transport and communications and reduced restrictions on trade and capital flows. Not only is this globalisation evident for the rich countries of the North, within which most of the internationalisation process is occurring, but less developed countries (LDCs) – which we will collectively refer to as the South – are increasingly entering this nexus.

The effects of globalisation on the North and the South are also attracting attention. While LDCs are usually attempting to establish closer trade links with rich countries and to attract FDI to their shores, it is often argued that globalisation adversely affects rich countries due to competition from producers in the South as Northern jobs move to low wage countries through FDI.[1]

One particularly important question is the effect that globalisation has on the gap between the North and the South. A large and growing empirical literature is concerned with whether or not per capita income levels in different countries is converging, using a variety of measures of convergence. A consensus seems to have emerged that there seems to be no convergence in levels of development between rich and poor countries, and despite some success stories among poor countries and convergence within the group of rich countries, the evidence appears to support divergence between rich and poor countries. There is some evidence (see Sala-i-Martin 1996) that rich countries appear to grow faster than poor countries (what is called β-divergence) and measures of dispersion of income across countries show a tendency to increase (an example of which is called σ-divergence), and frequency distributions of income levels of countries derived from transition matrices exhibit a thinning middle and an accumulation at both low and high tails, or what has come to be called the twin-peakedness of world income distribution (Quah 1993). However, some recent data seem to suggest that after 1900 there has occurred a slight fall (see Stocker 1999). Although it is too early to tell from this data alone whether the trend towards rising inequality has been reversed, the possibility that globalisation has reversed the trend towards divergence cannot be ruled out.

Most of the discussion on globalisation and its effects on international inequality have focused on trade and capital flows, with little attention being given to international migration.[2] This is not entirely surprising, since international migration appears to be the absentee in the globalisation process: while trade and FDI flows have increased at a faster rate than world production in the last two decades or so, migration flows have exhibited little change during that period if one excludes the temporary surge after the change in political regimes in Eastern Europe (see Faini, de Melo and Zimmerman 1999). The share of foreigners in the population changed very little over the 1980s in most advanced countries: from the early 1980s to the early 1990s this percentage changed from 6.8 to 6.3 in France, 7.4 to 8.5 in Germany, 2.8 to 3.5 in UK, and 6.2 to 7.9 in the US, and stayed at 16.1 in Canada (Faini, de Melo and Zimmerman 1999: 3). This contrasts with trade growing at 9.2 per cent and output at 2.9 per cent in 1994–1995 and with FDI growing between 1981 and 1993 at almost double that of exports. While there has generally been a liberalisation of restrictions on international trade and capital flows, the same cannot be said of labour flows, with most advanced countries severely restricting immigration.

However, the effects of South-North migration on international development patterns should not be neglected. In the North it is feared that immigration will worsen unemployment problems and exacerbate skilled-unskilled wage gaps, worsen income distribution, put excessive burdens on public services, and generally reduce the well-being of natives. The call for a relaxation of immigration of skilled workers, especially of workers trained in computer software engineering, in countries such as Germany, has set off a public debate on the immigration issue. Such a relaxation seems already to have occurred in the US. Regarding the South, it has long been feared that the emigration of workers, especially skilled ones, would lead to a brain drain and adversely affect development prospects (see Bhagwati 1979b, for instance). The recent emphasis on the role of human capital in growth, especially in the new growth theory literature, has brought about a revival of interest in this question, as evidenced by recent work by Haque and Kim (1995) and Wong and Yip (1999).

This chapter examines the effects of migration of labour from poor to rich countries. It does so by dividing the world into two parts, a rich North and a poor South, and examining the consequences of the migration of skilled workers from the South to the North on relative per capita income levels in the two regions and on income distribution within the two regions.

A Simple Model of Migration and Convergence

A useful point of departure for our analysis is a simple neoclassical model of migration between two regions which produce one good with homogeneous labour and possibly other factors (which do not flow between regions) and which consequently do not trade with each other. Production exhibits diminishing returns to labour, and the economies are perfectly competitive. Given the total supply of labour in the two regions, we can draw a standard diagram showing the average and marginal product curves of homogeneous labour, shown by APL_i and MPL_i, respectively, in each region, with the labour in the South measured from left to right and that in the North measured from right to left.

Now suppose that the initial allocation of labour is at E, so that the supply of labour in the South is given by $0_S E$ and that in the North is given by $E0_N$. Since labour demand in each region is given by the marginal product curve of labour, and since wages are perfectly flexible within each region, the wage in the South will be given by *DE* and that in the North, *CE*. Per capita income in the South and the North are given by *BE* and *AE*, respectively. Assume, now, that migration is allowed between the two regions, that there are no costs of migration to workers, and that workers choose to move to a region with a higher wage. Since the wage is higher in the North than in the South, workers in the South will therefore migrate to the South. As labour supply is reduced in the South and increased in the North, the wage in the South will rise and that in the North will fall, till wages are equalised at *EC'*, at which point migration will cease, and the allocation of labour will be given by point *E'*. As a result of migration, per capita income in the South has increased from *BE* to *E'B'*, while in the North it has fallen from *AE* to *A'E'*.

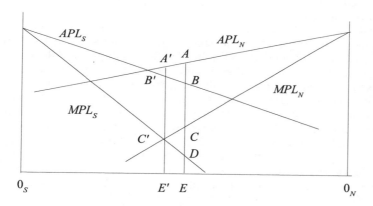

Figure 8.1   Migration and convergence

This implies that migration leads to convergence in levels of per capita income, which is the sense in which South-North migration is equalising.[3] This convergence result will be obtained even if we take into account the fact that unrestricted immigration is not allowed by the North, and that it restricts migration to an amount less that *EE'*.

The model just discussed, from which the convergence result is obtained, makes three major assumptions: first, there is only one kind of homogeneous labour in the two regions; second, there are diminishing returns to labour; and third, perfect competition prevails everywhere. All three assumptions are arguably inappropriate for analysing South-North migration in the modern world. Most Northern countries not only control the total amount of migration, but attempt to restrict it mostly to skilled workers (apart from family members of residents and those granted political asylum). The assumption of diminishing returns has increasingly been dispensed with in the international economics and the growth theory literature, with the increasing popularity of the so-called new trade and new growth theory models. More generally, the importance of distinguishing between skilled and unskilled labour has been stressed in recent analyses of trade between rich and poor countries (see Wood 1994). Increasing returns has long played in important role in development economics, as shown by the early work of Rosenstein-Rodan (1943). Closely related to the growing popularity of increasing returns is the rise of models of imperfect competition in the trade, growth and development literatures. Only if scale economies are external to the firm is the assumption of perfect competition compatible with increasing returns. It is no wonder then that the new trade theory and new growth theory literatures have increasingly relied on models of imperfect competition. Krugman (1993) has drawn attention to the importance of the assumption of imperfect competition in the early theories of coordination failures and low level traps in development economics. The empirical importance of imperfect competition in developing countries, especially in the non-agricultural sectors of semi-industrialised countries in which skilled workers are employed, has also attracted much attention. For instance, LDCs – given their smaller markets – have been found to have higher seller concentration ratios than developed countries (see Lee 1984).

There is reason to believe that these assumptions of the model bias our results towards producing the result of convergence due to migration. The literature on the brain drain has drawn attention to the fact that the emigration of skilled workers can have adverse effects on the development prospects of LDCs, because of the dearth of human capital in these countries. Skilled workers may generate positive externalities in the countries in which they work, so that the loss in output that results from their emigration can exceed their 'private' marginal product. Endogenous growth models imply that brain drain can reduce the growth rate of LDCs. Haque and Kim (1995) show that migration results in LDCs lose workers who are the most skilled in the sense of having the greatest efficiency due to their educational potential, and therefore leads to lower growth and levels of income. Wong and Yip (1999) show that the migration of skilled workers results in a decrease in the ratio of skilled workers (who also train unskilled workers) to unskilled labour and total population, which has an adverse effect on efficiency growth, and hence on the growth rate, in LDCs. By ignoring the distinction between skilled and unskilled workers, the simple model of this section is unable to take these effects into account. The role of the assumption of diminishing returns and the associated assumption of perfect competition is clearer still: the movement of labour from the poor country to the rich reduces productivity in the rich country due to diminishing returns, and raises it in the poor country, leading to convergence of income levels. In general, it is widely recognised in the economics literature that in general diminishing returns leads to negative feedbacks which bring regions closer together when they interact with each other, while increasing returns leads to positive feedbacks which results in divergence (see Arthur 1990). Models of regional migration within countries which assume increasing returns also produce the result of industrial concentration in one region (see Krugman 1991).

Accordingly, the next section develops a simple model which departs from the previous one by introducing skilled labour, by allowing for increasing returns, and by assuming imperfect competition, to see whether such a model also implies convergence due to migration.

Skilled Labour, Increasing Returns and Imperfect Competition

There are a number of different ways in which skilled labour, increasing returns and imperfect competition can be introduced into the model discussed in the previous section.

As far as increasing returns and imperfect competition are concerned, we follow the approach developed by Romer (1987, 1990) and used extensively in the new growth literature, such as in the model developed by Rivera-Batiz and Rivera-Batiz (1991). In this approach, the production of the final good reflects the benefits of specialisation in the use of intermediate inputs, and the production of intermediate inputs reflects increasing returns. The final good is produced under conditions of perfect competition, and there are not internal scale economies in its production. The benefits of specialisation are formalised by using a CES production function of the type which was used by Dixit and Stiglitz (1977) to show that consumer utility increased with product variety. The intermediate inputs – which we interpret as services – are, however, produced by monopolistic competitors who face scale economies due to the existence of fixed costs. Since these assumptions have become quite standard in the literature, we need not spend further time discussing them. Suffice it to note that there are alternative ways of introducing increasing returns available in the literature. For instance, Panagariya's (1992) model of factor flows in an open economy assumes that scale economies are output generated and external to the firm, and that producers are perfectly competitive. However, because of the empirical importance of internal scale economies and imperfect competition, we adopt our version which incorporates them.

Skilled labour can be introduced into the model in a variety of ways. One approach is to assume that skilled labour is simply a more productive version of unskilled labour. This approach is followed by Haque and Kim (1995), who assume that there are workers with many different skill levels, and that unskilled workers can be transformed into skilled workers by schooling and that the skill level of workers depends on their learning ability, or the extent by which a given amount of time spent on schooling leads to an increase in efficiency. While this approach can yield a number of useful insights, it does not take into account the arguably qualitatively very different roles that skilled and unskilled workers play in the economy.

An alternative approach treats the skilled and unskilled workers as two different inputs. This approach is followed by Wood (1994), in whose analysis the supplies of labour of the two kinds are taken to be given in a model which analyses trade patterns and the effects of reductions to trade barriers in which the skilled worker to unskilled worker endowment ratio plays a major role. While Wood's approach merely treats the two as separate factors with one receiving a higher wage than the other, they do not have distinctive roles in the production process. Wong and Yip (1999) provide different roles to the two kinds of labour in their overlapping generations' model in which workers in their first period are unskilled and those in their second, after obtaining schooling, become skilled. Although the two kinds of labour just appear as two inputs in production, only skilled workers can also serve as educators. Although the model gives skilled workers as educators an important role in the dynamics of productivity growth since a higher educator-student ratio makes education more effective, it does not give the two kinds of workers a distinctive role in production at a point in time. Panagariya's (1992) model mentioned earlier, which has three factors – skilled labour, unskilled labour and capital – does provide the two kinds of labour different roles in production. The model has two sectors of production in the two regions, the North and the South: sector 1 produces a modern, high technology good, has output-generated economies of scale external to the firm, and sector 2 produces a traditional good exhibiting constant returns to scale. The simple version of the model assumes that skilled labour is specific to the modern sector, and that capital is specific to the traditional sector, and unskilled labour is used in both sectors, but these strong assumptions can be generalised without changing the main results of the analysis if assumptions about relative factor intensities and elasticities of substitution between factors are made to ensure that skilled labour is used more intensively in the modern sector and capital is used more intensively in the traditional sector, when all three factors are used in both sectors. The model produces the interesting result that skilled labour will wish to migrate from the South to the North where it will receive a higher wage (with the assumption that the two regions have identical factor endowment ratios and technologies, but larger absolute factor endowments), but actual migration are likely to make those left behind in the South worse off and Northerners better off, since it will reduce production of the modern good in the South with a resultant loss in scale economies and increase its production in the North with the opposite effect.[4] However, its results require the questionable feature that Southern exports to the North are relatively capital intensive along with the more acceptable one that Northern exports are relatively skilled worker intensive.[5] The approach followed here departs from the other models by assuming that unskilled labour is involved in the assembly of the final good using intermediate goods, while skilled labour is involved in the production of intermediate services. This formulation arguably captures an essential difference between skilled and unskilled labour, with the former producing differentiate services under conditions of scale economies, while the latter takes the products of skilled labour and combines them into a homogeneous product.

Turning to the model, we first consider a closed economy in isolation, which produces one final good. Unskilled workers produce this good with a variety of intermediate services with a constant return to scale production function, while intermediate services are produced with skilled workers under conditions of increasing returns.

We assume that final output is produced with unskilled labour and a composite intermediate service using the Cobb-Douglas production function

$$Y = L^\beta V^{1-\beta} \tag{1}$$

Where L is the employment of unskilled labour and V is the amount of the composite intermediate service used. We define the composite intermediate service with the Dixit-Stiglitz CES function as

$$V = \left(\sum_{i=1}^{n} Q_i^\sigma \right)^{1/\sigma} \tag{2}$$

Where $0 < \sigma < 1$ and Q_i is the quantity of each intermediate service used, there being n services in existence.[6] We will introduce assumptions that make the level of use of each intermediate service to be equal, so that

$$Q = n\,Q_i \tag{3}$$

Where Q is a measure of the total quantity of intermediate services, which implies that

$$V = n^{(1-\sigma)/\sigma}\,Q \tag{4}$$

Substituting this equation into equation (2) we get

$$Y = L^{\beta}\,Q^{1-\beta}\,n^{\,(1-\sigma)(1-\beta)/\sigma} \tag{5}$$

which implies that $\partial Y/\partial n > 0$, which states that an increase in the number of intermediate services, given labour and the total quantity of intermediate services, there is will be an increase in the output of the final good, that is, a greater variety of intermediate services increases final output. This results from the technology assumed in equation (2), where the elasticity of substitution between intermediate services, given by $1/(1 - \sigma) > 1$.

Now we turn to the production of the final good which, as noted above, has a perfectly competitive market structure. Profits are given by

$$\Pi = L^{\beta}\,V^{1-\beta} - wL - \sum\nolimits_{i=1}^{n} P_i\,Q_i$$

Where V is given by equation (2), P_i denotes the price of the ith intermediate service, and the price of the final good is set equal to unity. Since firms maximise profits by choosing L and Q we get the first order conditions

$$\beta\,Y/L = w \tag{6}$$

and

$$Q_i = [(1-\beta)\,Y/P_i V^{\sigma}]^{1/(1-\sigma)} \tag{7}$$

Using this equation, summing over all services and using equation (2),

$$\sum\nolimits_{i=1}^{n} P_i\,Q_i = (1-\beta)\,Y \tag{8}$$

Substituting equation (5) into (6) we also get

$$w = \beta\,n^{(1-\beta)(1-\sigma)/\sigma}\,Q^{1-\beta}\,L^{-(1-\beta)} \tag{9}$$

Which shows that the real wage of unskilled workers depends positively on the number of intermediate services, (since a larger number of producer services increases the productivity of unskilled workers) and on the quantity of intermediate services, but negatively on the employment of unskilled workers.

We now turn to the market for the intermediate services. As noted earlier, such services require only skilled labour in production, and we assume that the skilled labour required for producing an intermediate service is given by

$$X_i = F + b\,Q_i \tag{10}$$

Where F is the fixed amount of skilled labour required producing each intermediate good and b the amount of skilled labour required to produce each additional unit of each service. Note that since the services enter the production function given in (2) symmetrically, and since they have identical technology given by equation (10), we are entitled to treat them symmetrically, as assumed in equation (3). From equation (10) it follows that the total cost of producing service i,

$$TC_i = w_X F + w_X b\,Q_i$$

Where w_X is the wage of skilled workers, so that the average and marginal costs are given by

$$AC_i = (w_X F / Q_i) + w_X b$$

and

$$MC_i = w_X b$$

This shows that the former falls with output, reflecting increasing returns to scale and the latter is constant. We assume that firms producing intermediate services operate in a monopolistically competitive market, maximising profits taking the output levels of other firms as given, with each firm producing one differentiated service. This implies that they set marginal cost equal to marginal revenue, so that

$$MC_i = P_i\,[(\epsilon_i - 1)/\epsilon_i]$$

Where, ϵ_i is the absolute value of the price elasticity of demand. Firms take equation (7) to be the demand curve for their product, with Y and V given, so that $\epsilon_i = 1/(1 - \sigma)$, which implies that this equation can be rewritten as

$$MC_i = P_i\,\sigma$$

This can be substituted into the expression for the marginal cost to yield

$$P_i = b\,w_X / \sigma \tag{11}$$

This is the standard result that firms use a fixed mark-up on marginal costs to set price. Free entry and exit imply that the number of firms adjust to ensure that for each intermediate service producer, profit is zero, or

$$w_X F + w_X b\,Q_i = P_i\,Q_i$$

Which, using equation (11) implies

$$Q_i = F\sigma/b(1 - \sigma) \tag{12}$$

This gives the production level of each intermediate service. Combining this equation with equation (8) and (11) we get

$$(1 - \beta)\, Y = n\, w_X\, F/(1 - \sigma) \tag{13}$$

Finally, we have the factor market clearing conditions

$$\sum_{i=1}^{n} X_i = X \tag{14}$$

Where X is the exogenously fixed supply of skilled labour, and condition that the employment of unskilled labour is equal to its exogenously-fixed supply, which we also represent by L.

We are now in a position to solve for the equilibrium values of all variables in the model. By symmetry, equation (14) implies

$$X = n\, X_i$$

Which, using equations (10) and (12) implies

$$n = (1 - \sigma)\, X/F \tag{15}$$

This shows that the equilibrium number of intermediate services will be larger the smaller are the importance of fixed costs (so that it is possible to have many varieties despite the fixed costs) and the smaller the elasticity of substitution between the services (so that it is less possible to substitute between them in production). From equations (3), (12) and (15) we get

$$Q = \sigma X/b \tag{16}$$

Substituting equation (15) and (16) into equation (5) we get

$$Y = (\sigma/b)^{1-\beta} \, [(1 - \sigma)/F]^{(1-\sigma)(1-\beta)/\sigma} \, L^{\beta} \, X^{(1-\beta)/\sigma} \tag{17}$$

Substituting this into equation (6) we get

$$w = \beta \, (\sigma/b)^{1-\beta} \, [(1 - \sigma)/F]^{(1-\sigma)(1-\beta)/\sigma} \, L^{\beta-1} \, X^{(1-\beta)/\sigma} \tag{18}$$

Substituting equations (15) and (17) into (13) we get

$$w_X = (1 - \beta) \, (\sigma/b)^{1-\beta} \, [(1 - \sigma)/F]^{(1-\sigma)(1-\beta)/\sigma} \, L^{\beta} \, X^{(1-\beta-\sigma)/\sigma} \tag{19}$$

The unskilled-skilled wage differential is given by using equations (18) and (19),

$$w/w_X = [\beta/(1 - \beta)] \, X/L \tag{20}$$

Which of course follows from the Cobb-Douglas production function of equation (1), noting that profit in the intermediate service sector is zero in equilibrium, so that the expenditure on intermediate services is entirely received by skilled workers. We will assume that unskilled workers receive a wage lower than skilled workers, which requires that $(1 - \beta)/\beta > X/L$, which implies that $(1 - \beta) > X/(X + L)$.

Effects of South-North Migration

We now consider two economies, the North and the South, which we denote by subscripts N and S, both of which produce the final good with the intermediate services and labour and the intermediate services with skilled labour. We assume that the intermediate services are non-traded, so that there is no trade between the two regions at all. Moreover, we assume that unskilled labour does not move between regions, but that skilled labour can. We assume that for a given level of X_i, the wage of skilled labour in the North, w_{XN}, is higher than that in the South, w_{XS}. This can be due to a number of reasons, including the fact that they are identical economies other than that fact that $X_N > X_S$, that is, that the supply of skilled workers is higher in the North than in the South. To fix ideas we assume that it is due to better technology in service production (implying a lower F and lower b).

We analyse the interaction between the two economies using Figure 8.2, where the horizontal axis measures skilled labour in the North from left to right and skilled labour in the South from right to left, and the distance $0_N 0_S$ measures the total quantity of in the two regions. The N and S curves show the level of w_X for each region. Two cases must be distinguished. In one, we have $(1 - \beta) > \sigma$. In this case, as equation (19) shows, the relation between X_i and w_{Xi} is a positive one, as shown in Figure 8.2. A rise in X_i increases output by increasing both the total quantity of intermediate services and the number of services produced, and with skilled workers receiving a constant share of the value of output, skilled wages increase with X if the share of intermediate services and income of skilled workers in income is high and σ and the elasticity of substitution among services is high, which makes the number of services have a large impact on total output.

We start with an allocation of skilled labour between regions at A, with the skilled worker wage in the North given by BA and that in the South by CA. We assume that since $w_{XN} > w_{XS}$, skilled labour moves from the South to the North, so that the allocation of labour between North and South moves rightward from A, as shown by the arrow on the horizontal axis. This implies that w_{XN} increases along the N curve and w_{XS} falls along the S curve. Equation (18) shows that the wages of unskilled workers, w_N, also rises in the North, while w_S fall. If we measure the equality of income distribution by the ratio of unskilled to skilled worker wage, w_i/w_{Xi}, equation (20) shows that equality increases in the North and falls in the South. Finally, output per worker in region i, which we can also identify as per-capita income (assuming that everyone works), is given by

$$y_i = [L_i/(L_i + X_i)] \, w_i + [X_i/(L_i + X_i)] \, w_{Xi}$$

Which, using equations (19) and (20) can be written as

$$y_i = \Psi_i \, L_i^{\,\beta} \, X_i^{\,(1-\beta)/\sigma}/(L_i + X_i) \tag{21}$$

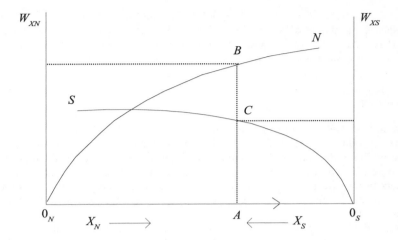

Figure 8.2   Divergence due to migration of skilled labour

Where $\Psi_i = (\sigma/b_i)^{1-\beta} [(1-\sigma)/F_i]^{(1\neq\sigma)(1-\beta)/\sigma}$. Differentiating (21) with respect to X_i we find that

$$dy_i/dX_i \overset{>}{_<} 0 \iff (1-\beta)/\sigma \overset{>}{_<} X/(L+X) \qquad (22)$$

Since our assumption that $w/w_X < 1$ implies that $(1-\beta) > X/(L+X)$, and since $\sigma < 1$, we must have $(1-\beta)/\sigma > X/(L+X)$, so that we must have $dy_i/dX_i > 0$. Thus, the per capita income of the North rises, and that in the South falls, with the migration of skilled workers. We therefore have an unequivocal case of uneven development due to migration. Not only is the South relatively immiserised, but it is absolutely immiserised as well. And this continues to happen as the migration continues to occur, as long as unskilled workers are paid less than skilled workers in both regions.[7]

In the other case, with $1-\beta < \sigma$, equation (19) shows that w_{Xi} falls with X_i, so that the upward-rising N and S curves in Figure 8.2 have to be replaced by negatively sloped curves. In this case, it is obvious that if we start with an initial allocation of skilled labour at which $w_{XN} > w_{XS}$, and as X_N rises and X_S, w_{XN} will fall and w_{XS} will rise till migration ceases when $w_{XN} = w_{XS}$. As equation (18) shows, the wage of unskilled workers, w_N, rises in the North, while w_S falls. This implies that income equality as measured by w_i/w_{Xi} increases in the North and falls in the South. Per capita income must rise in the North and fall in the South even in this case so that uneven development in the sense of per capita income will still occur.

A hybrid case may also be considered, in which in the North we have $(1-\beta) > \sigma$, while in the South $(1-\beta) < \sigma$, which is possible if the share of intermediate goods and skilled labour in total output is large in the North than in the South because $\beta_S > \beta_N$. In this case, the N curve will be upward rising as in Figure 8.2, while the S curve will be falling from right to left as in the case just discussed. Starting from an initial situation in which $w_{XN} > w_{XS}$, X_N will rise and X_S will fall as skilled workers migrate from the South to the North, and this will cause w_{XN} and w_{XS} to rise. Equation (18) shows that the unskilled worker wage in the North, w_N will rise, and that in the South, w_S, will fall. Equality and per capita income rises in the North and fall in the South, again implying uneven development.

Conclusion

Our simple model of skilled worker migration from the South to the North implies that migration may increase or reduce the wages of skilled workers in the North and the South, but will increase the wage of unskilled workers in the North and reduce it for the South. Moreover, it will reduce the inequality between skilled and unskilled workers in the North while increasing it in the South. Finally, such migration will cause uneven development in the sense that per capita income will fall in the poor South and rise in the rich North.

Of course these results are obtained from a model which makes a number of simple and specific assumptions, including that of Cobb Douglas technology in final good production which fixed the factor shares between skilled and unskilled workers. Nevertheless, it does suggest that lobbies in the North which attempt to limit the immigration of skilled workers from the South may well be short-sighted. Even if such migration adversely affects skilled worker wages there (which is unlikely, given the high share of intermediate inputs), it is likely to increase per capita income and reduce wage inequality, which has been a cause of much concern in recent years. If anyone has a cause to worry about the migration of skilled workers from the South, it is the South, where such emigration is likely to worsen income distribution and reduce per capita income. While democratic countries in the South will find it difficult to control this brain drain directly, a case can be made for the taxation of migrants to pay for Southern development or for transfers from the North to the South from taxes paid by such migrants in the North, requiring a return to themes that were brought to the fore by Bhagwati (1979) and others several decades ago.

This simple model of skilled worker migration and uneven development can be extended and modified in a number of ways. Three important issues which can be taken into account with such modifications are briefly discussed.

One, it is sometimes argued that the emigration of skilled labour from the South is not a problem, and may in fact serve as a safety valve which guards against expressions of political discontent, if there are unemployed skilled workers in the South. It is sometimes argued that countries in the South, such as India, have overextended their higher education systems with the result that they have an oversupply of skilled workers. This issue can be analysed by assuming that the skilled labour wage in the South, w_{XS}, is exogenously fixed, and above the market-clearing level, so that the entire skilled labour force, $\bar{X}_S$, is not employed, so that $\bar{X}_S - X_S$ are unemployed. In this case equation (13) gives a relation between Y and n for the exogenously-fixed level of w_X, and equations (3), (6), (9) and (12) give us another relation between Y and n, which is

$$Y = [F\sigma/b(1 - \sigma)]^{1-\beta} L^\beta n^{(1-\beta)/\sigma}$$

This can simultaneously solve for the equilibrium levels of Y and n. Since Y is independent of $[X]_S$, as is w, there will be no change in Y_S, but a rise in per capita production, y_S, when $[X]_S$ falls, but no change in per worker production. Thus in this case it is possible for per capita income to rise in both North and the South when skilled labour migrates. However, as argued by Bhagwati and Hamada (1974), if one takes into account the process of transferring labour from unskilled through skilled through higher education which requires real resources, and assumes that the reduction of unemployment in the South due to migration increases the expected return to higher education, it is possible that migration can in fact reduce the per capita income in the South and even serve to increase the level of unemployment in the South by converting more unskilled workers into skilled workers. Moreover, even if there was a general oversupply of skilled workers several decades ago, it is not clear that at present such an oversupply of appropriate skilled workers of high quality exists in the South.

Two, except in the comment just made, we have abstracted from the dynamics of L and X over time. Our model can be extended to incorporate the dynamics of changes in L and X in each region. The growth in the supply of unskilled labour, L, reinterpreted to denote the change in unskilled labour in efficiency units, can be assumed to depend on an exogenous rate of population growth, and on spending on primary and secondary education. The growth in the supply of skilled labour, X, also reinterpreted in efficiency units, can be assumed to depend on the supply and demand for higher education. The supply of higher education can be assumed to depend on government spending on higher education, while that of demand can be expected to depend on the relative wages of skilled and unskilled workers. Government spending on education can be taken to be equal to tax receipts from skilled workers. The migration of skilled workers, in this context, can result in a reduction in the growth of the supply of skilled workers because of a reduction in the educator-student ratio as a result of emigration of skilled workers, as in the overlapping generation's model developed by Wong and Yip (1999). These dynamic effects can therefore exacerbate the problems discussed in our simple model, which does not take these dynamic issues into account.

Three, a crucial assumption made in the model is that services are not tradable. If services (or at least goods made from services) were tradable, for instance, via the Internet, then final good producers in both countries could all import all services, wherever they are produced, and thus reap the advantages of a larger variety of intermediate goods. The reason for assuming that services are not tradable is that the use of services requires close contact between the service producer and the final good producer, because of frequent changes and improvements necessary in the nature of the services, which is difficult or impossible to achieve when the products are trade long distance. It can be conjectured that even if trade in intermediate goods and services is allowed, as long as there are productivity gains to be made through having the skilled workers in the home country, our results discussed in this model would continue to hold.

Notes

1   See *The Economist* (1994), Schwab and Smadja (1994) and Wood (1994); but see Krugman (1994) for a contrary view.
2   There are exceptions. See, for instance, Baker, Epstein and Pollin (1998), which devotes three out of its nineteen chapters on different aspects of globalisation to the discussion of labour migration, and Faini, de Melo and Zimmerman (1999) which is concerned specifically with migration.
3   Two caveats must be made about this result. First, this analysis implies convergence in per capita income levels, in contrast to some of the empirical analysis which examines the convergence issue in terms of rates of growth of per capita income. However, this analysis does imply that we have σ-convergence. Second, even this neoclassical model can be shown to imply that those who are left behind in the South lose as a result of emigration, and the natives of the North gain because of immigration, if it is assumed – as the analysis implicitly assumes – that the migrating workers only receive wages (and no portion of non-wage income) in the South (before migration) or the North (after migration). This is because those left behind in the South lose the non-labour income which was generated by employing the workers in the South and the Northern natives gain the non-labour income generated by employing them in the North. Looking at per capita income figures ignore these distributional issues (see Bhagwati 1979a). If we assume that workers always receive a share of non-labour income, wherever they reside, then per capita income will be the correct indicator of welfare, but migration will be in response to differences in the average product of labour and not the marginal product of labour; our convergence result, however, will still hold.
4   Since terms of trade effects also come into play, the effects are ambiguous.
5   It has already been noted above that we also opt for an approach in which scale economies can be internal to the firm and in which firms are imperfectly competitive, over Panagariya's approach in which scale economies are external to the firm and firms are perfectly competitive.
6   This form of technology is used commonly in models with a variety of inputs. See, for instance, Rivera-Batiz and Rivera-Batiz (1991). The analysis of the final goods sector follows the presentation in that paper.
7   This is a sufficient, and not necessary condition, since even if $(1 - \beta) > X/(X + L)$ and hence $w/w_X < 1$ we can have $(1 - \beta)/\sigma > X/(X + L)$ and hence $dy/dX > 0$ satisfied.

References

Arthur, Brian (1990), 'Positive Feedbacks in the Economy', *Scientific American*, Vol. 262, February, pp. 92–9.

Baker, Dean, Gerlad Epstein and Robert Pollin (eds) (1998), *Globalization and Progressive Economic Policy*, Cambridge University Press, Cambridge.

Bhagwati, Jagdish (1979a), 'International Factor Movements and National Advantage', *Indian Economic Review*, No. 14(2), October, pp. 73–100.

Bhagwati, Jagdish (1979b), 'Economic Migration of the Highly Skilled: Economics, Ethics and Taxes', *Third World Quarterly*, Vol. 1, No. 3, pp. 17–30.

Bhagwati, Jagdish and Koichi Hamada (1974), 'The Brain Drain, International Integration of Markets for Professionals and Unemployment. A Theoretical Analysis', *Journal of Development Economics*, Vol. 1, pp. 19–42.

Bhagwati, Jagdish and Carlos Rodriguez (1975), 'Welfare-theoretical Analysis of the Brain Drain', *Journal of Development Economics*, Vol. 2, pp. 195–221.

Dixit, Avinash and Joseph E. Stiglitz (1977), 'Monopolistic Competition and Optimum Product Diversity', *American Economic Review*, Vol. 67, No. 3, pp. 297–308.

The Economist (1994), 'A Survey of the Global Economy', October, Vol. 1, pp. 1–38.

Faini, Riccardo, Jaime de Melo and Klaus Zimmerman (1999), 'Trade and Migration: An Introduction', in Riccardo Faini, Jaime de Melo and Klaus Zimmerman (eds), *Migration. The Controversies and the Evidence*, Cambridge University Press, Cambridge.

Haque, Nadeem U. and Se-Jik Kim (1995), '"Human Capital Flight": The Impact of Migration on Income and Growth', *IMF Staff Papers*, 42(3), September, pp. 577–607.

Krugman, Paul (1991), *Geography and Trade*, MIT Press, Cambridge, MA.

Krugman, Paul (1993), 'Toward a Counter-counterrevolution in Development Theory', *Proceedings of the World Bank Annual Conference on Development Economics, 1992*, supplement to *The World Bank Economic Review* and *The World Bank Research Observer*, pp. 15–38.

Krugman, Paul (1994), 'Does Third World Growth Hurt First World Prosperity?' *Harvard Business Review*, July–August, pp. 113–21.

Lee, N. (1984), 'Business Concentration in LDCs' in C.H. Kirkpatrick, N. Lee and F. I. Nixson (eds), *Industrial Structure and Policy in Less Developed Countries*, George Allen and Unwin, London.

Panagariya, Arvind (1992), 'Factor Mobility, Trade and Welfare: A North-South Analysis with Economies of Scale', *Journal of Development Economics*, Vol. 39, No. 2, October, pp. 229–45.

Quah, Danny T. (1993), 'Empirical Cross-section Dynamics in economic growth', *European Economic Review*, Vol. 37, Nos 2–3, April, pp. 426–34.

Rivera-Batiz, L. Francisco and Luis A. Rivera-Batiz (1991), 'The Effects of Direct Foreign Investment in the Presence of Increasing Returns Due to Specialization', *Journal of Development Economics*, Vol. 34, pp. 287–307.

Romer, Paul (1987), 'Growth Based on Increasing Returns Due to Specialization', *American Economic Review*, Vol. 77, No. 2, pp. 56–62.

Romer, Paul (1990), 'Endogenous Technical Change', *Journal of Political Economy*, Vol. 98, No. 5, S71–S102, Part 2.

Rosenstein-Rodan, P.N. (1943), 'Problems of Industrialization in Eastern and South-Eastern Europe', *Economic Journal*, June–September, pp. 202–11.

Sala-i-Martin, Xavier (1996), 'The Classical Approach to Convergence Analysis', *Economic Journal*, Vol. 106, pp. 1019–36.

Schwab, Klaus and C. Smadja (1994), 'The New Rules of the Game in a World of Many Players', *Harvard Business Review*, November.

Stocker, Herbert (1999), 'Globalization, International Inequality and Economic Development', Department of Economics, University of Innsbruck, unpublished.

Wong, Kar-yiu and Chong-Kee Yip (1999), 'Education, Economic Growth and the Brain Drain', *Journal of Economic Dynamics and Control*, Vol. 23, Nos 5–6, April, pp. 699–726.

Wood, Adrian (1994), *North-South Trade, Employment and Inequality*, Oxford University Press, Oxford.

Chapter 9

Ethical Issues for Multinationals in the Age of Globalisation

Keith Lehrer

Introduction

This chapter attempts to analyse the extent to which underlying forces other than economic need to be addressed in order to explain the duress of low-paid workers in low technology industries worldwide. A value of life approach is used as a start-off point, and is widened into a discussion of the impact of an attenuation of social values, which would otherwise provide social cohesion, as social distance is increased.

An historical perspective on free trade and globalisation is sketched, and conditions in England in the time of Marx and Engels' writings will be paralleled to those of underdeveloped countries and low-tech industries in developed countries, one and a half centuries later. The behaviour and a tentative suggestion of the underlying value-sets of the diverse actors in the international economy are explored e.g. supranational retail and marketing companies, contracting companies, subcontractors, unions, homeworkers, NGOs, 'Northern' and 'Southern' governments, and international institutions such as the World Bank: and the ILO. The main context of the exploration is in the clothing and footware industries, so that the simultaneous use of high-tech control and marketing systems are juxtaposed with the use of labour-intensive and low-capital technologies. Current conflicts around appropriate auditing and monitoring procedures to reduce non-transparency are used to illustrate the profound schisms in underlying value-sets of the different actors.

An underlying theme of the chapter is to suggest that the so-called inevitability of globalisation through freer trade, and the transitional hardships it necessarily imposes on less powerful economic actors, is by no means a modern phenomenon. Similar interests are served now as before but with the potential of forms of long-distance exploitation being exposed by an array of increasingly globalised countervailing forces. Of course their power and sophistication is different from those available and relied upon in the eighteenth and nineteenth centuries. Whether these forces will prove more or less effective at closing the gap of global inequality, or become the unwitting instrument of even greater inequality, remains a central but unresolved issue. However, there are some grounds for hope.

Mexico

On Sunday 23 May 1999, the *Toronto Star* reported the latest toll in the murder of teenage girls, in the city of Juarez, most of them maquiladora workers: 187, up from the 100 last reported in late 1997. Many of the bodies remain unidentified.

Juarez is in the State of Chihuaha, Mexico, on the border of the US across from El Paso, Texas. Since the advent of free trade, in just a few years, the town has grown from a few hundred thousand to 2 million, and continues to act as a magnet for young unemployed rural people, mostly female, in search of work. The police have solved none of the murders. The government has not thought fit to establish a task force to focus on the issues, and the maquiladora owners state it is not their responsibility to ensure the safety of their workers.

El Salvador

Excerpts from a report by the National Labour Committee, New York, on the 'Violations of Women's Rights and the Abuse of Minors in El Salvador's Maquiladora Sector'.

> Gabo, a Korean-owned maquilador, uses over 500 young women to sew garments for export to the U.S. to a number of large retailers including Marshalls, Sears, Wal-Mart, Nordstroms and K-mart. Overtime at Gabo is mandatory. For example, last December, Gabo instituted 21 hour work days, twice a week … [At 4 a.m. when the women are let out] there is not public transportation … [At work] women have been hit; have had their skin pinched and twisted; have had their noses grabbed and pulled by managers screaming at them … Anyone who would like to continue their schooling is told to quit … there is no clean-filtered drinking water at Gabo. If you drink from the water you get sick. Nor is there any toilet paper in the bathrooms … As is typical throughout the maquiladoras, you are granted permission to use the bathroom only twice a day. If you ask to use it more, you get a warning, and the third time you are fired … There are a lot of minors at Gabo … the majority of workers are women 18 years old and younger. Mr. H-, one of the supervisors, likes to touch the breasts and buttocks of the young women. The girls have to learn to laugh at this, because if they showed their anger they would be fired …
>
> Every way Gabo management can cheat the workers it does so … what Gabo frequently does is to deduct social security from the workers' pay, but then pocket the money, rather than pay it into the government program … Gabo did this to Julia Esperanza Quintinnia … on March 1, 1995, Julia felt desperately sick [her supervisor refused to let her go home, calling her a liar, but she was too sick to stay] … She couldn't go to the social security clinic, because despite the fact that Gabo had deducted social security payments from her check for the last seven months, they never issued her social security medical card … At 2 a.m. she was dead of gastroentitis.

Guatemala

Report from US/Guatemala Labour Education Campaign, c/o UNITE (Update #14, September 1995):

> Because of continuing violence against maquila workers, US/GLEC is initiating a new campaign to begin leafleting Sears, K-Mart, and JC Penny. Developments since the last

Update include: On May 17 1995, Flor de Maria Salguero de Laparra was abducted and repeatedly raped by unknown men, following a series of death threats and intimidating telephone calls to her home. Ms. Salguero, who is an activist for Guatemala's Federation of food workers' unions, last year came to the U.S. to speak about abuses of maquila workers in Guatemala.

These and countless similar situations too numerous to report, form the backdrop of this analysis, which attempts to put into a sociological and organisational framework the in-some-ways new, in some ways familiar, economic infrastructure of maquiladoras. The maquiladora system was, if not spawned by, at least given its main raison d'etre by, the movement towards freer trade and the trend to strategies of globalisation in labour-intensive industries, such as clothing and footware. For example, in Mexico alone, 'the maquiladora sector has grown from 1,120 plants and 330,000 workers in 1987 to 3,700 plants and 1 million workers a decade later'. (*Toronto Star*, 23 May 1991)

In El Salvador, while the aggregate numbers are smaller, the growth rate is far greater: a 5 times increase in maquila jobs, from 1992 to 1997 (Yanz, Jefcott et al. 1999). In all, some 27 million people are now employed in the maquila sector – more than the total working population of Canada and Australia, combined. By far the greatest numbers of those employed are very young women, and children, i.e. the most vulnerable members of the work force.

The increased publicity concomitant with setting up internationally controlled sweatshops in underdeveloped countries, has focused the spotlight on related issues, concerning labour practices, as well as wage levels, occupational health and safety issues, environmental issues etc. In the excerpts highlighted above, the central issues can be considered at least as much from a sociological as an economic perspective, and revolves around the role and social status of vulnerable workers, such as young women and children, in what has been described as the fastest-growing sector of the economy of the poorer developing countries. In particular:

1   Why is so much violence and abuse tolerated, condoned or possibly encouraged against young women and children who work in low technology industries?
2   Who is responsible?
3   What can be done to improve conditions?
4   What is being done, and by whom?
5   Are conditions improving or deteriorating, and why?

Violence and Values

For a human to value others, s/he must first value him/herself. How much does one value one's own self; in extremis, one's own life? The life of others? Which 'others'?

Suicide, the taking of one's own life, can be thought of as a profane act; a wanton destruction of God's holy creation (classical Jewish interpretation); the result of a personal self-devaluation, to be considered as the result of psychological duress/ emotional imbalance; the result of a personal evaluation, which assesses more or less rationally the value of one's future life, and finds it not worth the hardship of survival; the ultimate act of sacrifice (literally 'making sacred'), thus placing a higher value on some outside source of reference –one's community, one's society, one's family, the honour of one's name, or that of the group to which one most closely identifies, than one's own life. This last category is often associated with the violation and destruction of an outsider ('the enemy'), for which no remorse would be felt. The use of suicidal fighter pilots by Japan in World War II led to the adoption of the word 'kamikaze' in Western language, and informs Western terms of reference. Guerilla fighters in many arenas have since adopted the same tactics, which rely on a similar set of values for success.

What are the linkages between valuing oneself, and valuing others; between violating oneself, and violating others? A reasonable possibility is that the more one has been valued/devalued oneself, especially in early childhood, the more one will be predisposed to value/devalue others: similarly with violation, abuse, violence. To the extent that this is true, the first 'others' from whom we learn these values would normally be the closest 'others' – traditionally the mother and father. Each might transmit a different variant on the norm of acceptable behaviour with regard to violating and being violated.

Whether a child is male or female may make a substantial difference in learning about the acceptability of being violent, and being violated. A key part of the gender-differentiating learning process will be the observed interaction between mother and father, and the degree of violence experienced by the female as distinguished from the male child. The conventional wisdom is that the father is predisposed to act out violence towards the mother, and that this pattern may be intergenerationally transmitted. The InterAmerican Development Bank (IADB) has embarked on an ambitious programme in Latin America and the Caribbean to address the issue of violence from this perspective, at the domestic level.

'Close Others'

Who are most likely to be violated? Those whom a person has most ready access can be expected to bear the brunt of violent acts. These could be labelled 'close others', such as spouse and children, but the 'closeness' may have more to do with physical proximity than with emotional connection. An alternative explanation might be that these are the relationships with the greatest intensity, which pose the greatest challenge to a person with problematic self esteem, and hence a convenient release might be one's favourite form(s) of substance abuse, as socially sanctioned self-violation, followed by violation of others.

The other aspect of family or domestic abuse is that until recently it has been shrouded in secrecy. This may be because there is a degree of shame or humiliation in admitting to it. It may also be related to the values aptly captured in the old English adage: 'An Englishman's home is his castle'; i.e. what goes on there is no-one else's business but his own. The home is his private property, and by extension all who reside therein. This value might be held even more strongly in cultures other than the Anglo-Saxon, such as in some Latin, Middle-Eastern and Asian societies. Violation of 'close others' within a family system can also be explained by the women and children being considered the 'property' of the head of the family, whose paternal authority would be judged in patrimonial societies as more or less inviolable.

Distant Others

Any person not belonging to the nuclear family could be labelled as belonging to more or less 'distant others'. In more traditional societies extended family, kin and clan might impose many nuclear family-like claims on members, and give mutual rights and obligations or responsibilities. At the same time there is the potential to exploit the most vulnerable group members, through ready access. The exploitation could take many forms: economic, as a means of production, sexual and physical, as uncles, aunts and older siblings and cousins are given custody of and therefore access to young children etc. By the same token, an obligation to protect a member of the extended family/kinship group/clan (and tribe) against outsiders would give a measure of security to those within the group, creating the bonds which form the cement of 'social cohesion'.

As societies have industrialised and become increasingly urban-based, the bends of extended family, kin, clan and tribe have been eroded, yet there is still expected to be some level of mutual obligation and responsibility, cemented by a voluntary subscription to shared value system, and often based on shared ethnicity, religion, language and historical traditions. The responsibilities are likely to be less onerous than in a kinship system, as relationships are less intense and person bonds and obligations less strong. The less the commonality in the shared value system, the greater the attenuation of social obligations one can expect, especially if cleavage develops along kinship/clan or tribal lines.

This trend to attenuation can be expected to become far more pronounced, as a society's class and economic lines break in the same places as its lines of ethnicity, religion and/or language. Not only is there less sharing of a common value system; often the value systems are mutually exclusive and antagonistic. In this sort of context, one can expect a degree of tolerance and latitude to the violation of 'distant others', since there is a more or less attenuated acceptance of a shared humanity. At the extreme the 'other' is bestialised or demonised, with the sanction of the state, and/or the authority of the political regime, as in the Spanish Inquisition and the Nazi regime, and most recently in Yugoslavia.

In less extreme forms, within the framework of international economic relationship we might simultaneously expect an extension of some strongly held values from a society of origin, coupled with an attenuation of obligations, when operating in an 'alien' society. Thus the Asian societies from which many of the owners of Latin American maquiladoras hail, such as the Korean-owned company operating in El Salvadore, whose operation was described above, are considered to be still highly family-oriented, yet strongly patrimonial. Working conditions for the most vulnerable workers, such as children and young women, which might not be tolerated in Western countries, might be considered as more or less acceptable, given the social status of these groups in the owners' countries of origin. This, coupled with a sense of far less responsibility for social cohesion, in the 'host society', might help account for some of the conditions outlined above. The walls around plants provides owners and managers easy and uncensored access to women and children who have become vulnerable prey. Abuse is as easily perpetrated in the plant as in the home; but without the social/moral ties of obligation which act as a break on domestic abuse. A further compounding factor, which may help set the tone for the social dynamics outlined within the business context of sweatshop industries, is the value system of the host country. The first article from the *Toronto Star* ('Murder most foul'), which attempted to come to grips with the wholesale killing of teenage girls in a maquila-dominated shanty town, talked of the phenomenon of 'Mexican machismo' as underlying the murders of the teenage girl workers. The Mexican Human Rights Commission has itself accused the city of Juarez of 'sexist contempt for the lives of women to the point that what's happening is not even considered to be exceptional'. It might be possible, given the IADB's findings, with regard to the pervasiveness of 'domestic violence' to extend the label of 'misogyny' to much of the culture in Latin America.

How much is this changing, as more women get elected into public office? How much of this misogynous, patrimonial value-set is institutionalised, in the workings of the police, the Ministries of Labour, the Judicial systems, and other relevant agencies of government? These vital questions must be addressed on a country-by-country basis.

Value of Life and Value of Work

According to Kurt Salmon Assoc. (1999), the wages and benefits of manual workers in the apparel industry in the US was roughly $8.00, those in Mexico were $0.85, and those in Indonesia $0.15. If the price of labour in Indonesia is less than 2 per cent of an equivalent employee in the US, it may become extremely easy for the owners and managers of foreign-owned businesses to fall into the trap of undervaluing the living human being who is at the behest of economic conditions which ascribe these monetary values. Because of the demographics of Mexico, Indonesia, and indeed of many underdeveloped countries in Latin America and Asia, there is no shortage of young people lacking formal education, mostly female, whose best recourse for work off the streets is working in a sweatshop. Since their social status begets their low economic status, the value of their life itself has been all too often treated as cheap, in extreme cases as in Juarex, Mexico, as more or less expendable.

A Look Over our Shoulders

The 'deja-vu' quality between the economic and social conditions at the dawning of the twenty-first century, for some two-thirds of the world's population, and the situation of the populations in the first countries to undergo wholesale industrialisation and urbanisation, in the nineteenth century, is uncanny. The earlier scenario of rapidly expanding industrialisation, internationalisation of trade, and the hardships endured by the new labour force, was reported perhaps most analytically by Marx and Engels, as they observed the sewing machine sweatshops in and around Manchester. These miserable conditions were portrayed perhaps most vividly and easily understood in human terms, by Dickens' fictional work in England, and by Zola in France. Working hours in the new factories were long and uncontrolled, conditions were unsafe and in many cases inhuman, pay was by piecework and geared to produce what came to be known as 'sweat shops'. An increasing proportion of the labour force consisted, not just of previously rural in-migrants to cities, but also of women and children, who would provide a more compliant labour force, and again, as history repeating itself, in one of the biggest industries, that of manufacturing clothes, much of the work could be 'effectively and efficiently' shunted to the home, where low capital, high labour input and minimalisation of overhead and employer responsibilities, contributed to the growth of the homeworker industry, with its attendant lack of outside monitoring potential. Throughout the nineteenth and the early part of the twentieth century, the government was nudged into introducing incremental reforms, to humanise the above scenario, with factory safety laws, hours of work legislation for adults and for children, the introduction of mandatory child education, and rights of collective organising.

None of this came easily or fast. Much of it was spearheaded by 'activist groups', or 'reformers' as they were then labelled, many of whom were religiously based, like the Society of Friends (Quakers), as well as socialist groups (forerunners of our contemporary NGOs, and many still operating today). At the same time, the major manufacturers found ways to locate and exploit 'offshore locations', usually conveniently located in poor, highly populated, more slowly industrialising colony countries sharing some public administrative umbrella for better control.

Thus the 'distancing' process, not just on the physical, but more profoundly on the social plane, was honed as a control technique over a century and a half ago with the advent of serious levels of international trade. This process was dominated by one economic super power, deploying the standardisation tools of a hegemonisation of its language, English, for trade, and its legal, financial and public administration structures to help underpin the international economic infrastructure – all well before the currently vogue discussion of globalisation.

Present Trends

In the US alone, apparel imports comprise 61 per cent of a $101bn wholesale apparel market, up substantially from 47 per cent of the US market in 1987 (*Business Week*, 3 May 1999, op. cit.). These economic facts of life put in the forefront the actions of all the US-based actors in the 'globalised' apparel industry: supranatural manufacturers, trade unions, media, NGOs, consumers, both active and passive, and the government, to mention only the more obvious. There are likely to be at least four separate governments in a regular maquiladora set-up: 1) the government of the major customer/supplier; 2) the government of the contracting company; 3) the national host government; and 4) the local legal systems, public administrative systems, plus four sets of macro-norms of social procedure and control.

However, the US is home base for a) the majority of the largest supranational corporations involved in the globalised system of manufacturing and marketing of clothing and footware, and b) a huge portion of consumer demand and therefore revenue for those industries' more expensive brand-name products, e.g. Nike, the Gap, Van-Heusen etc. Given these facts, the US government can be thought of as having a potentially crucial role in how the interconnected system of so many international organisational actors actually evolves, in much the same way that Great Britain (in simpler times) was instrumental in influencing and overseeing the huge expansion of international trade in the eighteenth and nineteenth centuries, together with the economic apparatus and social conventions involved.

In terms of market power, then, the US dominates the rest of the world. This has been compounded by the financial power provided by the strength of the US dollar, as the most readily accepted international currency, again in much the same way that the pound sterling fulfilled that role, and thereby gave the UK an extra international edge, in its days of economic pre-eminence. The American government can be considered ipso facto to become the most powerful government in the world, thereby able, to a greater or less extent, to dominate other governments, and their policies, at a global level.

Because the US is also a politically pluralistic democracy, with high levels of freedom of expression, articulated public opinion can be expected, sooner or later, to have an impact on public policy and ultimately the actions of government institutions. NGOs can therefore gain significant levels of influence, if able to successfully sway the hearts and minds of a critical mass of the articulate electorate, which generally requires the consistent support of influential branches of the media. To the extend that this process succeeds, the values of the latter-day reformers, the NGOs, may have a significant impact on the nature and pace of policy change.

But the political machinery of any democratic government, and the US is perhaps the prime example, needs to be sensitive to the articulated interests of its many lobbying interest groups. It will therefore often find itself leading with one foot and trailing with another, in an effort to maintain an uneasy balance of forces. Often a crisis and or scandal is required, which pointedly exposes a breach of the values to which most Americans profess to subscribe, in order to precipitate a proactive policy. Thus, the media-supported campaign against such apparel supranationals as Phillips-VanHeusen and Nike, led by such internationally respected NGOs as the Global Exchange, and supported by such legitimate media as the *New York Times* (e.g., 'Nike's Boot Camp', *NYT*, 31 March 1997), culminated in creating sufficient public pressure on the US government, to have a Presidential Task Force created, in order to discuss the working conditions and pay of non-US workers. In itself, the establishment of the Fair Labour Association (FLA), under the auspices of the presidential task force, might have taken some of the immediate, uncomfortable spotlight pressure off the specific supranationals which have participated in its creation, in particular Nike and Phillips-Van Heusen.

One could argue then that the most powerful government in the world is still able to ultimately constrain the actions of its most powerful corporations, according to values underwritten by a liberal democracy, despite the global nature of their operations. One would also be correct in pointing out that the US government, in setting up its Presidential Task Force, was more proactive than its Canadian counterpart, which has resisted the exhortations of NGOs north of the border to establish a similar government body.

However, too much faith in the system operating consistently at a worldwide or global level, might be premature. Instead, it might be more accurate to identify a 'mercury effect', where an excess of pressure in one area will result in movement of resources to another. For example Nike moved production orders and resources from less malleable to more malleable contractors and from less coercive to more coercive host countries. As Naomi Klein explained: 'In countries like Indonesia and China, where anti-sweatshop activists have focused on their campaigns, conditions are so bad and the wages so paltry that it's painless for Nike to swoop in and look like a hero for handing out one cent raises and better lunches' (*Toronto Star*, 2 April 1999).

One might still wish to argue that the most powerful government in the world does what it can, despite the institutional and ideological constraints within which it operates, to help the most vulnerable in the work forces of the rest of the world. A recent OECD report on overseas aid provides a different slant on official US government action in this area of supporting the most vulnerable members of the global work force: 'The U.S. cut its overseas aid budget to a historic low of 0.09 per cent of GDP in 1997, a cut of 28.1 per cent over 1996, at a time when the economy was booming'. The US in fact led the aid cuts among OECD members: 'Most OECD members have pledged to grant 0.7 per cent of their economic output to the world's poorest countries, but only Denmark, Norway, Sweden and the Netherlands reached the target' (OECD's 1997 Development Co-operation Report).

The US government was thus leading the world in cutting aid most drastically, such that its contribution was roughly one eighth that of the Nordic countries of Europe, as a proportion of GDP. According to the Executive Director of UNICEF, when commenting on the report, those who suffered most from the US cuts were the most vulnerable in the work force, i.e. children (*Globe and Mail*, 23 February 1999). An ideology of free enterprise and its twin free trade may tend to support the US government position on aid. This might provide scant comfort for starving children.

Free trade advocates might argue that 1) globalising trends represent the fostering of a greater commonality of the value systems of diverse societies, and that 2) the 'global village' phenomenon manifestly reduces distance. To the first argument, of greater commonality, a response might include a) an analysis of the degree of collusion between elites in supranational marketing and retail corporations, owners of smaller, but still transnational contracting companies, and in the relevant agencies of the host governments; and b) a discussion of the shrinkage in the diversity of recognised value systems, until only the lowest common denominator of economic materialism is ultimately accepted as having recognisable social value. To the second argument, of globalisation shrinking distance, it is impossible to ignore the impact of modern communication and information technologies on the cost and availability of data. This however does not address the issue of who controls the content of the data, in whose language and according to whose cultural framework it is transmitted, and what constitute the barriers to transmission as well as to reception. For one group of persons, the world may well become an intimate and increasingly comfortable crucible. It is easy to visualise the internet and its ever-cheaper and more available access as the essence of a modem democratisation process at work. However, it behoves one to appreciate the ease of dissemination of mis-information, and the inevitability of cultural bias in favour of the transmitter, which results, intentionally or not, in reinforcing and compounding elements of prejudice and social control. The end result may be the illusion of commonality, since it is sharing only at the most superficial levels of value, amid the reality of a greater distancing – with all the echoes of Marx's analysis of the many dimensions of alienation.

Power, Values and the Monitoring Conundrum

Given that free trade zones, maquiladoras and homeworking are facts of life, regardless of the morality and deja vu quality of their existence, how are they to be monitored, if at all, and by whom?

The Malaysian Prime Minister Mahathir Mohamad is quoted by Aaron Bernstein (Commentary, in *Business Week*, 3 May 1999) as 'long arguing that such standards (as a living wage) would price them out of global markets. Low-wage countries would lose investment and jobs, ... hurting the local economy and the workers the standards are intended to help'. This free trade argument can also be posed as the Friedmanite argument of 'freedom to choose' (Friedman 1990). Thus monitoring would be self-defeating.

The problem with this argument is the lack of a level playing field in which the lowest level players have to contend, thus making the choice one with severely limited alternatives. 'Accept inhuman working conditions or starve' can be considered a form of neo-slavery, rather than freedom of choice: 'On March 8 1997 (International Women's Day) 56 women employed by a Nike contractor in Vietnam were forced to run around the factory in the hot sun until a dozen of them collapsed. They were being punished for not wearing regulation shoes to work'.

In the first two years Nike contract factories have been operating in Vietnam, one factory official has been convicted of physically abusing workers. A second has fled the country during investigation of sexual abuse charges. A third is under indictment for abusing workers' (Labour Behind the Label Coalition 1997). Despite the Malaysian Prime Minister's comments, given high levels of capital mobility, coupled with highly restricted mobility of labour, an important avenue to improve conditions would appear to be to again go through some process of social legislation at the national level, together with means of enforcement, similar to that which Britain found it necessary to introduce and to implement, in the last century. As the Labour Behind the Label Coalition (1997) noted with regard to the use of child labour in Honduras: 'In Honduras, for example, youths between 14 and 17 are legally permitted to work only six hours a day, and they are prohibited from working at night. They are also legally guaranteed the right to an education. THE PROBLEM IS THAT THIS LEGISLATION ISN'T ENFORCED'. Multinational companies such as Nike can be thought of as supranational precisely because they have more power than the countries in which they operate. For example, Nike in 1997 had $9.9 billion of revenue, more economic clout than that of 70 individual nations, as measured by the GNP (Cox 1998).

If small, weak and/or dictatorial governments are unwilling or unable to protect their more vulnerable citizens from exploitation, by other citizens or by foreigners whose economic power may exceed that of the entire national economy, then other, more global forms of countervailing power may be deemed urgently necessary, for the survival of a humane society in an era of increasingly mobile capital and constrained labour. The United Nations, and prior to the advent of that institution, the League of Nations, have been looked to, in this century of the globalisation not just of free trade, but equally of violence, as just such a countervailing power. The ILO, as one of its agencies, has as its major mandate the improvement of working conditions of the world's working population, especially its more vulnerable constituents.

Further to this end, on 19 June 1999, the ILO 'adopted a treaty banning the worst forms of child labour, including slavery and forced military recruitment ... . The pact was passed by the ILO's 174 member states ... The Worst Forms of Child Labour Convention 1999 aims to protect those under 18 by targeting child slavery, forced labour, trafficking, debt bondage, serfdom, prostitution, pornography and exploitive work in industries using dangerous machinery and hazardous substances'.

The ILO estimates that in developing countries alone, 250 million children aged between 5 and 14 work. About half are believed to work full-time' (*Toronto Star*, 18 June 1999, p. A18). Given such huge numbers, it may be totally unrealistic to have any expectations of detailed monitoring and policing by such a tiny umbrella organisation as the ILO. However, if enough publicity is raised by such august umbrella organisations, in addition to the efforts by NGOs, then the larger, more public relations-sensitive organisations may deem it in their interest to comply with international pressure for standards higher than those minimally required to host countries. This would be done, not out of any absolute moral ethic, but out of a revised understanding of enlightened self-interest. Thus Nike, which alone provides work to off-shore contractors employing about half a million workers, appears in the 1990s to have been sufficiently affected by adverse publicity, that it changed its philosophy regarding responsibility for its contractors' pay and working conditions. Following the inflation in Indonesia in 1997, Nike raised its wages above the nationally legislated minimum wage, actually an increase of 30 per cent, for 80,000 workers. As Professor Philip Rosenzweig (1998) argues: 'For Nike, it was the cumulative effect of bad publicity, often from investigative reporters and watchdog agencies, that finally led Phil Knight to take workplace standards seriously ... To this end, non-governmental agencies such as Global Exchange and Multinational Monitor are crucial pressure on multinationals'.

Naomi Klein, however, puts a slightly different spin on the same events. In her article 'Trying to feel good about Nike' (*Toronto Star*, 2 April 1999), she outlines how Nike has pulled orders from factories in the Philippines, precisely because 'unlike Indonesia, where organising an independent trade union can land you in jail, in the Philippines the union is both legal and militant. Most significantly, unions have made inroads into the export zones where Nike's contractors are located'. In similar fashion, she damns other forefront apparel and show manufacturers, such as Levi Strauss, Reebok, and Phillips-Van Heusen, for 'spouting new age rhetoric (but engaging in) a global race to the bottom'.

Hope for the Future?

According to an article in *The Economist* (Business Ethics – Sweatshop Wars', 1999):

> Multinationals have greatly improved the working conditions in their Asian factories ... (despite adverse reports from the Asia Monitor Resource Centre, which allege that some workers making Disney products are forced to work up to 16 hours a day, seven days a week, and are paid almost no overtime, and an equally adverse report on four subcontractor plants for Mattel, the largest toy maker.) ... Disney and Mattel have done more than most other firms to improve working conditions in their Asian plants (most of them contractors

or licensees), that make products under their name. Both have codes of conduct. Disney has carried out 10,000 inspections to date ...

Are large publicity-sensitive supranationals being deliberately targeted then, by most foreign activists, ignorant of local conditioners? Again, according to *The Economist*: 'Don Douglas, who runs a health program in Jakarta [states] "my impressions differ quite a bit from what I read from the critics. My sense is that a lot of this is driven by US groups with an axe to grind. They risk sacrificing jobs for perfection"'.

The central issues revolve not around whom to believe, the NGOs such as Global Exchange and the Asia Monitor Resource Centre, or political leaders such as Mahathir Mohamad; rather it is about values or, if we think of them as implicitly set up in a hierarchy, which value set takes priority, in which context?

One can make a very good case for stating that sweatshop jobs, low incomes and questionable conditions in maquilas and their ilk, still beat the reality of everyday existence for the vast majority of vulnerable workers, especially young women and children, in the poorer countries of the world, for whom the alternatives are far more ghastly; e.g. the child slaves used by the Military in Burma, 'the abduction of ... women and children, their subjection to the slave trade, including traffic in and sale of children and women' in Sudan (reported by Law Professor Biro of Budapest in a report to the UN Commission on Human Rights – *Toronto Star*, 13 June 1998). According to a recent article in *The Economist* ('Children in the Boiler Room', 7 October 2000), 'in Morocco, where 2.5 million children are out of school, many of them 5-year-old girls huddling over looms, row upon row of them, weaving carpets for tourists ... a seamstress rapping knuckles when attention slips. Parents receive about $10 a month for their daughters' 10-hour days [which computes to roughly 3 cents per hour – KL] ... And the number of child-maids is estimated at up to 1m. The only difference between their lot and slavery is the payment, probably to their parents, of $14 a month. Abuse is rampant, murder occasional'.

Indeed, despite a widespread belief among social activists that globalisation erodes both the rights and the incomes of the poor (e.g., V. Shiva's address from the World Court of Women, March 2001), a recent report published by the World Bank strongly suggests that the growth generated by global capitalism 'really does help the poor: in fact, it raises their incomes by about as much as it raises the incomes of everybody else' (Dollar and Kraay 2000). It is reasonable to take these findings with a grain of salt. As Jean-Pierre Lehmann (1998) argues in his article in *Mastering Global Business*: 'The forces of globalisation are forces of polarisation – not so much between states but within states. The most obvious manifestation of this polarisation is the growing gap in incomes that all countries are experiencing'.

A way of reconciling the two positions is to make the distinction, as the World Bank has done in its world development reports, between absolute and relative poverty. It is possible then that a growth of 1 per cent in an economy will raise the income of the poor by roughly that percentage, as argued by Dollar and Kraay; however, to the extent that it raises the income of the more affluent by a higher percentage, the poor end up being relatively worse off. This may be less than just in Rawls' terms. However, it may still be better than other local alternatives on offer.

A final sanguine note, to help counterbalance our introductory account of violence in the context of maguiladoras in Mexico. The Zapatistan leader Marcos has jus proved, through his peaceful confrontation with the Mexican President, just how far Mexico has moved towards democratising its society, during the last decade. How much of this process is due to Mexico embracing free trade through NAFTA, is open to debate. But a reasonable argument can be made that the more open that trade becomes, the greater the chances for other openings into societies which have been traditionally both more closed and less liberal.

Conclusion

Market forces, free trade and globalisation do not operate in a vacuum. In some ways it has been convenient to blame these impersonal forces as responsible for the below-poverty level of pay, and the inhuman working conditions, of millions of vulnerable workers. It is both more honest and more analytically useful, in terms of generating better solutions, to identify the roles of the critical organisations and institutions, within a global framework. Only then does it become possible to discuss levels and limits to the responsibility of each organisational actor. Analysis of international action by global actors should not hide behind economic terminology such as profit maximisation, but should instead 1) attempt to unravel the dynamics of power among the actors, and 2) consider the behaviour of the organisations, in terms of the value sets which drive the actions.

References

Bernstein, A. (1999), Commentary, *Business Week*, 3 May, p. 192.

Cox, S. (1998), 'Nike's Detractors Ready to Rally', *The Georgia Strait*, 15 October.

Dickens, C. (1917), *David Copperfield*, Collier, New York.

Dollar, D. and A. Kraay (2000), 'Growth is Good for the Poor, World Bank, Analysed in Economics Focus', *The Economist*, 27 May, p. 82.

Friedman, M. and R. Friedman (1990), *Free to Choose*, Harcourt Brace Jovanovich, San Diego.

Kurt Salmon Associates (1999), cited in 'Sweatshop Reform: How to Solve the Standoff', *Business Week*, 3 May, p. 190.

Labour Behind the Label Coalition (1997), 'Child Labour and the Rights of Youth', Wear Fair Action Kit Issue Sheet 2, Maquila Solidarity Network, Toronto.

Labour Behind the Label Coalition (1997), 'Nike Doing it Just', Wear Fair Action Kit 1, Maquila Solidarity Network, Toronto.

Lehman, J.P. (1998), 'Who Writes Today's Economic Scripts?', *Mastering Global Business*, Supplement of the *Financial Times*, November.

Marx, K. (1912), *Das Kapital*, English trans., London, William Glaisher Ltd.

National Labour Committee (1995), 'Violations of Women's Rights and the Abuse of Minors in El Salvador's Maquiladora Sector', New York.

Organization for Economic Co-operation and Development (OECD) (1999), 'Development Co-operation Report, 1998', summarised in the *Globe and Mail*, 23 February, pp. A4 and A18.

Rawls, J. (1971), *A Theory of Justice*, Harvard University Press, Cambridge, MA.

Rosenzweig, P.M. (1998), 'How Should Multinationals Set Global Work Standards?', *Mastering Global Business*, Part 9, Supplement of the *Financial Times*, pp. 8–14.

Shiva, V. (2001), 'Globalisation: The War against Women', Address to World Court of Women, South Africa, reported in Hindu, 25 March.

Yantz, L., B. Jefcott, D. Ladd and J. Atlin (Maquila Solidarity Network) (1999), *Policy Options to Improve Standards for Women Garment Workers in Canada and Internationally*, Status of Women Canada, Ottawa.

Chapter 10

The Governance of Regional Networks and the Process of Globalisation

Riccardo Cappelin

R32, J80, L14 F02 P16, F23

Introduction

The debate on global capitalism is polarised between the fear of globalisation and the belief in the virtues of free trade. Economists agree that countries tend to prosper when they are open to trade and that direct foreign investment, which goes into long-term productive enterprises, brings similar benefits. However, this act of faith in the virtues of the free market has been pushing rigid doctrines, slashing the state's role in industry, accelerating the restructuring of the formerly state-owned companies. In order to revamp the banking system it is necessary to apply a solid macro-economic management, strengthen the legal system which protects property rights and adopt business friendly fiscal policies. The only concession to social aspects is to advocate good educational standards and provide a relatively fair distribution of income and political stability. The belief that open markets will magically produce prosperity in all conditions is erroneous since the global economy is pretty much in the robber-baron age. The classical capitalist medicine cannot avoid a long list of the negative effects of globalisation. It can hardly be denied that multinationals have contributed to labour, environmental and human rights abuses including: the exploitation of the labour of women and children, sixteen hour workdays, no overtime pay, limits to the freedom of movement of the workers, the use of toxic materials and lax safety standards, the spread of international sexual tourism, the trade of human beings through massive immigration, environmental damage. The risk of a recurrent international financial crisis, such as indicated by the examples of Mexico, the Far East and Russia, increases with the globalisation process and dependence on short-term foreign capital. It is a model of development pushed in a cumulative way by foreign investment and often by speculative monetary flow from abroad. It does not allow any realistic evaluation of the fundamentals of individual projects, such as many enormous investments in so called global cities and it inevitably increases the macro-economic instability and danger of financial collapse.

The search for an alternative has led to the support for the idea that multinationals should endorse a set of basic human right, environmental and labour principles and allow private (not government) groups to monitor their compliance. Otherwise multinationals should accept the local rules and local governments should have the power to enforce regulations on multinationals. Thus in countries where the rule of law is weak, international efforts should aim to strengthen local institutions in a gradual process of institutional building. This chapter illustrates the economic development process in the model of territorial networks and it also investigates the role of institutions in a bottom-up approach of integration aimed at tackling the negative impact of the globalisation process in less developed countries and regions.

The Increasing Integration between Firms within Networks

The model of industry that emerges at the threshold of the twenty-first century is deeply different from the model of mass industrialisation, on which traditional economic theory is based. In a modern industrial economy, the old model of industrial organisation (based on the concept of economies of scale), has been replaced by a new organisational model based on an increasing integration, cooperation and competition between different firms that belong to the same wide sector of activity.

The model of multinational companies, which is implied in the traditional analysis of the globalisation process, strongly vertically integrated and controlling various foreign branch plants specialised in labour-intensive productions, does not seem to correspond to the actual structure of most firms, which are highly internationalised in the developing countries.

The creation of strategic alliance joint ventures, consortia and groups has become the almost standard practice in all sectors, including production, distribution, finance and technological research. The prospects of development of the individual firm depend on the increasingly articulated and complex relations of integration with other firms, not only those belonging to the same financial group, but also many external firms.

This transformation, which characterises the world of industry and the organisation of firms, is mainly linked to the new dimensions of the process of innovation (Nonaka and Konno 1998, Cappellin and Orsenigo 2000, Rubenson and Schuetze 2000). The role of the small and medium sized firms has increased in recent years, due to the process of outsourcing and subcontracting, linked with the increasing focus of firms in which they have a specific competitive advantage. The development of a regional and national production system does not proceed incrementally with the growth of the existing firms, but is determined especially in the medium and long term by the turnover of firms and the birth and death of many firms. In fact, the most dynamic regions are those where the negative impact on the employment levels determined by the inevitable closures and downsizing of the existing firms is compensated by the birth and fast development of many new small and medium sized firms, often into new sectors of activity.

The process of searching for better flexibility by the large firms, that adopt a more decentralised structure, corresponds to the searching process of small firms to find new forms of integration through networks and clusters, which may have a rather formalised and stable character. From a methodological perspective, a production system may be analysed according to different perspectives. The meso-economic perspective of those interested in the networks or clusters is similar to that of those who have entered the forest and analyse the intricate webs of the various plants, their different sizes, functions and the shared symbiotic relationships. Some may observe that the individual plants compete for air and soil, but this would miss the point that their individual and overall survival and development depend first of all on their diversity and complex integration. A modern industrial economy is characterised by a tight and quickly changing web of financial participations, mergers, spin-offs and co-operative relationships between various industrial groups. Thus, the traditional paradigm of the firm, which is usually adopted in the traditional microeconomic models, differs in many aspects from the model of the networks of firms (see Cappellin 1991 and 1998, Cappellin and Orsenigo 2000). Therefore, a thorough analysis of the mechanisms of crucial importance in the organisation of modern industry will consider:

- the mechanisms of financial control and the process of strategic decision;
- the mechanisms of decision of the labour demand and of the labour investigation;
- the processes of production growth and the decisions of investment;
- the mechanisms related with the growth of productivity, the decrease of costs and the adoption of process innovations. The processes of adoption of product innovations or of product diversification;
- the processes of expansion at the international scale or of internationalisation demonstrate that these mechanisms are very different, when the perspective of analysis is enlarged from the case of the individual firm, which vertically integrates the various phases of a specific production process, to the case of a system or a network of firms, which are rather autonomous among them.

This model of networks is related to the concept of transaction costs (Williamson 1981) and lies between the market of the neoclassical approach and the hierarchy of the business economics. Therefore, as indicated also by the modern economics of institutions (North 1990), the governance of the economic relations require the role of a facilitator and 'network steering' by the national state, the regional and local governments and by the various public-private 'intermediate organisations'.

The International Openness and the Governance of Local Networks

The new model of network organisation of modern firms, which has been described above, seems to represent the extension of the case of the large firms at the national and the international level of model of network organisation, which for several decades have existed at the local production systems of small and medium sized firms. This model of analysis has been the focus of many studies of the 'industrial districts' of new industrialised regions in Italy and in various other countries (Pyche et al. 1990, Cossentino et al. 1996, Brusco and Paba 1997).

Moreover, the vast international literature in the process of innovation at the local and regional level has elaborated various concepts, which are tightly linked to the concept of the industrial district, such as: the concept of the 'milieu innovateur' (Maillat 1995, Maillat and Kebir 1999), of 'regional innovation system' (RIS) (Cooke and Morgan 1998), of 'learning regions' (Lundvall and Johnson 1994, Morgan 1997), of 'dynamics of proximity' (Rallet and Torre 1998) or of 'institutional thickness' (Rullani 1998). In particular, the new scenario of the diffusion of modern information and communication technologies (ICT) and the gradual transformation of the national and regional economies of the most developed countries into a 'knowledge economy, imply a rethinking of the traditional paradigms of development strategies.

These different concepts along with the concept of 'integration' (Cappellin 1997a, 1997b, 1998) may be adopted in order to design a new approach to regional development, which may be defined as the approach of 'territorial networks'. This approach allows the establishment of a direct relationship between three dimensions of the regional development, such as the economic/industrial dimension of the sectoral structure of the regional economy, the territorial dimension of the physical structure of the regional territory and the institutional dimension of the architecture and the governance of the local institutions and organisations. From an economic perspective, the model of the territorial networks indicates that the process of economic development is the result of the tight interaction between the process of local networking and of the process of inter-regional and international networking. It also includes four crucial processes such as: the growth of the regional product and employment, the dynamics of productivity or the adoption of innovation, the accumulation of the local technological and organisational know-how and the process of birth, growth and closure of local firms. In particular, the analysis of the current evolution of the local production systems of small and medium size firms in the already developed economies allows the identification of various cumulative processes, which may have a virtuous character. This explains the persistent success and international competitiveness of these production systems, notwithstanding the recurrent alarms, which have been raised by its critics during the last thirty years. The adoption of process innovation and the growth of productivity lead to a decrease of employment and labour costs and to an increase in profits, which has a positive impact on investment, especially in the creation of new firms. This allows an increase in employment and an assurance of the reconversion of production capabilities, which were made temporarily unemployed. The maintenance of a low level of unemployment promotes a high social consensus and it lowers the resistance to the adoption of innovation by the workers, thus promoting the increase of productivity. Moreover, the creation of new firms promotes the diversification and integration of the local production system, which decreases the obstacles to innovation within firms.

Secondly, the development of the local economy stimulates the demand of local services by the population and the specialised subcontractors of the firms and thus leads to the creation of new firms. The higher number of firms in the local economy implies a greater competition, a greater diversification of the organisational and technological know-how and the development of entrepreneurial capabilities. This stimulates the adoption of product innovation and increases in the quality of local production and competitiveness on the external markets. It also promotes the growth of exports, which represents the most dynamic component of the demand of local productions. Thirdly, the tight integration between the local firms within the networks of subcontractors and the increased complementarity of the local firms increases the efficiency of the local production system and facilitates the innovation process and the competitiveness of local production. On the other hand, the increased international openness stimulates the cooperation between the local firms, in order to jointly face the challenges of the international competition. Fourthly, the development of local networking and especially of the subcontracting networks facilitates the creation of new firms, which, as indicated above, promotes the diversity of the technological and organisational know-how and entrepreneurial capabilities. This facilitates the innovation process which stimulates the networking and cooperation between the local firms, since it promotes the outsourcing and the creation of subcontracting agreements.

Clearly, the dynamic relationship between these six variables defines a development model, which is completely general and which may assume different forms in the various local economies. In particular, these relationships also explain a process of cumulative decline in some areas of old industrialisation, where these relationships work in an opposite direction. In fact, the withering of local know-how, due for example to the lack of strong research efforts or insufficient professional education may decrease innovation, the growth of productivity, the competitiveness of regional exports and the production capacities of local industry. The process of globalisation and increased international competition may determine the crisis of some local firms and constrain the surviving firms to deep restructuring processes with negative effects on local employment. This initial effect may determine a cumulative decline of service and industrial firms which are oriented toward the local demand. Similarly, the closure of some large firms may determine the crisis of the local subcontracting networks. This decreases the diversification of the local production system and limits the development of local know-how.

Crucial factors of the developmental process are international openness and local integration. Regional development strategies increasingly require the capability to adopt a 'local but global' perspective. Thus there is a tight complementarity between endogenous development and international openness. The development of each region is affected by its competitive and complementary relationships with other increasingly distant regions. In particular, this model of territorial networks indicates the conditions required in order to make a technological jump from the base represented by initial foreign investments. The development of an industry specialised in the assembly for foreign firms and state of the art production machines from the most developed regions and countries, gradually allows the generation of a local part-supply industry and the broadening of the industrial base. Moreover, firms which initially grew as specialised subcontractors, in order to serve a local growing market, may in a later phase, allow the broadening of the local export base.

A valid development strategy is based not only on the capability to attract foreign capital and firms, but rather promotes the local exports and the investment of endogenous production capabilities. The investment of foreign firms is important in order to import know-how, modern machines and technology, rather than just to finance the expansion of foreign controlled traditional production capacities. Foreign capital is certainly essential but it should not be the final aim of development policies. It is only an instrument that facilitates the expansion of local production capabilities, while the crucial problem to be tackled is to identify what to produce and where to invest. On the contrary, economically lagging regions and countries often lack an investment strategy in production activities, which are competitive on international markets. They lack the capability to promote an 'intensive' mode of development which promotes the gradual evolution of the local firms toward more advanced productions, rather than an 'extensive' mode of development, based on foreign investment which replicates the existing specialisation.

In fact, the model of territorial networks underlines the institutional dimension of the local development process. The concept of 'institutional thickness' is based on the idea that economic development is not the result of the completely endogenous dynamics of the economy, but is the result of a long term and gradual process of institutional building that implies institutional reforms such as the regional decentralisation and federalism, the creation of new instruments of economic policy such as business service centres, development agencies and new legal schemes of public-private cooperation, etc. In this new approach to local and regional policy, a crucial role is assigned not only to the national, regional and local governments, but also to the actors, the networks and the 'intermediate institutions: which organise the relations between the local actors.

The 'institutional thickness' is a factor of strength in the process of international competition. In fact, when the internationalisation process is affecting the overall national and regional economic systems, the role of public institutions are that of a partner in the development of international projects and joint ventures with private organisations. A crucial problem for the local and regional governments in their efforts at 'network steering' is to understand the internal relations between the local actors and to identify which actors should be involved in the collective decision-making process. In fact, the borders of the networks are rather soft or have a flexible geometry according to the specific problem which is being considered. Local and regional government should identify the obstacles which hinder the promotion of the integration and cooperation between the local actors, such as the cases of missing links or of uncoupling which is the result of reciprocal mistrust between these actors. The aim of the local and regional governance is to extend the temporal and geographic perspectives of the programmes of action agreed upon by the policy networks of local actors. In particular, it is necessary to promote the development of medium range development strategies and the increasing openness and integration of local networks at the inter-regional and international level.

The Nature of the Process of Integration and the Evolving Structure of Networks

The process of local networking has a complex character and may be illustrated as the interaction of firms and the local actors within different types of networks, each of which facilitates a different form of integration. These different types of networks between firms and actors may also characterise the process of international networking. According to the approach of 'territorial networks' a local production system may be characterised by the following types of integration relations (Cappellin and Orsenigo 2000):

*   *technological integration*, marked by the development of local production know-how, the sharing of knowledge and values promoted by on the job learning processes, continuous education of workers, vocational education of young workers, joint investments in R&D by local firms and technological cooperation with external firms;
*   integration *of the local labour market*, related with the cooperation between the workers and the firms and the mobility of workers between the firms of the same

sector and also the capability to attract qualified workers from other regions and from other sectors;

- *production integration between the firms*, through subcontracting relationships between the firms which play a crucial role in promoting the gradual diversification of the local productions;
- *integration between the service sectors and manufacturing firms*, related to the development of modern commercial distribution services, transport and logistical services and also qualified services in the certification of the quality of production and in the diffusion of modern technologies;
- *financial integration of the firms*, as it is indicated by the creation of groups made by several firms belonging to the same entrepreneurial family and by pro-active bank-industry relationships, which promote the creation of spin-off and the capability to attract external investments or the investments of local firms in other countries and regions;
- *territorial integration at the local level*, which requires an improvement in the infrastructure endowment and it is linked to an effective physical planning aiming to defend the quality of the territory;
- *social and cultural integration*, which determines the existence of a local identity and the creation of consensus within the local community or shared development projects;
- *territorial integration at the inter-regional and international level*, which leads to a greater openness from an inter-regional perspective, to the development of 'foreign policy' or of 'territorial market' measures, which are crucial in attracting external investments and in promoting the internationalisation of local firms.

Therefore, the process of integration concerns also the complex and indirect relationships between actors which belong to different networks, which may have an economic, technological/knowledge, physical/geographical and social/institutional character. These relationships between different networks may be described as in the example of. The relationship between two networks is characterised by a precise direction, which identifies a relationship of control or of dependence of a node with respect to another node. This implies that the relationships within a network usually have a hierarchical character. Secondly, each node has a specific function, which depends not only on the relationship with another node, but also its position in the overall network. Thirdly, the relations existing in space or in a network are normally linked to relations in other spaces or networks. Therefore, the relations of financial control between the firms within a financial group, as indicated in the space A, may be linked to the relations of subcontracting between the same firms.

Fourthly, the relations existing in a specific space or network are normally affected by the relations existing in the previous period in the same space or network due to the existence of cumulative processes of learning and of path dependence.

A matrix representation can allow us to illustrate in a clearer way some crucial characteristics of a network and of the relationship between different networks. In fact, one may show the existence or the absence of relations between the same nodes. On the other hand, the transition of interconnection matrices indicates first of all, the correspondence between the number of a node in a network and that of the same node in another network and vice-versa. Since the networks normally have a hierarchical structure, it may be observed that the matrices normally have a triangular shape. However, in some cases a relationship of cooperation may exist. Matrices may be used to represent two crucial dimensions of the relations between the nodes of a network, such as the intensity of the flows and the level of the reciprocal distance. In particular, the flows (xij) from a node (i) to a node (j), which are represented by two firms, may consist of goods, financial flows, information, workers, or other factors and they may be measured in monetary or physical terms according to the nature of the considered flow. On the other hand, the distance (dij) between two nodes may have a geographical, organisational or social and cultural nature and it may thus be measured according to the nature of the relations represented in the specific network considered and the unit of measurement of the particular flows (xij).

According to the specific space or network considered the coefficient (dij) may represent the time required for transferring a unit of the flow from the node (i) to the node (j). It may also represent the speed of connection between these two nodes, the unit transport cost or also a measure of the differences in organisational terms, or the institutional obstacles or of the cultural barriers between the actors (i) and (j). In particular, the distance (dij) indicates that the relations between two nodes should face barriers or costs. These depend on the material infrastructures, such as transports and ICT, or the immaterial infrastructures, such as the existence of institutions, organisations and rules which coordinate those relations and decrease the transaction costs, existing between those nodes. Moreover, these infrastructures may also be represented as networks, which have a physical nature or an institutional/organisational nature and which are complementary and tightly linked to the previously considered economic, financial, technological and social networks when up to two consecutive intermediate nodes (s) and (z) are considered. However, the indirect link between two nodes, which belongs to two different networks, may occur through an intermediate node, which belongs to both networks and has a direct link with both nodes. Otherwise, the indirect link between two nodes which belong to the same network may occur through two intermediate nodes, which are directly connected between them within another network. In general terms, the cost of the relation between two nodes (j) and (z), which respectively belong to different networks are only indirectly connected through various intermediate node(s), may be measured as:

Where the coefficient (ABds) indicates the element of the interconnection of the transition matrix and the flows (aij) and (bij) respectively indicate the elements of different matrices. The coefficient (ABds) allows converting the cost of distance between two nodes measured in one network in the measurement unit of distance in another network, in order to compute the total transaction cost. Therefore, the model of networks allows identifying relations, which may be measured in quantitative terms, not only within the same network but also between different networks, such as networks indicating economic, geographical, institutional/organisational relations between various firms both within a regional production system and an international framework. This model of networks clarifies the tight complementarities between local networks, such as the subcontracting network, and international networks, such as the financial network, and it demonstrates the tight complementarity between external openness and local embeddedness.

The structure of a network is continuously changing due to the establishment of new links between couples of actors and the change or rupture of the existing bilateral links. It may be stated that the iterative adaptation both of the direct links (dyadic ties) and of the indirect links (weak ties) between a couple of actors or nodes depends on the distance (dij) and the distance (ABdjj) and it is stimulated by the gradual search by each actor for the most opportune integration or cooperation with other actors. In particular, the incentive by a couple of actors to establish a new link or to change an existing link depends not only upon the distance existing between them, but also on the existence of a cumulative learning process and on the respective perception of the other actor's characteristics, such as its position within the overall network or its distance with respect to third actors. The network model is based on an evolutive approach and it allows the establishment of relations between the structure of a network in a given period and the structure of the same network and of complementary networks in the previous periods. In the model of the networks the firms, all different and integrated, through different types of relations, have an intentional character. Within a network, a crucial role is performed by relations and processes of exchange, negotiation, conflict, agreement and integration between actors which are different and potentially complementary, such as in the relations of vertical integration between clients and suppliers and in the contracts of joint investment and of the creation of a new firm by different actors, which allocate particular resources for the achievement of a common aim.

The Concepts of Distance and the Different Forms of International Integration

The analysis of the process of territorial agglomeration/diffusion, both from an inter-regional and international perspective, may apply the useful distinction between 'geographical distance', 'organisational distance' and 'institutional distance' (Rallet and Torre 1998, Bellet et al. 1993). In fact, the territorial proximity is the intersection of these three different concepts of proximity. In particular, the geographical proximity considers the links in terms of physical distance and it refers to the natural borders and to the effects of transport and telecommunication infrastructures. The organisational proximity considers the links in terms of production organisation and is based on the logic of organisational belonging and to the intrinsic seeming less of the actors, which belong to the same organisation. Finally, the institutional proximity indicates the sharing of representations, models and rules of thought and policy by various actors. It also includes forms of collective action and the creation of formal and informal institutions, which often perform a crucial role in the mechanisms of interaction between the economic actors. The geographical proximity allows knowledge interactions only whether it encompasses an appropriate organisational and institutional context. In fact, the experience accumulated in the international technological transfers has demonstrated that geographical distance is less important as an obstacle to international cooperation, when the organisational or technological distance is limited. The transfer of the tacit knowledge that is required by the innovation process is above all influenced by the organisational and institutional proximity, from which it is possible to act with various tools also at the inter-regional level, such as in the inter-regional agreements between firms and programmes of inter-regional cooperation. The joint consideration of the two concepts of 'geographical' distance and of 'organisational/institutional' distance illustrates four different cases of international and inter-regional integration and different forms of the relationships between the firms of different regions and that it poses both opportunities and challenges. It is also clear that these technological, policy, institutional, ideological and cultural developments that have led to globalisation are still very active. Thus, barring a radical move in a different direction, these trends toward greater globalisation will likely continue or even accelerate in the future. One important aspect of these trends will be the growth in international trade, in services that have already substantially increased, but promises even greater growth in the future, especially in such areas as telecommunications and financial services. The result will be continued moves toward a more open and more integrated world as it moves closer and closer to a planet without borders and to a more integrated, open and interdependent world economy. The result will be an even greater worldwide flow of goods, services, money, capital, technology, people, information and ideas when strong geographical obstacles and strong organisational/institutional barriers exist. The prevailing form of international or inter-regional economic integration has only a commercial character.

If instead, both the geographical distance and the organisational/institutional distance are very limited, modern forms of 'network integration' become possible and convenient, as within the internal market of the most developed countries. Among these relations are commercial and production partnerships between the firms belonging to the same filiere or production cluster, financial groups encompassing various firms and the acquisitions or the minority financial participation in external firms. These network relationships characterise the modern model of industrial organisation and they are especially diffused in the industrial districts of the most developed regions. However, they have started to develop also as the inter-regional level between contiguous regions, and even at the international level, especially in the case of the large firms and between the regions, which are leaders at the European level.

Particularly interesting are two intermediary cases, where the two concepts of geographical distance and of organisational/institutional distance do not correspond. In fact, if the geographical distance can be decreased though investments in transport and communication costs, while a strong organisational/institutional distance persists, a tight technological and financial cooperation between the local and the not local firms is not possible. In this case, at the inter-regional level, the existence of low transport and transaction costs allows only tight production integration, through the specialisation and the outsourcing of intermediate productions. This case is very important for the regions of South Europe and of East Europe, which are very close to the most industrialised regions of the European Union and may benefit from the process of decentralisations of intermediate productions from these regions. It may also be important for the areas in Mexico that are close to the US border. At the international level, these forms of very tight but mainly commercial integrations determine the so-called 'intra-industry trade'. In particular, a tight integration of the industrial firms of the economically lagging regions in South Europe within the inter-regional networks of subcontracting is favoured by the construction of highways and more recently by the improvement in logistic services, the use of containers and the integration of road transport with railway and maritime transport. It may also be strengthened by a wider use of the Internet, which is promoting 'business to business' electronic commerce and an easier exchange of technological and organisational information, which allows a tight integration of the supply chain.

However, even more interesting for the perspectives of economic development in the peripheral regions is another type of intermediary case, which occurs when the organisational/institutional distance has been reduced in a crucial manner, while a great geographical distance still persists. At the inter-regional level, this is the case illustrated by very dynamic areas in Europe, like Ireland, Scotland and Wales and also the Italian regions of the Centre North, which have been very successful in attracting foreign qualified investments. At the international level this case may be represented by the Far East countries, which are certainly distant from the European and American markets, but are tightly embedded in the networks of international alliances between firms and are clearly characterised by a strong openness to international relations. In fact, the process of internationalisation of firms is different from the growth of exports and it is based on a tight integration, not only of the product markets, but also of their internal organisation and their internal processes. The internationalisation process of firms requires a high decentralisation of the operative functions and the creation of flexible alliances with foreign firms. This allows large industrial groups to become strategically articulated, which may be defined as 'localisation' or of 'local-but global' (Cappellin 1998). In this case, the local firms may maintain a considerable level of autonomy, due to their different sectoral specialisation and the existence of great geographical distance. The international groups may decentralise to the local firms, even the R&D activity. They may also assign to them the responsibility for a market area that could be much wider than just the respective regional or national market. This could encompass a wide regional basin at the transnational level, such as South Europe or the Mediterranean countries or the Far East region.

Federalism as a Model of a Bottom-up Process of International Integration

The forms of the process of networking and integration at the international scale tend to become increasingly complex, with respect to the traditional flows of international trade and of branch plant investment. They become gradually similar to the forms of networking and integration, which exist within an internal market at a regional or national level. In fact, international integration is characterised by various mechanisms, which are similar to those analysed in the case of local production systems, such as the production integration between industrial firms, their increasing demand for customised, high quality services, complex financial participation links, the relations of technological cooperation between firms, the process of interactive learning related to the mobility of workers between firms, the relationships of socio-cultural integration, the development of infrastructural networks on the territory and the development of institutional or inter-governmental relations.

On the other hand, there are major differences between the case of inter-regional and international disparities. In particular, the ethical refusal of protectionist and nationalistic closure, should not undermine the critiques of the negative aspects of the globalisation process, such as: the disequilibria between the world of financial speculations and the world of the 'real' economy, the exploitation of the labour of women and children, extremely low wages and long working hours, the increase in social inequalities, the loss of national identities and jobs and the consequent migrations toward foreign countries and larger metropolitan areas, damage to the natural environment and increasing risks for consumers.

Clearly, the globalisation process has not yet achieved the same level of economic, territorial, social and institutional integration in the relations between the most developed and least developed countries. In particular, the experience in the most developed countries indicates that the process of globalisation does not only have an economic dimension, as the result of the market mechanism, but it also has a political and institutional dimension. Economic development at the international level is linked to the creation of institutions, both within each country and at the international level, or to the development of 'institutional thickness'. Thus, there is a need to design new rules and institutions, which may represent the most appropriate environment at the international level, within which the individual actors, firms and private and public organisations may discuss, learn and take the most appropriate initiatives.

In fact, first of all, the revolution of technological innovations has unevenly led the economic integration between the most developed countries and the least developed countries, beyond the framework of pure international trade. In particular, the development of the networks of technological cooperation and the integration of financial networks has required a gradual and time consistent effort of institutional harmonisation through joint bodies created by the governments or even by private actors, aiming to decrease the 'organisational/institutional distance'. Secondly, without a common institutional framework between two countries, such as a permanent 'Council', it is impossible to interconnect the different productive, technological, financial, social and institutional networks and that it poses both opportunities and challenges. It is also clear that these technological, policy, institutional, ideological and cultural developments that have lead to globalisation are still very active. Thus, barring a radical move in a different direction, these trends toward greater globalisation will likely continue or even accelerate in the future. One important aspect of these trends will be the growth in international trade in services, which have already substantially increased, but promises even greater growth in the future, especially in such areas as telecommunications and financial services. The result will be continued moves toward a more open and more integrated world as it moves closer and closer to a planet without borders and to a more integrated, open and interdependent world economy. The result will be an even greater worldwide flow of goods, services, money, capital, technology, people, information and ideas in order to promote a harmonious or balanced development of the integration process. Finally, without the sharing of common values and the sense of belonging to a common institution, such as international association, it is not possible to assign a long term perspective to the network relations between two or more countries, as it is required whether these relations should overcome the commercial and opportunistic perspective of the instantaneous exchange for that of a cooperative game.

Thus, the crucial difference between inter-regional and international trade is due to the existence of the state. Regional and inter-regional economic relations (unlike international relations) are subject to the rules of law and are managed by a complex set of powerful institutions, such as a central bank, antitrust and other regulatory authorities, industry associations, trade unions, consumer associations and various other councils, committees, foundations and associations. International relations are usually regulated by short-term bilateral agreements, which may be considered similar to the 'exchange contracts' in a market and are only based on the respective self-interest or on the identification of 'ad hoc' common objectives. On the contrary, inter-regional relations in a federal or unitary state are based on the reciprocal acknowledgement of a common identity or a sense of belonging, which makes the inter-regional agreements similar to long term 'uncompleted contracts'. This leads the individual regions to accept the power of common national/federal institutions and to adopt various procedures of mutual coordination, which imply some limits to the self-interest in the achievement of common long-term goals.

From this perspective, the process of economic and political integration in Europe represents perhaps the most significant effort which has ever taken place in order to overcome (in a wide or continental framework) the national barriers and borders to create a set of common rules and institutions between countries which have different languages, very old traditions and differences among the most consolidated economic and institutional structures. The European Union actually includes fifteen countries and it represents 370 million inhabitants. Within the next few years it will extend to twenty-seven countries and will include 480 million inhabitants. In the short run, it may also be extended to all countries in the Balkans and to Turkey, and in the long term, may possibly extend to some Mediterranean countries and to Russia. The process of European integration may be interpreted according to three different principles: competition and market exchange, equity or hierarchical relations and reciprocity or associations (Cappellin 1993). The process of European integration, according to a market approach mainly consists in the removal of obstacles which hinder the integration of the national markets of goods, services, capital and labour. The abolition of customs tariffs, the creation of the European Single Market, the free mobility of capital and the European Monetary Union represent various stages in this perspective (Cappellin 1991 and 2000a). Secondly, according to an institutional approach, the process of European integration may be understood as the gradual transfer of legislative and administrative competencies from national authorities to the European institutions. This process implies the design of new regulations in many different fields, which allow the governance of the increasingly tight interactions between the various national economies and societies (Molle and Cappellin 1988). These institutional mechanisms explain the profound differences between the working of the international relations in the European context and those occurring between other countries, where international relations are only governed by the rules of the market mechanism. This also explains why the process of international integration in Europe does not have the same negative effects, which are clear in the case of the negative impact of the globalisation process on the less developed countries.

Regulations and institutions allow the gradual shift from the perspective of the international market to that of an internal market. These examples indicate that the development of international rules to govern international economic relations requires the harmonisation of national regulations into new fields as required by the evolution of technology and the demands of the citizens. The European Union has clearly been an effective model in tackling the problem of the negative impact of the internationalisation process on the European economies and in the promotion of economic development, at least in the case of already industrialised countries. On the contrary, the political issue is still open to whether the European Union should transform itself into a new state or a Federation, and especially how and when or which balance should be achieved between federal, national and regional institutions and according to which intermediate phases. In fact, the process of institutional integration within the European Union is almost inevitably leading to the gradual development of a sort of federal or confederal constitution, which implies both the design of a coherent architecture of common institutions and also the common recognition of some fundamental legal principles, such as those indicated in the Chart of Fundamental Citizen Rights, which has been approved in Nice by the Heads of States in December 2000 and which may later evolve into the adoption of a formal European constitution.

Thus, an important approach to international integration has a territorial perspective (Cappellin 1993, 1995 and 1999), as indicated by the concepts of territorial networks, or of the 'Europe of Regions'. In fact, the process of European integration has always had a spatial character and it has been characterised by the gradual extension of the borders of the European Union through successive accessions of new countries, such as Denmark, Ireland and the UK in 1973, Greece in 1981, Portugal and Spain in 1986, Austria, Sweden, Finland in 1995 and the German reunification in 1989. Formal negotiations have already started in order to enlarge the European Union to the countries of Central and Eastern Europe, and also to Cyprus and even to Turkey, in the Mediterranean rim.

A regional perspective is at the base of the funds created in order to promote cooperation with external countries, such as the Phare regulation and the Intas Fund with Eastern Europe, the Tacis regulation with the Russian federation, the Cards regulation and the Stability pact with the Balkan countries and the Meda programme with the Mediterranean countries. All these regulations and funds adopt a very similar approach, leading to the creation of new institutions and the strengthening of existing national institutions, as they are based on the principle negotiation of strategic plans with national institutions and the partnership with private actors, intermediate bodies and local institutions. In fact, these regulations have been designed as an instrument to adjust the internal institutions of the developing countries to the rules adopted within the European Union in the organisation of the Structural Funds. These regulations and funds aim to promote the creation and restructuring of firms in the external countries, the development of transport and communication networks, a better organisation of the territory, the fostering of technology and the investment in human potential. However, in contrast to the approach of international institutions such as the IMF, which are only interested in macroeconomic convergence, the European Union is tightly linking these development programmes with the timely adoption of major institutional reforms in third world countries with the establishment of democratic rules (the support of a civil society) and the regional decentralisation of centralist nation states. Thus, the strengthening of the national and local institutions and the modernisation of national regulations should accompany the progress in international economic integration, in order to define the institutional and social framework, which is required by a modern market economy.

The perverse effects of the globalisation process in the relations between the developed and the less developed countries are certainly due to the automatic effect of the market mechanism. However, they should not be blamed on the policies of the multinationals, which in fact are changing their internal organisation (Vazques Barquero 1999). Neither can they effectively be changed though the benevolent adaptation by various individual companies of internal codes of social responsibility. The size of the world economy and the complexity of the industrial networks would make these individual actions similar to mere window-dressing exercises. On the contrary, a much more systematic and gradual effort based on the design of common institutions and the enforcement of common regulations is clearly needed. In particular, the adoption of a federalist or of a regional approach in the governance of the globalisation process, suggests the necessity of tackling the problem gradually according to a 'bottom-up' model, rather than wait for the improbable establishment of supranational institutions. This may imply, first of all, the development of multilateral agreements, as in the case of the 'macro-regions' (Ohmae 1990, Chen 2000), aiming at defining common rules which will promote a common identity. In fact, a greater economic integration and institutional and social cohesion within a macro-region would certainly decrease the zero-sum competition between neighbouring states in attracting foreign investments and create a defence against the economic power of multinational companies.

Secondly, it may require a consistent effort both within each country and through common programmes with each macro-region, such as a common regional policy, aiming to reinforce the national and the local institutions, which as previously mentioned, are a crucial factor in promoting endogenous development, integration of local networks and the development of productivity and new productions. The major obstacles to a regional or federal approach in the governance of the globalisation process seem however, to be the existence of old-fashioned, nationalistic ideologies and of a short-sighted defence of the national autonomy, which is often leading to political tensions and military conflicts, especially between countries which have only recently achieved their independence or regained their freedom, such as the Balkans. Moreover, weak, corrupt and authoritarian governments or also the insufficient development of the civil society and the lack of various 'intermediate institutions' certainly facilitate the power and the abuses of multinational companies in many less developed countries and regions.

The approach to international integration, which during the last half century, has been gradually extended to almost all European countries, even those with a per capita income which is half or even a quarter of that of the European average, may represent a model for the management of international relations in other world areas. This has been demonstrated by the development of various schemes of international cooperation as the macro-regional level in North America, South America and Asia. However, the institutions which regulate and promote the transnational inter-regional integration should arise from an historic and evolutive process, which is specific to each area. 'Institutional thickness' has a precise evolutive character and the building of an institutional framework is the result of a long and gradual process of institutional learning.

References

Bellet, M., G. Colletis and Y. Lung (1993), 'Economie de proximites', Numero Special, *Revue d'Economie Regionale et Urbaine*, No. 3.

Brusco, S. and S. Paba (1997), 'Per una storia dei distretti producttivi italiani dal secondo dopoguerra agl anni novanta', in F. Barca (ed.), *Storia del capitalismo italiano dal dopoguerra a ogg*, Donzellu Editore, Roma, pp. 263–333.

Cappellin, R. (1991), 'The European Internal Market and the Internationalization of Small and Medium Size Enterprises', in D.E. Boyce, P. Nijkamp and D. Shefer (eds), *Regional Science: Retrospect and Prospect*, Springer Verlag, Berlin.

Cappelin, R. (1993), 'Interregional Co-operation in Europe: An Introduction', in R. Cappellin and P. Batey (eds), *Regional Networks, Border Regions and European Integration*, Pion Editor, European Reseach in Regional Science, London, pp. 1–20.

Cappelin, R. (1995), 'Regional Development, Federalism and Interregional Co-operation', in H. Eskelinen and F. Snickars (eds), *Competitive European Peripheries*, Springer-Verlag, Munich.

Cappelin, R. (1997a), 'Regional Policy and Federalism in the Process of International Integration', in K. Peschel (ed.), *Regional Growth and Regional Policy within the Framework of European Integration*, Springer-Physica Verlag, Heidelberg.

Cappelin, R. (1997b), 'Federalism and the Network Paradigm: Guidelines for a New Approach in National Regional Policy', in M. Danson (ed.), *Regional Governance and Economic Development*, Pion, London.

Cappelin, R. (1997c), 'The Economy of Small and Medium Size Towns in Non-metropolitan Regions', document prepared for OECD, Programme of Dialogue and Co-operation with China SG/CHINA/RUR/UA(97)3.

Cappelin, R. (1998), 'The Transformation of Local Production Systems: Interregional Networking and Territorial Competitiveness', in M. Steiner (ed), *From Agglomeration Economies to Innovative Clusters*, Pion Editor, European Research in Regional Science, London, pp. 57–80.

Cappelin, R. (1999), 'The Enlargement of the European Union and the Future of the European and National Regional Policies', *Regional Contact*, 13, Vol. 40, pp. 14–29.

Cappelin, R. (2000a), 'The Impact of the Euro on Regional Disparities: The Case of the Italian "Mezzogiorno"', in J. Brocker (ed.), *Euro: Knosequennzen fur die Regionen, Heidenheimer Schriften zur Regionalwissensxhaftern*, August Losh in Memoriam, Stadt Heidenheim and der Brenz, Heidenheim, pp. 9–25.

Cappelin, R. (2000b), 'Urban Agglomeration and Regional Development Policies in an Englarged Europe', in J. Bröcker and H. Herrman (eds), *Spatial Change and Inter-regional Flows in the Integrating Europe-Essays in Honour of Karin Peschel*, Physica-Verlag, pp. 117–29.

Cappelin, R. and L. Orsenigo (2000), 'The Territorial Dimension of Modern Industry and the Scope of Regional Industrial and Labour Market Policies', in P. Klemmer and R. Wink (eds), *Preventing Unemployment in Europe. A New Framework for Labor Market Policy*, Elgar, Cheltenham, UK and Northampton, US, pp. 166–87.

Chen, X. (2000), 'The Geoeconomic Reconfiguration of Semiperiphery: The Asian–Pacific Transborder Subregions in the World System', in G.M. Derlugian and S.L. Greer (eds), *Questioning Geopolitics: Political Projects in a Changing World System*, Greenwood, Westport, CN, pp. 185–205.

Cooke P. and K. Morgan (1998), *The Associational Economy: Firms, Regions and Innovation*, Oxford University Press, Oxford.

Cossentino, F., F. Pycke and W. Sengenberger (eds) (1996), *Local and Regional Response to Global Pressure: The Case of Italy and its Industrial Districts*, International Institute for Labour Studies, ILO, Geneva.

European Commission (1999), 'European Spatial Development Perpsective-ESDP, Toward Balanced and Sustainable Development of the Territory of the EU', Final discussion at the Meeting of the Ministers responsible for Regional/Spatial Planning of the European Union, Potsdam, 10–11 May.

Lundvall, B.A. and B. Johnson (1994), 'The Learning Economy', *Journal of Industrial Studies*, Vol. 1, No. 2, pp. 23–42.

Maillat, D. and L. Kebir (1999), '"Learning region" et sytemes territoriaux de production', *Revue Regional Development*, No. 7, pp. 157–65.

Maillat, D. (1995), 'Territorial Dynamic, Innovative Milieus and Regional Policy', *Entrepreneurship and Regional Development*, No. 7, pp. 157–65.

Molle, W. and R. Cappellin (eds) (1998), *Regional Impact of Community Policies in Europe*, Avebury, Aldershot.

Morgan, K. (1997), 'The Learning Region: Institutions, Innovation and Regional Renewal', *Regional Studies*, Vol. 31, No. 5, pp. 491–504.

Nonaka, I. and N. Konno (1998), 'The Concept of "Ba": Building a Foundation for Knowledge Reaction', *California Management Review*, Vol. 40, No. 3, pp. 40–54.

Ohmae, K. (1990), *The Borderless World*, Harper and Row, New York.

Pycke, F., G. Becattini and W. Sengenberger (1990), *Industrial Districts and Inter-firm Co-operation in Italy*, International Institute for Labour Studies, ILO, Geneva.

Rallet, A. and A. Torre (1998), 'On Geography and Technology: Proximity Relations in Localized Innovation Networks', in M. Steiner (ed.), *From Agglomeration Economies to Innovative Clusters*, Pion Editor, European Research in Regional Science, London, pp. 41–56.

Rubenson, K. and H.G. Schuetze (eds) (2000), *Transition to the Knowledge Society: Policies and Strategies for Individual Participation and Learning*, Institute for European Studies, Vancouver.

Rullani, E. (1998), 'Riforma delle istituzioni e sviluppo locale', *Sviluppo Locale*, Vol. V, No. 8, pp. 5–46.

Vazquez Barquero, A. (1999), 'Inward Investment and Endogenous Development: The Convergence of the Strategies of Large Firms and Territories?', *Entrepreneurship & Regional Development*, Vol. 11, pp. 79–93.

Williamsom, O.E. (1981), 'The Modern Corporation: Origin, Evolution, Attributes', *Journal of Economic Literature*, Vol. 19, pp. 1537–68.

Chapter 11

Globalisation of the Cooperative Movement

Tapani Köppä

Taking Care for Profits, Nature or Human Societies?

Technological development, in particular the opportunities offered by information technology for on-line connections over the Internet, is the foundation for the explosive progress of globalisation. Major investors and large-scale multinational companies are the engines of globalisation, with world-economy stock exchanges as the arena for their operations. In their world, growth of business and market position in the international competition are measures of success. In order to make profit for their shareholders, the companies seek the most favourable operational conditions: they minimise the labour costs, pay the least possible price for raw materials, and would rather not pay unreasonable taxes or duties. If national governments wish to have international high-technology companies operating in their territories, they are forced to face tough competitive bidding and to prioritise the allocation of public funding. Such prioritisation inevitably affects citizens' social security, sustainable development and economic autonomy. When searching for a profitable investment or bridgehead in a new market, the companies should make the ethical goals of their operations transparent. Governments should be aware of these goals when making contracts in order to avoid undesirable surprises. The connections of the business operation with the development of the host country should also be considered.

The fundamental principles for sustainable development have been discussed and accepted at many international forums.[1] They should also provide guidelines for the operations of global market economy. An aware consumer movement has already contributed to the establishment of ethical markets, with examples of global trade and production arrangements (fair trade networks through which the producers in developing countries can market their products in the industrialised countries, Body Shop as a representative of ethical production, etc.). It is, however, naïve to trust that the maximisation of interests by private companies would automatically – through the magic power of the 'invisible hand', as Adam Smith put it – lead to a harmonic world economy which takes the prerequisites of ecologically, socially and culturally sustainable development into consideration.

Jeremy Rifkin states that 'community precedes markets, culture precedes commerce' (2000: 255–60). This means, that without proper social capital that is accumulated in institutional structures, operational practices, shared values and patterns of mutual behaviour, market economy lacks an essential ground of trust and empathy between people, the actors of economic exchange. Rifkin speaks strongly for the third sector as a vital factor in transition from the industrial capitalism towards the 'cultural capitalism', of the information society. Without a true civil society, there is a danger of capital flow to the fourth sector, the illegal and shadow economy as happened in Russia after the collapse of the Soviet Union. This is also a risk in many developing countries in Africa, Latin America and Asia.

To put society first, before money, is not self-evident in the Western democracies, either. There is thin elite of speculators whose example of making money is followed by the ordinary people as the highest goal of their lives. Thus, capitalism is disturbing the communities, pointed out by Karl Polanyi. Short term calculations and commercialisation of social relationships do not nourish empathy and trust, the basic elements of sustainable social life in human communities. More and more people are ready to sell even their grandmother for a few dollars more.

The modern Cooperative Movement, which began to get organised in the middle of the nineteenth century in England, represents a human-centred way of doing business. In the pioneering years of industrialisation, cooperative enterprises were established to protect the producers' and consumers' interests against market distortions. The idea was that cooperation can correct failures of markets and provide an economically ethical alternative to business operations that aim solely at maximised returns on private capital and profit seeking. Today the International Cooperative Alliance (ICA), which has operated globally since 1895, has member associations in more than one hundred countries. With its membership of over 700 million individuals in cooperatives, ICA is the world's largest NGO. Ever since its foundation, ICA has striven to build a common identity for the Cooperative Movement, with the international basic principles of cooperation as the historic background and continuously renewable guidelines. Most recently, these basic values of cooperation were recorded in the ICA declaration of the identity of cooperation in 1995 (for example, MacPherson 1996).

In today's global information society, the basic cooperative principles offer a valid solution for a harmonic and peaceful fusion of technological revolution and socioeconomic development. The cooperative 'network community', based on the international organisation of Cooperative Movement, opens huge visions into global influence reinforcing ethical management and mutual trust in the world economy (see for example Rifkin 2000).

In the following, I will review the opportunities of this human-centred alternative for economic development, based on combined participation and ownership. The principles of cooperation are in the focus, illustrated with examples of this form of enterprise in a small European country, Finland. The text refers mainly to the experiences of new emerging cooperative undertakings established during the last 10–15 years. The general cooperative model is recognised, however, as a common feature shared by the 'cooperative sector of the economy' as a whole, including established cooperatives, too, i.e. consumer co-ops, co-op banks, mutual insurance companies, farmers' dairy co-ops, slaughterhouse and forest-owners' co-ops, having important roles in the Finnish economy. Emphases given to new SME co-ops points to the roles of grass root membership and cooperation on the level of learning by doing.

Growth Illusion of the Mammon: Never-ending Treadmill

Hopes and expectations of the blessings of globalisation, lean strongly on the doctrine of the guiding 'invisible hand', as presented in classical economic theories. The 'invisible hand' is assumed to produce miraculous prosperity in free market conditions and to distribute welfare maximally both within and between nations. The absolutely superior measure of economic development is gross national product, and its level and growth is repeatedly cited in economic comparisons. The way we calculate the national product is, however, extremely simple and biased. The goods and services included in the GNP are priced according to the exchange value of products of companies and public institutions or according to an administrative value, without considering whether they promote individuals' or families' quality of life, working or local communities' wellbeing, or the diversity or survival of nature and environment.[2] Growth of alcohol consumption, costs of corrective treatment of prisoners and sales of entertainment based on violence are included in the GNP equally with expenditure related to production of food, maintenance of law and order, or education. The economic growth logic is unable to see anything weird in the fact that the GNP is increased both by the use of technology causing pollution and the publicly funded measures to correct the harm caused to the environment by the said production technology. On the other hand, plenty of unpaid performances, which individuals and households exchange reciprocally, fall outside the national product statistics. These outputs are not recorded as statistical quantities until the performance is transferred from the unofficial exchange economy to the official monetary economy. The extent of the grey economy or black market is obviously not seen in the national accounting either. It is the laundering – in other words, circulation of the profits from illegal drug or arms trading in the official economy – that 'contributes' to the growth of national product.

The following dialogue between a young Finnish researcher specialising in the study of rural life and an experienced Polish agricultural economist illustrates the development optimism created by the GNP based growth logic in 'new' market economy countries and the importance of not falling behind the development for them. Getting the Polish agriculture and countryside into 'Euro shape' for application of membership in the EU is the issue:

- The criteria of economic growth constitute the central terms and conditions which the Eastern and Middle European countries with transitional economies are expected to meet in order to be accepted as members of the European Union. According to the agricultural economist from Poland, the special problems of the country from the point-of-view of agriculture are the following: There are about 2 million farms, and the proportion of agriculture of labour force is about 10 per cent. The share of agriculture of GNP is 4–6 per cent, indicating that the productivity of agriculture is lower than that of other branches. In order to get the Polish agriculture into 'Euro shape', the number of farms must be reduced to 300,000. This means a drastic drop in the number of farms, leading to rural depopulation. The change, however, is voluntary because young people seek for recognition and want to keep up with the pace of modern life. The reduction in the number of farms does not affect the level of production, since the remaining farms will be modern and efficient. They will produce top crops using the state-of-art production technologies and chemical fertilisers, herbicides and pesticides. The crops of genetically modified corn exceed by far the best harvests of traditional cultivation. The farmers will have cultivation and marketing contracts with Monsanto type multinationals, which schedules each farm's cultivation, supplies the required (genetically modified) seeds, fertilisers and plant protecting agents together with detailed instructions of use, leases necessary machines and equipment, and finally, guarantees the markets for the products.

- Bewildered, the Finnish expert of the EU rural policy pointed out that the European Union has set strict restrictions for the production and marketing of genetically modified food; trusts controlling or monopolising the production chain are not allowed because of their restraints of competition; and the rural development projects are encouraged towards diversity, many-sided structure of industry and trade, and enhanced local processing of primary products to promote local employment. Furthermore, the costs of uncontrolled migration of population will be multiplied because the infrastructures existing in the countryside become useless while new buildings and infrastructures need to be constructed in the towns. The European consumers are also becoming increasingly aware, and the demand for fresh, clean and organically produced foodstuffs is increasing. By developing the agriculture along the narrow line based on the growth of GNP, Poland will end up with a desolated countryside, fading social networks and dying cultural identity. The fading of social capital will eventually jeopardise the prerequisites of sustainable economic development.
- But, people in Poland are poor, they feel inferior in comparison with other European nations, and want to show as soon as possible GNP figures that they can present 'without having to look at the tips of their shoes'! This was the plea of an experienced economist whose sincerity we have no reason to question. (Helsinki, October 2000)

Use of GNP as the measure of economic growth has been criticised profoundly. Other measures have been developed to replace it, which better indicate the quality of socioeconomic development and its multiple dimensions, for instance, the Index of Sustainable Economic Welfare (ISEW) (Douthwaite 2000: 20–22). Nevertheless, the GNP and percentage of economic growth in practice are still the figures that motivate decisions in economic policy: 'Unemployment can be reduced, provided that the annual growth of economy is at least 3.5 per cent. Supply of services cannot be guaranteed, unless the economic growth reaches at least 3.5 per cent'. Economic growth has resulted in a rat race and there seems to be no alternative solution, although the benefits of economic growth are often questionable as far as the quality of life and survival of the environment are concerned. In the early 1970s, the proportion of real capital in international business operations was 90 per cent and the speculative capital 10 per cent, but by the year 1995 the ratio was quite the opposite: real capital accounted for less than 10 per cent of the daily international monetary flow of over one billion US dollars, while over 90 per cent was the movement of speculative capital. Individuals whose lives are affected by these capital movements have become helpless bystanders, while the 'invisible hand of market competition' is arranging the economic division of work to an optimal position in the eyes of international major investors and multinational companies.

With saturating markets, increasing environmental liabilities and an ever 'too high' share of the public sector leading to increasing expenses, companies are forced to seek better profit margins from operating environments where the labour and raw material costs are low and the attitude towards environmental hazards is indifferent. The neo liberal economic policy of the Western countries seems in practice to trust the alliance between government and large-scale companies more than the free market competition: consider the number of top executives accompanying presidents and prime ministers during their state visits. It is the state that prepares the way and acts as guarantor and sponsor in trade and development aid contracts. The companies share the risks with the public government, but the profit remains private (for example, Chomsky 2000).

Growth of Risks: Limits of the Planet and Development Gap

Globalisation seems to benefit mostly major investors and multinational companies, which are able to utilise the business tools offered by the information technology, to establish worldwide networks and to exploit national or supranational investment and assistance programmes. The losers are the societies that use their supplies of raw materials sparingly, and have low technological and wage levels, the poorest countries, and societies without inherent operating structures and know-how of market economy.

What, then, is so bad in the current globalisation process? Do the major companies and neo liberal economic policy not know the operational logic of market economy and its demands best? In the hands of economic experts and with the instruments of modern technology, the development of nations, economic communities and the whole world is under better control than ever before in history. The less the laymen interfere in the complex and sensitive machinery of economic and social policy, the better the development can be led towards wealth and prosperity! Besides, the majority of ordinary people want to be able to increase consumption, to have more leisure and to advance to better paid positions in their career. With a population of slightly over five million, haven't Finland and the Finnish Nokia shown that inherent know-how and the ability to develop it are sufficient grounds for success? There is, however, a well-grounded reason to claim, that the Finnish experience of flexibility and successful new technology advancement has been made possible by the strong commitment of the Finnish state to its two-fold role as the promoter of enterprises and as a welfare society (Castells and Himanen 2002).

The Limits to Growth, a report published in the early 1970s for the Club of Rome, caused a permanent crack in the basic logic of economic growth (Meadows et al. 1972). Although many of the conclusions by Dennis Meadows and co-workers about the exhaustion of natural supplies and the collision between the expansive population growth and the food production falling behind were later shown to be inaccurate – by looking for new supplies of raw materials deeper under the Earth's surface, by advancing food production technologies, by controlling the growth of population etc. – the fundamental claim has not been disproved: in a limited space growth cannot continue without limits. Raising the living standard of the developing countries with large populations up to the Western level means multiplied energy consumption, growth of food consumption and the need to increase cultivated area in excess of the capacity of our planet. No parallel is found in earlier history to the environmental risks caused by the storage of nuclear waste, global warming resulting from the greenhouse effect or pollution or drying out of groundwater. Decisions on measures to stop environmental deterioration should be taken without delay.

It is understandable that the governments of poorer countries, the business inspired by the opportunities of market economy and the consumers, who are caught by the images created by modern advertising and media, all feel that warnings about the risks of economic growth, when they come from the more developed countries with thriving market economies, are hypocritical. It is equally hard to demand that major companies struggling to keep their market position in the tightening international operating environment should delegate decision-making power from the headquarters to the staff of their production plants in the developing countries or to representatives of local communities. There have, however, been presented serious proposals about political income transfer schemes on international level targeting to cut a part of capital flows of multinational firms to the benefit of more even global economic development, like the proposal made by Nobel Laureate James Tobin (Tobin 1978, European Parliament 1999). Jointly accepted targets to increase the share of the development cooperation budgets by the states have proved to be less effective, until now. Solidarity movements and campaigns have shown that it is possible for private citizens to voluntarily collect major contributions to development aid, the amount of which may exceed official government assistance.

From the Dominance of Centralised Capital and Power towards Participatory Networks

Two contradictory processes, one of economic concentration leading to improving competitiveness on the globalising markets, and the other of mobilising the society to rely on decentralised resources and local needs, are restructuring society. During this process, values are changing, too. Firstly, the positive values of welfare state, emphasising social equality, justice and solidarity have made room for more critical voices blaming public services of top heavy care-taking, bureaucratic control and over-standardised rules of distribution. Secondly, emphasis is given to individual self-interest seeking and free competition as a driving force of the development of the private market and the privatisation of public services. Thirdly, the widening gap between those strong enough to benefit from the concentration of economic benefits on the markets, and those who are not able to compete in the hardening market conditions, calls for a new revival of charity and altruistic care-taking for those excluded from the markets. Fourthly, there are trends which strengthen the consciousness of the common interests of people globally as well as locally. Striving for ecologically, economically, socially and culturally sustainable ways of life and fighting for local communities are expressions of both global solidarity and local responsibility and bring people together to start cooperative activities.[3]

a) *Cooperation Correcting Market and Public Failures*

Cooperatives as economic actors and the Cooperative Movement as a whole have been referred to as corrective factors of the failures of the markets. Nowadays, the labour markets in all industrial countries show decreasing numbers of permanent salaried personnel. Both private and public employers are searching for possibilities to reduce labour costs. The mechanisms of the labour markets tend to lead towards permanently high unemployment rates and an increase of atypical work relations i.e. non-permanent employee relations. Seasonal or part-time jobs, short term contracts, freelance work, self-employment and entrepreneurship are becoming more and more common. Networks are created between small entrepreneurs and between small and big enterprises to achieve economies of scale with lower administration costs. Local partnerships are established to unite public, private and third sector needs and capabilities to mobilise economic activities into entrepreneurship and employment.

The age of information society has been described by several futurologists and philosophers as a turning point, where the previously dominant hierarchical or centralised capital driven forms of organisation will become less competitive. Open, flexible, flat hierarchy networks will respond better to the changing values and inspire enthusiasm and creativity at work (for example, Himanen 2001, Jensen 1999, Rifkin 2000).

The role of new forms of economic cooperation may be interpreted as a means to correct the failures of globalising markets as well as failures of the public sector, too. Cooperatives may contribute to firstly create jobs – employment, secondly increase earnings – income, and finally motivate their members to participate actively in taking care of their common undertaking – joy.[4]

i) *Concrete utopias 1: to create jobs*

One hundred years ago, economic cooperation played an important role in correcting market failures. Today it may take the same task. Nowadays are also failures of the public regulation, where cooperation may offer alternative or additional solutions to the production of different welfare services.

The failures of the labour market are obvious, and cooperation may be needed to correct them. In Finland, as will be shown, the establishment of worker cooperatives by the unemployed during the deep recession in the early 1990s has shown how cooperative self-help may give people an opportunity to keep working even when they were ignored by the mainstream markets. Since then, new cooperatives have been organised by various groups of people, including the unemployed or disabled, as well as by highly educated people, entrepreneurs, farmers etc. On one hand, cooperatives have proved to be a sound reaction towards globalising markets, which threaten to leave masses of labour force unemployed and socially excluded, while on the other hand, new structures of labour markets have opened new fields of growth and development for cooperatives. One of the most important developments has been the reinvention of local communities to further entrepreneurship.

ii)   Concrete utopias 2: to create income

Cooperatives are intended to further their members' economic needs and aspirations. This means that cooperatives have to be taken care of economically effectively and profitably. There is, however, a large variation among cooperative organisations according to the economic value of their activities to the members. If a member of a workers' co-op earns all his/her salary through the cooperative, he/she certainly values the membership highly. In a consumers' cooperative, membership fee may be very low, and you may be able to choose where you shop between the co-op store and a nearby private shop. In this case, commitment to membership may be much lower than in the workers' co-op. Benefits of cooperation for an individual member can be calculated directly from the economic exchange relations between the member and the co-op.

The situation is different, however, if we look at the economic benefits of a larger community. Cooperatives return their profits back to their members. Even small amounts of income returned by local co-op to its members may improve the local economy considerably. Instead of following the so called global change agents' advice to close down local shops, production plants or community service co-ops, maintaining local activities may help to keep local money in local use instead of it all going to outsiders' pockets.[5]

In the globalising markets, cooperative networks based on the local utilisation of resources may be the most powerful counter-force against multinational investor driven markets. Cooperative ethical trading (fair trade) networks are one example of activities, where even small enterprises can participate globally.

iii)   Concrete utopias 3: to create joy

People do not live on bread alone. According to the interview studies made among new cooperators in Finland, membership in a cooperative means not only an opportunity to gain employment or income, it also means the chance to share common needs and aspirations with others, to learn from other people's experiences, to earn respect and trust from others etc. Cooperatives offer their members communality, togetherness, belongingness, which private small-scale entrepreneurs often lack; feeling themselves isolated and alone with their own problems.

Cooperative management methods and principles have many properties making it compatible with emerging ethics and practices of innovative network organisations, described by Pekka Himanen in his visionary book about the hacker ethic (Himanen 2001). In business markets, while capitalistic firms motivate their top management by big bonus and option benefits, employee-owned co-ops may become competitive working-places, dividing benefits to the worker-members on an equal and just basis. People enjoy their work more, if they can participate in the decision-making and division of incentives, too. Encouraging enterprises to develop employee-ownership is a future trend in global competition (for example, Jensen 1999: 133–45).

b. *Cooperation and Diffusion of Innovations: People-centred Development of Technology*

Economic cooperation may be in a key position representing new types of social capital needed to create a human information society, where networks are based on trust and empathy (e.g. Etzioni 1996: 62–96, Putnam 1993). This is certainly very important, if the benefits of new technology are to be distributed evenly among the people inside national borders as well as on a global scale.

Historically, cooperatives have played a decisive role in the furthering of technological innovations, for example in agriculture. Common ownership and utilisation of the means of production have made it possible for owners of small farms to make use of the newest techniques and farming methods as well as organising the most modern marketing systems for their products. Why not use cooperation as a means of distributing the innovations of information society for the benefit of ordinary people, SMEs and public welfare services, too? This might be even a priority historical challenge for Cooperative Movement of our age. How can it be done? Sectoral big Cooperatives are not interested in taking more holistic responsibilities, innovations are first applied by big money holders, small-scale knowledge intensive workers' co-ops are a marginal phenomenon among IT businesses. To develop alternative, people centred use of technology, based on participatory, shared ownership of the basic means of production – the human skills and know-how – the means of public policy are needed urgently. This requires new partnerships between public and cooperative sectors to develop an information society based on participation and shared ownership.

Different processes of the diffusion of innovations seem to be related to different cultural contexts, community traditions – or social capital. The question is how the information technology and opening global networks could be introduced into communities with a small amount of social capital. Perhaps because of the Internet, this is no more needed? We return to Rifkin's notion that community comes before markets.

An interesting example is South Savo in Eastern Finland, a province with 200,000 inhabitants. It is sparsely populated and an economically slowly developing area with high unemployment and high migration rates. Due to historical and geographic reasons, especially the traditional burn-clearing culture that lasted there until the early twentieth century, as well as a multitude of lakes and forests, the settlement structure in South Savo consists of relatively isolated farmsteads and decentralised villages. According to some studies, there seem to be interesting differences between South Savo and more concentrated western settlements concerning the spread of innovations, too. New ideas find their way rapidly into public debates in Savo. There are always interested people ready to make their remarks about and express their support for all good innovations, but very few are ready to realise these ideas in practice. The diffusion process is very slow. In general, the cooperatives have found their way to South Savo later than to other areas in Finland (e.g. Inkinen 2000, Tauriainen 1970). The diffusion process in western village settlements is different: first the reactions of people are usually reserved, suspicious and even negative; but after some experimenting by a handful of successful innovators, others very soon follow, and the new method or equipment is taken into common use.

Differences related to the diffusion of innovation processes between collective village settlements of western Finland and more individualistic scattered settlements in East can be interpreted as a difference of learned social capital. Long tradition of living in villages in western Finland has created trust and encouragement between the people, needed to share ideas and take the risk to start new activities. Everyone's contribution is accepted and needed to increase the common good. In a community, where individualistic orientations dominate, common benefit comes later, only if your own share is first granted. Sharing knowledge becomes more threat than opportunity, and competition may make the common cake smaller, instead of increasing it (see Etzioni 1996: 62–91).

There are situations, where the application of new technical or organisational solutions can be realised through the establishment of partnerships with other entrepreneurs or large companies, shifting to employee buy-outs, or other cooperative ways, including the use of public authorities as partners. The role of local actors is important, because the innovations are considered not only as a matter of business, but also that of the community. There is a need to develop practices of 'community governance' instead of narrow 'corporate governance' to stress the point of view of local sustainability in the application of technology.

In applying new technology, however, direct profits often seem to be much more interesting goals than slow learning and community involvement for both entrepreneurs and development support authorities. This may, however, result in isolated attempts to establish nonviable undertakings with short-sighted, unsustainable exploitation of the most easily utilised opportunities. Partnerships of local authorities, local entrepreneurs and technological knowledge centres, i.e. universities or polytechnics, are needed as a basis for transferring technological innovations from theory into practice, but also as a new model for community governance building up the route towards sustainable information society.

Utopian Energy of Emerging Cooperatives towards Twenty-first Century: Finland[6]

In Finland the rise of new cooperatives coincided with the great depression of the Finnish economy and large-scale unemployment at the beginning of the 1990s. To cope with the unexpected situation there was a need to find new employment opportunities. Labour cooperatives, organising rent-out or leasing work contracts were invented by the unemployed themselves as an innovative means to organise work for skilled people with various occupational backgrounds. More business oriented workers' co-ops have developed successfully in different fields of activities. The branches of workers' cooperatives are widening from construction work to architecture, publishing to entertainment and show business, home-aid services to knowledge intensive consulting etc. Over the past few years, the spectrum of new co-ops has dispersed from workers' co-ops to marketing, supplying, community development and energy. In rural areas, new cooperatives often function in new fields such as tourism, marketing of organic or ecological production, the processing of natural products like berries and mushrooms, small-scale handicrafts, carpentry and the production of wood energy. Due to the lower earnings from traditional farming there has been an urgent need to find new sources of income. Cooperation is a suitable way of organising and experimenting with new types of economic activities because the economic risks involved are not so high.

Table 11.1   Number of new cooperatives established in Finland 1987–December 2001

Workers' co-ops	503
Marketing co-ops	249
Purchasing co-ops	76
Cultural, media and publishing co-ops	107
Social, health and welfare co-ops	62
Travel industry co-ops	51
Development co-ops	43
Energy industry co-ops	44
Other co-ops	53
Water supply and sewerage co-ops	500
Total number of established co-ops	1687

Source: Finnish National Board of Patents and Registration and Pellervo, Confederation of Finnish Co-operatives, 31 December 2001.

About half of the workers' cooperatives can be considered to be of the traditional type, working in one or two industrial sectors, with business ideas based on specific products, or more often services. The other half consists of multi-sectoral labour or work cooperatives, often established by unemployed professionals. In these cooperatives, members are not permanently employed by the cooperative, but have temporary work contracts. In the periods between work contracts they have the right to receive unemployment benefit from the state. The cooperatives can produce a meaningful environment for their members to practice and develop their skills and participate actively in society. At the same time, they can also form social communities where the depressing effects of unemployment can be minimised and new social capital can even be produced between them.

Labour cooperatives and other new cooperatives can be viewed as new initiatives both in employment policy and in economic life. In economic life, they represent a new way of viewing business where people take their destiny in their own hands without depending on the public sector or large private enterprises. In work integration they have produced both new labour opportunities and opportunities to renew or improve vocational skills for thousands of unemployed people for minimal public sector inputs. With a little more financial and other support from the public sector Finnish society would benefit greatly from the employment and financial effects of the cooperatives in work integration.

In the field of producing welfare services, there are good grounds for estimating a strong increase of cooperative solutions. On the other hand, the Finnish Welfare State is still considered to have the main responsibility for social welfare and health care services. The public sector still has the old habit of absorbing new ideas from the associations and including these services in the services produced by the public sector. It is estimated that the re-integrative actions of associations will become gradually more important and more abundant over the next few years.

In rural Finland, the main motives for establishing cooperatives have been both economic and social. Creating new marketing channels, supplementary income and a meaningful way of working were all important factors. In a recent questionnaire study, opinions as to how the co-op had helped its members, differed according to the type of cooperative. In worker cooperatives, the most significant positive impacts focused on increased work satisfaction, new employment and additional income. In supply cooperatives, the main benefits were gained through savings in the cost of farm inputs. In marketing cooperatives, the cooperative had helped to expand markets and increased social togetherness and communication. In most of the studied cases, the cooperative had, at least partially fulfilled the expectations initially set for them.

Cooperation between independent farmers has also changed in Finland. This includes the collective use of machines, machine rings, milk producing rings, jointly owned cow sheds and dryer cooperatives. Cooperation has been used as a means of increasing efficiency and use of agricultural machinery, reduces fixed expenses and has created social relations (Kallioniemi 1998).

The overall impact of cooperatives on rural development is hard to assess empirically because it is almost impossible to control any other factors, and we do not know about the opportunity costs of other solutions. New cooperatives often enter the picture as the last resort or appear in regions where other ways of resolving problems are scarce. That is why cooperation is called the child of need and distress. Still, we can say that cooperation has played a crucial role in improving the vitality of many rural communities in the past and continues to do so today.

The studies carried out in Finland confirm that new cooperatives have had a positive impact on their members' self-confidence and belief in the future. Most of the respondents to the questionnaire believed that new cooperatives help to keep the countryside inhabited. They believed also that cooperatives are able to support the weaker members. Cooperation is a way of creating networks between small enterprises and establishing larger marketing units that are competitive in centralised distributing markets of food products. In cooperatives even small producers can benefit from returns of scale. About half of the representatives of new rural cooperatives believed that their activities would not have started at all without the cooperative form of enterprise. New cooperatives have not only replaced or preserved existing entrepreneurship but they have been able to create new economic activities in rural communities. According to the opinions of cooperative members, demand for new cooperatives in the Finnish countryside is most evident in social services and marketing (Rantanen 1998).

The unemployment rate in Finland was, at its worst, almost 20 per cent of the labour force at the beginning of the 1990s and currently is still around 10 per cent. The situation has led politicians to look for new ways of arranging job opportunities and promoting entrepreneurship. By establishing worker cooperatives unemployed blue and white-collar workers have been able to set up small enterprises using their own resources, produce new products and services, and thus employ themselves. In rural Finland the villagers' activities have been an embodiment of citizens' own initiatives and mutual self-help since the 1970s. This will be a sound basis for organising services and establishing new entrepreneurial activities in a new cooperative way.

Conclusion

The revival of cooperation in the 1990s can be seen as a solution to recent shortcomings of the functioning of both market and public sector institutions. In modern society cooperation represents an opportunity to combine the principles of the free market economy with the ethic of social care-taking. Within the mixed system of free markets and social services cooperative practices provide a multitude of options, the weight of which depends upon the needs in society and the adaptability of the cooperatives themselves.

Cooperation has gained a new popularity among the population in the face of the challenges of increasing globalisation and liberalisation in Finland. The necessity of grass roots collective action is becoming more and more obvious when centralised government support is in retreat and has been retrenched. But cooperation is a precarious enterprise when there is insufficient member commitment and external support. Bad experiences tend to have a long influence on people's opinion of cooperation and it is hard to re-convince them of its usefulness.

The great advantage of economic cooperation is, that it can combine job, joy and income around common ownership and entrepreneurship. If the capital is given all power in the markets, ownership, job, joy and income are taken away from the peoples' hands and given to a small number of powerful speculators to play with. It could be said, that access to job, joy and income as well as to the blessings of new technology are an ethical imperative of people in the globalising world. Without a cooperative ethic, globalisation is threatening job, joy and the income of millions of people in developed as well as developing countries. The deepening gap between rich and poor, centre and periphery, town and country is a growing global threat on all levels: regional, national, as well as inside and between economic blocks. Globalisation begins at home. Without more concern for the human factor, care for nature and environment, food, energy and other basic values, the world will be turned into a battlefield of blind profit searching for market forces.

Notes

[1] For the leading document, where the principles of sustainable development have been laid down, see World Commission on Environment and Development 1987.

[2] For a comprehensive, polemical and critical analysis of the concept and use of economic growth as a measure of 'development' see especially Douthwaite 2000.

[3] These structural changes related to the shift from industrial to post-industrial or information society have been a topic of lively debate among futurologists, among them Castells (1996), Jensen (1999) and Rifkin (2000).

[4] The following analysis is based on a series of seminar lectures by the author, see, for example, Köppä (1999: 95–8).

[5] For a brilliant analysis of the role of cooperatives in the local economy, see Fairbairn et al. (1991).

6   This chapter is largely based on Köppä et al. (1999: 88–96).

References

Castells, Manuel (1996), 'The Rise of the Network Society: Economy, Society and Culture', *The Information Age*, Vol. I, Blackwell, Oxford.
Castells, Manuel and P. Himanen (2002), *The Finnish Model of the Information Society*, Oxford University Press, Oxford.
Chomsky, Noam (2000), *Profit over People: Neoliberalism and Global Order*, Europa Verlag, Hamburg and Wien.
Douthwaite, Richard (2000), *The Growth Illusion. How Economic Growth has Enriched the Few, Impoverished the Many, and Endangered the Planet*, rev.d edn, The Lilliput Press Ltd, Montreal.
Etzioni, Amitai (1996), *Die Verantwortungsgesellschaft. Individualismus und Moral in der heutigen Demokratie*, Campus Verlag, Frankfurt and New York.
European Parliament (1999), 'The Feasibility of an International "Tobin's Tax"', *Economic Affairs Series*, ECON 107 EN (PE 168.215).
Fairbairn, Brett, Jane Bold, Murray Fulton, Lou Hammond-Ketilson and Daniel Ish (1991), *Co-operatives and Community Development, Economics in Social Perspective*, Centre for the Study of Co-operatives, University of Saskatchewan, Saskatoon.
Finnish National Board of Patents and Registration and Pellervo, Confederation of Finnish Co-operatives (2001), *The Number of New Co-operatives Established in Finland 1987*, Pellervo, Helsinki, 31 December.
Hickens, G.R. (1981), *Leading Organizations: Perspectives for a New Era*, SAGE Publications, Thousand Oaks, London and New Delhi.
Himanen, Pekka (2001), *The Hacker Ethic and the Spirit of the Information Age*, Random House, London.
Inkinen, Kari (2000), 'Diffuusio ja fuusio. Osuuskauppainnovaation levinneisyys ja sen dynamiikka 1901–1998' ('Consumer Cooperatives in Finland: Diffusion of an Innovation and its Dynamics 1901–1998'), Dissertation thesis, Helsinki School of Economics and Business Administration, Acta Universitatis Oeconomicae Helsingiensis, A–181.
Jensen, Rolf (1999), *The Dream Society: How the Coming Shift from Information to Imagination Will Transform your Business?*, McGraw-Hill, New York.
Kallioniemi, Marja (1998), 'Kolmisäikeinen köysi ei katkea. Tapausesimerkkejä maatilojen välisestä yhteistyöstä' ('Cooperation between Farms, Case Studies'), Mikkeli, University of Helsinki, Institute for Co-operative Studies, Publication No. 20.
Köppä, Tapani (1999), 'Cooperation Creating Job, Joy and Income' in Tapani Köppä (ed.), *Concern for Community in a Globalizing World*, Conference Report, Mikkeli, University of Helsinki, Institute for Co-operative Studies, Publication No. 24.
Köppä, Tapani, Pekka Pättiniemi and Markus Seppelin (1999), 'Emerging Co-operatives in Rural Finland in New Rural Policy', *Finnish Journal of Rural Research and Policy*, 2/99, English supplement, available at http://www.mtkk.helsinki.fi/mua.html.
MacPherson, Ian (1996), *Co-operative Principles for the Twenty-first Century*, International Co-operative Alliance, Geneva.
Meadows, Donella, Dennis Meadows, Jorgen Randers and William Behrens (1972), *The Limits to Growth*, Earth Island, London.
Putnam, R.E. (1993), *Making Democracy Work: Civic Traditions in Modern Italy*, Princeton University Press, Princeton.

Rantanen, Seppo (1998), 'Maaseudun uudet osuustoiminnan ideat' ('The Ideas of Rural New Cooperation'), Mikkeli, University of Helsinki, Institute for Co-operative Studies, Publications.

Rifkin, Jeremy (2000), *The Age of Access. The New Culture of Hypercapitalism. Where All of Life is a Paid-for Experience*, Jeremy P. Tarcher/Putnam, New York.

Tauriainen, Juhani (1970), 'Kehitysalueiden muuttuva maatalous', Publications of the Marketing Research Institute of Pellervo Society, No 12. Helsinki.

Tobin, James (1978), 'A Proposal for International Monetary Reform', *Eastern Economic Journal*, Vol. 4, pp. 14–19.

World Commission on Environment and Development (1987), *Our Common Future*, Oxford University Press, Oxford.

PART B
ECONOMIC ISSUES OF GLOBALISATION

Chapter 12

International Aviation: Globalisation and Global Industry

Peter Forsyth   R40,   L93 L83

F23

(*authors' comments*)

F02

Introduction

Globalisation is a process of breaking down barriers between countries and regions around the world. Hitherto distant countries are brought together, as the tyranny of distance is reduced. The transactions costs of doing business between nations has been falling; these costs include money costs as well as costs in terms of other resources such as time. Costs have fallen in a number of fields, such as:

- the costs of communications, which involve both voice and data;
- the costs of capital flows;
- the costs of transport of goods, people and technology.

We shall concentrate on the latter in this chapter. Transport costs have been falling gradually over the centuries. The result has been the increased scope for trade between distant nations, and the possibility of intensification of trade between close neighbours. Changing transport costs have been a potent force shaping the development of economies around the world. This is no more evident than in Australia. As a remote and large country, transport costs within the economy, and between Australia and its markets have always been high. How transport costs moulded the development of Australia is explored by Blainey in his 'the tyranny of distance' (1966).

One of the most pervasive revolutions in transport of recent years has been the post war development of air transport. This has revolutionised the movement of people over medium and long distances. Travel has become much cheaper and much quicker, and thus there has been a boom, which continues unabated, in international travel. In this chapter, two aspects of the aviation boom are considered: firstly, the role of air transport as a force facilitating globalisation and secondly, the emergence of aviation as a global industry.

Aviation as a Globalisation Force

Before World War II, the aviation industry was small. International air services were available, but they were slow (by current standards; a flight from Australia to Britain took over a week) and extremely expensive. The post-war period has been one of very rapid technical progress in aviation, leading to a transformation in the product and an enormous increase in productivity. Now air is a very quick way to travel, and it has become very cheap. Air transport has more or less completely replaced sea transport for passengers on long haul routes, and it is very competitive with rail and private car on medium haul routes where these exist. These developments have had profound effects on trading patterns.

These changes in aviation have led to the creation of the international tourism industry. International movements by people were quite limited prior to the War Holiday tourism took place, but mainly to nearby countries. For example, people from the UK would visit France or perhaps Italy, and people from the US would visit Canada or Mexico. Air travel was for the very rich or for business. Nowadays, there are very large flows of leisure tourists, within and from Europe and North America and flows of tourists within the Asia Pacific region are growing very rapidly. Tourism is now, by various measures, the world's largest industry. Also for many countries tourism is the largest single export or import.

The progress in aviation has essentially created a very large, and growing industry international tourism. Quick and affordable travel has transformed the tourism industries within countries into tradable industries. The range of goods and services that tourists purchase, such as hotel and transport services, restaurant meals and admissions to attractions have become tradable and traded products. Beyond tourism aviation has made other services, such as education and health more tradable. Students are more willing to travel to other countries for their education, and it is feasible to visit countries for medical procedures.

The development of the tourist industry, as a large and tradable industry, is having impacts on economies. In some countries there has been a boom in the export of tourism; this is so for the popular tourist destinations. This booming sector leads to offsetting changes in other tradable sectors, such as declines in traditional export sectors such as manufacturing and primary products. In other countries there has been a reverse process going on; this has been so for Japan, which does not attract many tourists, but which has been experiencing a rapid growth of overseas tourism by its citizens. This boom in an import industry has been having the effect of moderating the rise in its exchange rate, and thus helping traditional export industries such as manufacturing.

The growth of tourism has been having a tangible impact on the development process in some lower income countries. Trade tends to produce factor price equalisation. Aviation has opened up more industries to trade. This is especially true of countries which have the potential to export tourism services. Thus countries like Singapore and Thailand have been able to export tourism services very effectively these industries account for sizeable proportions of trade. Tourism has been an export industry which has not had to overcome barriers to trade such as tariffs. To the extent that growth in these countries has been export led growth, aviation and tourism have contributed positively to growth in per capita incomes.

While the development of leisure tourism has been the most obvious consequence of aviation changes, business travel has also boomed. This is having an indirect impact on flows of goods and services. Business travel between countries is now quicker and easier, and this is having an effect in strengthening links between industries in different countries. Trade follows travel. Better transport has also facilitated direct foreign investment, since it is now much more easy for a head office to monitor performance of subsidiaries in distant countries. Another effect has been that on labour flows between countries. Medium term flows of labour from one country to another have been present for many years. However, the development of quick and affordable air travel has meant that travelling internationally for work is no longer the very long term commitment it used to be. It is possible for a worker in a foreign country to maintain good contact with family in the home country through periodic visits. It is also economic for employers to offer shorter term contracts. The lower cost of travel has had impacts on the flows on knowledge and technology. Flows of technology are related to flows of people. Conventions and conferences facilitate the international dissemination of knowledge. Specific expertise can move from country to country at short notice. Human capital becomes mobile when transport is cheap and quick. People can travel to gain information, for example when industry associations arrange trips to other countries to observe practices in their industries. When firms invest overseas, they can monitor their investments and enable rapid adoption of innovations developed in the home country (or other branches of the firm). The impact of aviation on flows of goods has hitherto been modest. Air freight only accounts for a relatively small proportion of goods carried overseas, and in value terms, the revenue from air freight is only a small proportion of the revenue from passenger services. Air freight is predictably concentrated in high value commodities. It is significant for specific types of goods flows, however. With the development of just-in-time methods of production, there is a premium on reliability of parts flows. Air freight plays a role here. For some higher value processes, air freight is used extensively for much of the inputs. For other processes, air freight can be used as a back up, lessening the risks of operating on a just-in-time basis. Thus, if crucial parts from another country are held up in shipping delays, they can be air freighted in and production can be maintained. Another trade in which air freight has become significant is in the trade in fresh produce, such as foods and flowers. With these time is of the essence, and rapid transport is of necessity if the trade is to take place.

Australia's Experience

Given its isolation from world markets and population centres, the revolution in aviation has had a particularly strong impact on Australia. Prior to World War II international travel was very slow and quite expensive. Trips to Europe took six weeks and for the few that undertook them they were a once in a lifetime experience. Australia is still an expensive destination, but it is quite affordable for most people in higher income countries. The impact of the aviation revolution was first upon travel from Australia. From the 1970s on, more and more Australians began to travel abroad, many making leisure trips overseas every few years. For a time, Australia was primarily an importer of tourism services. As a holiday destination it was not competitive with other countries; North Americans could travel more cheaply to Hawaii or Mexico, and Northern Europeans could travel more cheaply to Spain. While Australia remains a more expensive destination for these origin countries, the additional cost is much reduced. This is illustrated in Table 12.1: Australia is now quite a competitive tourism destination for some distant origin countries. Over the same period incomes in closer countries such as Japan and Singapore have reached Western levels, and people from these countries have begun to travel. Since the early

1990s there has been a sustained boom in travel to Australia. By the early 1990s, Australia became a net exporter of tourism services, and at the end of the century, it has a substantial positive balance of trade in tourism. By some measures tourism is Australia's largest export industry.

Table 12.1   Tourism competitiveness, 1997: selected origin and destination countries inclusive of ground and air components

Origin country	Japan	US	UK	Singapore
Destination country				
Australia	100.0	100.0	100.0	100.0
US	99.7	–	111.4	101.5
UK	86.2	87.6	–	77.8
Spain	84.8	104.2	121.4	74.3
Thailand	325.6	223.6	241.9	280.8

Note: A higher index indicates greater price competitiveness.

Source: Dwyer, Forsyth and Rao (1999).

The aviation revolution has facilitated Australia's participation in several other aspects of the global economy. Business travel has boomed along with leisure travel, assisting trade in other commodities and capital flows as well as flows of direct foreign investment. Improved movement by people has meant that it has been feasible for Australia to participate in trade in human capital intensive industries, such as the information technology industry.

Will the Trends Continue?

There are good prospects for the downward trend in prices of aviation services to continue. Technical progress continues to be fairly rapid in the aircraft industry, leading to prospects for lower operating costs. However some of the more important changes are taking place behind the scenes. Airlines are basically information technology companies with wings. Much of the expense in running an airline is in coordinating passengers, goods and aircraft with flight schedules. One of the main sources for the fall in airline prices has been the improved performance of this task. Airlines have been able to make more effective use of their fleets, and to fill their aircraft more effectively. Yield management has meant that the excess capacity inherent in operating scheduled services has been reduced, and products have been able to be matched more closely to passengers' preferences.

There has been a sustained, if slow, movement towards more liberalisation of international air transport, and this has put pressure on airlines to lower costs and lower prices. There is still some scope for further liberalisation. As airlines become more of a global industry than they are at present, air transport prices will continue to fall.

Airlines: A Global Industry?

At first sight it might appear that international airlines are the quintessential global industry. The products they offer are transport services between different countries, they have networks which span many countries, and they market their services across a wide range of countries. These days we hear much about global alliances between airlines.

In reality, things are rather different. In spite of their product, airlines are very much nationally based industries. They are prevented from becoming global by several restrictions. Until recently, it was either impossible or extremely difficult for a foreign investor to invest in an international airline of another country, and even today, although investment has been somewhat liberalised. It is more difficult to invest in the airlines of most countries than it is to invest in culturally sensitive firms such as media corporations. Airlines have been strictly limited in the products and routes which they have been permitted to offer. This is changing: economic forces are pushing airlines to be more global, and governments have been liberalising the industry, making it possible for airlines to become more globally integrated. The international airline industry stands as a marked contrast to the international shipping industry. This industry is barely regulated. Foreign investment is usually unrestricted, and shipping companies are free to offer services on almost any route they wish to operate, regardless of national boundaries. They can and do source their inputs from the cheapest source; they do not have to employ mainly labour from the home country. Indeed the 'home country' of a shipping line which has a head office in one country, is owned by investors and registers its ships elsewhere, employs its crews from other countries and operates services between none of these countries, is difficult to determine. Airlines have changed substantially over the past decade. Consider the typical international airline of 1990. It was fully owned by home country investors – in fact it was probably government owned. It operated almost exclusively to and from the home country. Its hub for operations was in the home country. It employed only such foreign labour as was necessary for operations. It faced little competition on most routes; probably an airline from each country it flew to, but no other airlines from the home country. Any formal agreements it had with other airlines were probably standard and of relatively minor significance.

The Regulatory Framework

Airline regulation effectively prevented them from becoming global. Home country policies, such as those on investment, hindered the development of global airlines. Also the international regulatory system, which operates on a bilateral basis, hindered globalisation. The bilateral system is one in which the two countries at either end of an international route set the terms and conditions under which airline services operate. Typically the number of airlines which could operate was limited, and the capacity they could offer was also limited. The cities which airlines could fly from were specified, and in many cases, prices were regulated. This bilateral approach restricted the development of networks. An airline from one country, such as Australia could fly to another such as the US, but it would normally not be permitted to fly on to a third country, such as the UK. If it did, it would be tightly constrained.

The system had some flexibility. For example, there was some competition over different routes; to fly from Australia to Europe, there are several alternative routings. This is less feasible for other routes, for example from Australia to South Africa. Sometimes countries which lay geographically between others could break into their markets; thus the airlines of the South East Asian countries were able to operate services between Australia and Europe (so-called sixth freedom traffic). Some countries were liberal; Singapore has been an example. Overall, however, regulation has prevented airlines from developing as a global industry. The limits on competition and trade has enabled prices to be higher and productivity to be lower than feasible. Airlines which could service routes efficiently were not allowed to do so. Airlines were prevented from developing route networks which were cost effective and which met passenger demands. Countries which had a comparative advantage in the operation of airline services were restricted from exercising their advantage.

Airline Economics

There are several features of airline economics which need to be taken into account when efficient patterns of airline services are being devised. An efficient airline system is one which keeps costs low and which provides the services which passengers want. Scale economies, per se, are not important in the airline industry. However, economies of market density are. Larger aircraft are cheaper to operate, per passenger, than smaller aircraft. However, larger aircraft mean lower frequencies, and passengers value high frequency. Airlines which are able to achieve high market shares on a route are able to offer frequent services at low prices, and thus they have an advantage. Connections are important; passengers want convenient connections if they have to make multiple flight journeys. They will prefer airlines which are able to offer good connections to a wide range of destinations. The costs at which different airlines are able to produce can vary considerable across countries. One reason for this is differing factor prices. While the prices paid by airlines for fuel and aircraft are much the same for all airlines, the prices paid for labour and materials can differ widely. These account for about half an airline's costs. Airlines from low income countries enjoy much lower prices for labour than do airlines from high income countries. On the other hand, airline efficiency differs amongst airlines (see Table 12.2). In the past it tended to be the airlines from low income countries which were less efficient. Thus they were not able to take advantage of their lower input costs. However, from about the 1980s on, some airlines from these countries were able to match or nearly match the efficiency of the airlines from high income countries, and they were able to become highly cost effective. Airlines such as Singapore Airlines and Korean Air became amongst the lowest cost airlines in the world. Other airlines such as Thai International have also become very cost competitive. As incomes grow, the competitive advantage of airlines from countries like Singapore will be eroded unless they can maintain the growth in productivity.

Table 12.2   Efficiency and cost competitiveness (% deviation from American Airlines): selected airlines, 1993

	Efficiency	Unit costs
American Airlines	0.0	0.0
United Airlines	+3.8	−0.1
Canadian Airlines	−13.7	+5.0
Japan Air Lines	−14.3	+52.7
Singapore Airlines	−3.9	−16.3
Korean Air	-0.8	−22.9
Cathay Pacific	−2.6	−3.8
Qantas	-11.6	−9.3
Thai International	−42.9	+2.7
Air France	−12.4	+21.2
Lufthansa	−3.8	+20.6
British Airways	−10.8	+7.3

Source: Gum and Yu (1998): 161.

Granted that the regulatory system has been inimical to efficiency, why has it persisted? One main reason lies in protection; countries have persisted with regulation to protect their airlines from foreign competition. For example, Japan's airlines have high costs (see Table 12.2), and the Japanese government has sought to protect them. In many countries producer interests have been stronger than consumer interests. As leisure travel booms, the political clout of consumer interests is increasing, and governments have been more willing to liberalise. Another reason for regulation may be to extract rents from foreign nationals.

Regulation works as an optimum tariff, since it can raise the prices at which a home country industry sells to a foreign country. Thus a country like Australia may be happy for Japan to be restrictive if Australian airlines are able to charge high fares on the Japan route, which is mainly travelled by Japanese nationals.

Liberalisation and Globalisation

Currently, within the international airline industry there are major changes taking place. Some of these have their origin in firms trying to adapt to the underlying conditions. Other changes, such as liberalisation of regulation have their origin in government attempts to improve the performance of the industry. Perhaps the most prominent of the firm based changes has been the move to strategic alliances. Airlines around the world are seeking to link up with other airlines, to form global alliances. By doing this they are able to offer more frequent services and take advantage of economies of density. They are able to offer coordinated and well connected services around the world, and an enhanced range of destinations. They are able to make more efficient use of their fleets, and to take advantage of lower cost airlines to supply particular routes. To some extent, these alliances provide a way around regulations. Alliances may also result in less competition; for this reason, competition authorities are wary of them At the same time, governments are being more willing to liberalise. This is partly a reflection of the greater relative strength of consumer interests, but is also a reflection of the greater acceptance of market solutions across a whole range of industries. Governments, such as that of Australia, are allowing more airlines (such as Ansett) to compete on international routes, through multiple designation of routes. They are privatising their airlines, and allowing foreign firms to invest in airlines. This is facilitating equity links between airlines in strategic alliances. Most countries are still somewhat reluctant to allow much trade in airline services; while they encourage more competition on routes, they are not willing for this competition to come from countries not actually on the route. Thus the US, which is pro-competition, would be hesitant to allow Singapore Airlines to compete on the Australia–US route. Also they are ambivalent about allowing sourcing of inputs, like labour, on international markets. There have been some shifts in input sourcing however; airlines from high income countries have been outsourcing their labour intensive data processing to lower income countries.

The outcome has been a considerable shift in regulation over the past decade. There has been extensive liberalisation though this has taken place within the framework of the bilateral system. Some countries, especially in Asia, remain quite protectionist. North America has been the most liberal region, and Australia and New Zealand have been forming a single aviation market. Europe is currently liberalising intra Europe air transport, though several countries maintain tight regulation on non-European routes. There have been some very liberal countries in Asia, such as Singapore, but overall, liberalisation in Asia has been slow. This partly reflects the pressure of producer interests in countries such as Japan, and the fact that until recently, leisure travel had yet to take off in many medium income, but rapidly growing countries. There are growing pressures for further liberalisation in Asia however.

International aviation is becoming a global industry, although there is still room for improvement. Airlines, as firms, are becoming more integrated internationally. Progress in liberalisation in Asia has mainly been made within a bilateral framework, which has limited the possible reforms, especially since there are some countries which are reluctant to liberalise. One option canvassed in the recent Productivity Commission Report (1998) is for groups of countries to liberalise amongst themselves, effectively creating free trade areas for aviation. These areas might then expand to include more countries.

Another possibility for change is through multilateral trade negotiations. Up to now, aviation has only been included in minor ways in multilateral negotiations such as the Uruguay Round. Other services, such as telecommunications have been tackled through the GATS process. The advantage of multilateral negotiations is that they include more than one type of trade, and there is scope for trade-offs between one area and another. Thus a country which is reluctant to liberalise aviation might be persuaded to do if it can gain benefits in other areas which it has been seeking. There is the potential for aviation to be addressed seriously in the forthcoming Millennium Round, something which would facilitate its becoming a global industry.

References

Blainey, G. (1966), *The Tyranny of Distance*, Sun Books, Melbourne.

Dwyer, L., P. Forsyth and P. Rao (1999), 'The Price Competitiveness of Travel and Tourism: A Comparison of Nineteen Destinations', *Tourism Management*, Vol. 11, pp. 38–59.

Gum, T. and C. Yu Hand (1998), *Winning Airlines: Productivity and Cost Competitiveness of the World's Major Airlines*, Kluwer Academic Publishers, Boston.

Productivity Commission (1998), *International Air Services*, Report No 2, Ausinfo, Canberra.

Chapter 13

Internet and Globalisation

Neil Warren

F02 F13
H87, / L86 K33

New Age Globalisation

The trend towards the globalisation of markets and the liberalisation of trade is not a new phenomenon. During the nineteenth century there was a strong push for free trade between nations. In the twentieth century, considerable success was had in liberalising the trade in goods and capital with more limited success in the case of trade in services. In the twenty-first century, there is every reason to expect that the pace of globalisation will accelerate down an even more challenging path than that in the past. While globalisation until now has been restricted largely to the trade in goods and capital flows, the rapid expansion of the information revolution through the growth of the Internet will give a whole new meaning to the concept of globalisation in the twenty-first century.

Those institutions that have served the global community well over the past fifty years will be sorely challenged in the next decade as the Internet is rolled out across the world. In fact, it is reasonable to expect that the pressures imposed through the growth of the Internet will largely overtake the role of these institutions. These pressures will not just be economic but will also be social and political and herein lies the new challenge from globalisation.

The growth of the Internet has such broad ranging implications for individual countries and their people that it is almost inevitable that there will be concern at social, cultural, and political impact of this Internet inspired globalisation. A foretaste of events to come was witnessed at the 1999 WTO round in Seattle, Washington State, where there were major riots in protest at the impact of globalisation on labour and environmental standards and for society in general. This is a situation not assisted by the perceived lack of transparency in the deliberations of the WTO, IMF and World Bank.

It is reasonable to expect that these institutions will continue to be at the forefront of the push towards a global economy and they can expect an escalation in community level concern about the implications of increasing international interdependencies and the subsequent loss of national sovereignty and local identity. The danger is that this concern will result in growing nationalism and protectionism.

This chapter will outline how globalisation in being spurred on by the growth of the Internet and how this new phase of globalisation has the potential to change every facet of our lives. It will influence everything from how and what we read, to how we work, how governments function, to issues such as maintaining a country's cultural identity. It is therefore not surprising that so much attention has been given to the growth of the Internet.

Collapsing Frontiers

For centuries, nations have waged wars over the control of trade routes. With control over these routes, a country would not only been able to demand substantial premiums for traded goods in international markets but it also had effective if not actual control over those territories which produced these goods. The response of those countries forced to import these goods was to positively discourage their consumption, this being achieved through a combination of tariffs and physical import restrictions. These barriers to trade were effective because traded commodities were often bulky and had a clear physical presence.

Throughout the nineteenth century there was a concerted push for free trade. English economist, David Ricardo (1817), has shown as early as 1817 that nations could benefit from international trade if they specialised in the production of that good in which they have comparative advantage. John Stuart Mill amongst others also strongly argued the case for free and open trade between countries. These calls grew stronger in the early twentieth century and while some progress towards global free trade was made, problems began to occur with the international trade settlement regime. An essential complement to any free trade regime is an international monetary system capable of enabling an efficient balance of payments adjustment mechanism. Prior to World War I, the international gold standard was the prevailing international monetary system with countries specifying the value of their currencies relative to gold. Since gold was the international reserve asset, trade flows could be settled using gold and trade imbalances accommodated by adjusting a country's rate of exchange for gold.

While these rates of exchange remained stable up until World War I, this system began to break down in the 1920s as countries more frequently adjusted their exchange rates. With the onset of the Great Depression and the dramatic decline in economic activity, those countries with overvalued currencies experienced difficulties in meeting their trade obligations. In response, some governments sought to increase exports by selling their national currency below its real value combined with undercutting trade in similar commodities by other countries. This practice of competitive devaluation by one country, not surprisingly, resulted in retaliatory action by their trading partners, primarily through a matching devaluation.

The uncertainty this created resulted in nations hoarding both gold and those currencies that could be readily converted into gold. The result was a contraction in the amount and frequency of transactions between nations which obviously meant reduced international trade. This undoubtedly served to prolong the depressed level of economic activity throughout most of the 1930s.

The advent of World War II saw economic activity increase but left largely unresolved the need for an alternative system of international payments. Much thought was given to deciding how a new and more liberal international economic order could be achieved which was characterised by:

- trade liberalisation;
- a new international payments system which would avoid the policy adjustments to economic shocks evident in the 1930s; and
- increased economic development.

John Maynard Keynes in Britain and Harry Dexter White in the United States had long been strong advocates of a new and liberal international trade environment and their thinking formed a major foundation for the discussion at the historic conference at Bretton Woods, New Hampshire, in July 1944.

Bretton Woods led to the recommended establishment of three institutions: the International Monetary Fund (IMF) (fiscal and monetary issues), the World Bank (financial and structural issues) and the International Trade Organisation (ITO) (international economic cooperation). The objective was to create a number of key international institutions which would oversee the development of an international economic framework that was supportive of free-trade and would result in the trading nations overcoming their isolationist and beggar-thy-neighbour policies, replacing them with multilateral rules and obligations.

While the IMF and World Bank[1] came into operation in 1944, the ITO was slower to gain acceptance. The problem for the ITO was that its charter was ambitious. It extended beyond world trade disciplines, to include the issues of employment, commodity agreements, restrictive business practices, international investment, and services. The all embracing nature of this ITO charter slowed its acceptance and resulted in only 23 countries agreeing to accept some of the trade rules in the draft ITO charter as a matter of priority. As a result, these countries moved swiftly and 'provisionally' to sign (in 1947) the General Agreement on Tariffs and Trade (GATT which came into force in January 1948).

While the ITO charter was agreed at a UN conference on Trade and Employment in Havana in March 1948, it was not ratified in some national legislatures, especially in the US Congress, which effectively made this agreement ineffective. While GATT remained a provisional agreement it was not until 1995 when the World Trade Organisation (WTO)[2] was formed following the Uruguay Round, that it became the sole international body dealing with the legal ground rules for international commerce.

GATT/WTO and Global Trade

The most fundamental principle underlying WTO agreements is the principal known as most favoured nation (MFN) treatment. This requires each member to treat all other members the same way they would their 'most-favoured' trading partner. This is the basic condition of free-trade underlying the WTO. The WTO monitors three areas of agreement amongst members:

- GATT: General Agreement on Tariffs and Trade (which relates to trade in goods);
- GATS: General Agreement on Trade in Services; and
- TRIPS: Agreement on Trade-Related Aspects of Intellectual Property Rights

While GATT is comprehensive, GATS is not nor is TRIPS. Compounding the challenge for the WTO is that what worked for the twentieth century will not necessarily work in the twenty-first. Technology and in particular the Internet is now revolutionising the economies of the globe and global commerce.

In effect, the Internet is challenging all of our past understandings of what are trade routes and the notion of a trade barrier. For example, over-zealous pursuit of ownership or interference in the new digital trade route by one country is largely counterproductive since it may simply result in that country losing access to those routes rather than giving them any power or influence over them.

What a Difference the Internet Makes!

To appreciate the fundamental challenges posed by the Internet, it is important to first understand what it is, how it works and why it is so threatening to individual countries. At its most basic, the Internet is technically nothing more than a series of computer networks linked together by a series of telephone lines, communicating between each other using a set of agreed protocols. It constitutes a revolution because it offers a simple framework for bringing together all electronic media into one delivery mechanism – whether it is simple data retrieval, telephony or video. Using this digital network, the business of banking, shopping, training, working or just being entertained, is all possible.

The Internet was originally developed by the US government to encourage communications between scientific communities and to provide a computer network that would be indestructible in any Cold War nuclear strike on the USA by the USSR. It was not until the Internet was given a user-friendly interface (called the World Wide Web) that the Internet's growth began to increase exponentially. This growth has meant that the future of the Internet is now largely beyond the control of any one country and any attempt to influence or direct this technology by one country is futile.

For governments, this Internet inspired internationalisation of the global economy offers up major challenges which are far from easily (if at all) solved. What resulted has been a flurry of reports produced by governments and international organisations focusing on examining the potential implications of this new technology.[3]

Of particular concern has been the growth of global e-commerce. This issue alone has resulted in an unprecedented level of international cooperation between governments which highlights the seriousness with which they view Internet developments. Despite this cooperation, governments are still largely playing 'catch-up'. What is proving difficult to accept is the idea that no country is an island in the Internet sea. Any attempt by one government to take unilateral action against the Internet is largely fruitless since only multilateral actions have the potential to have an impact and even then, unless *all* nations agree, the actions of a few may be quite ineffective.

At the core of the challenge posed by the growth of the Internet is an information revolution. The revolution is affecting the way not only goods and services markets operate, but also global financial and labour markets. While considerable attention has been given to the development of global goods markets via the Internet though B2C[4] and B2B[5] portals, it is the potential it offers for a revolution in the other markets that is the real revolution associated with the Internet.

Individuals' selling their labour services globally or service companies selling their business and financial services into global markets, free off the traditional international barriers, is the challenge posed by the Internet. In the case of the labour market, this is occurring at two levels – through the provision of Internet based domestic employment agencies[6] and through the actions of individuals selling their labour services directly via the web.

The Internet is also forcing a revolution onto capital markets which although characterised by high capital mobility, have been restricted to B2B and B2C activity. What the Internet offers is C2B and C2C[7] revolution in financial markets. With the Internet, global comparative information is now readily accessible through any web search engine and individuals and businesses can obtain this information almost cost-free.[8]

From an economic perspective, the Internet facilitates increased capital and labour mobility and considerably improves the competitiveness of markets for goods and services. In fact, it is likely that the Internet would do more for trade in the coming decade than the WTO has been able to do in the past half-century. While the Internet offers significant global economic efficiency gain, it poses potentially major threats to established practices and government institutions.

Threats to Government

The globalisation inspired by the Internet poses a broad challenge to governments. Some are of a fundamental nature such as the challenge posed to current tax systems and other more subtle impacts such as the challenge to cultural identity and diversity.

a) Tax System Integrity

An all-important question is 'Can current tax rules and tax designs live harmoniously with the new electronic trade routes and if not, what are the solutions?' Tax authorities have sound reasons to be less enamoured by the prospect of globalisation than those with global economic efficiencies only in mind. The thought of undecipherable (encrypted) communications between millions of highly mobile businesses and individuals trading their goods and services in cyberspace sends a shiver down the spine of tax administrators. Tax administrators also know that despite their protestations about the difficulties likely to be encountered in administering the tax system, the governments will demand they enforce the laws and raise the revenue needed to meet the electoral promises of politicians.

This issue is receiving an unprecedented level of international attention. In the USA, Congress has passed the Tax Freedom Act in response to the proliferation of State taxes on e-commerce. The recently released *Report to Congress* (2000) by the Advisory Commission on Electronic Commerce[9] gave considerable attention to the taxation issue in terms of both its domestic and international implications. Similarly, the European Union,[10] the OECD[11] and various other governments[12] have released reports on e-commerce and its implications for taxation and trade.

Different views have been taken and these can be divided into those who are the immediate beneficiaries of the Internet such as the USA and those who are less significant beneficiaries such as the European Union. In the case of the USA, the

Federal government has declared a moratorium on the taxation of Internet trade as well as removing taxes which act as impediments to the growth of the Internet such as telecommunication taxes.

In contrast, the European Union discussion on the taxation of the Internet has examined the possibility of imposing a bit tax, an indiscriminate tax on digital data flows. The OECD has sought to take a more balanced approach by reviewing how current tax systems can be made to work in the new Internet based global trading environment. This has involved setting up a number of technical advisory groups (TAG) whose task is to discuss key taxation issues in electronic commerce and work towards mutually agreeable solutions.[13]

b) Domestic Compliance with International Obligations

Governments are signatories to a raft of international treaties on issues as diverse as trade, the environment, humanitarian and civil liberties issues, and the conditions of employment for labour. Globalisation inspired by the Internet has the potential to impact on compliance with these undertakings. A person living in one jurisdiction and working in another cannot call upon their own government to ensure their labour rights are protected in another jurisdiction. This might be possible if both countries are members of international organisations with a common set of agreed principles, such as with the International Labour Office (ILO),[14] of which conventions and recommendations seek to promote social justice and human and labour rights.

Founded in 1919 following the signing of the Treaty of Versailles, the ILO became in 1946, the first specialised agency of the UN, with a mandate to formulate international labour standards in the form of conventions and recommendations designed to set minimum standards for basic labour rights.[15] By June 2000, it had 174 member States which clearly gives it scope for making recommendations regarding labour engaged across borders via the Internet. What is probably now required is to give employees in one jurisdiction the power to act locally against employers in another jurisdiction. It is here that the ILO could develop conventions that apply to those non-residents who are tele-working. This obviously has important implications for the regulation of the domestic labour markets because it implies governments accept the presence of a global market for labour services.

c) Domestic Regulation

Equally difficult for government will be enforcing consumer protection laws for its citizens when consumers purchase goods directly from other jurisdictions via the Internet. Similar questions arise in the case of enforcing domestic intellectual property rights in a global Internet based economy. Equally difficult will be attempting to regulate domestically the delivery of financial services via the Internet from other countries.

d) Online Government

One might conclude from much of the above discussion that governments are reactive rather than proactive in their response to the growth of the Internet. This is not the case in their own take up of the Internet as a means of improving their communication with and services to residents.[16] The great strength of the online delivery of government services is the ease with which the full range of government information can be made available immediately it is released at both a national and global level. This has significant benefits from both an efficiency and equity perspective. Not only is online delivery highly cost-effective, it also ensures a common standard of available material which is accessible on demand, searchable and downloadable. This enables comparative information on governments, their taxes, expenditure programmes and legislative framework to be globally accessible. A recognised consequence of this freely available information is the potential for destructive competition between governments, an issue which is attracting increasing international attention.[17]

e) Democratic Institutions

The Internet has been called both the epitome of democracy and the height of anarchy because it empowers individuals. Increased ease of communication through the Internet has meant that public opinions and outrage can be communicated with considerable force and impact through Internet discussion groups, email spams, viruses targeted at government organisations and at worst, by hacking into and the downloading of important information from government computer networks.

The Internet also gives residents in one jurisdiction easy access to governments and politicians in other jurisdictions that enables them to articulate any grievances at a global level. This empowerment of the individual has dramatic implications for political parties and politicians who will become less relevant if they are unable to respond to these new pressure groups. It will also mean that there is greater scope for polarisation within the community on numerous issues – including whether globalisation is preferable to protectionism.

f) Macroeconomic Policy

With globalisation comes pressure to conform to international standards and this is no more prevalent that in relation to macroeconomic management. Governments must now comply with the fiscal and financial rules which have implicitly become the pre-requisites for any one country to engage in global trade. These rules require countries to maintain low inflation and stable prices, a reduced size of government, balance budgets, and a liberal financial environment with minimal protective barriers. This inevitably means constraints on a government's use of fiscal policy for economic management and the scope for central banks to manage monetary policy.

One area that has concerned governments about the growth of global e-commerce has been the apparent development of e-money, particularly in the form of stored value cards (SVC).[18] At issue here is not just what the potential SVCs offer to the growth of the underground economy across international frontiers, but also to the potential loss of seigniorage (see Harper and Slyzys 1996) and the effectiveness of monetary policy.

g)   Barriers to Trade

An important outcome from GATT and more recent WTO negotiations has been a progressive reduction in the level of tariff and non-tariff barriers to trade. Pressures will always exist for increased protectionism but globalisation will inevitably mean such actions are futile. At the root of this call for protectionism is a concern about levels of employment and the vulnerability of those unable to benefit from the new Internet based global economy.

The fact is that increased protectionism will not solve this problem – but an effective safety net for those who could be perceived as the victims of globalisation could assist. While ever there are those who argue for no or a minimal safety net, there will be found those advocating barriers to global commerce.

What the discussion in this part highlights is the challenge to government from the Internet inspired impetus to globalisation. It is clear that the challenge posed is wide-ranging and will extend to issues such as the challenge of globalisation to cultural identity and diversity or to the possibility of a government funding crisis arising from widespread tax evasion using the anonymity of the Internet.

Challenges to Businesses

The economic attraction of the Internet is profound – offering domestic producers and consumers, simple and cheap access to global market information. In effect, it vastly improves consumers' and producers' access to information flows and therefore has the potential to revolutionise the way commodity, capital and labour markets operate.

For the economist, this improved information access means greater scope for improving the economic efficiency of domestic and global markets.[19] Traditionally, countries have been able to limit international competition and their potential global economic efficiency gains by using tariffs, subsidies, quotas, joint venture requirements, labelling rules, and tax holidays to export sectors to name but a few. What the Internet offers is a framework for business (and consumers) to circumvent many of these impediments to trade.

a)   Disintermediation

Disintermediation is the process of removing the middlemen from the production and distribution process. Using the Internet, a producer in one country can go directly to the consumers in another country without having to go through intermediaries or contend with government regulations designed to act as barriers to trade. Not surprisingly, some countries see the Internet as a major threat to their national sovereignty (which it is) and have restricted or monitored Internet access of its citizens.

Typically, these restrictions have been applied by limiting access to telecommunications (or by making it very expensive). However, new technology is being developed that will overcome even this barrier such as a low cost satellite phone network which is accessible from cheap handheld mobile phones. Nations might legislate against their citizens using such phones, but it may be a case of 'catch-us-if-you-can'.

b) Labour Productivity

Of particular significance for business has been the labour productivity gains arising from the adoption and use of B2C and B2B portals. Less warehousing and related support and sales staff has meant that a business can reduce its labour costs without reducing its service. These savings have also been complemented by those arising from the greater the use of intranets – which is effectively a secure company-wide Internet. Intranets facilitate improved communication within a company which in turn results in potential organisational benefits such as improved accounting practices and information flows between divisions, regardless of their global location. Intranet therefore can enable the location of production process in disparate global locations without imposing significant organisational burdens on Parent Corporation.

The Internet and the opportunities it offers for reorganising business practices has been seen as an explanation for the recent US high growth/low inflation phenomena and their can be no doubt that the existence of the Internet is changing the way companies organise and carry on their business. More ominously for governments is that this new globalisation of the production process also provides companies significant scope for tax minimisation through transfer pricing (and more blatantly, tax evasion which is potentially almost undetectable).

Challenges to Individuals

a) The 'Digital Divide'

The explosive growth of the information revolution and in particular, the widespread take up of access to the Internet, has raised the spectre of what the US Department of Commerce's National Telecommunications and Information Administration (NTIA) calls the 'digital divide'.[20] This is the disparity between those individuals (and countries) that have access to computers and especially the Internet, and those without such access. This disparity is not just age and education related, but also results from economic, cultural and geographic differences. Without general access to this information revolution, we are potentially creating a digital revolution underclass that will miss out on new avenues for education, commerce and communication.

In a NTIA report released in July 1999, it noted that the following examples highlight the breadth of the digital divide today:

- Those with a college degree are more than *eight times* as likely to have a computer at home, and nearly *sixteen times* as likely to have home Internet access, as those with an elementary school education.
- A high-income household in an urban area is more than *twenty times* as likely as a rural, low-income household to have Internet access.
- A child in a low-income White family is *three times* as likely to have Internet access as a child in a comparable Black family, and *four times* as likely to have access as children in a comparable Hispanic household.

- A wealthy household of Asian/Pacific Islander descent is nearly *thirteen times* as likely to own a computer as a poor Black household, and nearly *thirty-four times* as likely to have Internet access.
- Finally, a child in a dual-parent White household is nearly *twice* as likely to have Internet access as a child in a White single-parent household; while a child in a dual-parent Black family is almost *four times* as likely to have access as a child in a single-parent Black household.

Fortunately, the falling price of computer hardware and the prevalence of free Internet access is helping to enable those who previously could not afford such access, to now log on to the information revolution. However, just as workers in the seventeenth and eighteenth century cottage industries felt threatened by the coming of the industrial age, there are those who feel threatened by this new information revolution and this could potentially create a divide between those who are and are not computer literate. A part solution is to provide ready access to the Internet through libraries and schools, particularly in poorer regions, but unless all citizens have equal and open access to the Internet, a broad range of learning, employment, commerce and communication opportunities will be unavailable to these non-participants.

A factor potentially exacerbating the 'digital divide' is the possible imposition of taxes on e-commerce. Such taxes have been argued against (see GAO 2000) because they are regressive and potentially impose barriers to increased internet access for those on low incomes. What is clear is that the threat of a growing 'digital divide' is a new social problem which nations must urgently address.

b)   Consumer Sovereignty

As noted earlier, the Internet empowers individuals with dramatically improved access to information about global markets. Not only is this information now more easily accessible through the Internet, it is relatively cheap to obtain.

By searching the World Wide Web directly or by joining news groups or online chat sessions, market information can be obtained at a low cost. As a result, the long held ambition of having markets that are characterised by near perfect information by consumers is one step closer. The subsequent use of spam (or e-mail) wars against those who threaten this new market environment is a clear demonstration of consumer empowerment at a global level in a way that was not possible before the introduction of the World Wide Web. Witness for example, the outrage by users of the Napster website when it was forced to close down following a challenge by the rock band, Metallica to it offering free download of Metallica's songs.[21]

Challenges to International Institutions

What should be clear from the above discussion is that the Internet will provide the catalyst for a dramatic change in the role of international institutions such as the WTO, OECD,[22] IMF, World Bank, and the ILO. New and equally powerful international institutions will need to be developed including agencies charged with responsibilities such as taxation cooperation, the monitoring of environmental degradation, consumer protection and the development of the Internet.

Of particular concern for those who are supportive of the new economy and free trade is the push for 'fair trade' rather than 'free trade'. This, combined with a persistent criticism of the power of the IMF and the World Bank, has seen these institutions on the defensive. The protests at the July 1999 WTO meeting in Seattle, Washington State, over civil issues such as the domestic impact of globalisation, the place of labour and environmental standards in trade agreements and the lack of transparency in the WTO processes, clearly highlighted the challenges ahead for the WTO and for other institutions. The real dilemma is however that while ever developing countries wish to benefit from the advantages of growth, they ultimately have little alternative but to engage in trade.

Conclusion

The considerable international attention currently being given to how governments can work with and harness the new Internet technology is testimony to the rapid, although sometimes grudging recognition, that the Internet is a force with which countries must learn to live and therefore must make work for the collective good. What is clear is that there is currently no consensus between countries about how to respond to the fundamental challenges to currently accepted axioms posed by the Internet. This will be the global challenge of the future brought about by the growth of the Internet.

Notes

[1] See http://www.imf.org and http://www.worldbank.org. Also visit the Asian Development Bank website at http://www.adb.org.

[2] See http://www.wto.org for more information.

[3] There exist a number of important ecommerce gateway websites documenting these reports including http://www.ispo.cec.be/ecommerce/Welcome.html (European Union), http://www.oecd.org/subject/e_commerce/ OECD), http://www.ecommercecommission.org/site map.htm (US), http://e-com.ic.gc.ca/english/index.html, http://www.noie.gov.au (Australia), http://e-com.ic.gc.ca/english/index.html (Canada) and http://www.internetpolicy.org/research/directory.html.

[4] 'Business to Consumer'.

[5] 'Business to business' such as http://www.perfectmarket.com portal.

[6] Numerous Australian examples exist, including http://www.seek.com.au, http://www.mycareer. com.au, http://www.monster.com.au, http://www.jobs.com.au, http://www.job network.gov.au, http://jobsearch.dewrsb.gov.au.

[7] 'Consumer to Business' and 'Consumer to Consumer'.

[8] For example, see http://www.cannex.com.au.

[9] http://www.ecommercecommission.org.

[10] http://www.ispo.cec.be/ecommerce/Welcome.html and http://www.ei.gov.bc.ca/Trade& Export /FTAA-WTO/ecommerce.htm.

[11] http://www.oecd.org/freedoc.htm.

[12] Examples include the Australian Taxation Office which has released two substantial reports on this issue, http://www.ato.gov.au/content.asp?doc=/content/businesses/tidcal.htm.

13 See the OECD TAG outline at http://www.oecd.org//daf/fa/e_com/tag.htm and draft reports at http://www.oecd.org//daf/fa/first_en.htm and http://www.oecd.org//daf/fa/treaties/tce commpay.htm. All ecommerce TAGS were created in January 1999 are due to report in late 2000.

14 See the ILO website http://www.ilo.org for a comprehensive overview of its mission and agenda.

15 See http://www.ilo.org/public/english/about/mandate.htm.

16 Examples include http://www.business.gov.au, http://www.firstgov.gov and http://www. business.gov. See also the US government ecommerce website at http://www.ec.fed.gov.

17 See the discussion that for OECD website on harmful tax practices at http://www.oecd. org//daf/fa/harm_tax/harmtax.htm. Numerous websites also exist enabling interstate tax comparisons such as the http://www.treasury.nsw.gov.au/trpindex.html for Australian states.

18 See http://www.mondex.com.

19 An efficient market is one where social welfare is being maximised given available scarce resources. Put differently, to have a socially efficient market outcome, it must not be possible to make someone (firm/persons) better off without hurting someone else (Pareto efficiency).

20 See http://www.ntia.gov.au, http://www.digitaldivide.gov, http://www.ecommerce.gov, http:// www.firstgov.gov, http://www.digitaleconomy.gov, http://www.ecommerce.gov/apec/, http:// ec.fed.gov and see other links at http://www.doc.gov for other US government publications on electronic commerce and the Internet. For e-commerce actions by other countries, see http://www.ecommerce.gov/internat.htm.

21 Napster.com was forced to close at midnight 28 July 2000 following the imposition of an injunction.

22 The OECD like other international organisations has an active research programme into what they have termed the new economy. In its first report from the OECD's Growth Project http://http://www.oecd.org/subject/growth/.

References

Ricardo, David (1817), *On the Principles of Political Economy and Taxation.*

GAO (2000), 'Sales Taxes: Electronic Commerce Growth Presents Challenges; Revenue Losses Are Uncertain, United States General Accounting Office, GAO Report to Congressional Requesters, June, GAO/GGD/OCE-00-165 at http://www.gao.gov.

Harper, I. and Slizys, N. (1996), 'Measuring Seigniorage in Australia', *Economics Papers*, Vol. 15, No. 2, pp. 20–27.

Chapter 14

Financial Development and Growth: The APEC Experience

Debasis Bandyopadhyay

Introduction

We ask if a member of APEC must choose, under pressure from opposing political groups, between a better national financial system and better access to the global financial system, which policy would stimulate greater economic growth. The chapter compares empirically the relative contributions of those two channels on the growth of per capita income among the members of APEC.

King and Levine (1993a, 1993b) use four special indicators to measure financial development. We identify one of those indicators, the degree of privatisation of the domestic financial intermediaries, to most closely reflect the development of the domestic financial sector. We use a combination of the remaining three indicators to measure how easily the private sector can access the international credit market. We then compare the relative contribution of the two parallel sources of financial development to growth given above. The common experience in APEC includes increased privatisation of banks and insurance companies due to a lower government share in the total assets of the domestic financial intermediaries as well as increased internationalisation of the credit market due to trade liberalisation. In some of the member countries, however, the effect of privatisation seems to be somewhat offset by their regime of 'financial repression'.[1] This regime refers to a system of government policies designed to protect the profit of domestic financial institutions against international competition. These policies increase the domestic interest rate above the internationally available rate. The interest gap may help mobilise capital within the economy but hinders technology diffusion by limiting the number of innovators in the economy. Our regression results corroborate that conjecture. In particular, we find that the contribution of financial development to growth in the APEC economies has come mainly from greater access to the global financial system that presumably has reduced the interest rate gap without reducing the volume of available capital in the economy. We also find that the greater privatisation of domestic assets has only led to a higher rate of saving and a higher rate of accumulation of capital without any significant change in the overall efficiency or the total factor productivity. The latter finding goes well with Solow's (1956) model of growth where a higher rate of saving does not produce higher long run growth. It, however, poses a puzzle for the recently developed models of endogenous growth. Those models link financial development to long run economic growth through its beneficial effect on the total factor productivity in the economy. Examples of such models include Greenwood and Jovanovic (1990), Benceivenga and Smith (1991), Saint-Paul (1992) King and

Levine (1993a) and Pagano (1993). They model different functions of the financial intermediaries such as diversifying liquidity risk, diversifying project risk, efficient financing and evaluating innovative projects that raise the long run growth rate by acting as a kind of 'lubricant' for their respective growth engines (see King and Levine, 1993b). The lubrication effect comes from a more efficient allocation of resources together with a reduced consumption of resources by the financial intermediaries.

This chapter extends that general framework by linking national economic growth to two distinct channels through which entrepreneurs can finance their innovation in a country. The twin channels refer to the national versus global financial systems. Greater efficiency in the national financial system due to privatisation allows innovators to have more capital given the amount that a nation saves. The regime of financial repression that keeps the domestic interest rate at an artificially high level also helps to increase national saving. A greater access to the international credit market, on the other hand, helps the entrepreneurs to finance projects at a lower interest rate. The opportunity of borrowing at a low interest rate augments the relative proportion of innovators[2] and hence the total factor productivity[3] in the economy. In other words, we assume that privatisation fosters efficiency in the capital mobilisation process. Financial repression also adds to capital accumulation but only at a price measured by forgone efficiency of capital. If, however, funds for undertaking innovation can enter relatively more freely from other countries, innovators would feel less constrained by the volume of credit generated by their domestic financial institutions. In addition, access to low interest loans from the international market increases the relative proportion of innovators in the economy. This expedites technology diffusion and thus augments overall efficiency in the economy.

Following introduction we briefly review the theoretical background and describe the data and methodology of the empirical analysis conducted in the chapter. Next we study the main findings and a few concluding remarks which are followed by the complete list of references. Appendix A contains Tables 14.1–14.8 that present a summary of findings from several regressions. Appendix B contains Tables 14.9–14.10, the complete data set used in this chapter.

Theoretical Background

Members of APEC provide an excellent background for this study because of the significant increase in the degree of openness that accompanies various degrees of development in the domestic financial systems of the member nations. It is also helpful to note that the sample period of this study is from 1964 to 1993. Most of these countries were developing countries during this period with a relatively low stock of capital to labour ratio and, hence, a higher marginal product of capital. It is, therefore, expected that funds mainly flow into these countries contributing to their development in conjunction with the funds generated at home by the domestic financial institutions.

Endogenous growth literature highlights various ways a greater privatisation of the domestic financial intermediaries that presumably improves their efficiency may not only foster capital accumulation but also the growth of total factor productivity. King and Levine (1993b) argue that a more efficient financial intermediary sector channels a larger fraction of saving to finance a greater number of innovative projects. This increases the technological advancement rate and the growth rate of final goods. Saint-Paul (1992) emphasises the role of the financial intermediaries in diversifying the risks of investment through technological and financial diversification. In the model the introduction of the financial sector reduces the risk of specialised investment and, hence, increases the expected return from it, encouraging a higher rate of saving and investment in fully specialised capital that raises productivity in the economy. Benceivenga and Smith (1991) highlight the role of diversification of liquidity risk. Financial intermediaries pooled savings together to keep the level of liquid assets that investors prefer to leave to meet their unforeseeable liquidity risk to a minimum possible level. Consequently, it is possible to allocate a higher proportion of funds to finance innovative projects and this raises the total factor productivity or overall efficiency in the economy. Greenwood and Jovanovic (1990) emphasise the benefit of economies of scale in the processing of information on the marginal efficiency of investment and hence growth that the financial intermediaries bring in as they develop over time. Pagano (1993) concludes that a greater efficiency of the financial intermediaries implies a higher proportion of available savings in the economy would be channelled to augment the economy's capital stock.

The regime of financial repression, however, offsets the beneficial effects on the total factor productivity by discouraging potential innovators from undertaking risky ventures. Stiglitz and Weiss (1981) models an economy with a continuum of entrepreneurs where credit rationing arises endogenously and a small increase in interest rate drives a large number of relatively risk-averse entrepreneurs out of the market. If the total factor productivity varies directly with the relative proportion of entrepreneurs in the economy then financial repression would be harmful for growth. Relatively less protection of domestic financial industries through financial repression or more relaxed constraints on international borrowing lowers the domestic interest rate without limiting the total volume of credit that an entrepreneur can borrow to innovate a new technology. Consequently, the total volume of capital as well as the marginal efficiency of capital increases in the economy.

Data and Methodology

The data set for this chapter has been compiled using various data sources as described in this section. The methodology used in this study basically follows that of King and Levine (1993b) but this study focuses on only the members of APEC. Also, unlike King and Levine (1993b) who use thirty-year averages between 1960–1990, we use ten-year averages for the period 1964–1993 to expand the data set and to allow for paradigm shifts over time. After adjusting for the missing information we have a total of thirty-seven data points in the sample consisting of seventeen members of APEC.[4]

Four financial indicators are used to measure financial development.[5] They are as follows: LLY[6] measured by the ratio of liquid liabilities to GDP, BANK[7] measured by the share of the domestic assets of private financial intermediaries in the total domestic assets of the private financial intermediaries and the central bank, PRIVATE[8] measured by the fraction of credit received by private enterprises to total credit received by the government and the public and private enterprises, and PRIVY[9] measured by the ratio of credit received by private enterprises to GDP. The four financial indicators described above help us to examine different aspects of financial development. LLY measures the overall liquidity per unit of GDP. BANK measures the extent of private control over the domestic financial intermediaries. PRIVATE measures the fraction of overall liquidity available to private enterprises. PRIVY measures the private access to the total volume of national and international credit per unit of GDP.

There are four growth indicators:[10] GYP denoting real per capita GDP growth rate,[11] GK denoting real per capita physical capital stock growth rate,[12] INV denoting the ratio of investment to GDP and EFF denoting growth rate of overall of total factor productivity'. Also, we include following King and Levine (1993b) a set of other economic factors[13] to control for the macroeconomic condition in examining the effect of financial development on economic growth rate. They are TRADE[14] measuring degree of openness, GOV[15] measuring the share of government expenditure in GDP, (INF)[16] denoting the inflation rate, LYO denoting the log of per capita GDP level in the initial year and LSCH denoting the log of secondary enrolment rate in the initial year.

There are two parts to the analysis, contemporary and initial-year analysis. Contemporary analysis examines the relationship between the state of financial development and growth rate in the same period of time whereas initial-year analysis examines that of the state of financial development in the first year of each ten-year period and the ten-year average growth rate. The initial year analysis aims at examining the lagged effect of financial development. For this part of the analysis, LLYI, BANKI, PRIVATI, PRIVYI, TRADI, GOVI and INFI that are the initial-year data for LLY, BANK, PRIVATE, PRIVY, TRADE, GOV and INF are constructed.

Main Findings

Table 14.1 shows the correlation coefficients among the four financial indicators. Note that LLY and PRIVY are highly correlated while BANK and PRIVY are very weakly correlated. Recall that LLY is a measure of overall liquidity in proportion to GDP, PRIVY is a measure of the private access to the international credit market and BANK measures the degree of privatisation of the domestic financial sector. The high correlation between LLY and PRIVY, therefore, suggests that the source of a greater volume of liquidity in APEC is greater private access to the international credit market. A low correlation between BANK and PRIVY suggests, however, that greater privatisation is not related to greater private access to the international credit market. It is important to note that BANK relates to the assets of domestic financial inter-mediaries. It neither includes funds directed overseas by domestic financial intermediaries nor that channelled into the domestic economy from overseas financial intermediaries. The other three financial indicators are not confined to measuring financial development in the domestic financial intermediary sector. Since the portion of financial services provided by overseas financial intermediaries is significant in the APEC economies, BANK stands out as a distinctive financial indicator in APEC measuring mainly the state of the domestic financial sector.

We note from Table 14.2 that the correlation coefficients between BANK and growth indicators are significantly different from that between other financial indicators and growth indicators. In particular, BANK is negatively correlated to both the growth rate of per capita income (GYP) and the total factor productivity or the overall efficiency (EFF). Also, the regression results presented in Table 14.3 and Table 14.4 show that BANK does not have a significant effect on GYP and EFF whereas the other financial indicators do. There is weak evidence, however, that BANK positively influences the investment rate (INV) and the resulting growth rate of capital (GK). These findings isolate BANK as a poor predictor of growth in the APEC and stand in sharp contrast with the findings of King and Levine (1993a). King and Levine (1993a), however, sceptically note, 'The variable BANK does not measure to whom the financial system is allocating credit'. Also, governments in many countries attempt to indirectly influence the credit channelling decisions of the domestic banks and distort the allocation of credit even after liberalisation. In this context we note that King and Levine (1993b) also report a weakly negative relationship between their measure of financial development in Latin America and growth. They conclude that the result is due to 'financial liberalisation in a poor regulatory environment' and 'the main channel of transmission from financial development to growth is the efficiency rather than the volume of investment'. Interestingly, we note from Table 14.5 that the amount of loans channelled to government as a percentage to GDP (GL)[17] actually decreases with higher BANK. There is further evidence that a higher BANK also accompanies a higher ratio of Ml to GDP as described in Table 14.6. We consider this as evidence for the fact that government has a greater tendency to resort to seigniorage that increases MI following a greater degree of privatisation. It does so possibly facing the new reality of little chance of getting automatic loans below the market interest rate from the privatised banks to finance its expenditure.

Theoretical models suggest that financial development can take two forms, improvement in efficiency and increase in size. The above discussion suggests that the privatisation of domestic financial intermediaries indicated by BANK possibly measures only the latter. In open economies, greater access to the competitive international financial market induces both a greater volume of financial services as well as a better efficiency of allocation. We argue the financial indicator PRIVY is the best measure of such development among all four financial indicators that we considered. The financial indicator LLY measures the amount of all loans but includes the stock of domestic currency as well. The latter does not correspond to the volume of financial services. Moreover, as noted above if the government has a tendency to finance its expenditure by increasing money supply, LLY would overestimate the beneficial aspect of financial development on growth. The indicator PRIVATE is a measure of the efficiency in allocating funds only with the traditional assumption that a higher portion of loans directed to government represents a lower efficiency in allocating resources. It does not, however, capture the size of the financial development. The indicator PRIVY, on the other hand, is a combination of a size indicator such as LLY as well as an efficiency indicator such as PRIVATE. Moreover, by definition it accounts for only the loans received by private firms and, therefore, excludes the currency part of the liquidity that is related to seigniorage but inherently present in LLY. Precisely, PRIVY can be expressed[18] as PRIVATE *

(LLY-Currency/GDP), where currency represents the part of the liquidity measured by LLY that is primarily utilised by the government.

Empirical findings presented in Table 14.7 show that PRIVY has a significant positive effect on four growth indicators in the APEC countries. The effect is transmitted through three channels. They are; a higher real per capita physical capital growth rate, improved efficiency in other production factors and a higher investment rate. For the initial-year analysis related to PRIVYI, we find that there is lagged effect of PRIVY (i.e. PRIVYI) on GYP, EFF and INV at a 95 per cent confidence interval and that of GK is at a 90 per cent confidence interval. This set of results is attached in Table 14.8. So, it can be concluded that the increase in the ratio of loans channelled to private firms to GDP does causes growth. If PRIVY is an appropriate financial indicator for the open economies such as APEC, then there is evidence that financial development cause growth; their relationship is not simply a correlation.

Concluding Remarks

The above analysis reveals that financial development in APEC has led to economic growth but through a conspicuous channel. A greater privatisation of domestic financial intermediaries may have increased the volume of saving and capital but it has not necessarily increased the overall efficiency in those economies. Despite the inefficiencies in the domestic sector, however, a greater flow of credit through internationally competitive channels has led to growth in efficiency and per capita output. There are a few lessons that we can learn from this experience.

The growth in open economies with open access to the international credit market is not constrained by the state of development of the domestic financial intermediaries. This explains why the domestic financial indicator BANK is a poor predictor of economic growth in APEC. We should not expect, therefore, the long run growth in the Asia-Pacific region to be hampered by the recent crisis in the domestic financial systems in some of the East Asian countries. We should not expect any major problems in the long run as long as the governments of those countries do not limit the private access to international financial intermediaries out of unwise concern for the fate of the domestic financial intermediaries. Such policies would likely lower the efficiency of resource allocation and hinder growth. Unfortunately, however, East Asian members of APEC maintain significant entry barriers to foreign providers of financial services. Consequently, the credit ratings of the domestic banks in those countries depend to a large extent on the quality of the expected support from the State rather than on the quality of banks' balance sheets and profitability. This chapter suggests that a key to economic growth for these East Asian countries is freer access to the international credit market. The international competition would precipitate the quality of domestic financial institutions and hence total factor productivity. The privatisation of domestic financial intermediaries does help an economy to generate a high level of saving and, therefore, to accumulate a country's physical capital stock. In a protected economy, however, the privatisation of the financial institutions fails to inject a sufficient growth spur. Consequently, this policy is not a substitute for free access to the international credit market that expedites a free flow of international capital from other countries. The later policy makes the former much less important in promoting economic growth in the long run. After all, financial development in the world has injected growth in APEC because of its openness while the privatisation of domestic banks has not in itself stimulated economic growth in the same region.

Notes

[1] McKinnon (1973) provides a good reference for the idea of financial repression.

[2] Stiglitz and Weiss (1981) also conclude a positive effect of a lower interest on the total number of innovators in the economy.

[3] Bandyopadhyay (1997) models an economy where growth of total factor productivity due to technology diffusion increases with the relative proportion of the workforce that conducts innovative activities.

[4] We cannot collect any relevant information from Brunei. So, the number of countries involved in this study is seventeen instead of the eighteen members of the APEC countries.

[5] Information of financial indicators are collected from International Financial Statistics (IFS) published by International Monetary Fund (IMF) except Chinese Taipei and Hong Kong. The information of Chinese Taipei is collected from *The Statistical Yearbook of the Republic of China* published by Administrative Yuan of the Republic of China whereas that of Hong Kong is obtained from *Hong Kong Statistics* published by Statistic Department of the Hong Kong Government.

[6] LLY is calculated by dividing the sum of IFS line 34 and line 35 by GDP for each year. Then, ten-year averages are calculated. For Chinese Taipei and Hong Kong, LLY is calculated with dividing M2 by GDP

[7] BANK is calculated by dividing the sum of IFS lines 22a to 22f by the sum of IFS lines 12a to 12f and 22a to 22f. Each data point is constructed by the respective ten-year average. There is no information on BANK for People's Republic of China, Chinese Taipei, Hong Kong and Singapore.

[8] PRIVATE is calculated by dividing IFS line 32d by the sum of IFS line32a to 32d and 32f and ten-year averages are used to construct data points. There is no information on PRIVATE for Hong Kong and Indonesia.

[9] PRIVY is calculated by dividing IFS line 32d by GDP. Ten-year averages are used as data points. There is not enough information to construct PRIVY for Hong Kong and Indonesia.

[10] The information on growth indicators are collected from World Data published by World BANK unless specified.

[11] GYP = [Ln real GDP per capita$_{t+10}$ − Ln real GDP per capita$_{t+1}$]/10.

[12] GK = [Ln real per capita Capital Stock$_{t+10}$ − Ln real per capita Capital Stock$_{t+1}$]/10. The information on real per capita physical capital stock is from Nehru-Dhareshwar (1993), *Rivista de Analysis Economic*, 108 (1): 37–59, hhtp://www.worldbank.org/html/prdgm/grthweb//ddnehdha.htm, for all countries except Chinese Taipei, Hong Kong and Papua New Guniea. For Chinese Taipei, the information is from *The Statistical Yearbook for the Republic of China*. For Hong Kong and Papua New Guniea, their information is collected from King-Levine (1994), 'Capital Fundamentalism, Economic Development and Economic Growth', *Carnegie-Rochester Conference Series on Public Policy*, Vol. 40, http://www.worldbank.org/html/prdmg/grthweb/datasets.htm. Depreciation rate and gross investment data are calculated and collected respectively to facilitate extrapolation of the data. In the process of calculating the depreciation of Mexico, it is found that its annual depreciation rates are 0.00006 and 0.00013 whereas that of the other countries is between 0.05 and 0.22. It is expected that the data on real gross domestic fixed investment

in Mexico is represented in thousands and so it is multiplied by 1,000 for adjustments. Following King-Levine (1993), EFF is constructed by GYP – 0.3 (GK)

[13] These controlling factors are constructed by information from World Data.

[14] TRADE is calculated by dividing the total value of exports and imports by GDP and ten-year average is used to construct data points.

[15] GOV is the amount of government expenditure divided by GDP and ten-year average is used.

[16] INF is constructed by $[1n(_{Dt+10}) - Ln(D_{t+1})]/10$.

[17] The ratio of loans channelled to government to GDP (GL) is constructed by: the ratio of total loans to GDP (TL) – the ratio of loans received by private firms to GDP (PRIVY).

[18] TL is constructed by PRIVY/PRIVATE.

PRIVY = Loans received by private firms

GDP = (Loans received by private firms/Total Loans) * (Total Loans/GDP).

References

Bandyopadhyay, D. (1997), 'Distribution of Human Capital and Economic Growth', Department of Economics Working Paper, No. 174, University of Auckland, Auckland.

Benceivenga, V.R. and B.D. Smith, (1991), 'Financial Intermediation and Endogenous Growth', *The Review of Economic Studies*, Vol. 58, pp. 195–209.

Greenwood, J. and B. Jovanovic, (1990), 'Financial Development, Growth, and the Distribution of Income', *Journal of Political Economy*, Vol. 98, No. 5, pp. 1076–107.

Jappelli, T. and M. Pagano, (1994), 'Savings, Growth and Liquidity Constraints', *Quarterly Journal of Economics*, Vol. 109, pp. 93–109.

King, R.G. and R. Levine, (1993a), 'Finance and Growth – Schumpeter Might be Right', *Quarterly Journal of Economics*, Vol. 108, (Issue 3), pp. 717–37.

King, R.G. and R. Levine, (1993b), 'Finance, Entrepreneurship, and Growth Theory and Evidence', *Journal of Monetary Economics*, Vol. 32, pp. 513–42.

McKinnon, R.I. (1973), *Money and Capital in Economic Development*, Brookings Institution, Washington, DC.

Pagano, M. (1993), 'Financial Markets and Growth – An Overview', *European Economic Review*, Vol. 37 (Issue 2–3), pp. 613–22.

Saint-Paul, G. (1992), 'Technological Choice, Financial Markets and Economic Development', *European Economic Review*, Vol. 36, pp. 763–81.

Solow, R. (1956), 'A Contribution to the Theory of Economic Growth', *Quarterly Journal of Economics*, Vol. 70, pp. 65–94.

Stiglitz, J.E and A. Weiss (1981), 'Credit Rationing in Markets with Imperfect Information', *American Economic Review*, Vol. 71, pp. 393–410.

White, H.L. (1980), 'Heteroskedasticity-consistent Covariance Matrix Estimator and a Direct Test for Heteroskedasticity', *Econometrica*, Vol. 80, pp. 817–38.

Appendix A

Table 14.1   Financial correlations, A

Correlation	LLY	BANK	PRIVATE
BANK	0.500		
PRIVATE	0.218	0.3256	
PRIVY	0.878	0.1145	0.1809

Table 14.2   Financial correlations, B

Correlation	LLY	BANK	PRIVATE	PRIVY
GYP	0.3018	−0.2342	0.4587	0.3756
GK	0.3196	0.0290	0.4476	0.4123
EFF	0.1867	−0.3725	0.3234	0.2250
INV	0.3401	0.1050	0.4741	0.4917

Table 14.3   Sources of economic growth: regression results, A

Dependent	GYP	GYP	GYP	GYP
Independent Financial	LLY	BANK	PRIVA	PRIVY
	0.0298	0.0000	0.03618	0.0448
	(0.0130)	(0.0482)	(0.0175)	(0.0142)
TRADE	0.0061	−0.019	−0.0024	0.0067
	(0.0045)	(0.0204)	(0.0075)	(0.0045)
GOV				
INF				
LYO	−0.0099	−0.0079	−0.0079	−0.0104
	(0.0030)	(0.0051)	(0.0031)	(0.0030)
CONSTANT	0.0939	0.1017	0.06803	0.0915
	(0.024)	(0.0409)	(0.0293)	(0.0247)
Adjusted R2	0.3164	0.0346	0.2837	0.3872
F-statistics	6.5540	1.3110	5.2240	7.7400

(Standard errors)

Table 14.4   Sources of economic growth: regression results, B

Dependent	GYP	GK	EFF	INV
Independent				
BANK	0.0000	0.2175	0.0534	0.2126
	(0.0482)	(0.0785)	(0.0310)	(0.0819)
TRADE	−0.019	0.0129	−0.0247	0.0463
	(0.0204)	(0.0291)	(0.0122)	(0.0346)
GOV				−0.6678
				(0.1646)
INF			−0.1018	
			(0.0474)	
LYO	−0.0079	−0.0391	−0.0046	−0.0066
	(0.0051)	(0.0107)	(0.0030)	(0.0084)
LSCH		0.0618		
		(0.0186)		
CONSTANT	0.1017	−0.0758	0.1165	0.2073
	(0.0409)	(0.0732)	(0.0295)	(0.0673)
Adjusted R^2	0.0346	0.323	0.2464	0.3904
F-statistics	1.3110	4.1010	3.1250	5.1630

(Standard errors)

Table 14.5   Regression results and standard errors, A

GL=0.38494 − 0.31629 BANK

(Standard errors) (0.1180) (0.1360)

Adjusted R^2 = 0.1499   F-statistics = 5.410

Table 14.6   Regression results and standard errors, B

M1 = −0.2645 + 0.4933 BANK

(Standard errors) (0.1049) (0.1182)

Adjusted R^2 = 0.3697   F-statistics = 17.43

Table 14.7   **Private access to international credit market as a source of economic growth, A**

Dependent	GYP	GK	EFF	INV
Independent				
PRIVY	0.0448	0.0763	0.0219	0.1082
	(0.0142)	(0.0265)	(0.0103)	(0.0290)
TRADE	0.0067	0.0242	−0.0006	0.0381
	(0.0045)	(0.0085)	(0.0033)	(0.0093)
GOV				
INF				
LYO	−0.0104	−0.0116	−0.0069	−0.0121
	(0.0030)	(0.0056)	(0.0022)	(0.0061)
CONSTANT	0.0915	0.0978	0.0622	0.2879
	(0.0247)	(0.0459)	(0.0179)	(0.0503)
Adjusted R 2	0.3872	0.3897	0.2221	0.5396
F-statistics	7.7400	7.8100	4.0460	13.5020

(standard errors)

Table 14.8   **Private access to international credit market as a source of economic growth, B**

Dependent	GYP	GK	EFF	INV
Independent				
PRIVYI	0.0417	0.0508	0.0220	0.0860
	(0.0149)	(0.0284)	(0.0099)	(0.0316)
TRADI		0.0267		0.0404
		(0.0095)		(0.0105)
GOVI				
INFI				
LYO	−0.0106	−0.0109	−0.0068	−0.0120
	(0.0032)	(0.0060)	(0.0021)	(0.0067)
CONSTANT	0.10309	0.1078	0.06272	0.3037
	(0.0256)	(0.0490)	(0.0170)	(0.0546)
Adjusted R 2	0.2995	0.2912	0.2537	0.4475
F-statistics	7.8410	5.3830	6.440	9.6360

(standard errors)

Appendix B

Table 14.9   Data set for contemporary analysis

COUNTRY	LLY*	BANK*	PRIVATE*	PRIVY*	GYP[+]	GK[x]
AUSTRALIA I	0.4974	0.9316	0.5551	0.2529	0.0260	0.0343
AUSTRALIA II	0.4239	0.9075	0.6728	0.2898	0.0126	0.0227
AUSTRALIA III	0.5101	0.9582	0.8276	0.5408	0.0123	0.0138
CANADA I	0.3770	0.9696	0.7556	0.2529	0.0325	0.0293
CANADA II	0.4582	0.9314	0.8608	0.4195	0.0139	0.0384
CANADA III	0.4825	0.9618	0.8765	0.4895	0.0083	0.0271
CHILE III	0.7236		0.9792	0.8042	0.0713	0.0748
CHINA III	0.3908	0.4404	0.6649	0.8464	0.0465	0.0198
CHINESE TAIPEI I	0.4020		0.7183	0.3186	0.0638	0.1107
CHINESE TAIPEI II	0.6501		0.7863	0.5740	0.0560	0.0883
CHINESE TAIPEI III	1.2540		0.8449	0.9834	0.0588	0.1582
HONG KONG I	0.7266				0.0617	0.0392
HONG KONG II	0.8218				0.0542	0.0618
HONG KONG III	1.7819				0.0454	0.0464
INDONESIA III	0.3146	0.6899	0.0370	0.0639	0.0179	0.2877
JAPAN I	0.7645	0.9373	0.9213	0.8282	0.0702	0.1087
JAPAN II	0.8522	0.9358	0.8372	0.8690	0.0266	0.0508
JAPAN III	1.0563	0.9469	0.8569	1.1352	0.0291	0.0462
KOREA I	0.2530	0.7449	0.8678	0.2481	0.0727	0.1082
KOREA II	0.3282	0.7623	0.8843	0.3843	0.0568	0.1001
KOREA III	0.3748	0.7993	0.9543	0.5269	0.0652	0.0892
MALAYSIA III	0.7046	0.9723	0.8849	0.6775	0.0333	0.1268
MEXICO III	0.2459	0.7905	0.5214	0.1844	−0.0034	0.0097
NEW ZEALAND I	0.2269	0.7834	0.7765	0.1153	0.0174	0.0227
NEW ZEALAND II	0.2670	0.7994	0.6945	0.1723	0.0035	0.0245
NEW ZEALAND III	0.4927	0.9178	0.8811	0.4748	0.0041	0.0367
PHILIPPINES III	0.3176	0.7025	0.7451	0.1931	−0.0020	0.0056
PAPUA NEW GUINEA II	0.2935	0.9259	0.9403	0.1598	−0.0136	−0.0006
PAPUA NEW GUINEA III	0.3557	0.8801	0.8820	0.2759	0.0272	−0.0085
SINGAPORE I	0.6118		2.4016	0.4335	0.0819	0.1341
SINGAPORE II	0.6343		1.8501	0.6795	0.0614	0.0932
SINGAPORE III	0.8364		1.2483	0.8488	0.0492	0.1607
THAILAND II	0.3813	0.7910	0.6920	0.3005	0.0385	0.0553
THAILAND III	0.6546	0.8895	0.8260	0.5724	0.0628	0.1279
UNITED STATES I	0.6462	0.8735	0.7365	0.5516	0.0236	0.0224
UNITED STATES II	0.6342	0.9000	0.8033	0.6374	0.0135	0.0140
UNITED STATES III	0.6602	0.9115	0.8326	0.6932	0.0133	0.0175

I   indicates the period of 1964 to 1973
II   indicates the period of 1974 to 1983
III indicates the period of 1984 to 1993

Sources:* International Financial Statistics by International Monetary Fund;
            + World Data published by World Bank;
            x King-Levine data set or Nehru-Dhareshwar data set.

EFF[+]	INV[+]	TRADE[+]	GOV[+]	INF[+]	LYO[+]	LSCH[+]	M1/GDP
0.0157	0.2680	0.2947	0.1536	0.0520	8.9834	4.1271	0.1752
0.0058	0.2454	0.3194	0.1713	0.0865	9.2412	4.4659	0.1252
0.0081	0.2282	0.3579	0.1780	0.0422	9.4026	4.5433	0.1251
0.0237	0.2392	0.4140	0.2116	0.0416	9.0282	4.0254	0.1817
0.0023	0.2358	0.4998	0.2136	0.0735	9.3759	4.5109	0.1237
0.0002	0.2060	0.5335	0.2015	0.0271	9.5656	4.6347	0.1494
0.0489	0.3627	0.3446	0.0918	0.0753	5.1912	3.6109	0.0829
0.0406	0.2266	0.5848	0.1057	0.1660	7.2762	4.1897	
0.0306	0.2565	0.4930	0.2009	0.0453	7.1846	3.5978	
0.0295	0.3159	0.8633	0.2159	0.0727	7.9217	4.1503	
0.0114	0.3314	0.7926	0.2603	0.0685	8.3248	4.3581	
0.0500	0.2440	1.6700	0.0781	0.0457	7.6610	3.3673	0.2899
0.0356	0.2902	1.7551	0.0758	0.0764	8.2771	3.8918	0.1931
0.0315	0.2623	2.4647	0.0701	0.0721	8.8960	4.2767	0.1864
0.4864	0.0975	0.0689	5.9733	3.6636	0.1086		
0.0376	0.3569	0.1958	0.1090	0.0535	8.8157	4.4067	0.3160
0.0114	0.3175	0.2603	0.1012	0.0398	9.4940	4.5109	0.3166
0.0152	0.3013	0.2016	0.0905	0.0119	9.7920	4.5433	0.2897
0.0402	0.2247	0.3676	0.1729	0.1101	6.3975	3.5553	0.1038
0.0267	0.2978	0.6784	0.1355	0.1431	7.1981	4.0254	0.1083
0.0385	0.3294	0.6487	0.1019	0.0552	7.8364	4.5109	0.0955
−0.0048	0.3020	1.3327	0.1493	0.0160	7.5864	3.9703	0.2141
−0.0063	0.2130	0.3018	0.0851	0.3490	7.5437	3.9703	0.0824
0.0106	0.2492	0.4576	0.1543	0.0563	9.0189	4.3175	0.1752
−0.0038	0.2554	0.5896	0.1677	0.1182	9.2332	4.3944	0.1249
−0.0069	0.2299	0.5728	0.1614	0.0592	9.3051	4.4543	0.2245
−0.0036	0.2011	0.5684	0.0862	0.0859	6.4333	4.2195	0.0801
−0.0134	0.2379	0.9056	0.2902	0.0663	6.8857	2.4849	0.1169
0.0297	0.2319	0.9319	0.2193	0.0312	6.7226	2.3979	0.1123
0.0416	0.2997	2.4060	0.1159	0.0332	7.3969	3.8067	0.2827
0.0334	0.4331	3.5473	0.1118	0.0387	8.2634	3.9512	0.2565
0.0010	0.3921	3.4056	0.1131	0.0245	8.8977	4.2627	0.2328
0.0219	0.2749	0.4744	0.1151	0.0608	6.3038	3.2581	0.1424
0.0244	0.3419	0.6517	0.1054	0.0387	6.7277	3.4340	0.1075
0.0169	0.1961	0.1091	0.2075	0.0396	9.3940	4.2485	0.2400
0.0093	0.1981	0.1825	0.1798	0.0658	9.6167	4.4188	0.1791
0.0081	0.1816	0.2017	0.1774	0.0288	9.7654	4.5433	0.1727

Table 14.10   Data set for initial-year analysis

COUNTRY	LLYI*	BANKI*	PRIVATI*	PRIVYI*	GYP+	GKx
AUSTRALIA I	0.5261	0.9071	0.4681	0.2180	0.0260	0.0343
AUSTRALIA II	0.4571	0.9602	0.6669	0.2842	0.0126	0.0227
AUSTRALIA III	0.4031	0.9366	0.7460	0.3116	0.0123	0.0138
CANADA I	0.3569	0.9818	0.7240	0.2163	0.0325	0.0293
CANADA II	0.4065	0.9533	0.8494	0.3238	0.0139	0.0384
CANADA III	0.4432	0.9320	0.8678	0.4527	0.0083	0.0271
CHILE III	0.5193		0.9790	0.6377	0.0713	0.0748
CHINA III	0.3805	0.4609	0.7463	1.0865	0.0465	0.0198
CHINESE TAIPEI I	0.3144		0.6258	0.2112	0.0638	0.1107
CHINESE TAIPEI II	0.4658		0.7990	0.4624	0.0560	0.0883
CHINESE TAIPEI III	0.9109		0.8134	0.6991	0.0588	0.1582
HONG KONG I	0.6572				0.0617	0.0392
HONG KONG II	0.7294				0.0542	0.0618
HONG KONG III	1.2245				0.0454	0.0464
INDONESIA III	0.1889	0.5748			0.0370	0.0639
JAPAN I	0.7030	0.9308	0.9436	0.7848	0.0702	0.1087
JAPAN II	0.7946	0.9265	0.9120	0.8650	0.0266	0.0508
JAPAN III	0.9209	0.9441	0.8249	0.9562	0.0291	0.0462
KOREA I	0.0895	0.5465	0.7222	0.0918	0.0727	0.1082
KOREA II	0.3246	0.7228	0.9046	0.3783	0.0568	0.1001
KOREA III	0.3357	0.7891	0.8963	0.4644	0.0652	0.0892
MALAYSIA III	0.5765	0.9183	0.8312	0.5277	0.0333	0.1268
MEXICO III	0.2834	0.5761	0.3423	0.1150	−0.0034	0.0097
NEW ZEALAND I	0.2543	0.6345	0.7096	0.1173	0.0174	0.0227
NEW ZEALAND II	0.2598	0.7708	0.8149	0.1540	0.0035	0.0245
NEW ZEALAND III	0.2755	0.8137	0.9706	0.1993	0.0041	0.0367
PHILIPPINES III	0.2782	0.6748	0.6223	0.2447	−0.0020	0.0056
PAPUA NEW GUINEA II	0.3077	0.9830	0.9651	0.1463	−0.0136	−0.0006
PAPUA NEW GUINEA III	0.3521	0.9799	1.0064	0.2368	0.0272	−0.0085
SINGAPORE I	0.5738		3.2848	0.3823	0.0819	0.1341
SINGAPORE II	0.5520		2.6121	0.5454	0.0614	0.0932
SINGAPORE III	0.6772		1.0781	0.8891	0.0492	0.1607
THAILAND II	0.3176	0.8186	0.7467	0.2279	0.0385	0.0553
THAILAND III	0.5444	0.8141	0.6744	0.4394	0.0628	0.1279
UNITED STATES I	0.6655	0.8713	0.7029	0.5104	0.0236	0.0224
UNITED STATES II	0.6275	0.8933	0.7990	0.6494	0.0135	0.0140
UNITED STATES III	0.6579	0.9142	0.8139	0.6674	0.0133	0.0175

I   indicate the period of 1964 to 1973
II   indicate the period of 1974 to 1983
III indicate the period of 1984 to 1993

Sources:* International Financial Statistics by International Monetary Fund;
       + World data published by World Bank;
       x King-Levine data set or Nehru-Dhareshwar data set.

EFF+	INV+	TRADI+	GOVI+	INFI+	LYO+	LSCH+
0.0157	0.2680	0.3153	0.1427	0.0274	8.9834	4.1271
0.0058	0.2454	0.3162	0.1619	0.1706	9.2412	4.4659
0.0081	0.2282	0.3480	0.1762	0.0544	9.4026	4.5433
0.0237	0.2392	0.3786	0.2019	0.0266	9.0282	4.0254
0.0023	0.2358	0.4980	0.2152	0.1378	9.3759	4.5109
0.0002	0.2060	0.5363	0.2041	0.0309	9.5656	4.6347
0.0489	0.3627	0.2281	0.0921	0.0454	5.1912	3.6109
0.0406	0.2266	0.4958	0.1334	0.1190	7.2762	4.1897
0.0306	0.2565	0.3356	0.1797	0.0497	7.1846	3.5978
0.0295	0.3159	0.8608	0.1571	0.2939	7.9217	4.1503
0.0114	0.3314	0.8830	0.2215	0.1007	8.3248	4.3581
0.0500	0.2440	1.5631	0.0798	0.0516	7.6610	3.3673
0.0356	0.2902	1.7112	0.0763	0.1127	8.2771	3.8918
0.0315	0.2623	2.0918	0.0748	0.0940	8.8960	4.2767
0.0179	0.2877	0.5082	0.1006	0.0794	5.9733	3.6636
0.0376	0.3569	0.1913	0.1303	0.0488	8.8157	4.4067
0.0114	0.3175	0.2795	0.0976	0.1840	9.4940	4.5109
0.0152	0.3013	0.2726	0.0993	0.0228	9.7920	4.5433
0.0402	0.2247	0.1918	0.1928	0.2846	6.3975	3.5553
0.0267	0.2978	0.6686	0.1471	0.2428	7.1981	4.0254
0.0385	0.3294	0.7181	0.1114	0.0298	7.8364	4.5109
−0.0048	0.3020	1.0663	0.1591	0.0540	7.5864	3.9703
−0.0063	0.2130	0.2693	0.0875	0.4636	7.5437	3.9703
0.0106	0.2492	0.4466	0.1499	0.0395	9.0189	4.3175
−0.0038	0.2554	0.5546	0.1535	0.0293	9.2332	4.3944
−0.0069	0.2299	0.6998	0.1625	0.0788	9.3051	4.4543
−0.0036	0.2011	0.4923	0.0807	0.4276	6.4333	4.2195
−0.0134	0.2379	0.8673	0.3313	0.0854	6.8857	2.4849
0.0297	0.2319	0.9259	0.2408	0.0738	6.7226	2.3979
0.0416	0.2997	2.5631	0.1024	0.0258	7.3969	3.8067
0.0334	0.4331	3.1909	0.1172	0.1412	8.2634	3.9512
0.0010	0.3921	3.2496	0.1076	0.0062	8.8977	4.2627
0.0219	0.2749	0.4556	0.0916	0.1858	6.3038	3.2581
0.0244	0.3419	0.4807	0.1289	0.0144	6.7277	3.4340
0.0169	0.1961	0.0966	0.2108	0.0178	9.3940	4.2485
0.0093	0.1981	0.1728	0.1865	0.0816	9.6167	4.4188
0.0081	0.1816	0.1868	0.1765	0.0394	9.7654	4.5433

Chapter 15

Strategic Management of Operating Exposure

Robert Grant and Luc Soenen

F31

G30   F23

Introduction

We identify operating exposure as the most important and difficult to manage component of exchange risk. Our model identifies three components of foreign exchange exposure: direct operating exposure, the market demand effect, and the competitive effect. The size and relative importance of these components depends critically upon international market structure and firm strategies. We derive implications for managing foreign exchange exposure. Internationalisation of the economies of most nations has meant that companies are increasingly subject to the risk associated with exchange rate movements. Despite consensus over the importance of exchange rate risk, the ability of companies to effectively manage these risks has been limited by confusion over the definition of such risk and the appropriate tools for managing exchange rate risk. In terms of both defining and controlling exchange rate risk, a fundamental distinction is between accounting exposure and economic exposure (Lessard and Lightstone 1986, Oxelheim and Wihlborg 1987). Accounting exposure arises from the need to report the firm's financial condition and results in a common currency. The financial statements of foreign operations are converted from the local currencies involved to the reporting currency.[1] Accounting exposure is the variance in the book value of the firm resulting from changes in the home currency value of foreign currency-denominated assets and liabilities. Although accounting exposure has received considerable attention in the international finance literature, its relevance to managerial decision making is doubtful. Since management's goal is supposedly to operate in the interests of its owners by maximising the market value of the firm, the basic problem with accounting exposure is that book values bear little relation to shareholders' wealth maximisation.

From the viewpoint of the wealth-maximising firm, economic exposure, defined as the sensitivity of a firm's economic value to changes in the exchange rate (Oxelheim and Wihlborg (1987), is the relevant exchange rate risk. Since the market value of the firm is the discounted value of net cash flows to the firm, the critical issue in determining economic exposure is establishing the impact of exchange rate movements on net cash flow. Economic exposure comprises two components: transaction and operating exposure. Transaction exposure is the fluctuation in the home currency value of foreign currency-denominated contracts for which the price has been fixed. Operating exposure is the fluctuation in future operating cash flows (whether denominated in home or foreign currencies) in response to variations in real exchange rates. For most firms, operating exposure is far more important source of risk than transaction exposure.

While transaction exposure is short-term, relating to the period between entering and settling contracts, operating exposure affects any firm with foreign buyers, suppliers or competitors (or whose domestic suppliers or customers have foreign suppliers, buyers or competitors) through its impact on sales revenues and input costs. Operating risk arises not only because revenues and costs are denominated in different currencies (direct operating exposure), but also from the fact that costs of competing firms are in different currencies (competitive operating exposure).

While techniques for managing accounting and transaction exposure are well-established (see, for instance, Soenen 2000), approaches to managing operating exposure are less developed. Actually, this short-term focus on foreign exchange management has been documented in the Wharton Survey of Derivatives Usage by US Non-Financial Firms. Bodnar, Hayt, and Marston (1996), report that firms worry most about the impact of financial risk on current cash flows and less about distant cash flows. However, the more fundamental question of preserving the firm's overall earnings potential requires a long-term view of exchange risk management. Management needs to concentrate on the management of the firm's operating exposure. An important feature of managing operating risk is its strategic character, because operating risk is associated with a stream of transactions rather than individual transactions, the time horizon for hedging extends beyond that provided by conventional hedging instruments. As a result, managing operating exposure raises organisational issues. The strategic aspect of exchange risk management means that it cannot be relegated to the firm's treasury department. Managing exchange rate risk becomes a general management issue.

The purpose of this chapter is to investigate the determinants of operating exposure arising from unpredictable foreign exchange movements. We place particular emphasis on the relationship between market structure and operating exposure. While the competitive structure of international markets has been generally recognised as important in determining the extent and characteristics of exchange rate risk, there has been little in the way of systematic analysis of the relationship between market structure and exchange rate risk. Having analysed the determinants of operating exposure, we then develop a set of propositions concerning the management of these risks. Our research contributes to the analysis and management of exchange risk in two ways. First, it provides an analysis of exchange rate risk that incorporates a range of different market structures and assumptions about pricing policy and, in doing so, extends the work of Von Ungern-Stenberg and Von Weizsacker (1990) and Luehrman (1990). Second, it links the analysis of exchange rate risk to strategies for managing this risk.

Before analysing the determinants of operating exposure and drawing predictions for its strategic management, let us first explain the importance of a strategic approach to managing operating exposure by discussing the shortcomings of conventional hedging procedures.

Inadequacies of Financial Hedging

The international financial literature is increasingly coming round to the view that, for the purpose of managing economic exposure, conventional hedging techniques are of dubious value, and may even be value-reducing (Lessard and Lightstone 1990, Grant and Soenen 1991). There are four main arguments here:

a) The Dangers of Incomplete Hedging

Conventional approaches to exchange risk management focus upon hedging against accounting and transaction exposures, but such techniques provide no solution to operating exposure. For example, forward purchases of yen by General Motors to cover its payments for car imports from Japan provide a hedge for GM's transaction exposure but not against operating exposure. Any persistent change in the value of the yen relative to the dollar changes GM's competitive position vis-à-vis its Japanese rivals thus impacting GM's cash flows. Indeed, in this case, hedging transaction risk exacerbates GM's operating exposure to yen/US dollar volatility. GM's sourcing of cars in Japan provides a partial operating hedge against changes in its competitive position in the US market relative to Japanese automobile makers. By hedging its yen position, GM defeats that natural hedge, in the short term at least.

Similarly, hedging accounting exposure by means of financing foreign assets in the local currency may increase operating exposure. The subsidiaries of the Royal Dutch/Shell Group are financed mainly by dollar loans. Since the currency of reporting is the British pound and the Dutch guilder, any appreciation in the dollar causes a translation loss. However, the economic exposure of the Group is not determined by the currency of denomination of its assets but by the currency of price determination for the products generated by the assets. As the prices of oil and oil products are set in US dollars, financing foreign activities with dollar loans helps to hedge operating exposure: debt servicing in dollars partly offsets dollar-denominated revenues. Financing in any other currency might reduce accounting risk but would create operating exposure.

Operating risk may exist where the firm has no accounting or transaction exposure, and may even arise where a firm has no international transactions. Until recently, Harley-Davidson Inc. had limited international activity; nevertheless, a major determinant of its competitive position relative to its Japanese rivals was the yen/US dollar exchange rate. As we shall see, for many firms this competitive exposure is the main component of operating exposure.

b) Nominal Versus Real Exchange Rate Movements

One of the oldest theorems in international finance, purchasing power parity (PPP), implies that gains or losses from exchange rate changes tend over time to be offset by differences in inflation rates. If a company's revenues and expenses increase in accordance with the general price level, real profits should be left unchanged, making exchange risk unimportant in the long run. Hence, conventional financial hedging against operating risk encounters the problem that the relevant exchange rate for hedging operating exposure is the real exchange rate. If nominal exchange rates adjust to offset differences in inflation rates between countries – thus maintaining purchasing power parities – then operating exposure is non-existing and hedging is unnecessary. Because nominal exchange rate movements are closely correlated with inflation rates, real exchange rates are far more stable than nominal rates. So long as the company makes purchases and sales on a spot basis and avoids long-term contracts fixed in terms of foreign currencies, operating risk is modest. However, by attempting to hedge nominal exchange rates, that company would open itself to considerable risk.

There is an extensive empirical literature (for instance, Roll 1979 and Protopapakis and Stoll 1983) that documents deviations from PPP, i.e. changes in the real value of currencies. Adler and Lehman (1983) and Abuaf and Jorion (1990), among others, have reported significant long run deviations from PPP. Hence, if the firm's planning horizon is shorter than what is needed for PPP to hold, the firm is exposed to exchange risk. The firm's relative competitive position changes as changes in the nominal exchange rate are not offset by the difference in inflation rates between the two countries. The firm must, therefore, cope with risk arising from both changes in the general price level and in relative prices of specific inputs and outputs. Since financial derivatives exist in individual commodities but not in a representative basket of goods and services, it is not easy to hedge against changes in real exchange rates.

c) The Problem of Undefined Transactions Extending Long into the Future

The ability of the firm to use financial instruments to hedge cash flows runs into the problem that the financial instruments are specific with regard to amount and timing, while cash flows are uncertain and extend far into the future. The use of short-term hedging instruments to hedge continuous cash flows does not reduce operating risk; it simply lags it by the period of the hedge. In general, hedging is not useful for activities for which the firm's planning and action horizon extends beyond that of the hedging instrument. Consider a US firm that is always importing finished products from Japan for distribution in the US. Assume that the yen-payables are on terms net 30 days. Here, the firm is faced with a continuous cash outflow denominated in yen. A financial hedge consist of buying yen forward, going long in yen futures, buying yen calls or writing yen puts, or creating a yen deposit. As the exposure is long-term, one would have to repeatedly roll over the hedge. When the yen appreciates against the US, as has been the case since mid-1985, both spot and forward rates will rise. Each successive forward yen purchase comes at a higher dollar price, making the relief provided by hedging at best temporary and at worst illusory (Soenen 1991). To the extent the forward exchange rate is an unbiased estimator of the future spot rate, if we enter into a financial hedge or not, the firm will on average end up with the same exchange rate, that is the actual future spot rate. Although the financial hedge takes care of the short-term exposure (i.e. transaction exposure), repeated hedges do not reduce the exchange risk for the firm in the long run.

d) Risk Hedging and Shareholder Value

Finally, in a world of efficient currency and securities markets there is doubt as to whether any kind of hedging activity creates value for shareholders. If shareholders can hold internationally-diversified portfolios, or if they themselves can hedge the exchange risks associated with their shareholdings, then there is no reason why hedging creates value for the shareholder. Stated in terms of the capital asset pricing model, if share prices are determined by a firm's expected return and its non-diversifiable (systematic) risk, then activities such as exchange rate hedging which only reduce diversifiable (unsystematic) risk, do not increase the share price. Indeed, to the extent that hedging activities by firms incur administrative and financial costs in excess of the cost of comparable hedging activities by institutional or individual investors, then hedging by a company actually reduces its market value.

Once we introduce imperfections into financial markets, then these arguments do not necessarily hold. Suppose a firm faces a borrowing constraint. An adverse movement in the exchange rate that is sustained over several years may permanently impair a firm's competitive position. Consider the weighted average of the foreign exchange value of the US dollar against the currencies of a broad group of US trading partners (Figure 15.1).

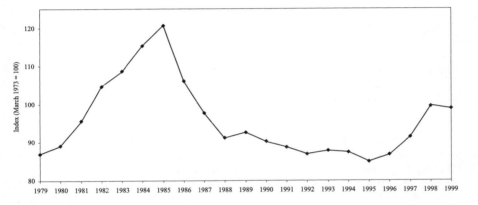

Figure 15.1 Real value of the US dollar

Over-valuation of the US dollar (relative to its PPP rate of exchange) extending from 1980 to 1985 depressed the net cash flows of many export-dependent US firms. For some, accompanying loss of market share and reduced investment in R&D and facilities may also have had a permanent impact on future cash flows. For instance, Caterpillar, the leading maker of earthmoving equipment, was driven to the brink of bankruptcy at that time because of the strength in the US dollar versus the yen (especially Komatsu) and European currencies (Poclain, Liebherr). In the same way, the current strength of the British pound has made it very hard for any manufacturer in the UK to compete in the global arena. This was recently announced by several leading Japanese firms, for example, Toshiba has described the level of sterling as 'unbearable' and warned its continued strength could force the closure of its last UK manufacturing base (Ibison and Brown 2000). In the same *Financial Times* article, it is reported that Komatsu, the construction equipment manufacturer said that it was considering siting a new plant in the euro-zone instead of the UK, while Nissan recently urged the British government to move towards euro membership.

Moreover, even if it is possible for shareholders to control exchange rate risk by means of holding internationally-diversified portfolios, such diversification opportunities may not be available to other stakeholders – including employees, distributors, customers and suppliers.

Determinants of Operating Exposure

The value of the firm is the sum of the present values of its expected future net operating cash flows converted to the home currency. These operating net cash flows correspond to net profits from operations: operating profits net of interest and tax, but including depreciation and other accounting items not involving actual cash flows. We shall refer to net operating cash flows as 'profits'. Thus the present value of the firm at time 0, V_0, is given by:

$$V_0 = \sum_{t=0}^{T} \Pi_t\, r^{-t} \tag{1}$$

where: T = the last (termination) period of the firm
$\quad\quad\ \ r$ = the rate of discount over the period
$\quad\quad\ \ \Pi_t$ = net operating cash flow during period t, after conversion to the home currency.

We have defined economic exposure as the sensitivity of a firm's net operating cash flows to movements in the exchange rate between its home currency and foreign currency i. Following Hodder (1982) and Oxelheim and Wihlborg (1987), we can measure this exchange rate risk in a manner analogous to the way in which the capital asset pricing model measures asset risk. The firm's cash flow comprises a portfolio of cash flows in different currencies. The contribution of exchange rate fluctuations to fluctuations in the firm's cash flow can be measured as the covariance between the exchange rate (e_{it}) and the net cash flow (Π_t) relative to the variance of the cash flow:

$$\frac{\text{cov}(e_{it}\Pi_t)}{\text{var}(\Pi_t)} \tag{2}$$

where e_{it} = exchange rate of currency i in terms of the home currency at time t.

However, equation (2) simply defines economic exposure and provides a formula for its estimation. In order to identify methods for managing risk, we need to understand the covariance between e_{it} and Π_t i.e. the relationship between changes in the exchange rate and changes in net cash flows, that is:

$$\frac{\Delta\Pi_t}{\Delta e_{it}} \text{ which, in the limit, } = \frac{d\Pi_t}{de_{it}}$$

Note that our definition of economic exposure includes both transaction and operating exposure, i.e. net cash flow (Π) includes both contractual and non-contractual transactions. To focus attention on operating exposure, we shall assume that all transactions are non-contractual.

Since net cash flow in each equals revenues less costs, the key issue is to determine how exchange rate changes influence the margin between revenues and costs. Thus, ignoring taxes, profit in period t in terms of the home currency may be expressed:

$$\Pi_t = \sum \left(p_{it} \cdot q_{it} - c_{it} \cdot q_{it} \right) e_{it} \tag{3}$$

where: q_{it} = quantity of goods sold in period t denominated in currency i
p_{it} = unit price charged for goods sold during time period t denominated in currency i
c_{it} = cost per unit of output incurred in currency during period t

The demand function facing the firm relates the quantity of goods sold to the price set by the firm and the prices set by other firms (p'_{it}). Following Henderson and Quandt (1971), we dichotomise the impact of price on quantity demanded into a constant market share effect that shows the effect of changes in the firm's price where the price differential with competitors remains constant, and a market share effect which shows changes in quantity demanded arising from changes in price differentials causing shifts in market share.

$$\Delta q_{it} = Q_{it} \left[\Delta p_{it}, \Delta \left(p_{it} - p'_{it} \right) \right] \tag{4}$$

where p'_{it} = the price charged by competitors in country i.

The impact of a change in the value of currency i on the firm's profits can be found by taking the partial derivative of equation (3) with respect to the rate of exchange, e_i (for simplicity, we shall ignore the time subscripts):

$$\frac{d\Pi}{de_i} = p_i q_i - c_i q_i + e_i \frac{\delta q_i}{\delta e_i} \cdot \frac{\delta p_i}{\delta e_i} + e_i \frac{\delta q_i}{\delta(p_i - p'_i)} \frac{\delta(p_i - p'_i)}{\delta e_i} \tag{5}$$

$$\frac{d\Pi}{de_i} = p_i q_i - c_i q_i + E_{qi,pi} \cdot E_{pi,ei} \cdot q_i + e_i \frac{\delta q_i}{\delta(p_i - p'_i)} \frac{\delta(p_i - p'_i)}{\delta e_i} \tag{6}$$

| direct operating exposure | market demand effect | competitive effect |

where: $E_{qi,pi}$ = the price elasticity of demand for the firm's sales in currency area i, and
$E_{pi,ei}$ = the elasticity of the firm's price in country i with respect to the domestic currency price of cone unit of currency i.

The impact of exchange rate changes upon the profitability of the firm therefore depends upon the following factors:

a) Direct Operating Exposure

The direct impact of exchange rate changes upon profit depends upon the extent of imbalance in the firm's cash inflows and outflows in each currency. Thus, consider the first two arguments in equation (6). If $(p_i q_i - c_i q_i) > 0$, the firm has a long position in currency i, implying that, in the absence of other factors, $d\prod/de_i, > 0$, i.e. a strengthening of the currency increases the firm's profits in terms of its own currency. This situation would exist for any firm which exports from its home base to another country. To a much smaller degree, it would also exist for a 'multi-domestic' firm – one that comprises independent national subsidiaries, each producing for its home market. To the extent that the subsidiary i is profitable, an increase in currency i's exchange rate has no effect upon the subsidiary's profits as measured in currency i, but they are converted to the home currency at a higher rate.

Where $(p_i q_i - c_i q_i) < 0$, the firm has a short position in currency i for period t implying that, in the absence of other factors, $d\prod/de_i < 0$, that is, a strengthening of currency i reduces the firm's profits. This situation would exist for a company sourcing its products or raw materials from country i. The greater the proportion of the firm's costs incurred in country i, the greater is the reduction in profits from a rise in e_i.

b)   The Market Demand Effect

The 'market demand effect' shows the impact of changes in price upon quantity demanded in the absence of any competitive effects. The starting point for predicting the direction and magnitude of this effect is examination of the impact of an exchange rate change upon the prices charged by the firm. This depends upon the pricing policy of the firm. To establish the range of $E_{pi,ei}$ consider three situations:

i)   If the firm is a price-follower, where the price leaders are domestic suppliers, then, to the extent that domestic competitors are unaffected by changes in the exchange rate of their domestic currency, $E_{pi,ei}$ can be expected to equal zero.
ii) If the firm is a price leader, following cost-plus pricing, and is operated as a multi-domestic firm where each national subsidiary is a stand-alone entity, then all the costs of supplying products in country i are incurred within country i, hence, we can expect that $E_{pi,ei} = 0$.
iii) If the firm is a price leader, following cost-plus pricing, and serves overseas markets by exporting from its home base, then any change in e_i will change unit costs (measured in currency i) by an equal and opposite proportion. Thus,

$$E_{pi,ei} = 1.$$

We can therefore expect that $0 \geq E_{pi,ei} \geq 1$.

The impact of any change in price, assuming that all competing suppliers move their prices together, is determined by the constant market share elasticity coefficient $(E_{qi,pi})$, which is equal to the normal price elasticity of market demand. Since the elasticity of price with regard to the exchange rate is normally negative and the price elasticity of market demand is also negative, the implication is that the market demand effect is positive (i.e. changes is exchange rates are positively correlated with changes in profitability), and the greater the elasticity of demand – in absolute terms – the greater is the impact.

c) The Competitive Effect

The competitive effect of an exchange rate change refers to the change in the firm's profit caused by a currency rate change affecting the competitive position of the firm relative to its rivals. Our model shows that the competitive effect comprises two terms: the impact of exchange rate changes upon price differentials, and the impact of changing price differentials upon sales as measured by the sensitivity of sales to relative prices. Let us consider each of these relationships separately.

The impact of exchange rate changes upon price differentials If we assume that prices are cost determined, then exchange rate changes will give rise to changes in price differentials between the firm and its competitors whenever the currency composition of costs is different between them.

$$p_i = (1 + g)\frac{\sum_i e_i c_i}{e_i}$$

and $p_i' = (1 + h)\dfrac{\sum_i e_i c_i'}{e_i}$

where: c_i is the unit cost incurred in country i
c_i' is the equivalent unit cost incurred by the firm's competitors in country i
g is the cost markup used to determine price
h is the equivalent markup used by competitors.

Hence: $\dfrac{d(p_i - p_i')}{de_i} \quad \dfrac{(1 + h)\sum_i e_i c_i}{e_i^2} - \dfrac{(1 + g)\sum_i e_i c_i'}{e_i^2}$

We observe, therefore, that the direction and magnitude of the competitive effect depends upon the firm's allocation of its costs across currencies, compared to competitors' allocation of their costs. Consider the following situations:

- If the firm and its competitors incur equal allocations of their costs between country i and the rest of the world, i.e. $\sum_i e_i c_i = \sum_i e_i c_i'$, then change in the exchange rate i leaves relative costs and relative prices unaltered, i.e. $d(p_i - p_i')/de_i = 0$.
- If the firm has less of its costs incurred in country i than its competitors, i.e. $\sum_i e_i c_i < \sum_i e_i c_i'$, then an increase in the exchange rate of i tends to increase the firm's costs and prices relative to those of its competitors, i.e. $d(p_i - p_i')/de_i > 0$.
- If the firm has more of its costs incurred outside of country i than its competitors, i.e. $\sum_i e_i c_i > \sum_i e_i c_i'$, then an increase in the exchange rate of i tends to decrease the firm's costs and prices relative to those of its competitors, i.e. $d(p_i - p_i')/de_i < 0$.

An implication of the competitive effect is that a firm with no direct involvement in international business can be vulnerable to operating exposure. The example given above of Harley Davidson's exposure to movements in the dollar/yen rate can be examined within this framework. Denote currency i as the Japanese yen. Harley Davidson has none of its costs in yen (i.e. $c_i = 0$). Assume that Japanese motorcycle manufacturers incur 75 per cent of their costs in yen (i.e. $c_i'/\sum_i c_i' = 0.75$). A rise in the yen against the dollar will tend to raise the price of Japanese motorcycles relative to those of Harley, therefore, $d(p_i - p_i')/de_i < 0$.

In reality, the situation is somewhat more complex. To fully examine the competitive effect of exchange rate changes we need to know, not only the currencies in which costs are incurred, but also how input prices are determined. Consider Chevron competing with Atlantic Richfield (Arco) in the California gasoline market. Arco's primary source of crude oil is Alaska; Chevron's production is more heavily concentrated in Canada and Venezuela. A depreciation of the Canadian dollar and Bolivar against the US dollar might be expected to give Chevron a cost and price advantage over Arco. However, because oil is an internationally traded commodity, it is priced in dollars worldwide (as are most of the inputs required for oil production), hence although oil companies differ in their sources of crude, exchange rate movements have only minimal effects upon competitiveness.

The sensitivity of quantity demanded to price differentials The extent to which an increase in the differential between the firm's price and that of competitors because quantity demands to fall depends upon market structure. The greater the number of competitors and less differentiated are their products, then the greater the sensitivity of demand to price differentials. In the case of a firm supplying a homogeneous product with many competitors, then the ratio elasticity of quantity demands with respect to relative price might approach infinity, that is, the emergence of a small price differential might cause quantity demanded to drop to zero. Conversely, for a highly differentiated product in a concentrated market, the elasticity might approximate zero.

Table 15.1 summarises the predictions of our model concerning the determinants of operating exposure to currency rate fluctuations.

Implications for the Strategic Management of Operating Risk

Before we can begin to identify strategies for managing operating exposure, we need to clarify companies' objectives with regard to exchange risk. The critical strategic choice for the firm is between hedging and opportunism with regard to exchange rate variation. Hedging involves trading off reduced earnings variability against lower expected earnings caused by the cost of hedging. Opportunism is the quest for profit opportunities from exchange rate fluctuations, usually at the cost of a higher level of earnings volatility. We can expect the firm's strategic orientation with regard to currency risk as determined by top management's risk aversion, the total level of risk to which the business is subject, and the operational flexibility of the firm. Let us explore these three factors.

1   *Ownership and Control*

We argued above that, if securities markets are efficient, hedging exchange rate risk would not, in general, enhance the value of the firm. To provide a rationale for risk aversion we need to assume either independence of managers from owners, or, that securities markets are subject to imperfect information. The more dispersed is

Table 15.1 Summary of predictions concerning the determinants of operating exposure

The impact of changes in exchange rate i upon the firm's profit (π) depends upon the following variables

The direct exposure effect	The firm's net cash flow position in currency i	The sign and the size of the impact of changes in exchange rate e_i depend upon the sign and size of the firm's net cash flow in currency i. The more country i is a market base for the firm, then the greater is the positive impact of any increase in e_i. The greater the extent to which country i is a production base for the firm, then the greater is the negative impact of any increase in e_i.
The pricing policy effect	The pricing policy of the firm	The pricing policy of the firm influences the extent to which a change in exchange rate e_i results in changes in the firm's price in country i, p_i. In particular, whether the firm is a price leader or price follower, and if a leader, whether the firm sets a single world price or price discriminates by country.
Market structure effects	The price elasticity of market demand	The greater the (absolute value of the) price elasticity of market demand for the firm's product, the greater the profit impact of any change in exchange rate e_i.
	Seller concentration in the market for the firm's product	The greater is seller concentration, the more sensitive is the firm's demand to changes in the price differential between the firm and its competitors, hence the more sensitive are profits to changes in exchange rates.
The competitive effect	The differentiation of the firm's product from those of competitors	The more a firm's products are differentiated from those of its competitors, the less sensitive is the demand for the firm's product to changes in price differentials, and hence, the greater the sensitivity of profits to changes in exchange rates.
	The currency composition of the firm's costs relative to that of competitors	The greater the similarity in the currency structure of costs of the firm and its competitors, the smaller the effect of exchange rates in changing the competitive position of the firm. The greater the proportion of costs denominated in currency i (relative to competitors), the greater the reduction in profits arising from a deterioration in the firm's competitive position.

ownership, the greater is managerial independence. To the extent that managerial performance is measured in terms of short-term profit movements and downward movements have a bigger impact upon perceived performance than upward movements – then increased profit stability over time increases managerial utility. Alternatively, if managers do aim to maximise shareholder wealth, but securities markets overreact to new information and react particularly strongly to adverse news – then this also provides an incentive to managers to 'smooth' reported earnings. Hence, as a result of either mechanism, companies whose shares are listed on a stock exchange and/or which have widely distributed share ownership are more likely to hedge exchange rate exposure than companies with unlisted shares and/or with concentrated ownership.

2   The Firm's Overall Level of Risk

Both for owners and managers, as the marginal cost of risk tends to rise, i.e. after a certain point, the firm requires steadily increasing amounts of additional return in order to compensate for additional increments of risk. Risk has numerous sources of which currency exposure is just one. Hence, a firm's propensity to hedge exchange rate exposure is positively related to the level of risk it faces from market demand, competition, and technology.

3   The Costs of Flexibility

An opportunistic approach to exchange rate fluctuations requires that a firm is capable of adjusting its production and marketing activities in order to take advantage of movements in exchange rates. The greater is the capital intensity of production, the greater are scale economies and exit costs, and more established are customer relations in the firm's markets, and the more costly is the shifting of production and marketing activities between countries. Consequently, the more likely a firm is to adopt a hedging rather than an exploitation approach to currency fluctuations. In other words, a firm's propensity to hedge currency exposure is positively related to the costs of geographical flexibility in production and marketing activities.

Hedging of direct operating exposure involves a balancing of a firm's cash flows in each of the currency areas in which the firm operates. Such an approach is likely to be effective in reducing, even neutralising, operating risk in situations where there is no conflict between direct hedging and hedging competitive risk. This is normally the case when in each country i that the firm markets in, competitors have their costs denominated in currency i. This would mean either that competitors are all domestically-based, or that they are multinationals which pursue a multi-domestic strategy. The greater the globalisation of the industry, the less effective is direct hedging likely to be. Hence, hedging direct operating exposure in the form of cash flow matching is most effective in international markets where competition is from domestically-based firms and/or multinational enterprises pursuing a multi-domestic approach.

To the extent that competitors within the same markets have costs comprised of different currencies, then exchange rate movements will change the relative costs of competitors. The essence of strategic hedging against competitive exposure, therefore, is for the firm to restructure its costs such that it matches the currency cost structure of its leading competitor(s). For companies facing global competition from overseas rivals, competitive risk represents the primary source of operating exposure, and hedging such exposure requires a firm to emulate the currency cost structure of its main competitors.

Our model predicts that operating exposure is positively related to the intensity of competition in a firm's product market as indicated by the price elasticity of market demand, seller concentration, and product differentiation. Hence, the more competitive the firm's product markets, the greater the level of operating exposure that the firm is subject to. Consequently, the firm may reduce exposure by pursuing strategies of product differentiation and relocating to fewer prices sensitive market segments.

Our theoretical analysis points to a number of market structure variables which determine operating exposure, and these in turn, suggest several instruments for managing that exposure. For the sake of simplicity, we identify a small number of configurations of industry structure and risk orientation each associated with a distinct strategic approach. In terms of risk orientation, we have already identified two basic orientations: risk aversion that is associated with a hedging approach, and opportunism that is associated with a risk-exploiting approach. In terms of market structure, the critical distinction is between industries where competition is nationally fragmented (multi-domestic industries) and those where competition is global. Within these dimensions we can identify three distinct strategic approaches (see Table 15.2).

Conclusion

The analysis presented identifies economic exposure as the exchange rate risk relevant to the wealth-maximising firm. Of the two components of economic exposure, operating exposure and transactions exposure, for most firms operating exposure is the more important, and it is the more difficult to hedge. In particular, we show that conventional financial instruments for exchange risk hedging are ineffective in managing operating exposure.

We argue that management of foreign exchange risk does not necessarily involve risk reduction through hedging activities. As with any unpredictable variable impacting profits and returns, a firm can either pursue risk reduction or it can adopt an opportunistic stance by relocating its cost and revenue activities in response to movements in real exchange rates.

Our model identifies two primary components of operating exposure, i.e. direct operating exposure and competitive (or indirect) operating exposure. The relative importance of these two components depends upon the structure of international markets: where competition is nationally fragmented, direct operating exposure is most important; where competition is global then competitive exposure is of primary importance. More generally, market structure emerges as critical to the analysis of the sources and the extent of operating exposure. The firm's vulnerability to exchange rate movements depends upon the sensitivity of its prices to exchange rates and then on the sensitivity of its sales to price changes.

Table 15.2   Strategies to manage operating exposure: a simple classification

International market structure

	Fragmented/multi-domestic	Global
Hedging	Hedging direct operating risk through balancing cash flows in each currency	• Hedging competitive risk through emulating the currency cost structure of competing firms. • Hedging competitive risk through strategic alliances with competitors in different currency area. • Reducing vulnerability to competitive risk through product differentiation and relocating in less price-sensitive market segments.
RISK ORIENTATION Opportunism	Exploring profit opportunities arising from exchange rate fluctuations by means of shifting cost activities to countries with currencies below their PPP levels, and shifting revenue generating activities to countries with currencies above PPP levels.	

The analysis reveals clear predictions as to the strategies appropriate to managing operating exposures:

- in nationally fragmented markets, firms should seek to hedge direct operating exposure by matching costs and revenues;
- in global industries, firms should emulate competitors' currency cost structure;
- to reduce sensitivity to exchange rates firms should differentiate their products and seek price insensitive market segments.

The central issue of exchange rate risk concerns the competitive position of the firm, and managing this risk is a strategic issue. The implication therefore, is that managing operating exposure is a general management responsibility that cannot easily be delegated to the treasury department.

Note

[1]   For a more detailed analysis of the accounting translation process, we refer to Arpan and Radenbaugh (1985), and Eun and Resnick (1998).

References

Abuaf, N. and P. Jorion (1990), 'Purchasing Power Parity in the Long Run', *Journal of Finance*, Vol. 45, pp. 157–74.

Adler, M. and B. Lehman (1983), 'Deviations from Purchasing Power Parity in the Long Run', *Journal of Finance*, Vol. 38, pp. 1471–87.

Arpan, J.S. and L.H. Radenbaugh (1985), *International Accounting and Multinational Enterprises*, Wiley, New York.

Bodnar, G.M., Hayt, G.S., and R.C. Marston (1996), 'Wharton Survey of Derivatives Usage by US Non-financial Firms', *Financial Management*, Vol. 25, No. 4, Winter, pp. 113–33.

Eun, C.S. and B.G. Resnick (1998), *International Financial Management*, Irwin McGraw-Hill, New York.

Grant, R.M. and L.A. Soenen (1991), 'Conventional Hedging: An Inadequate Response to Long-term Foreign Exchange Exposure', *Managerial Finance*, Vol. 17, pp. 1–4.

Henderson, J.M. and R. Quandt (1971), *Microeconomic Theory: A Mathematical Approach*, 2nd edn, McGraw-Hill, New York.

Hodder, J.E. (1982), 'Exposure to Exchange Rate Movements', *Journal of International Economics*, November, pp. 375–86.

Ibison, D. and K. Brown (2000), 'Chief Warns of "Unbearable" High Pound', *Financial Times*, 4 May.

Lessard, D.R. and J.B. Lightstone (1986), 'Volatile Exchange Rates Can Put Operations at risk', *Harvard Business Review*, July/August, pp. 107–14.

Lessard, D.R. and J.B. Lightstone (1990), 'Management of Operating Exposure', in A. Boris (ed.), *Management of Currency Risk*, Euromoney Publications, London, pp. 89–96.

Luehrman, T.A. (1990), 'The Exchange Rate Exposure of a Global Competitor', *Journal of International Business Studies*, pp. 225–42.

Oxelheim, L. and C.G. Wihlborg (1987), *Macroeconomic Uncertainty: International Risks and Opportunities for the Corporation*, Wiley, New York.

Protopapakis, A. and H.R. Stoll (1983), 'Spot and Futures Prices and the Law of One Price', *Journal of Finance*, Vol. 38, pp. 1431–55.

Roll, R. (1979), 'Violations of Purchasing Power Parity and their Implications for Efficient International Commodity Markets', in A. Sarnat and G. Szego (eds), *International Finance and Trade*, Vol. 1, Ballinger, Cambridge, MA.

Soenen, L.A. (1991), 'When Foreign Exchange Hedging Doesn't Help', *Journal of Cash Management*, Vol. 11, No. 6, pp. 58–62.

Soenen, L.A. (2000), Foreign *Exchange Management: A Managerial Approach*, McGraw-Hill, New York.

Von Ungern-Stenberg, T. and C.C. Von Weizsacker (1990), 'Strategic Foreign Exchange Management', *Journal of Industrial Economics*, Vol. 38, pp. 381–95.

Chapter 16

Foreign Shareholding and Trade Policy

Arijit Mukherjee, Sugata Marjit and Sarbajit Sengupta

Introduction

Researchers have already discussed various aspects of strategic trade policies. For a representative sample, one may look at Brander and Spencer (1984, 1985), Spencer and Brander (1983), Dixit (1984), Lee (1990), Dick (1993), Neary (1994) and Das (1997). However, the previous contributions have paid little attention to an important issue of integrated equity markets. The previous works, except Lee (1990) and Dick (1993), have considered that the residents of a country own 100 per cent share of that country's firm. However, in today's world, this assumption helps to focus on trade policies for a subset of firms. With the emergence of integrated equity markets and high percentage of foreign equity shares in domestic firms, it is important to look at a situation where the residents of that particular country do not own 100 per cent share of a firm. Hence, it is important to examine the implications of trade policies of different countries when people of different countries hold equity shares in a firm.

With the emergence of international equity markets, foreign shareholding in firms as indirect investment has increased drastically. Under this type of foreign ownership, an investor takes part in the equity markets and is mainly concerned to maximise the return from its total portfolio rather than controlling the decisions of a firm. In other words, in case of portfolio investment, an investor helps to finance a firm but does not interfere with the workings of the firms.

In a related contribution Lee (1990) has also examined the effects of foreign shareholdings on trade policies and welfare. Considering equity participation by the residents of competing countries,[1] Lee (1990) has concluded that outputs and prices are independent of the shareholding patterns. Thus, it implies no possibility of arbitrage in international equity markets. The present chapter differs from Lee (1990) in the following way. This chapter allows shareholdings by the residents of competing as well as by the non-competing countries. While considering integrated equity markets, we feel the assumption of shareholdings by the residents of the competing countries only is a restrictive one. With the emergence of integrated equity markets, it is more realistic to consider equity participation by the residents of non-competing countries also. The present chapter takes this issue and highlights the importance of ownership by the residents of competing and non-competing countries. Thus, the present chapter generalises Lee (1990) by introducing shareholdings from the non-competing countries. We show that the shareholdings from the rest of the world affect the outputs, trade policies, firm-values and also the welfare of these countries. Thus, it creates the incentive to manipulate the extent of foreign ownership, which is in sharp contrast to Lee (1990). It shows that the shareholdings from the rest of the world to the exporting firm and import-competing firm can lead to different conclusions. Hence, this analysis may have implications for government policies towards foreign shareholdings. Further, unlike Lee (1990), we consider more policy variables by introducing output subsidies along with trade policies. In a chapter, Dick (1993) has examined the effect of cross-ownership when the firms from two different countries compete in a 'third country'. Therefore, Dick (1993) has focused only on the exporting firms. The present chapter, however, focuses on a different scenario with exporting firm and import-competing firm.

In what follows, the part on 'model and results' considers a situation where the firms from two countries compete in one of these countries and see the effects of shareholdings on outputs and prices. We find that world production does not depend on the shareholdings pattern by the residents of competing countries but it depends on the shareholdings by the residents of the non-competing countries. Further, we demonstrate that if the shareholdings by the residents of the non-competing countries increase in the import-competing firm, then world production increases. Conclusions are opposite if the shareholdings by the residents of the non-competing countries increase in the exporting firm.

In the section on 'Welfare Implications' we look at the welfare implications of foreign shareholdings. We find that foreign investments to the exporting firm or from the exporting country are likely to increase the welfare of the exporting country. However, a rise in investment to the exporting country from the non-competing countries may reduce the welfare of the exporting country. But, more foreign shareholdings to the import-competing firm or from the importing country reduce the welfare of the importing country.

Then the section on 'Industrial Policy' considers the possibility of other types of government policies along with trade policies. In particular, we consider the possibility of output subsidy along with the import tariffs and export subsidies. Thus, it focuses on the combinations of trade policies and industrial policy. With this larger policy set, it is found that the outputs depend on the shareholding patterns of the competing countries. Hence, it creates the arbitrage possibilities even if there is no equity participation from the non-competing countries. Thus, it highlights the importance of different policy instruments and shows that the results of Lee (1990) are not robust when one considers more policy variables.

In sum, we find the following main results of this chapter:

1   The outputs of these firms are responsive only to the shareholdings by the residents of the non-competing countries.

2   Higher shareholdings by the importing country to the exporting firm reduces (increases) the welfare of the importing (exporting) country. We find similar effects for higher shareholdings of the exporting country to the import-competing firm.

3   We find that, under linear demand and symmetric marginal costs of productions, the effect on the welfare of the exporting country is positive (ambiguous) for higher shareholdings by the non-competing countries to the import-competing (exporting) firm. But, the welfare of the importing country reduces for higher shareholdings by the non-competing countries to the exporting or import-competing firm.

Hence, our results have important implications for globalisation policy. For example, if liberalisation by either the importing country or the exporting country attracts investments from the non-competing countries then it reduces the welfare of the importing country but may benefit the exporting country. From the point of view of the exporting country, it is important whether these investments from non-competing countries are going to the import-competing firm or to the exporting firm. Even if we consider the movement of investments between the competing countries, it is important to see whether the importing country or the exporting country is increasing their share to the firms of the competing countries. Hence, while adopting the globalisation policy, it is important to consider the possible effects of the capital flows caused by this liberalisation policy. Our findings show that the type of liberalisation policy a country will adopt depends on the characteristic of the firms (i.e., whether these firms are exporting firms or import-competing firms) of that country. Further, the liberalisation policy of a country may depend on the policy choice of the competing countries.

Another main point of this chapter is to highlight that if the countries engage in strategic trade policies then arbitrage possibility in the international equity markets arise if there exist foreign ownership from the non-competing countries. While foreign ownership from the non-competing countries to the exporting firm are likely to reduce the welfare of the exporting country, any foreign investments to either of these firms reduce welfare of the importing country. Further, the possibility of industrial policy, such as output subsidy, along with the trade policies create arbitrage possibilities even with no foreign ownership from the non-competing countries.

Model and Results

Consider that there are two firms located in two countries. We label these countries and the respective firms 1 and 2. Assume that the residents of country 2 own a fraction u of firm 1's share and residents of other countries, except country 1, own a fraction l in firm 1. Therefore, the residents of country 1 own $(1 - u - 1)$ fraction of equities in firm 1. Similarly, assume that the residents of country 1 and other countries, except country 2, hold v and k fraction of equities in firm 2, respectively. Hence, the residents of country 2 own $(1 - v - k)$ fraction of equities in firm 2.

We assume that firm 1 and firm 2 compete in one of these countries 1 and 2.[2] Without loss of generality, we consider that they compete in country 2. Therefore, firm 1 behaves like an exporting firm while firm 2 becomes an import-competing firm. We assume that the firms compete like Cournot duopolists in the product market with homogenous goods. Consider that the inverse market demand function is:

$$p = p(x + y) \text{ with } p' < 0 \tag{1}$$

Here x is the export of firm 1 and y is the domestic production of firm 2. As in Brander and Krugman (1983), Dixit (1984), Lee (1990) and others, the marginal costs of production of these firms are constant and considered to be c^1 and c^2 for firm 1 and firm 2 respectively. Assume that there are no other costs of production.

Consider the following structure of the game. At stage 1, the governments of country 1 and country 2 announce their trade policies. In particular, government of country 1 commits to a specific export subsidy, s, and the government of country 2 commits to a specific import tariff, t, on the imports of country 1. We however, do not restrict the signs of s and t. Therefore, positive (negative) s and t implies export subsidy (tax) and import tariff (subsidy), respectively. Then, in stage 2, both firms choose their outputs to maximise profits.

We find that given s and t the profits of firm 1 and firm 2 are

$$\pi^1 = p(x + y)x - c^1 x + sx - tx \text{ and } \pi^2 = p(x + y)y - c^2 y. \tag{2}$$

The optimal outputs can be found by solving the following two first-order conditions:[3]

$$\pi^1_x = p'x + p - c^1 + s - t = 0 \tag{3}$$

$$\pi^1_y = p'y + p - c^2 = 0. \tag{4}$$

Following Dixit (1984), assume $\pi^1_{xy} = p''x + p' < 0$ and $\pi^2_{xy} = p''y + p' < 0$. It satisfies the Hahn's stability condition. Further, we have

$$\pi^1_{xx} = p''x + 2p' < 0$$

$$\pi^1_{yy} = p''y + 2p' < 0$$

and $D = \pi^1_{xx} \pi^1_{yy} - \pi^1_{xy} \pi^2_{xy} > 0$

since $p' < 0$. Hence, the second order condition for profit maximisation is satisfied.

Therefore, from (3) and (4), we see that as long as the difference between the specific subsidy and tariff is same, the optimal outputs of these firms will be same. The imposition of specific subsidy and tariff changes the effective marginal cost of firm 1 and affects the optimal output of firm 1, which, in turn, will affect the optimal output of firm 2. Therefore, if the difference between the specific subsidy and tariff remains same, the effective marginal cost of firm 1 also remains same and as a result does not affect the output choices of these firms.

Before going further, we will state comparative static results that will help us for the following results. Taking total differentiation of (3) and (4) we get

$$x_s = -x_t = \frac{(2p' + p''y)}{D} > 0 \tag{5}$$

$$y_s = -y_t = \frac{(p' + p''y)}{D} < 0. \tag{6}$$

Therefore, the effects of subsidy and tariff on export and domestic production are the same but opposite. If the rate of subsidy increases then it makes firm 1 more cost efficient and encourages firm 1 to increase its output, which will induce firm 2 to reduce its production. On the other hand, if the rate of tariff increases, it increases the effective marginal cost of firm 1 and hence, induces firm 1 to reduce its production, which, in turn, will increase the production of firm 2.

In equilibrium, (3) and (4) must be satisfied simultaneously. Given the values of marginal costs of production of these firms, one can implicitly define that export and domestic production depend on the values of $(s-t)$. The difference between $(s-t)$ acts as effective subsidy to the export and this, in turn, affects marginal cost of production of firm 1. Hence, the optimal outputs of these firms depend on the values of $(s-t)$.

Let us now consider the policy stage. The problem of the governments of country 1 and country 2 are, respectively

$$w^1 = (1 - u - 1)\pi^1 + v\pi^2 - sx \tag{7}$$

$$w^2 = \int_0^Q p(q)dq - p(Q)Q + (1 - v - k)\pi^2 + u\pi^1 - tx \tag{8}$$

where $Q = x + y$. Government of country 1 and country 2 maximise the respective welfare functions by choosing the values of s and t respectively. The Nash solution of the policy game can be found by solving the following two first-order conditions (using (3) and (4)):[4]

$$w_s^1 = (1 - u - 1)p'xy_s - (u + 1)x + p'xy_s - sx_s = 0 \tag{9}$$

$$w_t^2 = p'Q(x_t + y_t) + (1 - v - k)p'xy_t + tx_t + x + u[p'xy_t - x] = 0. \tag{10}$$

Assume that the second order and stability conditions are satisfied. Therefore, using (5) and (6), we can say that in equilibrium (since in equilibrium) $w_s^1 = w_t^2 = 0$.

$$w_s^1 - w_t^2 = -p'xx_g - p'yy_g - gx_g - x - p'lxy_g - p'kyx_g - lx = 0 \tag{11}$$

where $g = s - t$. From (11) we can solve for g as x and y are functions of g. The examination of condition (11) says that this expression does not depend on u and v but it depends on l and k. Therefore, one can say that the difference $(s-t)$ does not depend on the values of u and v but, it depends on l and k. Further, from (11) it is easy to check that g varies positively with k but negatively with l.

Consider the possibility of share redistribution between the competing countries only. For example, if the exporting country's shareholding reduces in the exporting firm, then it reduces the incentive for subsidy. As a result the exporting country will reduce the rate of subsidy. Since the redistribution of share increases the share of the importing country to the competing firm, it reduces the importing country's incentive for rent seeking through tariff. Therefore, this redistribution will reduce the rate of tariff also. Since both the subsidy and tariff will be imposed on the output of the exporting firm, we find that the incentive for lower subsidy exactly matches with the incentive for lower tariff. Hence, the difference between the rate of subsidy and the rate of tariff remains the same.

But, if the redistribution of shares occurs between the competing and non-competing countries then it creates an imbalance between the gains and losses due to the absence of counter policies of the non-competing countries. Hence, in this situation, a redistribution of shares has an impact on the difference between the rate of subsidies and tariffs.

We summarise these findings in the following proposition.

Proposition 1

a. $(s - t)$ is independent of the shareholding patterns between the competing
     countries (i.e. u and v).
b. $(s - t)$ is dependent on the shareholding from the non-competing countries (i.e.
     l and k) and $(s - t)$ varies positively (negatively) with shareholdings from non-
     competing countries to the import-competing firm (exporting firm), i.e. $k(l)$.

Since exports and domestic productions are functions of the difference of subsidy and
tariff, from Proposition 1 one can say that the outputs of these firms are independent
of the shareholdings by the residents of country 1 and country 2. Outputs are,
however, sensitive to the shareholdings by the residents of the rest of the world. So,
any reallocation of shares between the residents of competing countries, keeping the
shareholdings of the rest of the world unchanged, have no effects on the outputs, prices
and firm-profits. But, reallocation of shareholdings between the rest of the world and
the competing countries, keeping the total amount of foreign investment unchanged,
will change the outputs, prices and the profits. Combining these observations we may
say that changes in total foreign shareholdings are neither necessary nor sufficient for
affecting the outputs and prices of the products.

   Now, we are in a position to see how the outputs will be affected due to a change in
the shareholdings of the residents of the non-competing countries.

Proposition 2

a.   Firm 1's (firm 2's) production varies inversely (directly) with the shareholdings
     to the firm 1 from the non-competing countries (i.e. with l). Firm 1's (firm 2's)
     production varies directly (inversely) with the shareholdings to the firm 2 from
     the non-competing countries (i.e. with k).
b.   World production varies inversely (directly) with the shareholdings to the firm 1
     (firm 2) from the non-competing countries.

Proof: See Appendix A, available from authors upon request.   QED

From Proposition 2, one can see that if the shareholding to the exporting firm from the
non-competing countries (i.e. l) increases, then it reduces the outputs and profit of the
exporting firm (firm 1) but it increases the outputs and profits of the import-competing
firm (firm 2). For an increase in the shareholdings in the import-competing firm from
the non-competing countries (i.e. k), we get the opposite results. Thus, we find that
while some patterns of foreign shareholdings (i.e. u and v) leave the producers and
consumers unaffected, other types of foreign shareholdings (i.e. l and k) affect the
producers and consumers differently. More foreign shareholdings from the non-
competing countries to the domestic import-competing firm and less in the foreign
exporting firm make the consumers better-off.[5] But, more (less) foreign shareholdings
from the non-competing countries to the foreign exporting firm (domestic import-
competing firm) make the domestic import-competing firm better-off. Hence, more

foreign shareholdings do not make both the producers and consumers better-off in the domestic country. Further, assuming a positive relationship between outputs and inputs (e.g. labour) of a firm with sticky input prices, one may argue that if foreign shareholdings from the non-competing countries increase in a firm, then the input usage in the respective country (competitor country) decreases (increases). Thus, an increment of this type of foreign investments in a country with a large amount of unutilised resources may cause less employment to that country and may make the unemployment problem more severe. However, world employment may increase or decrease depending on the extent of these investments to the domestic import-competing firm and to the foreign exporting firm.

i) Welfare Implications

In this section, we devote our attention to highlight whether foreign shareholdings are welfare improving or not. It turns out that the answer depends on the identity of the sector (i.e. exporting firm or import-competing firm) as well as on the identity of the country (i.e. competing or non-competing country).

First, we see how the welfare of the countries 1 and 2 are affected by u and v. While considering this, assume that the change in u or v leads to a change in the shareholdings of the residents of countries 1 and 2, keeping the shareholdings of the residents of the non-competing countries unchanged. This helps us to see the effect on welfare when foreign investment does not change the outputs and prices. Otherwise, a change in the shareholdings of the residents of the non-competing countries will affect the outputs and prices. Thus, we look at the change in total foreign investment while outputs and prices are unaffected due to this change.

Proposition 3

Given the shares of the non-competing countries, a change in the importing (exporting) country's ownership of the exporting (import-competing) firm affects positively the exporting country's welfare and affects negatively the importing country's welfare.[6]

Proposition 3 shows that irrespective of the initial shareholdings, any rise in foreign investment to and from the foreign competing country, country 1, increase the welfare of that country. The opposite holds for the domestic country, country 2. For example, consider that, given the shares of the non-competing countries, the share of the exporting country has reduced in the exporting firm. This will reduce the earning of the exporting country as well as the subsidy payment by the exporting country. We find that the later effect dominates the former effect and increases the welfare of the exporting country. In contrary, this redistribution of shares increases the earning of the importing country but reduces the tariff revenue and on the balance it reduces the welfare of the importing country.

Hence, one may say that, given the foreign investments from the non-competing countries, if foreign shareholdings increase to the exporting sector or if the residents of the exporting country own more shares in the competing firm of other country then it increase the welfare of the exporting country. But, if foreign investment increases to the importing country or if the residents of the importing country hold more shares in the competing firm of another country then the welfare of the importing country decreases. Now, we look at the other side. In particular, we consider the effect of changes in the shareholdings of the residents of the non-competing countries, i.e. changes in l or k, keeping the values of u and v unchanged. Therefore, like the earlier case, this also focuses on a situation where total foreign investment increases. But, as shown earlier, these foreign investments affect the outputs and profits of the firms.

Proposition 4

Suppose the shares of the competing countries remain the same. Given linear inverse market demand function and symmetric marginal costs of productions, the welfare effects on the exporting country due to a change in investments from the non-competing countries to the import-competing (exporting) firm are positive (ambiguous), but, the welfare of the import-competing country is affected negatively with a change in foreign investments from the non-competing countries to the exporting firm or import-competing firm.

Proof: See Appendix B, available from authors upon request.   QED

From Proposition 4 we find that while higher shareholding by the non-competing countries reduce the welfare of the importing country, it is more likely to increase the welfare of the exporting country. In fact, higher shareholding by the non-competing country to the import-competing firm always increases the welfare of the exporting country.

Propositions 3 and 4 highlight that foreign investment to the import-competing firm or investment from the importing country, is likely to reduce the welfare of the importing country. Further, foreign ownership in the exporting firm provides a negative effect on the welfare of the importing country. On the other hand, investment from the exporting country or investment to the import-competing firm improves the welfare of the exporting country. While foreign ownership in the exporting firm from the competing country increases the welfare of the exporting country, the foreign investment from the non-competing country to the exporting firm is likely to reduce the welfare of the exporting country. Further, Proposition 4 implies that whether a rise in foreign investment from the non-competing country to the exporting firm increases the welfare of the exporting country depends on the foreign shareholdings in the competitor firm. Therefore, it may be important to look at the foreign investment flows to the competing countries while allowing foreign shareholdings to a country.

These findings of Propositions 3 and 4 suggest that one must be careful while adopting the globalisation policy. We find that it is more likely that an exporting country will be benefited due to the redistribution of shares. But, the share redistribution will adversely affect the importing country. So, globalisation could be a more preferable strategy from the point of view of the exporting country. However, the globalisation policy of the exporting country may also encourage the importing country to adopt a similar policy as a loss minimisation policy. Otherwise, the importing country may suffer from higher loss of welfare due to the adoption of the liberalised policy of the exporting country.

In Propositions 3 and 4, we consider an increment in total foreign investments. It may happen that total foreign investments and/or the composition of foreign ownership are changing. Then it will change u, v, l and k and may lead to different effects on welfare.

In sum, the above analysis shows that the involvement of the residents from non-competing countries in the equity market can create the arbitrage possibility in the international equity markets. Therefore, a disturbance in the world economy may create different types of foreign investment flows and may have different welfare implications. Further, it highlights that the welfare of the exporting country may as well decrease due to the foreign ownership.

ii)   Industrial Policy

So far we have concentrated only on the trade policies imposed by these countries. The purpose of this section is to highlight the importance of the availability of other policies. In particular, we will show that no-effect of shareholding patterns by the competing countries on the firm values and trade patterns are not robust with larger policy variables.

Assume that country 2 can give a per-unit output subsidy (tax, if negative) to the firm 2 along with its imposition of tariff on the output of firm 1.[7] Thus, assume that the government of country 2 imposes a per-unit import tariff l and gives the firm 2 a per-unit output subsidy s_2. Government of country 1 gives a per-unit export subsidy s_1.

Therefore, the profits of firm 1 and firm 2 are given by

$$\pi^1 = p(x+y)x - c^1x + s_1x - tx \tag{12}$$

and $\pi^2 = p(x+y)y - c^2x + s_2y.$ (13)

The first order conditions for profit maximisation are given by

$$\pi_x^1 = p'(x+y)x + p(x+y) - c^1 + s - t = 0 \text{ and } \pi_y^2 = p'(x+y)y + p(x+y) - c^2 + s_2 = 0. \tag{14}$$

Assume that the conditions for Hahn stability are satisfied. Therefore, it will satisfy the second order condition for profit maximisation. Notice that, given c^1 and c^2, the optimal outputs depend on $(s_1 - t)$ and s_2.

Next, consider the policy stage. The government of country 1 and country 2 will maximise the welfare functions, respectively

$$w^1 = (1 - u - 1)\pi^1 + v\pi^2 - s_1x \tag{15}$$

and $w^2 = \int_0^Q p(q)dq - p(Q)Q + (1 - v - k)\pi^2 + u\pi^1 + tx - s_2y$ (16)

The government of country 1 and country 2 will choose simultaneously s_1, t and s_2 to maximise w^1 and w^2, respectively. Therefore, the first order conditions for maximisation are given by (using (14)):

$$w^1_{s_1} = (1 - u - l)p'xy_{s_1} - (u + l)x + p'vyx_{s_1} - s_1 x_{s_1} = 0 \tag{17}$$

$$w^2_t = -Qp'(x_t + y_t) + (1 - v - k)p'yx_t + u(p'xy_t - x) + x + tx_t - s_2 y_t = 0 \tag{18}$$

and $w^2_{s_2} = -p'(xx_{s_2} + yy_{s_2}) - (1 - u)p'xy_{s_2} - (v - k)(p'yx_{s_2} + y) + tx_{s_2} - s_2 y_{s_2} = 0 \tag{19}$

We obtain an equation for $(s_1 - t)$ by subtracting (18) from (17). Therefore, we get

$$w^1_{s_1} - w^2_t = p'xx_g - p'yy_g - gx_g - x - p'lxy_g - p'kyx_g - lx = 0 \tag{20}$$

where $g = s_1 - t$. From (20) we see that g does not depend on the value of u and v. However, now the government of country 2 has another choice variable s_2. We will find g and s_2 simultaneously and the expression (19) shows that it depends on the values of u and v also along with l and k. As a result, now the optimal outputs are dependent on the values of u, v, l and k. Hence, we get the following proposition immediately.

Proposition 5

If the government of country 2 provides specific output subsidy to the firm 2 along with the trade policies taken by the governments of the countries 1 and 2 then the export, domestic production and world production depends on the shareholding patterns of the competing and non-competing countries.

The exporting country cannot provide any subsidy (or, impose tax) to the firm in the importing country. Hence, the exporting country cannot counter the policy of output subsidy (or, tax) to the import-competing firm by the importing country. Therefore, in this situation, the benefits and losses from share distributions cannot be balanced as it could be in the absence of subsidy (or, tax) to the import-competing country. As a result, the possibility of output subsidy (or, tax) to the import-competing firm along with the trade policies affects the outputs when there is a redistribution of shares between the competing countries only.

The possibility of output subsidy to the import-competing firm however may lead to zero production by firm 1, i.e., zero export. Suppose these firms are fully domestically owned. The provision of import tariff helps the importing country to extract some rents from the exporting firm. While this import tariff hurts the domestic consumers, the rent extraction from the foreign exporting firm makes positive amount of import tariff as an optimal policy. If the domestic government provides output subsidy also to the import-competing firm then this subsidisation helps to increase the competitiveness of the import-competing firm by reducing its effective marginal cost of production. At the same time, this subsidisation helps the domestic consumers by increasing industry outputs. Therefore, while the output subsidy to the import-competing firm increases the competitiveness of the import-competing firm and reduces the deadweight loss, the imposition of import tariff increases both the competitiveness of the import-competing firm and deadweight loss. Hence, from the point of view of the domestic country, output subsidy is preferable than import tariff. So, the domestic government will prefer subsidisation to reduce the deadweight loss. In this situation, the optimal export may be equal to zero. In fact, given the linear demand function considered in Proposition 4, optimal values for s_1, t and s_2 will be 0,0 and 1 when there is no foreign ownership in the import-competing firm and, therefore, optimal export equals to zero.[8] The foreign ownership of the domestic import-competing firm however creates divergence between the private and social valuation of subsidies.[9] Therefore, this reduces the incentive for subsidising the import-competing firm and creates deadweight loss. This can increase the welfare of the exporting country and can reduce the welfare of the importing country.

Conclusion

This chapter considers trade policies of two countries when the firms compete in a Cournot fashion. We consider equity holding by the residents of competing and non-competing countries in each of these firms.

The result shows that the production of the import-competing (exporting) firm varies directly (inversely) to the shareholdings by the residents of non-competing countries to the exporting firm. Opposite conclusions arise for shareholdings by the residents of non-competing countries to the domestic import-competing firm. But, world production varies directly (inversely) in the later (former) situation. However, productions do not depend on the shareholdings from the competing countries. The possibility of output subsidy to the import-competing firm, however, makes the outputs of these firms dependent on the shareholding patterns between the competing firms. Thus, shareholding by either the competing or non-competing countries creates an arbitrage possibility.

In this chapter we have taken the shareholding patterns as exogenous. Since this chapter highlights the incentive to manipulate the extent of foreign shareholdings, a more detailed analysis calls for the endogenous determination of shareholding patterns. Secondly, one may look at the oligopoly markets while focusing on the effect of foreign ownership in these exporting and importing firms. Another possible extension of this work may be to focus on the R&D decisions of these firms. In this respect, the trade policies and R&D policies along with the cooperative and non-cooperative R&D may be an interesting area for future research.

Finally, the findings of this chapter have important implications for the globalisation policies. We find that whether a particular country will encourage foreign shareholdings depends on the nature of firms of that country. For example, an importing country will be worse-off with higher foreign shareholdings. But, higher foreign shareholdings always increase the welfare of the exporting country except for the situation when it comes from the non-competing countries. However, if the exporting country opens its economy to foreign investment, the importing country may also prefer to adopt similar policy to reduce the loss of the importing country. Hence, a country's liberalisation policy may not be independent of the policy adopted by the competing country.

Notes

[1] In this chapter, by saying competing (non-competing) countries we mean those countries, the firms of which are competing (not competing) in the market.

[2] One can easily extend this analysis to consider that these firms compete in both the countries 1 and 2. However, for our purpose, this will not add much insight.

[3] The subscripts show the partial derivatives.

[4] All the profits are distributed to the shareholders as dividends.

[5] In this chapter the term 'domestic' and 'foreign' are used to imply the countries where these firms compete and do not compete, respectively, i.e. country 2 and country 1, respectively.

[6] Since this proposition is similar to the Proposition 5 in Lee (1990), we are omitting the proof of this proposition.

[7] One may assume that these firms take labour as the input of production. Assuming competitive labour market and one-to-one relationship between the labour input and output, one may think this subsidy as a wage subsidy rather than output subsidy.

[8] This result will hold even with asymmetric marginal costs of production provided the marginal cost of production of the exporting firm is not sufficiently low compared to the import-competing firm.

[9] For works on the divergence between private and social costs of subsidisation and strategic trade policy, one may look at Neary (1994).

References

Brander, J.A. and B.J. Spencer (1984), 'Trade Warfare: Tariffs And Cartels', *Journal of International Economics*, Vol. 17, pp. 227–42.

Brander, J.A. and B.J. Spencer (1985), 'Export Subsidies and International Market Share Rivalry', *Journal of International Economics*, Vol. 18, pp. 83–100.

Brander, J.A. and P.R. Krugman (1983), 'A Reciprocal Dumping Model of International Trade', *Journal of International Economics*, Vol. 15, pp. 313–21.

Das, S.P. (1997), 'Strategic Managerial Delegation and Trade Policy', *Journal of International Economics*, Vol. 43, pp. 173–88.

Dick, A.R. (1993), 'Strategic Trade Policy and Welfare: The Empirical Consequence of Cross-ownership', *Journal of International Economics*, Vol. 35, pp. 227–49.

Dixit, A. (1984), 'International Trade Policies for Oligopolistic Industries', *Economic Journal* (supplement), Vol. 94, pp. 1–16.

Lee, S. (1990), 'International Equity Markets and Trade Policy', *Journal of International Economics*, Vol. 27, pp. 279–82.

Neary, J.P. (1994), 'Cost Asymmetries in International Subsidy Games: Should Governments Help Winners or Losers?' *Journal of International Economics*, Vol. 37, pp. 197–218.

Spencer, B.J. and J.A. Brander (1983), 'International R&D Rivalry and Industrial Strategy', *Review of Economic Studies*, Vol. 73, pp. 707–22.

Chapter 17

Reciprocal Dumping: A Generalised Approach

Prabal Ray Chaudhuri and Uday Bhanu Sinha

F13

Introduction

The process of globalisation has led to a greater integration in the world economy. This integration has several manifestations. One important manifestation is the greater volume of world trade. Another crucial manifestation is an increasing vulnerability of individual nations to global business cycles. Given these facts it is natural to examine the linkage between business cycles and the volume of world trade. To be precise one can enquire if trade behaves pro-cyclically or counter-cyclically. In this chapter we try to address this question in a theoretical framework.

An important feature of globalisation in last few decades is the increase in trade among similar countries. A substantial portion of this trade is characterised by the intra-industry trade. That is countries sometimes export as well as import the same good. One of the most interesting explanations of intra-industry trade was provided by Brander (1981). He demonstrated that if firms behave in a Cournot fashion, and if they treat the domestic and the foreign markets in a segmented manner, then they would sell in each other's market, leading to 'cross-hauling'. Thus market imperfections may be sufficient to cause reciprocal dumping of goods among countries.

This chapter is an attempt to generalise the Brander (1981) result to more general cost functions and examine the impact of a change in world income on cross-hauling trade. Brander (1981) concentrated on the case of linear demand and cost functions. The extension to the case of general demand functions was provided by Brander and Krugman (1983). They also derive some welfare implications for the model with a general demand function. We seek to extend the model further by allowing for general cost (as well as demand) functions. As we are going to argue, the importance of general cost function lies in the fact that some of the comparative static results, that are held for linear cost functions, may not hold any longer.

We adopt the model developed in Brander (1981). There are two countries, each having a single firm. Thus, we essentially have a duopoly model with quantity competition where the firms consider the domestic and the foreign markets in a segmented manner. We, however, extend the earlier models by considering general demand and cost functions. Let us remark that our model contains the earlier ones as special cases.

We now come to the main findings of this chapter. To begin with we provide a simple and intuitive characterisation result regarding the existence of cross-hauling trade. We demonstrate that reciprocal dumping would occur if and only if the monopoly mark-up exceeds per unit transport costs. The sufficiency part of the above claim is mentioned in Dixit (1984: 6). We shall show that this condition is also related closely to the condition in Brander and Krugman (1983).

In addition to characterising the condition for reciprocal dumping, we study the impact of cyclical changes on cross-hauling trade. In our model, cyclical changes are going to enter via demand effects with the demand likely to increase during a boom period, and likely to fall during the bust. We find that, for a simple example, a demand increase may lead to a decline in world trade if the transport costs are large enough. Thus, somewhat surprisingly, cross-hauling trade may behave in a counter-cyclical manner. This result is specific to our model and cannot occur in a model with linear cost functions.

The Model

We consider two identical countries, one 'domestic' and the other 'foreign', with each country having one firm producing the commodity X. Therefore, under autarky, the firms act as monopoly producers in their respective countries. With the opening up of free trade the firms consider the domestic and the foreign markets in a segmented manner and sell their products in each other's market leading to duopoly competition in both countries, with quantity being the strategic variable.

Let the inverse demand function in each country be $F(X)$. Assume that the firms have the same cost structure $c(X)$, with $c'(X) > 0$. Notice that this specification allows for the Brander (1981), as well as the Brander and Krugman (1983) model as special cases. Transport costs are t per unit.

Let us introduce the following notations:

X^{dd}: Domestic firm's supply to the domestic market
X^{df}: Domestic firm's supply to the foreign market
X^{fd}: Foreign firm's supply to the domestic market
X^{ff}: Foreign firm's supply to the foreign market

Now the profit functions for the domestic firm, Π^d, and that of the foreign firm, Π^f, can be written as follows:

$$\Pi^d = X^{dd} F(X^{dd} + X^{fd}) + X^{df} F(X^{df} + X^{ff}) - c(X^{dd} + X^{df}) - t.X^{df}$$
$$\Pi^f = X^{ff} F(X^{df} + X^{ff}) + X^{fd} F(X^{dd} + X^{fd}) - c(X^{ff} + X^{fd}) - t.X^{fd}$$

Hence, the Cournot-Nash equilibrium conditions are:

$$\partial\Pi^d/\partial X^{dd} = X^{dd} F'(X^{dd} + X^{fd}) + F(X^{dd} + X^{fd}) - c'(X^{dd} + X^{df}) = 0$$
$$\partial\Pi^d/\partial X^{df} = X^{df} F'(X^{df} + X^{ff}) + F(X^{df} + X^{ff}) - c'(X^{dd} + X^{df}) - t = 0$$
$$\partial\Pi^f/\partial X^{ff} = X^{ff} F'(X^{df} + X^{ff}) + F(X^{df} + X^{ff}) - c'(X^{fd} + X^{ff}) = 0$$
$$\partial\Pi^f/\partial X^{fd} = X^{fd} F'(X^{dd} + X^{fd}) + F(X^{dd} + X^{fd}) - c'(X^{fd} + X^{ff}) - t = 0$$

We then assume that Cournot equilibrium exists and that it is unique. Notice that under the uniqueness assumption, the equilibrium outcome must be symmetric.

(Because, otherwise the mirror image of that outcome would constitute equilibrium as well, thus violating uniqueness.) This means both the countries would sell the same amount domestically and export the same amount to other countries. So the solution must involve $X^{dd} = X^{ff}$, and $X^{df} = X^{fd}$.

We require a few more definitions before we can proceed with the analysis. Let X^m denote the monopoly output. Clearly, the monopoly mark-up is given by $F(X^m) - c'(X^m)$. We are now in a position to state the main result of this study, which provides a characterisation theorem for the existence of reciprocal dumping.

As we have pointed out in the introduction, this condition is the same as the sufficiency condition in Dixit (1984, p. 6). We provide the necessity part, and to that extent this demonstration may be of some value.

Proposition 1

Cross-hauling occurs if and only if the monopoly mark-up exceeds per unit transport costs, that is $F(X^m) - c'(X^m) > t$.

The formal proof can be found in the appendix. Here we try to provide an intuitive re-interpretation of this result. Notice that the above proposition can be restated in terms of demand elasticity:

$$(P^m / \varepsilon^m) > t$$

Where ε^m denotes the elasticity of the inverse demand function at the monopoly output level and P^m denotes the monopoly price. (Note that we use the relation marginal cost (MC) = marginal revenue (MR) = $P(1 - 1/\varepsilon)$ to derive the above statement.)

This restatement is interesting as this is similar to the condition Brander and Krugman (1983) derive in their paper (316). Let us now relate the condition given in Proposition 1 to that in Brander and Krugman (1983). The sufficiency condition that they provide is $\varepsilon < 1/(1 - g)$, where transport costs are of the iceberg type. Therefore, the marginal cost of export is c/g, where c is the constant marginal cost of production and $0 \le g \le 1$. In their analysis ε is the demand elasticity measured at the equilibrium output level. This is somewhat unsatisfactory if we want to use the condition in order to predict whether cross-hauling occurs or not, since we have to first solve for the equilibrium itself. The condition derived here is, however, free of this criticism and since ε is always measured at the monopoly output level (under autarky) irrespective of what the equilibrium outcome would be.

While they only argue the sufficiency part, it is not difficult to show that their condition is necessary also. Let us begin by restating their condition in terms of linear, rather than iceberg type, transport costs. Under this reformulation, the condition for cross-hauling would be $\varepsilon < (c+t)/t$. We can now use equation (5) in Brander and Krugman (1983), to argue that their condition becomes $P/\varepsilon > t$, where both P and ε are evaluated at the equilibrium output levels. In order to establish the necessity part, we have to show that if the equilibrium is autarkic then $(P^m / \varepsilon^m) \le t$, where P^m and ε^m are evaluated at their autarkic monopoly levels. But this is the same condition as ours, and can be proved similarly.

This is somewhat surprising as two different (though related) sets of conditions appear to characterise the cross-hauling equilibrium. However, a closer look at the conditions suggests that they are indeed equivalent when the Cournot equilibrium is unique (the proof is given in the appendix).

We now use a simple example to verify that the characterisation is indeed correct. Let the demand functions in both the countries be $X = 10 - P$, and let the cost functions be $c = X^2/2$. We also assume that $t = 1$. Simple calculations would entail:

$$X^{dd} = X^{ff} = 12/5 \text{ and } X^{df} = X^{fd} = 7/5$$

This is a case of cross-hauling equilibrium.

In this example, the monopoly price $P^m = 20/3$, $c'(X^m) = 10/3$ and $t = 1$. Notice that in this case $P^m = 20/3 > 10/3 + 1 = c'(X^m) + t$, that is the proposed condition is satisfied. In the same example, one may verify that for $t = 4$, the unique equilibrium involves zero cross-hauling with both the firms acting as monopolists in their own countries. Thus, the characterisation of the cross hauling equilibrium demonstrates that the cost structure of the firms and the transport cost are the two crucial determinants of cross hauling trade.

Effect of World Income Change

We now relate the level of cross-hauling trade to world income levels. Such an analysis is of interest as it would allow us to predict the movement of cross-hauling trade during booms and busts. Since booms are associated with rising demand and busts with falling demand, our analysis allows us to see whether this movement is pro-cyclical or counter-cyclical.

Let us take the inverse demand and cost functions as $A - bX$ and $X^2/2$ respectively. We consider demand changes such that the new demand curve lies strictly above the old demand. A necessary condition for this to happen is that A/b, the demand at $P = 0$, increases; that is $dA/A \geq db/b$. Further, consideration of the other extremity of the demand curve, that is the price which chokes off demand viz., $P = A$, leads us to assume that $dA \geq 0$. Given these natural restrictions, we have the following cases (where we exclude the case considered by Brander (1981), that is only A changes and b does not change): (i) A increases and/or b decreases, (ii) A increases and b increases.

Our reason for considering changes in the slope parameter is as follows. Consider the case where an increase in world demand occurs via a replication of the domestic markets. Let us consider the case where the demand, to start out with, is $a - dP$. Thus the inverse demand function is $A - bX$, where $A = a/d$ and $b = 1/d$. Now assume that a market of equal size is added to the existing one. Clearly, for the same level of price the market demand should be twice the earlier level, that is, the new market demand is $2(a - dP)$. Hence the new inverse demand function becomes $A - bX/2$. Thus, the effect of market replication is captured by a decline in b, and hence our interest in this parameter.

Furthermore, Brander (1981: 6) has already demonstrated that an increase in the world demand, captured via a change in A, leads to an increase in cross-hauling trade. It would be of interest to see if the more general framework adopted here would lead to somewhat different conclusions.

Now observe that a demand shift can be represented in terms of the following parameter α defined by,

$$dA/A = -\alpha.db/b$$

Note that our cases of demand increase were: (i) A increase and/or b decrease, (ii) A increase and b increase. Given our natural restrictions the value of α would be for case (i) $\alpha \geq 0$, and for case (ii) $\alpha \leq -1$. The range $-1 < \alpha < 0$ is ruled out by our specification of demand shift.

Proposition 2 below examines the effect of a change in the world income on the volume of cross-hauling trade.

Proposition 2

Suppose that $dA/A = -\alpha.db/b$.

(i) Then for $0 \leq \alpha \leq \hat{\alpha} = 1/(2b+1)$, there is an interval $(\hat{t}, t^*)$ such that for all transport costs belonging to this interval, an increase in demand leads to a decline in the volume of cross-hauling trade. For $t < \hat{t}$, however, an increase in demand leads to an increase in the volume of cross-hauling trade.

(ii) If $\alpha > \hat{\alpha}$ or if $\alpha \leq -1$, if cross-hauling at all occurs, then an increase in demand would always lead to an increase in the volume of cross-hauling trade.

Again the formal proof has been relegated to the appendix.

Thus Proposition 2(i) demonstrates that if the demand shift can be essentially attributed to a shift in the slope parameter, then the Brander (1981) conclusion need not hold universally. The intuition for this result is as follows. Notice that with an increase in demand (either because of an increase in A, or a decline in b), profitability in the domestic as well as in the export market increases. This, however, sets up a tension between the production for the domestic market (X^{dd}) and the production for the export market (X^{df}) since an increase in X^{dd} leads to an increase in the marginal costs (as costs are convex), making exports less profitable. This tension is captured by the difference in the marginal profitability of the two markets, $\partial\Pi^d/\partial X^{dd} - \partial\Pi^d/\partial X^{df}$. One can easily check that this expression is independent of A, but it depends on b. Thus, a change in A does not affect the relative profitability of the two markets. Hence, if the demand change occurs through a change in A, X^{df} is going to increase as in this case there is no tension between X^{dd} and X^{df}. Since the difference in the marginal profitability depends on b, therefore, for high values of t, the difference in the marginal profitability of the two markets is larger, so that the tension is greater in this case. In fact, as we have demonstrated, for a large enough transport cost, the tension may be enough to offset the effect of the increase in the foreign demand leading to a decline in exports.

Notice that with a linear cost function, a decline in b would always lead to an increase in cross-hauling trade (see Brander (1981)). This is because with a constant marginal cost, the tension between X^{dd} and X^{df} is not there. Furthermore, notice that for b small enough, that is for $b < \dfrac{t}{A-2t}$, cross-hauling stops altogether. (Observe that this is the same condition that ensures that the monopoly mark-up is less than the per unit transport cost, that is $F(X^m) - c'(X^m) < t$.

Thus we find that if the demand increase comes mainly through a change in the slope parameter, b, then, for a range of transport costs cross-hauling trade would behave counter-cyclically. Moreover, for a large enough demand shift cross-hauling would stop altogether.

Conclusion

This chapter was motivated by the desire to understand the nature of trade shifts in a world that, because of globalisation, is much more integrated than before. In particular we were interested in understanding the impact of business cycles on trade volumes.

The analysis is carried out in the intra-industry trade framework pioneered by Brander (1981). We begin by extending the cross-hauling result to the case of general cost functions, thus establishing the robustness of the cross-hauling result to changes in the cost structure. The characterisation result derived here is also quite intuitive and simple, so that it may, possibly, be used as a test of the cross-hauling model.

More importantly, we establish conditions under which cross-hauling trade would behave in a counter-cyclical manner. Such counter-cyclical behaviour is not possible under linear cost functions, thus demonstrating the importance of considering non-linear cost functions. Our analysis demonstrates that in the age of globalisation any simplistic predictions regarding the impact of business cycles on the trade volume are unwarranted. This depends on many things like the production conditions, the nature of demand shifts etc.

References

Brander, J. (1981), 'Intra-industry Trade in Identical Commodities', *Journal of International Economics*, Vol. 11, pp. 1–14.

Brander, J. and P.R. Krugman (1983), 'A Reciprocal Dumping Model of International Trade', *Journal of International Economics*, Vol. 15, pp. 313–21.

Dixit, A. (1984), 'International Trade Policy for Oligopolistic Industries', *Economic Journal* Conference Chapters, Vol. 94, pp. 1–16.

Appendix

Proof of Proposition 1

Notice that since the equilibrium is symmetric, only two kinds of outcomes are possible:

1. No cross-hauling, that is $X^{dd} = X^{ff} = X^m > 0$ and $X^{df} = X^{fd} = 0$.
2. Cross-hauling, that is $X^{dd} = X^{ff} > 0$ and $X^{df} = X^{fd} > 0$.

We claim that outcome (2) occurs if and only if:

$$F(X^m) - c'(X^m) > t$$

We first show that this condition is sufficient for cross-hauling to occur. Suppose, to the contrary, that outcome 1 occurs and $F(X^m) - c'(X^m) > t$. In that case the domestic firm can, by expanding output by a small enough amount, increase its profit. This follows from the fact that the domestic firm's perceived marginal revenue in the foreign market, $F(X^m)$, exceeds its marginal cost of exports, $c'(X^m) + t$. (A similar argument holds for the foreign firm.) Thus outcome (1) is not sustainable in equilibrium.

To establish the necessity part we have to show that if outcome 2 holds then $F(X^m) > c'(X^m) + t$. Suppose not, that is let outcome 2 hold and also $F(X^m) \le c'(X^m) + t$. But this implies that the autarkic outcome can be sustained as an equilibrium as well, thus violating uniqueness.

Proof of equivalence between our condition and that in Brander and Krugman (1983)

The difference between our condition and that in Brander and Krugman (1983) can be resolved as follows. Notice that unless the demand curve is very convex, $P^d/\varepsilon^d > P^m/\varepsilon^m$, where superscripts d and m refer to duopoly and monopoly situations respectively. This follows from the fact that $X^d > X^m$ and $\dfrac{d(P/\varepsilon)}{dX} = \dfrac{d}{dX}(-X F'(X)) = -F'(X) - X F''(X) > 0$. For any demand function which is not too convex, that is if $F''(X) < -F'(X)/X$, then $-F'(X) - X F''(X) > 0$. We then note that the only way the two characterisations can differ is if $(P^d/\varepsilon^d) > t > (P^m/\varepsilon^m)$. But this violates the uniqueness of the equilibrium, since the first inequality, $(P^d/\varepsilon^d) > t$, implies the existence of a cross-hauling equilibrium according to the condition given by Brander and Krugman (1983), while the second inequality, $t > (P^m/\varepsilon^m)$, ensures the existence of autarkic monopoly equilibrium by our Proposition 1. Thus, this case can never arise. Therefore, we conclude that the two conditions are equivalent.

Proof of Proposition 2

As before, the cross-hauling equilibrium yields the following four equations:

$$A - 2\,bX^{dd} - bX^{fd} - (X^{dd} + X^{df}) = 0$$
$$A - 2\,bX^{df} - bX^{ff} - (X^{dd} + X^{df}) - t = 0$$
$$A - bX^{df} - 2\,bX^{ff} - (X^{ff} + X^{fd}) = 0$$
$$A - bX^{dd} - 2\,bX^{fd} - (X^{ff} + X^{fd}) - t = 0$$

Solving explicitly we find that:

$$X^{df} = X^{fd} = \frac{A - t(2 + 1/b)}{(3b + 2)}$$

and $X^{dd} = X^{ff} = \dfrac{A + t(1 + 1/b)}{(3b + 2)}$

Now, totally differentiating X^{df} we get:

$$dX^{df} = \partial X^{df}/\partial b . \, db + \partial X^{df}/\partial A . \, dA$$

Routine calculations would now yield that $dX^{df} < 0$ for case (i), if and only if,

$$t > \frac{(3Ab + 3\alpha Ab + 2\alpha A)}{(6 + 2/b + 6b)} = \hat{t}, \text{ say}$$

Next observe that $X^{df} > 0$, if and only if $t < t^*$, where $t^* = Ab/(2b + 1)$. Finally we can see that $t^* > \hat{t}$, if and only if,

$$\alpha < 1/(2b + 1) = \hat{\alpha}, \text{ say}$$

Thus, for all $0 \le \alpha \le \hat{\alpha}$, there is an interval of transport costs $(\hat{t}, t^*)$ such that, for all t belonging to this interval, $X^{df} > 0$ and $dX^{df} < 0$.

Similarly, routine calculations would yield that $dX^{df} < 0$ for case (ii), if and only if $t < \hat{t}$. But for $\alpha \le -1$, $\hat{t} < 0$, thus in this case $dX^{df} > 0$ always.

Hence the proposition is proved.

Chapter 18

Welfare in a Unionised Bertrand Duopoly

Subhayu Bandyopadhyay and Sudeshna C. Bandyopadhyay

F23, F13 D43, F12,
J51   L13

Introduction

With globalisation comes increasing degree of competition between exporting firms based in different nations. Third country markets (e.g., Asian markets) may be opened up to both domestic (e.g., US) and foreign (e.g., European) firms as a result of trade lliberalisation under the framework of WTO or due to preferential trading agreements that may encompass different exporting nations. To be successful in such international markets, firms need to be cost-efficient. Unionisation raises wage costs and may neutralise the competitiveness of exporting firms. This may adversely affect their market share and the welfare of their country. This chapter looks at these issues in the context of an oligopolistic model where a unionised domestic firm engages in price competition with a non-unionised foreign firm in a third nation's market. First, we focus on the case where both exporting nations follow free trade. Then we look at the case where each exporting nation employs an optimal trade policy to raise their nation's welfare. The interplay between unionisation, optimal trade policies and welfare (under price competition) is the subject of our investigation.

The area of optimal trade policy in imperfectly competitive markets has been widely researched in recent years. Since large oligopolistic firms are often unionised, researchers have also focused on the analysis of unionised oligopolies. Brander and Spencer (1988) focus on trade policy under unionisation for the cases of both export and import competition. Fung (1989 and 1995) investigates the role of profit sharing between the union and the firm on market share rivalry. Mezzetti and Dinopoulos (1991) analyse efficient contracting between a domestic firm and the union and its effects on import competition. Gaston and Trefler (1995) explore the effects of trade policy on union wages. Recent contributions of Santoni (1996) and Zhao (1995 and 1998) have focused on issues relating to sequential bargaining and foreign direct investment, respectively. Tanaka (1994) finds a rather remarkable result that in an otherwise level playing field the role of profit sharing is to reduce market share at a subsidy equilibrium.

Bandyopadhyay and Bandyopadhyay (1999, henceforth B&B) find a similar paradox in a standard unionised oligopoly model where rival governments (simultaneously) engage in profit shifting policies. In an otherwise symmetric model the unionised firm has a larger market share than its non-unionised rival. Recently, Bandyopadhyay and Bandyopadhyay (2001) show that paradoxical welfare results emerge under unionisation for both an *efficient bargaining model* and a *right to manage* model under Coumot competition Bandyopadhyay and Bandyopadhyay (2000) analyse a unionised Bertrand duopoly and show that unlike the non-union case the optimal policy does not revert from a subsidy to a tax for the domestic government. This establishes the robustness (to the mode of competition) of strategic trade policy under unionisation. In the light of these contributions a natural question is whether the welfare results are also robust to the mode of competition under unionisation. We address this issue by providing a welfare analysis for a unionised Bertrand duopoly.

We do not specify a particular model of union behaviour and can accommodate wage bargaining and profit sharing as special cases. The only restriction that we impose is that we have a three stage model like Brander-Spencer (1988) where the export subsidy, union wage and employment are chosen in stages one, two and three, respectively. We use a third country export rivalry model. The home firm is unionised while its foreign rival is non-unionised. A tax by the foreign nation under (differentiated good) Bertrand competition raises the foreign firm's price. This leads to a larger demand for the home firm's product and raises the demand for labour. In the normal case, this will raise the union wage (referred to as the 'wage effect' hereafter). Thus, the home firm's price is affected in two ways due to the rise in the foreign price. First, the home price will rise as a Bertrand reaction. In addition, the rise in the union wage raises the marginal cost of the home firm, thereby raising its price further. The 'wage effect' amplifies the domestic price reaction and causes the foreign nation to tax more aggressively. A larger foreign tax causes a positive spillover on the domestic nation, thereby raising its welfare. Thus, a rise in any unionisation parameter that amplifies the 'wage effect' must raise domestic welfare.

We should note that the results hinge on the foreign government's ability to gauge the effect of its subsidy (or tax) on the domestic wage. Admittedly, the information requirement of the foreign government regarding the precise model of union behaviour is quite demanding. In the same token, however, it is unreasonable for the foreign government to ignore the endogeneity of the union wage. A weaker and a reasonable interpretation of our results is that while the foreign government may not know the precise magnitude of the wage effect, it will recognise the positive relation between domestic labour demand and the union wage. Therefore, as we explain below, it will tax more aggressively in the Bertrand case. This implies that domestic welfare will increase with the foreign government's expectation regarding the union 'wage effect'.

The Model

A home firm (1) is assumed to compete with a foreign firm (2) in a third country market. The firms produce differentiated products q^1 and q^2, respectively. There is no domestic consumption of these goods in nations 1 and 2, where these firms belong. Each firm is assumed to maximise profits and employ the Nash-Bertrand assumption regarding its rival's price level. q^1 and q^2 are substitutes and follow the direct demand functions:

$$q^1 = q^1(p^1, p^2) \text{ and } q^2 = q^2(p^1, p^2), q^i_i < 0, q^j_i > 0 \tag{1a}$$

The production functions are:

$$q^i = L^i \text{ for } i = 1,2 \tag{1b}$$

Let α $(O < \alpha < I)$ be the share of profit given to the domestic union. Let the domestic and the foreign governments offer subsidies s and s.*, respectively to their firms. The net profit of firm-i is:

$$\pi^1 = (1 - \alpha)(p^1 - w + s) \, q^1(p^1, p^2) \text{ and } \pi^2 = (p^2 - b + s^*) \, q^2(p^1, p^2) \qquad (2)$$

The home firm's profit maximisation yields the following Nash-Bertrand reaction function:

$$(p^1 - w + s) \, q^1_1 + q^1 = 0 \leftrightarrow p^1 = p^1(p^2, w, s) \qquad (3)$$

The foreign firm's Bertrand reaction function is:

$$(p^2 - b + s^*) \, q^2_2 + q^2 = 0 \leftrightarrow p^2 = 2^1(p^2, s^*) \qquad (4)$$

The third stage Bertrand equilibrium is:

$$p^1 = p^{1B}(w,s,s^*) \text{ and } p^2 = p^2(p^{1B}(w,s,s^*)) = p^{2B}(w,s,s^*) \qquad (5)$$

The union wage is chosen in the second stage of the game and internalises (5) in its choice. Therefore, it is a function of the variables chosen in the first stage of the game and of the unionisation parameter y (which for example may be the union's bargaining power in the Nash bargain function *or* the degree *of* profit sharing, α, etc.):

$$w = w^B(s,s^*,\gamma) \qquad (6)$$

Let the domestic alternative wage be equal to the foreign wage b. This equalises the social opportunity cost of labour in the two exporting nations and neutralises the de Meza (1986) and Neary (1994) type effects. Domestic welfare W is the rent earned from exporting to the third nation. It is also measured by adding the rents earned and the tax burdens of the different agents in this model:

$$W = (p^1 - b)q^1(p^1, p^2(p^1,s^*)) \qquad (7)$$

This completes the description of the model structure. The free trade and the policy equilibrium can be obtained using this structure.

Welfare under free trade $(s = s^* = 0)$:

Using (4), (5) and (7), under free trade:

$$dW/d\gamma = [(p^1 - b))q^1_1 + q^1_2 p^2_1) + q^1]p^{IB}_w(dw/d\gamma) \qquad (8)$$

Using (3), (8) can be written as:

$$dW/d\gamma = [(w - b)q^1_1 + (p^1 - b)q^1_2 p^2_1]p^{IB}_w(dw/d\gamma) \qquad (9)$$

The first term inside the curly bracket reflects the labour market distortion and the second tend the strategic distortion. They are of opposite signs and *a priori* the sign of the bracketed term cannot be determined. However, B&B (2000) show that the labour market distortion dominates in a wide range of cases. Let us assume that to be the case for our purpose. Thus, the bracketed term is negative. It is easy to check using the first order conditions of the two firms that (p – B) is positive. Thus, we can state the following proposition.

Proposition 1

Under free trade, domestic welfare must rise if the domestic wage is reduced by a rise in a labour market parameter.

Proof and Comment

The proof is contained in (9) and the discussion following it. Consider a change in some labour market parameter, like union bargaining power or degree of profit sharing etc. If this leads to a fall in the domestic wage, the price of good-1 will fall (in response to the lower labour cost). The fall in price has two effects. First, since the rival firm's Bertrand reaction function is upward sloping, p2 will fall. Because goods 1 and 2 are substitutes, demand for good-1 must fall. This will tend to reduce the profit of firm-1 and hence domestic welfare. Secondly, the fall in pi will raise the demand for good-1 and will therefore increase employment. This reduces the labour market distortion caused by unionisation.

As long as the second effect dominates, a fall in the wage rate must raise welfare. It is possible that with globalisation the unions realise the importance of being competitive in international markets. This may be reflected in the unions demanding lower wages. Then (under free trade) the competitive positions of the unionised firms improve and the welfare of the relevant exporting nations rise. However, we see later that this finding may be reversed in an environment where exporting nations employ optimal trade policies.

Corollary 1

Under demand linearity and a rent maximising union utility function, a rise in the degree of profit sharing by the union must raise domestic welfare under free trade.

Proof and Comment

The proof is given in an appendix, available upon request from the authors.

Let us first state the wage determination problem for the general case where s and s* can assume any value. We will then obtain the free trade wage as a special case. The union's objective is to maximise the sum of rents and its share of profit (α is the degree of profit sharing). The wage is chosen by the union in the second stage of the game. To ensure subgame perfection the union must consider the effect of w on the third stage choice variables (p^1, p^2). Then, under free trade, we can show that the wage rate falls with the degree of profit sharing (see #1 in the appendix). Further, it is easy to check that the product of the remaining terms on the right hand side of (9) is negative. Thus, using (9) it is clear that domestic welfare W will rise with the degree of profit sharing (i.e., α). This finding is intuitive. As the degree of profit sharing rises, the union places a higher weight on profit income and balances its desire to obtain higher wages with ensuring healthy profits. This tilts the balance towards a reduction in wages. A lower wage helps the domestic firm to reduce its price and thereby raise domestic welfare (through the channels discussed under Proposition I). Therefore, we may conclude that profit sharing helps to raise international competitiveness of unionised firms under free trade and augments the welfare of the relevant exporting nation.

Welfare at the Policy Equilibrium

Using (7) we get:

$$dW = [(p^1 - b)(q^1_1 + q^1_2 p^2_1) + q^1]dp^1 (p^1 - b)q^1_2 p^2_s ds* \tag{10}$$

Under optimal subsidisation (or taxation), where s. is taken as given by the home government, the marginal effect on W will be neutralised. Therefore, using (3) and (10):

$$(p^1 - b)(q^1_1 + q^1_2 p^2_1) + q^1 = 0 \tag{11}$$

$$\text{or, } s = w - b + [(p^1 - b)q^1_2 p^2_1 /q^1_1] \tag{12}$$

This is the optimal subsidy formula derived in B&B (2000). As pointed out in that chapter the subsidy is likely to be positive for several demand and unionisation specifications, but the possibility of a tax cannot be ruled out. It turns out that the welfare results for the policy equilibrium that we derive below are independent of the sign of the trade policy.

Using (9) and (10):

$$dW/d\gamma = (p^1 - b)q^1_2 p^2_s \, ds*/d\gamma \tag{13}$$

The sign of $dW/d\gamma$ is the negative of $ds*/d\gamma$. The optimal subsidy rule for the domestic government implicitly defines:

$$s = s(s*,\gamma) \tag{14}$$

Proposition 2

At the trade policy equilibrium, if a rise in the domestic labour market parameter (γ) raises (reduces) the absolute value of the wage effect), domestic welfare rises (falls) with a rise in γ.

Proof and Comment

The proof is given in an appendix, available upon request from the authors.

A tax by the foreign government raises p^2. This has two effects on the price of good-1, both of which tend to raise p^1, First, since firm-1 's Bertrand reaction function is upward sloping, p^1 rises as a Bertrand reaction. Secondly, because good-1 is a substitute for good 2, the rise in p^2 leads to a rise in the demand for good-1. This raises the demand for domestic labour and leads to a rise in the union wage. The result is a rise in the (net) marginal cost of the domestic firm. This leads to a further rise in p^2, the second effect adds to the first, and therefore the response of p^1 to an increase in p^2 is amplified under unionisation. Consequently, the strategic tax which is set to exploit the Bertrand reaction will be larger.

The greater the magnitude of the wage change the greater will be the strategic foreign tax (i.e., lower will be the foreign subsidy). A tax on the foreign firm raises its price, and in turn raises the demand faced by the domestic firm. This benefits the latter and raises domestic welfare. Thus, the effects of unionisation on an increasingly integrated global economy is not clear. While proposition 1 tells us that a union that is more conservative in terms of its wage demand positively impacts the unionised firm (and the relevant exporting nation), exactly the reverse is observed here. The difference arises because of optimal trade intervention which changes the nature of the game between the firms. Indeed, it is the foreign government's aggressive trade policy which benefits the domestic firms.

Corollary 2

If demand is linear and if the union has a rent maximising utility function, then at the trade policy equilibrium a rise in the degree of profit sharing by the union must reduce domestic welfare.

Proof and Comment

The proof is in the appendix, available on request from the authors.

A rise in the degree of profit sharing makes the union care more about profits and therefore moderates its desire for wage hikes. An export tax by the foreign nation raises its firm's price (p^2). Through the wage effect discussed above (under proposition 2), this raises the union wage rate. However, for unions with higher degrees of profit sharing these wage hikes are smaller. Consequently, the hike in the domestic price (p^1) is smaller. In effect, the foreign government finds that taxing its firm (firm 2) leads to a smaller response from the domestic firm (firm 1) as the degree of domestic profit sharing rises. This reduces the strategic incentive for foreign taxation and leads to a lower tax imposed by the foreign government (on the foreign firm). As the magnitude of foreign taxation declines with profit sharing, the welfare of the domestic nation must fall. This result paradoxically reverses Corollary 1, one would expect that profit sharing should raise the domestic firm's profit and raise domestic welfare. We find that while this is true under free trade, the results are reversed at a policy equilibrium of a Bertrand duopoly. These findings complement the chapters of Tanaka (1994) and B&B (1999 and 2001) who find similar paradoxes under Cournot competition.

Conclusion

This chapter makes two contributions. To our knowledge it is the first work to present a systematic welfare analysis for a unionised Bertrand duopoly. Secondly, it finds that paradoxical welfare results obtain that are similar to the case of Cournot competition (analysed in the existing literature). This suggests that these results are robust to the mode of competition. Finally, we note that while the chapter highlights the case of profit sharing as an example, the propositions are more general and apply to any wage determination process (assuming that the same three stage Bertrand structure is used). These results have important implications for the global marketplace. One would normally expect that if unionisation leads to greater labour market distortions, it should reduce the welfare of the nation to which the unionised firm belongs. For example, profit sharing will be expected to reduce labour market distortions and raise welfare. While we find support for this idea under free trade, we find contrasting results under optimal trade intervention. This confirms the importance of careful analysis of international markets and also of obtaining greater information about the contexts in which these markets operate.

References

Bandyopadhyay, Subhayu and Sudeshna C. Bandyopadhyay (1999), 'Unionisation and International Market Share Rivalry: A Paradox', *Review of International Economics*, Vol. 7, No. 1, pp. 153–61.

Bandyopadhyay, Subhayu and Sudeshna C. Bandyopadhyay (2000), 'Unionised Bertrand Duopoly and Strategic Export Policy', *Review of International Economics*, Vol. 8, No. 1, pp. 164–74.

Bandyopadhyay, Subhayu and Sudeshna C. Bandyopadhyay (2001), 'Efficient Bargaining, Welfare and Strategic Export Policy', *Journal of International Trade and Economic Development*, Vol. 10, No. 2, pp. 133–49.

Brander, James A. and Barbara J. Spencer (1985), 'Export Subsidies and International Market Share Rivalry', *Journal of International Economics*, Vol. 18, pp. 83–100.

Brander, James A. and Barbara J. Spencer (1988), 'Unionised Oligopoly and International Trade Policy', *Journal of International Economics*, Vol. 24, pp. 217–34.

de Meza, D. (1986), 'Export-subsidies and High Productivity: Cause or Effect?', *Canadian Journal of Economics*, Vol. 19, No. 2, pp. 347–50.

Eaton, Jonathan and Gene M. Grossman (1986), 'Optimal Trade and Industrial Policy under Oligopoly', *Quarterly Journal of Economics*, Vol. 101, pp. 383–406.

Fung, K.C. (1989), 'Unemployment, Profit-sharing and Japan's Economic Success', *European Economic Review*, Vol. 33, pp. 783–96.

Fung, K.C. (1995), 'Rent Shifting and Rent Sharing: A Re-examination of the Strategic Industrial Policy Problem', *Canadian Journal of Economics*, Vol. 28, pp. 450–62.

Gaston, N. and D. Trefler (1995), 'Union Wage Sensitivity to Trade and Protection: Theory and Evidence', *Journal of International Economics*, Vol. 39, pp. 1–25.

Mezzetti, Claudio and Elias Dinopoulos (1991), 'Domestic Unionisation and Import Competition', *Journal of International Economics*, Vol. 31, pp. 79–100.

Neary, J.P. (1994), 'Cost Asymmetries in International Subsidy Games: Should Governments Help Winners or Losers?', *Journal of International Economics*, Vol. 37, pp. 197–218.

Santoni, M. (1996), 'Union-oligopoly Sequential Bargaining: Trade and Industrial Policies', *Oxford Economic Papers*, Vol. 48, pp. 640–63.

Tanaka, Y. (1994), 'Profit-sharing and Welfare in an export subsidy game', *Economics Letters*, Vol. 45, pp. 349–53.

Zhao, L. (1995), 'Cross-hauling Direct Foreign Investment and Unionised Oligopoly', *European Economic Review*, Vol. 39, pp. 1237–53.

Zhao, L. (1998), 'The Impact of Foreign Direct Investment on Wages and Employment', *Oxford Economic Papers*, Vol. 50, pp. 284–301.

Chapter 19

Corruption, Globalisation and Domestic Environmental Policies

Richard Damania

Introduction

Environmental issues are high among the litany of concerns about globalisation. Critics of globalisation contend that the competitive pressures resulting from increased openness and trade will induce a 'race to the bottom', with all countries lowering their environmental standards. In contrast, proponents of globalisation argue that trade restrictions are an inefficient and inappropriate way to resolve environmental problems. Efficiency considerations dictate that domestic environmental problems should be corrected using domestic environmental policy instruments, which internalise the environmental externalities (Esty 1994).

However, a growing body of recent literature suggests that in many developing countries widespread corruption has rendered domestic environmental policies ineffective. For instance, Desai (1998: 172) in a comparative study of ten countries concludes that: 'The practice of large scale corruption has at times stalled the implementation of pollution control laws to a significant extent. Industry owners commonly perceive that public servants are to be bought by monetary incentives'.

Similarly, in an econometric analysis of water pollution, Pargal, Mani and Huq (1997) find that corruption has resulted in routine non-compliance. More generally, as environmental regulations have increased over time, this has enlarged the sphere of activities through which corrupt administrators can extract bribes. Public support for the process of economic integration may well depend on the ability to resolve these environmental problems. The objective of this chapter is to propose a simple mechanism which can be used to deter corruption and make domestic environmental policies more effective.

Corruption arises when bureaucrats who enforce and administer policies are given discretionary powers. If the bureaucrats are assumed to be self interested, these delegated powers may be exploited for personal gain, rather than the purposes intended by the policy makers. Such problems abound, particularly in developing countries, where corruption has been shown to undermine government policy (Rose-Ackerman 1997), stifle the entry of new enterprises and technologies (Krueger 1990, Manion 1996) and impede economic growth (Mauro 1995).[1] However, the effects of bribery on environmental policy outcomes, remains one of the least researched aspects of economic behaviour.[2]

In this chapter we outline a new mechanism which may be employed to prevent corruption. It is shown that by injecting uncertainty into the relationship between a bribe giver and a bribe taker, the payoffs from corrupt behaviour can be substantially reduced, thereby making corruption easier to control. Intuitively, this follows from the fact that agents will choose to offer a bribe only if it is likely to be accepted. A bribe in turn will be accepted only if the recipient believes that the expected payoffs from acceptance of the bribe offer will exceed those from rejection of the offer. A sufficient degree of uncertainty at either of these stages may be sufficient to render honest behaviour the individually rational strategy. This chapter outlines a simple and usable way in which this may be achieved.

The remainder of this chapter is organised as follows. Section II provides a brief intuitive summary of the model and the results. The next section outlines the basic sequential model which we use as a benchmark to motivate the discussion in Section IV which deals with the case when the order of inspections is randomised. Section V provides a numerical example which gives an indication of the relative magnitudes implied by the model. Finally, Section VI concludes the chapter.

Model Description and Discussion

We consider a model in which a government regulator employs environmental inspectors to monitor pollution emissions from two firms labelled i and j.[3] The regulator cannot directly observe the level of pollution emitted by the firms. However, the regulator knows that the lower the aggregate level of *reported* emissions, the greater is the probability that a bribe has been paid to an inspector to underreport true emission levels.

The regulator may then choose to audit industry emissions. The likelihood of an audit being initiated is linked to the probability that emissions have been underreported. With some exogenously given probability, the audit unearths true emission levels and a fine is imposed on both the firm (briber) and environmental inspector (recipient of the bribe) for underreporting discharge levels.[4]

We begin by considering the incentives for bribe taking when the firms are inspected sequentially by different inspectors and the order of inspections is common knowledge. Since the probability of detection and prosecution increases with the degree of underreporting, the firm which is inspected first enjoys a strategic advantage. To see why, suppose that firm i, is inspected first and bribes its inspector to underreport the true level of discharge. Clearly, firm j's optimum response depends on firm i's report. The lower the level of emissions reported by firm i's inspector, the greater is the probability that an industry wide audit will be triggered, and the lower is the incentive for firm j to underreport its emissions. Thus, in equilibrium firm i and its inspector take advantage of their position and report a lower level of emissions than firm j. More importantly, it is demonstrated that corruption cannot be deterred in this situation.

We then extend the model by allowing the regulator to withhold information about the order in which the firms are to be inspected. It is demonstrated that if the regulator randomises the order of inspections and makes this known to all parties, bribe taking can be deterred. Intuitively, this reflects the fact that if each firm and inspector believes that there is a sufficiently high probability that they are to report second, this diminishes their collective incentive to underreport emissions. It is shown that there exists a feasible set of probabilities and fines such that the regulator can induce truthful reporting by the inspectors at both firms. This result reflects the fact that bribe taking is only feasible because the regulator (principle) is imperfectly informed about emission levels, while firms and their inspectors (agents) are fully informed. By generating uncertainty about the strategic position of each agent, the principle can partly mitigate the informational advantage of the inspectors. This in turn makes it easier to implement policies which deter bribe taking and induce truthful reporting.[5]

Formally, the game is one of incomplete information, where each inspector (and firm) is uncertain about the sequence of inspections and hence the rival's payoffs. Since the rival's payoffs are unknown, the best response functions must be based on expectations (i.e. announced probabilities) of the sequence of inspections. Given the informational structure of the model, there can be no learning or updating of probabilities, since an inspector has no way of determining whether a rival has undertaken an inspection.

These results are, however, predicated on the assumption that collusion and information sharing about the order of inspections can be prevented. Where institutional structures do not preclude communication, it is quite natural to expect agents to exchange information to protect their rents. We therefore outline a simple device which renders such communication unprofitable. Specifically, we consider a reward and punishment strategy where an inspector (or firm) who initiates unauthorised communication is fined with some probability, if reported by her rival. The rival in turn is offered a reward for disclosing this information to the authorities. It is demonstrated that if the reward and fine are sufficiently high the inspectors confront a standard prisoners' dilemma problem – the dominant strategy for each inspector is to divulge information, even though both would be better off by cooperating. Thus, neither inspector initiates communication.

While the model presented here bears some similarity to that of Koffman and Lawarree (1996), there are significant differences in structure and the mechanisms through which corruption is deterred. Firstly, Koffman and Lawarree analyse a situation where two inspectors police each other. In the current model there is only one inspector assigned to each firm. Moreover, Koffman and Lawarree do not consider the possibility of collusion between inspectors.[6] This issue is explicitly addressed in the current chapter. More importantly, the mechanisms through which corruption is prevented differ markedly. In the Koffman–Lawarree model, despite the use of two inspectors to police each other, double supervision is suboptimal since it is costly. Thus, the second inspector is sent with probability less than one, when the first submits a low (potentially fraudulent) report. Corruption is deterred when the principal offers the second inspector a high enough reward. This occurs because, once the first inspector has been bribed, the briber is left with insufficient rent with which to induce the second to collude. In contrast, in the current chapter uncertainty about the order of inspections diminishes the gains to each inspector and firm from submitting a dishonest report.[7] Since the expected gains from corruption are smaller, there exist a feasible set of probabilities and fines such that the regulator can induce truthful reporting by the inspectors at both firms.

The Model

An industry with two firms labelled i and j discharge pollution emissions $e_i \in [0, \bar{e}_i]$ ($i = 1, 2, i \neq j$). Each firm is visited by an environmental inspector who reports its emission levels to a regulatory agency. Firms pay an emission tax of t per unit on *reported* pollution emissions. Firms may, however, offer their inspector a bribe of B_i to under-report emission levels. An inspector who accepts a bribe, reports emission levels denoted $\hat{e}_i$ which may differ from actual emissions of e_i. We assume that $\hat{e}_i \leq e_i$, so that the inspector is unable to exaggerate true pollution levels.[8] The reward to each inspector for reporting emissions of $\hat{e}_i$ is given by $wt\hat{e}_i$. Thus, each inspector receives a proportion w of the tax paid by the firm. Not unrealistically, it is supposed that $w < 1$ so that some fraction of the emission tax revenue accrues to the government.

The inspectors' remuneration is linked to reported emissions ($\hat{e}_i$), since it is assumed that the regulator cannot observe the actual level of emissions (e_i). It is useful to note, that in order to encourage truthful reporting, the compensation schedule should be negatively related to the degree of underreporting (i.e. ($e_i - \hat{e}_i$)). However, such a schedule cannot be implemented here as the regulator has no knowledge of true emission levels (e_i), and must therefore condition the inspectors' remuneration schedule on reported emissions ($\hat{e}_i$).

While the regulatory authority cannot observe actual emission levels, it knows that *ceteris paribus* the lower the total level of reported emissions, the greater is the probability that at least one inspector has accepted a bribe to underreport true emission levels. Specifically, let the probability that the regulator attaches to a bribe being accepted by the inspectors be:

$$\sigma = \frac{K - \hat{e}_i - \hat{e}_j}{K} \tag{1}$$

where: $K > 0$ is an exogenously given parameter.[9]

It is assumed that σ also defines the probability that the regulator initiates an audit of emission levels.[10] Moreover, the probability that an audit successfully detects true pollution levels is exogenously given by $\beta \in (0, 1)$. Thus, β may be viewed as an indicator of the efficiency of the judicial process. An inspector found guilty of underreporting emissions is fined $P(e_i - \hat{e}_i)$ (where; $P \geq t$), while the firm is fined $F(e_i - \hat{e}_i)$ (where; $F \geq t$). The probability that an audit occurs and leads to successful prosecution is: $\lambda = \sigma\beta$.

Suppose that firm i decides to bribe its inspector an amount $B_i > 0$ to report emission levels of $\hat{e}_i < e_i$. The expected gains to the firm from offering a bribe are given by:

$$\Delta_i = te_i - (B_i + t\hat{e}_i + \lambda F(e_i - \hat{e}_i)) \qquad (i = 1,2), (i \neq j) \tag{2}$$

The first term in (2) represents the amount that must be paid in emission taxes if the firm does not offer a bribe. The remaining terms represent the expected costs of a bribe. Thus, a bribe of B_i induces the inspector to report $\hat{e}_i$, so that the firm pays emission taxes of $t\hat{e}_i$. With probability λ a successful audit is triggered and the firm is fined F on its unreported emissions of ($e_i - \hat{e}_i$).

Similarly, the gains to an inspector from accepting a bribe of B_i from firm i is given by:

$$\Omega_i = (B_i + wt\hat{e}_i - \lambda P(e_i - \hat{e}_i)) - wt\hat{e}_i \qquad (i = 1, 2), (i \neq j) \qquad (3)$$

The terms in parenthesis in (3) describe the expected payoffs from accepting a bribe. A bribe of B_i induces a report of $\hat{e}_i$, and the inspector receives a reward of $wt\hat{e}_i$ from the regulator. With probability λ a successful audit is initiated and leads to a penalty of P being imposed on unreported emissions.

We begin by considering a situation in which the firms are inspected sequentially by different inspectors and the order of inspections is common knowledge to all players. Without loss of generality, assume that firm i is inspected first.

By backward induction we begin by solving firm j's problem. Taking as given firm i's reported emissions, firm j and its inspector will choose to report a level of pollution which maximise their joint expected payoffs from a bribe of B_j. Specifically, the reported level of emissions $\hat{e}_j$ satisfies:

$$\underset{\hat{e}_j}{\text{Max}} \ (\Delta_j + \Omega_i) \qquad (4a)$$

Solving the associated first order condition for (4a), yields the following best response function for j:

$$\hat{e}_j(\hat{e}_i) = \frac{1}{2} \ (K(1 - \frac{t(1-w)}{\beta(F+P)}) - \hat{e}_i + e_j) \qquad (4b)$$

Given knowledge of its rival's reaction function in (4b), firm i and its inspector choose reported emission levels to maximise their joint payoffs:

$$\underset{\hat{e}_j}{\text{Max}} \ (\Delta_j(\sigma_i^*) + \Omega_i(\sigma_i^*)) \qquad (5a)$$

where $\sigma_i^* = \frac{1}{2} \left(\frac{(1-w)t}{\beta(F+P)} + 1 - \frac{e_j + e_i}{K} \right)$ is the quasi-reduced form probability of an

audit which is obtained by substituting (4b) for $\hat{e}_i$ in σ.

Solving the resulting first-order condition, equilibrium reported emission levels can be deduced to be:

$$\hat{e}_j = \frac{1}{2} \ (e_i - e_j + K(1 - \frac{t(1-w)}{\beta(F+P)})) \qquad (5b)$$

$$\hat{e}_j = \frac{1}{4} \ (3e_j - e_i + K(1 - \frac{t(1-w)}{\beta(F+P)})) \qquad (5c)$$

Once the reported emission levels have been decided, the equilibrium bribe is determined by a Nash bargain between the firm and each inspector. Each party is assumed to have equal bargaining power and the bribe is chosen to maximise the following Nash bargain:

$$\underset{B_i}{\text{Max}} \ (\Delta_j \Omega_i) \tag{6a}$$

This results in an outcome where the firm and inspector equally share the net benefits from underreporting the true level of emissions. The equilibrium bribe is thus:

$$B^*_i = \frac{1}{2} (e_i - \hat{e}_i)(\tau(P - F) + t(1 + w)) \tag{6b}$$

where: $\tau = \beta \dfrac{1}{4} \left(\dfrac{(1 - w)3t}{\beta(F + P)} + 1 - \dfrac{(e_j + e)_i}{K} \right)$

Firm j's bribe is determined in a similar manner and is given by:

$$B^*_j = \frac{1}{2} (e_j - \hat{e}_j)(\tau(P - F) + t(1 + w)) \tag{6c}$$

Lemma 1 below describes a useful property of the equilibrium. The proof of all the results is in the Appendix.

Lemma 1: If $e_i = e_j$ and $\beta \in [\ Kt(1 - w)/[(K + 2e)(P + F)], \ t(1 - w)/(P + F)]$ then $\hat{e}_i = 0$ and $\hat{e}_j \in [0, e_j]$ Lemma 1 informs us that, when both firms emit the same level of pollution, and if the probability of successfully prosecuting the corrupt parties lies in a certain range, then there exist equilibria in which firm i reports zero emissions, while j reports positive emission levels. This simply reflects the first mover advantage conferred upon firm i which allows it to capture a more favourable position and report lower emissions.

Having determined reported emission levels, Proposition 1 outlines the circumstances in which it is impossible to deter corruption.

Proposition 1

If $\beta \leq \beta^c$ then $\hat{e}_i < e_i$, $\hat{e}_j < e_j$ and $B^*_i > 0$ and $B^*_j > 0$.

Where: $\beta^c = tK(1 - w)/((P + F)(K - e_i - e_j))$

Proposition 1 is intuitively obvious. It reveals that if the probability of successfully prosecuting the corrupt parties (β) is sufficiently small, the expected payoffs from under-reporting emissions always exceed those from truthful revelation. It is therefore impossible to deter bribing.

It is of interest to note that all corruption can be eliminated if the regulator can adjust policies so that $\beta^c = 0$. This, however, cannot be achieved by simply raising the probability of audits (K), since $\underset{K \to \infty}{\text{Lim}} \ \beta^c = \dfrac{t(1 - w)}{\beta(F + P)} > 0$. Moreover, increasing the fines (F +P) only lowers β^c to zero as the fines approach infinity (i.e. ∞). Bribe taking can, however, be eliminated if all tax revenues are paid to the inspector (i.e. w = 1).[11] In the following Section we demonstrate that by introducing uncertainty into the sequence of inspections it is easier to prevent bribe taking.

Uncertainty

In this section we consider the consequences of introducing uncertainty about the sequence of inspections. Specifically, the regulatory authority randomises the order of inspections and informs all parties that with some probability $\theta[(1 - \theta)]$ firm i (j) will be inspected first. The game is thus one of incomplete information, where decision must be based on announced probabilities and the best responses depend on expectations.[12]

We initially assume that, there is no communication between the parties and the decisions are based on information about the sequence of inspections provided by the regulatory authority. This assumption is eschewed later in this section where we consider strategies which render communication between the parties unprofitable. It is demonstrated that the informational advantage accruing to the regulator makes corruption easier to control.

The expected payoff to firm i from offering a bribe of B_i to an inspector is:

$$\Theta_i = te_i - (B_i + t\hat{e}_i + \beta F(e_i - \hat{e}_i)(\theta\sigma_i^* + (1 - \theta)\sigma)) \tag{7a}$$

The first term represents the amount that must be paid in emission taxes if a truthful report is submitted. The remaining terms describe the expected costs of a bribe. A bribe of B_i induces a report $\hat{e}_i$, so that the firm pays emission taxes of $t\hat{e}_i$. With probability θ firm i is inspected first and as noted in Section II, the probability of an audit being initiated is defined by σ_i^*. Conversely, with probability $(1 - \theta)$ firm i is inspected second and the likelihood of an audit is given by σ. An audit leads to successful prosecution with probability β and the firm is fined F on its unreported emissions of $(e_i - \hat{e}_i)$.[13]

Similarly, the expected payoffs to an inspector from accepting a bribe of B_i from firm i are given by:

$$\Psi_i = (wt\hat{e}_i + B_i - \beta P(e_i - \hat{e}_i)(\theta\sigma_i^* + (1 - \theta)\sigma)) - wte_i \tag{7b}$$

Reported emissions are chosen to maximise the joint expected payoffs of firm i and its inspector:

$$\max_{\hat{e}_i} (\Theta_i + \Psi_i) \tag{7c}$$

Similarly, at firm j reported emissions are chosen to maximise joint payoffs:

$$\max_{\hat{e}_j} (\Theta_j + \Psi_j) \tag{7d}$$

where: $\Psi_j = (wt\hat{e}_j + B_j - \beta P(e_j - \hat{e}_j)((1 - \theta)\sigma_j^* + \theta\sigma)) - wte_j$
$\Theta_j = te_j - (t\hat{e}_j + B_j + \beta F(e_j - \hat{e}_j)((1 - \theta)\sigma_j^* + \theta\sigma))$

For computational ease we focus only on the symmetric case where both firms emit the same level of pollution $e_i = e_j = e$. It can be verified that in equilibrium reported emission levels are:

$$\hat{e}_i = \frac{e}{2}(1-\theta) + \frac{K}{4}\left(\frac{(-1+\theta(3-4\beta))(1-w)t}{\beta(F+P)} + 1 + \theta\right) \tag{8a}$$

$$\hat{e}_j = \frac{e}{2}\theta + \frac{K}{4}\left(\frac{(2-\theta(3-4\beta))(1-w)t}{\beta(F+P)} + 1 + \theta\right) \tag{8b}$$

Equations (8a) and (8b) reveal that the emission levels reported by each firm increases with the probability that the rival is inspected first. This suggests that it may be possible for the regulator to induce truthful reporting by manipulating the level of information made available to the parties, through the randomisation strategy which determines the sequence of inspections.

Lemma 2 specifies the range of values of θ over which truthful reporting is incentive compatible. All proofs are in the Appendix.

Lemma 2: $\hat{e}_i = e$ if $\theta < \theta_i(\beta)$ and $\hat{e}_j = $ if $\theta > \theta_j(\beta)$.

where: $\theta_i(\beta) = \dfrac{-Kt(1-w) + \beta(P+F)(K-2e)}{Kt(4\beta-3)(1-w) - \beta(P+F)(K-2e)}$

$\theta_j(\beta) = \dfrac{-Kt(1-2\beta)(1-w) + \beta(P+F)(K-2e)}{-Kt(4\beta-3)(1-w) + \beta(P+F)(K-2e)}$

Clearly, such a θ is only feasible if: $\theta_j(\beta) \leq \theta_i(\beta)$. Lemma 3a specifies the circumstances under which $\theta_j(\beta) \leq \theta_i(\beta)$.

Lemma 3a: $\theta_j(\beta) \leq \theta_i(\beta)$ iff $\beta \geq \beta^u$

where: $\beta^u = \dfrac{Kt(1-w)}{4Kt(1-w) + (-K+2e)3(F+P)}$

Lemma 3a informs us that if the probability of a successful prosecution exceeds a certain threshold level β^u then $\theta_j(\beta) \leq \theta_i(\beta)$, so that bribe taking can be deterred by setting a $\theta \in (\theta_j(\beta), \theta_i(\beta))$. This condition is analogous to that outlined in Proposition 1 where it was shown that corruption can be prevented in a sequential game with perfect information only if β exceeds the critical level β^c.

Observe that corruption can be eliminated with the randomisation strategy when $\beta^u = 0$. The circumstance under which this occurs is outlined in the following Lemma.

Lemma 3b: If either $K \geq \dfrac{6e(P+F)}{3(P+F) - 4t(1-w)}$, or if $(P+F) \geq \dfrac{4Kt(1-w)}{3(K-2e)}$ then $\beta^u \leq 0$.

Lemma 3b reveals that the critical threshold level β^u can be reduced to a level below any non-negative prosecution rate β, by either raising the frequency of audits (K) sufficiently, or increasing the fines (P + F). Corruption can therefore be eradicated either by adjusting the penalty or the frequency of audits. Lemmas 2, 3a and 3b thus combine to suggest the following result.

Proposition 2

If $\theta \in (\theta_j(\beta), \theta_i(\beta))$ and either $K \geq \dfrac{6e(P + F)}{3(P + F) - 4t(1 - w)}$, and /or $(P+F) \geq \dfrac{4Kt(1 - w)}{3(K - 2e)}$, then $\beta^u \leq 0$ so that $\hat{e}_i = e$ and $\hat{e}_j = e$.

Intuitively, the introduction of asymmetric information provides the regulator with an additional policy instrument with which to influence reported emission levels and bribe taking. Thus, Proposition 2 reveals that uncertainty about the sequence of audits allows the regulator to lower the payoffs from bribe taking and induce truthful reporting by either raising the penalty, or the frequency of audits. This contrasts with the results outlined in the previous Section where it was shown that when the sequence of audits is known, increases in either the penalty or the frequency of audits do not deter bribe taking.

The results thus far have been based on the assumption that institutional structures can prevent unauthorised communication between agents. Clearly, in the absence of such constraints, firms and inspectors could collude and share information about the actual sequence of inspections and thus frustrate the regulatory authority's attempt to inject uncertainty into the game. We therefore consider a simple strategy which is designed to deter information sharing.

Consider a confidentiality clause which forbids inspectors and firms from disclosing information about inspections to unauthorised personnel. This rule is enforced by using a system of rewards and punishments. An inspector or firm who is approached by an unauthorised agent, for information, is given a reward for disclosing this to the regulatory authorities if the information leads to successful prosecution. The guilty party in turn, is fined for seeking access to unauthorised information, if prosecuted. In the Appendix we demonstrate that by setting a sufficiently high set of rewards and penalty the regulator can deter unauthorised communication.

A Numerical Example

This section outlines a simple numerical example which provides an indication of the relative magnitudes implied by the model. The simulations are based on the following values. True pollution levels are assumed to be $e_i = e_j = 10$; $t = 0.2$ is the tax on reported emissions; $w = 0.5$ is the proportion of the tax revenue accruing to the inspector and $\beta = 0.4$ defines the probability of a successful prosecution. For simplicity we consider a randomisation strategy where $\theta = 0.5$ is the probability that i reports first.

We begin by exploring the impact of varying the fines for a given value of K. Table 19.1 below reports the equilibrium outcomes as the combined fines $(P + F)$ vary from 0.1 to 1. Table 19.1 reveals that under full information about the sequence of inspections firm j's reported emissions always exceed those of firm i (columns 2 and 3). Moreover for all values of the penalties in the considered range, underreporting occurs. Columns 4 and 5 report emission levels under uncertainty when $\theta = 0.5$. When the fine reaches $(F + P) = 0.3$ truthful reporting is induced. In contrast, under full information about the sequence of inspections, a fine of 0.3 induces firm i to reports only 20 per cent of its true emissions, while j reports 60 per cent of its discharge levels.

Table 19.1   Reported emissions with K = 25 and $e_i = e_j = 10$

(F + P)	$\hat{e}_i$ full information	$\hat{e}_j$ full information	$\hat{e}_i$ uncertainty	$\hat{e}_i$ uncertainty
0.1	0	0	7.1	7.1
0.2	0	3.4	9.5	9.5
0.3	2.08	6	10	10
0.4	4.7	7.3	10	10
0.5	6.2	8.1	10	10
0.6	7.2	8.5	10	10
0.7	8	9	10	10
0.8	8.5	9.2	10	10
0.9	9	9.4	10	10
1.0	9.1	9.51	10	10

Table 19.2 explores the manner in which reported emission levels vary with the frequency of audits (K) for a given punishment. It is assumed that the penalty is set at (F + P) = 0.5.

Table 19.2   Reported emissions with penalties (F + P) = 0.5 and $e_i = e_j = 10$

K	$\hat{e}_i$ full information	$\hat{e}_j$ full information	$\hat{e}_i$ uncertainty	$\hat{e}_i$ uncertainty
5	1.2	5.6	4.1	4.1
8	2	3.46	5.2	5.2
11	2.78	6.3	6.2	6.2
14	3.5	6.7	7.2	7.2
17	4.25	7.1	8.2	8.2
20	5	7.56	9.2	9.2
23	5.75	7.8	10	10
26	6.5	8.2	10	10
30	7.25	8.61	10	10

The frequency of audits associated with K = 23 induces honest reporting under uncertainty when the fines are set at (F+P) = 0.5. However, under full information about the sequence of inspections, at K = 23 firm i only reports 57 per cent of its true emissions, while j reports 78 per cent of its emissions. These numerical examples illustrate the significant role played by information about inspections in a sequential setting. Corruption cannot be prevented with either a fine or by raising the probability of audits under full information. However, under uncertainty the expected payoffs can be reduced sufficiently to deter corruption with either a fine or by increasing the frequency of audits.

Conclusion

Environmental concerns and the inability to address these concerns through domestic policies remain one of the major challenges facing globalisation. Recent evidence suggests that widespread corruption is a major impediment to resolving environmental problems in developing countries. This chapter has shown that the traditional approach of increasing penalties in response to corruption may not be sufficient to eliminate bribery. Instead, greater attention needs to be given to institutional structures and mechanisms which mitigate the informational advantage of corrupt agents. One such strategy outlined in this chapter is the randomisation of the sequence of inspections. It was shown that this simple device can be used to induce greater compliance with regulations.

It is of interest to briefly outline an example of such a randomisation rule that could be used in practice. Consider a monitoring system over say $t = 4$ periods. In odd periods firm i's inspector is required to submit a report and in even periods firm j's inspector reports emissions. The regulator announces that in period $t = 4$, with probability θ reported emissions from periods 1 and 2 will be used to determine whether an audit will take place. With probability $(1 - \theta)$ reported emissions from periods 2 and 3 are used to determine the probability of an audit. Clearly in the former case i enjoy a strategic advantage, while in the latter case the advantage accrues to j. Communication between agents can do little to overcome the uncertainty generated by this system. Thus from Proposition 2 for any given β, the regulator can vary K, P, and F to ensure that truthful reporting is induced.

Notes

[1] The literature on the control of corruption is rapidly developing. Rose-Ackerman (1978) pioneered the formal analysis of corruption by examining the link between institutional structures and the opportunities for rent-seeking. Following this lead, much of the existing theoretical literature on corruption deals with monitoring problems which arise in a hierarchical structure, where a principal (such as the government), confers supervisory powers upon a self interested agent (say an inspector). An issue, which has received considerable attention, is the use of incentive payments and fines to deter bribe taking. The central conclusions which emerge from the literature are that: marginal increases in a fine imposed on the bribe taker simply leads to higher bribes being paid in equilibrium (Mookherjee and Png 1995). In contrast, penalties imposed on the bribe giver, unambiguously reduce the level of corruption (Basu et al. 1992). Payment of a sufficiently high efficiency wage diminishes the gains from bribe taking and may under certain conditions deter corruption (Beasley and McLaren 1990). Where multiple supervisors police each other, corruption can at times be deterred by sending subsequent supervisors with probability less than one (Koffman and Lawarree 1996).

[2] The only exception appears to be Damania (2002).

[3] The model is similar to that outlined by Mokherjee and Png (1995).

[4] This structure is analogous to the water pollution case in Pargal, Mani and Huq (op cit.).

[5] The mechanism outlined in this chapter is analogous to that suggested by Maskin and Tirole (1990) where imperfect information generated by the principal allows a superior equilibrium to be sustained.

[6] Instead they examine in detail whether the agent has an incentive to inform each inspector about the report of her rival and the rival's position.

[7] Under uncertainty the bribe is chosen to maximise expected payoffs which are a weighted average of the bribes of the first and second mover.

[8] This implies that the firm can provide irrefutable evidence of emission levels to the regulatory agency if it so chooses.

[9] Observe that as K rises the probability of an audit being initiated increases. K may be seen to depend on the resources available to the regulator to conduct an audit. Conversely, as reported emissions rise, then σ declines.

[10] There are several other rules which could be used to trigger an audit. In a non-sequential setting with no corruption, Chander and Wilde (1998) show that auditing the low reports with higher probability is optimal. Similarly in this model an audit probability which declines with reported emissions leads to less corruption than either a constant audit rate, or, perversely, an audit rate which increases in reported emissions.

[11] If regulators are required to raise revenue to cover costs or confront budgetary constraints this is unlikely to be an appealing policy choice.

[12] Note that this game reduces to the full information sequential game of the previous section if $\theta = 1$. Moreover, as in the standard duopoly case, the imperfect information (i.e. Cournot) outcome only obtains when we require that neither firm is the leader and each therefore plays a simultaneous game.

[13] This objective function can be compared to a Stackelberg duopoly where the players know that firm i moves first with probability $\theta < 1$. Firm i will base its strategy on the expectation that it is leads with probability θ and follows with probability $(1 - \theta)$. For example let $q_i = $ firm i's output, and let inverse demand be given by $P = 1 - q_i - q_j$. Assume there are zero costs. Suppose that both players know that firm i leads with probability $\theta < 1$. Then i's expected payoffs are $\pi_i = \theta(1 - q_i - R_j(q_i))q_i + .(1 - \theta)(1 - q_i - q_i)q_i$, where $R_j(q_i) = $ firm j's best response function. Equation (7a) defines the analogous objective function in the current context.

References

Basu, K.S. and A. Mishra Bhattacharya (1992), 'Notes on Bribery and the Control of Corruption', *Journal of Public Economics*, Vol. 48, pp. 349–59.

Beasley, T. and J. McLaren (1990), 'Taxes and Bribery', *Economic Journal*, Vol. 103, pp. 119–41.

Chander, P and L. Wilde. (1998), 'A General Characterisation of Optimal Income Tax Enforcement', *Review of Economic Studies*, Vol. 65, pp. 165–83.

Damania, R., 'Environmental Policies with Corruption', *Environment and Development Economics*, forthcoming.

Desai, U. (1998), *Ecological Policy and Politics in Developing Countries: Economic Growth, Democracy and Environment*, State University of New York Press, Albany, New York.

Esty, D. (1994), *Greening the GATT*, Institute for International Economics, Washington DC.

Hillman, A. and E. Katz (1987), 'Hierarchical Structure and the Social Cost of Bribes and Transfers', *Journal of Public Economics*, Vol. 34, pp. 129–42.

Koffman, F. and J. Lawarree (1996), 'A Prisoners Dilemma Model of Collusion Deterrence', *Journal of Public Economics*, Vol. 59, pp. 117–36.

Krueger, A. (1990), *Perspectives on Trade and Development*, University of Chicago Press, Chicago.

Manion, M. (1996), 'Corruption by Design: Bribery in Chinese Enterprise Licensing', *Journal of Law Economics and Organization*, Vol. 12, pp. 167–95.

Maskin, E. and J. Tirole (1990), 'The Principal Agent Relationship with an Informed Principle', *Econometrica*, Vol. 58, pp. 379–409.

Mauro, P. (1995), 'Corruption and Growth', *Quarterly Journal of Economics*, Vol. 110, pp. 681–712.

Mookherjee, D. and I.P.L. Png (1995) 'Corruptible Law Enforcers: How Should they be Compensated', *Economic Journal*, Vol. 105, pp. 145–59.

Pargal S., M. Mani and M. Huq (1996), 'Inspections and Emissions: Puzzling Survey Evidence on Industrial Water Pollution', World Bank Policy Working Paper No. 1810.

Rose-Ackerman, S. (1978), *Corruption: A Study in Political Economy*, Academic Press, New York.

Rose-Ackerman, S. (1997), 'Corruption and Development', in B. Pleskovic and J.E. Stiglitz (eds), *Annual World Bank Conference on Development Economics*, World Bank, Washington DC.

Appendix

Lemma 1: Let $e_i = e_j = e$, then from equation (5b) in the text:

$$\hat{e}_i = \frac{1}{2} K(1 - \frac{t(1 - w)}{\beta(F + P)}))$$ (A1)

Solving (A1), observe that $\hat{e}_i = 0$ if:

$$\beta \leq \frac{t(1 - w)}{(F + P)} \equiv \beta^{ii}$$ (A2)

Moreover, from (5c) we have:

$$\hat{e}_j = \frac{1}{4} (3e + K(1 - \frac{t(1 - w)}{\beta(F + P)}))$$ (A3)

Observe that $\hat{e}_j = 0$ if:

$$\beta \leq \frac{t(1 - w)K}{(F + P)(K + 2e)} \equiv \beta^{ij}$$ (A4)

Clearly $\beta^{ii} > \beta^{ij}$. Thus if $\beta \in (\beta^{ij}, \beta^{ii})$ then $\hat{e}_i = 0$ and $\hat{e}_j > 0$.

Proposition 1

Rearranging (5b) it is readily verified that $\hat{e}_i \leq e_i$ if:

$$\beta \geq \frac{t(1 - w)K}{(F + P)(K - e_i - e_j)} \equiv \beta^{ij}$$ (A5)

Similarly using (5c) $\hat{e}_j \leq e_j$ if:

$$\beta \geq \frac{t(1 - w)K}{(F + P)(K - e_i - e_j)} \equiv \beta^c$$ (A6)

Moreover from (6b) and (6c) if $\hat{e}_i < e_i$ then $B_i^* > 0$ and if $\hat{e}_j < e_j$ then $B_j^* > 0$.

Lemma 2: Rearranging and manipulating (8a) $\hat{e}_i = e$ if:

$$\theta \leq \theta_i(\beta) \equiv \frac{-Kt(1 - w) + \beta(P + F)(K - 2e)}{Kt(4\beta - 3)(1 - w) - \beta(P + F)(K - 2e)}$$ (A6)

Similarly using (8b) $\hat{e}_j = e$ iff:

$$\theta \geq \theta_j(\beta) \equiv \frac{-Kt(1 - 2\beta)(1 - w) + \beta(P + F)(K - 2e)}{-Kt(4\beta - 3)(1 - w) + \beta(P + F)(K - 2e)}$$ (A7)

Lemma 3a: Using (A6) and (A7):

$$\theta_j(\beta) - \theta_i(\beta) = \frac{K(1 - w)(4\beta - 1) - 3\beta(P + F) + 3\beta e(P + F)}{K(-\beta(P + F) + (3 - 4\beta)(-1 + w)t) + 2\beta e(P + F)}$$ (A8)

Solving observe that $\theta_j(\beta) - \theta_i(\beta) \geq 0$ iff:

$$\beta \geq \beta^u \equiv \frac{Kt(1 - w)}{4Kt(1 - w) + (-K + 2e)3(F + P)} \tag{A9}$$

Lemma 3b: The numerator of (A9) is positive $\forall\ w < 1$.

If $K > \dfrac{6e(P + F)}{3(P + F) - 4t(1 - w)}$ the denominator of β^u is negative thus $\beta^u < 0$.

Similarly, if $(P+F) > \dfrac{4Kt(1 - w)}{3(K - 2e)}$ the denominator of β^u is negative thus $\beta^u < 0$.

Proposition 2

If either of the conditions in Lemma 3b hold and if $\theta \in (\theta_j(\beta), \theta_i(\beta))$, then $\beta^u < 0$ so that by Lemma 2 $\hat{e}_i = \hat{e}_j = e$.

Collusion Between the Firm and Inspector

Communication between inspectors will be deterred if the expected payoffs to each inspector from exposing a rival, who has communicated, exceed the expected payoffs from colluding and sharing information. Let γ_s be the probability that inspector s $(s = i,j, i \neq j)$ approaches inspector r $(r = i, j, s \neq r)$ for access to information about whether an inspection has occurred. Let α_r be the probability that inspector r exposes rival s for communicating. As before, β is the probability of successfully prosecuting inspector s, when exposed. Inspector s, if successfully prosecuted for breaking the confidentiality clause is fined an amount G, which is paid to rival inspector r for exposing the misdemeanour.

The expected payoffs to s from communicating with r are given by:

$$\Gamma^c_s(\alpha_s, \alpha_r, \gamma_s, \gamma_r) = \gamma_s((1 - \alpha_r)[\theta\hat{B}_i + (1 - \theta)] - \alpha_r\beta G) \tag{A9a}$$

where: $\hat{B}_i = B_i + wt\hat{e}_i - \sigma*\beta P(e - \hat{e}_i), \hat{B}_j = (B_j + wt\hat{e}_j) - \sigma\beta P(e - \hat{e}_j),]$

To interpret this expression, observe that s communicates with her rival with probability γ_s. With probability $(1 - \alpha_r)$ she learns the sequence of inspections. Under the randomisation strategy outlined earlier, the expected probability that $s = i$ reports first (second) is θ $((1 - \theta))$. If s reports first (second) her net payoffs are $\hat{B}_i$ $(\hat{B}_j)$. However, approaching a rival for information risks prosecution. With probability α_r the rival exposes the inspector, resulting in an expected fine of βG.

In contrast, inspector s decides not to collude with probability $(1 - \gamma_s)$. An inspector who does not share information is compelled to truthfully reports emissions when $\theta \in (\theta_j(\beta), \theta_i(\beta))$, and this yields a payment of Wte from the government. With probability γ_r the rival may approach inspector s for confidential information. The rival is exposed by s with probability α_s. Inspector s then obtains a reward of G if this results in a successful prosecution. Thus, the expected payoffs from a strategy of truthful reporting are:

$$\Gamma_s(\alpha_s, \alpha_r, \gamma_s, \gamma_r) = (1 - \gamma_s)(\text{Wte} + \gamma_r \alpha_s \beta G) \tag{A9b}$$

In what follows we focus only on equilibria where $\alpha_k = 0$ or 1 and $\gamma_k = 0$ or 1 ($k = s,r$). Each inspector either chooses to communicate with the rival (ie $\gamma_k = 1$) or not (ie $\gamma_k = 0$). If approached each inspector must then decide whether to expose her rival ($\alpha_k = 1$), or collude in information sharing ($\alpha_k = 0$). Other possible equilibria would require the use of mixed strategies, which do not appear to have an obvious interpretation in this context. Clearly the strategy chosen by each inspector must be *ex post* optimal. Lemma 4 below compares the payoffs from the various feasible strategies.

Lemma 4: If $G > (\theta \hat{B}_i + (1 - \theta)\hat{B}_j)/\beta$ then, $\Gamma^c_s(\alpha_s = 1, \gamma_s = 0, \gamma_r = 1, \alpha_r = 0) > \Gamma_s(\alpha_s = 1, \gamma_s = 0, \alpha_r = 0, \gamma_r = 1) > \Gamma_s(\alpha_s = 1, \gamma_s = 0, \gamma_r = 0, \alpha_r = 1) > \Gamma^c_s(\alpha_s = 0, \gamma_s = 1, \alpha_r = 1, \gamma_r = 0)$.

Proof

Substituting in (9a) and (9b):

$$\Gamma^c_s(\alpha_s = 1, \gamma_s = 0, \gamma_r = 1, \alpha_r = 0) = \theta \hat{B}^i + (1 - \theta)\hat{B}^j \tag{A10}$$

$$\Gamma_s(\alpha_s = 1, \gamma_s = 0, \alpha_r = 0, \gamma_r = 1) = \text{Wte} + \beta G \tag{A11}$$

$$\Gamma^c_s(\alpha_s = 0, \gamma_s = 1, \gamma_r = 0, \alpha_r = 1) = -\alpha_r \beta G \tag{A12}$$

$$\Gamma_s(\alpha_s = 0, \gamma_s = 1, \alpha_r = 1, \gamma_r = 0) = \text{Wte} \tag{A13}$$

Clearly, $\Gamma_s(\alpha_s = 1, \gamma_s = 0, \alpha_r = 0, \gamma_r = 1) > \Gamma_s(\alpha_s = 0, \gamma_s = 1, \alpha_r = 1, \gamma_r = 0) > \Gamma^c_s(\alpha_s = 0, \gamma_s = 1, \gamma_r = 0, \alpha_r = 1)$. Moreover if $G > (\theta \hat{B}_i + (1 - \theta)\hat{B}_j)/\beta$ then $\Gamma^c_s(\alpha_s = 1, \gamma_s = 0, \gamma_r = 1, \alpha_r = 0) < \Gamma_s(\alpha_s = 1, \gamma_s = 0, \alpha_r = 0, \gamma_r = 1)$.

Lemma 4 reveals that if the fine G is large enough then, each inspector gains from exposing a rival and honestly disclosing emissions, when a rival chooses to communicate. The inspectors therefore confront a standard prisoner's dilemma problem. Each gains by exposing its rival, even though both would be better off by communicating. Thus the best response of each is to set $\alpha_k = 1$ and expose a rival if approached. If each inspector expects the rival to behave in this manner, neither chooses to communicate so that $\gamma_k = 0$ and information sharing does not occur. Thus, unauthorised communication between the inspectors can be deterred by the simple and cost effective expedient of offering a sufficiently high reward which is funded by the penalty.

Even if communication between inspectors can be prevented, there remains the possibility that firms may exchange information about the sequence of inspections. It can be verified that firms confront similar incentives and can therefore be deterred from disclosing unauthorised information with a sufficiently large fine. This is summarised with greater accuracy in Lemma 5.

Lemma 5: If $H > (te - (\theta Q_i + (1 - \theta)Q_j))/\beta$ then, $\Sigma_i(\alpha_i = 1, \gamma_i = 0, \gamma_j = 1, \alpha_j = 1) < \Sigma_i^c(\alpha_i = 1, \gamma_i = 0, \gamma_j = 1, \alpha_j = 0) < \Sigma_i^c(\alpha_i = 0, \gamma_i = 1, \gamma_j = 0, \alpha_j = 1)$.

Where: $\Sigma_i = (1 - \gamma_i)(te - \gamma_j\alpha_i\beta H)$, and $\Sigma_i^c = \gamma_i[(1 - \alpha_j)(\theta\Delta_i + (1- \theta)\Delta_j) + \alpha_j\beta H]$

$\Delta_i = t\hat{e}_i + B_i + \sigma^*\beta F(e_i - \hat{e}_i)$; $\Delta_j = t\hat{e}_j + B_j + \sigma\beta F(e_j - \hat{e}_j)$, γ_i is the probability that i approaches j, α_i is the probability that i exposes j when approached (i = 1, 2, i ≠ j).

Proof

Let $\Sigma_i = (1 - \gamma_i)(te - \gamma_j\alpha_i\beta H)$, and let $\Sigma_i^c = \gamma_i[(1 - \alpha_j)(\theta\Delta_i + (1 - \theta)\Delta_j) + \alpha_j\beta H]$

Then:

$$\Sigma_i^c(\alpha_i = 1, \gamma_i = 0, \gamma_j = 1, \alpha_j = 0) = (\theta\Delta_i + (1 - \theta)\Delta_j) \tag{A14}$$

$$\Sigma_i(\alpha_i = 1, \gamma_i = 0, \gamma_j = 1, \alpha_j = 1) = te - \beta H \tag{A15}$$

$$\Sigma_i^c(\alpha_i = 0, \gamma_i = 1, \gamma_j = 0, \alpha_j = 1) = \beta H + (\theta\Delta_i + (1- \theta)\Delta_j) \tag{A16}$$

$$\Sigma_i(\alpha_i = 1, \gamma_i = 0, \gamma_j = 0, \alpha_j = 1) = te \tag{A17}$$

$\Sigma_i(\alpha_i = 1, \gamma_i = 0, \gamma_j = 1, \alpha_j = 1) = te - \beta H < \Sigma_i^c(\alpha_i = 1, \gamma_i = 0, \gamma_j = 1, \alpha_j = 0) = (\theta\Delta_i + (1 - \theta)\Delta_j)$ if $H > (te - (\theta\Delta_i + (1 - \theta)\Delta_j))/\beta$. Moreover, $\Sigma_i^c(\alpha_i = 0, \gamma_i = 1, \gamma_j = 0, \alpha_j = 1) = \beta H + (\theta\Delta_i + (1- \theta)\Delta_j) > \Sigma_i(\alpha_i = 1, \gamma_i = 0, \gamma_j = 1, \alpha_j = 1) = te - \beta H$. Thus the optimal strategy for firm i is $(\alpha_i = 1, \gamma_i = 0)$ if $(\gamma_j = 1, \alpha_j = 1)$.

Chapter 20

Globalisation and Market Integration: Spain as a Case Study

Fernando Barreiro-Pereira and Francisco Mochón

Introduction

Economic globalisation means that the international networks of trade, foreign direct investment (FDI), portfolio investment and information have intensified to such an extent that strong worldwide economic interdependence has resulted. The major driving force of economic globalisation is the reduction of the transport costs in the private sector, due basically to the fact that technological progress and innovation has reduced the costs of transport and communication. Another driving force is the reduction of policy barriers to trade and investment. In addition, the enormous advances made in computer technologies, the fall in computer prices and recent technical progress in telecommunications facilitate access to information and reduce the price of communication, especially in those countries where deregulation and privatisation has taken place. Similarly, the World Wide Web is reducing cross border barriers to zero. However, distance is still an important barrier to trade, not only due to the existence of transport costs but also due to the role of what is called social distance. International interdependence stemming from globalisation could be asymmetric, causing some disparities, which would explain why small countries are generally less exposed to the international economy than large countries.

Although globalisation was a defining term of the 1990s, O'Rourke and Williamson (2000) distinguish at least three waves of the phenomenon which have taken place through the modern and contemporary history: From 1400 to the eighteenth century, long distance trade was strictly limited to what might be called non-competitive goods, such as spices, sugar or gold, which were in very scarce supply. The second wave of globalisation started in the early nineteenth century when the rise of trade was centred in basic tradable goods, such as wheat or textiles. The third wave of globalisation applies to recent times in which trade takes place in both basic and highly differentiated manufactured commodities. Throughout this paper we use the term globalisation to refer to this third wave, which is characterised by the rising dominance of new skills and technologies. The most important stylised facts that appear in almost all the different waves of globalisation are the continuous fall in transport costs, the rise in the share of trade, commodity prices convergence, and a divergence-convergence process of real income per capita. These stylised facts are analysed by using a sample, which contains fifty-eight countries examined during the period immediately prior to the last wave of globalisation (1978–1990). In the last wave of globalisation proper we analyse other similar stylised facts concerning forty-six countries during the 1990s. These facts are foreign direct investment,

R&D expenses, the internationalisation of the multinational companies (MNCs), the production of information technologies, and the diffusion of high technology across different countries. We also examine the impact of globalisation in the European zone which contains Spain as a particular case.

Four Stylised Facts of Globalisation in the 1980s

The stylised facts that we analyse in this section are the fall in transport costs, the rise in the share of trade, commodity prices convergence and the real income per capita divergence-convergence process. We do not study facts such as the mobility of the capital flows and the financial integration.

Fall in Transport Costs

During any wave of globalisation technological progress and innovation are important factors in the reduction of the cost of transport and communication. In order to test this hypothesis it is usual to lump informational barriers to trade together with transport costs and model both using the iceberg assumption of Samuelson (1952), in which a proportion of the goods traded melts in transit from one place, country, or region to the other. The maximand in the iceberg assumption is known as the 'net social payoff' (W) and represents the sum of the surpluses of trade for both consumers and producers. It can be written as the sum of consumer satisfaction (integral of the demand function) less the total cost (integral of the supply function), minus the total transport costs:

$$W = \int_0^{y_1} P_D(y)dy - \int_0^{y_1} P_S(y)dy - CT \tag{1}$$

where y is the quantity of a composed good, y_1 is the quantity of goods that corresponds to market equilibrium, CT are the transport costs, and P_D and P_S are the inverse curves of demand and supply respectively. The variation of the transport costs causes a variation in the net social payoff and hence social welfare fluctuates (ΔW):

$$\Delta W = \int_{y_1}^{y_2} P_D(y)dy - \int_{y_1}^{y_2} P_S(y)dy - \Delta CT \tag{2}$$

Where y_2 is the quantity corresponding to a second equilibrium caused by the fluctuation in the aggregate supply. If we aggregate this problem for all consumers and producers and, considering it in the long run equilibrium, the aggregate supply will be vertical and the variation of the net social payoff can be written, following Small and Winston (1999), as follows:

$$\Delta W = \frac{1}{2} \Delta P \Delta y + P \Delta y - \Delta CT \tag{3}$$

Where P is the price at the equilibrium. Rearranging this equation and dividing both members by $P\Delta y$, we have that:

$$\frac{\Delta(W + CT)}{\Delta y} = \left(\frac{\pi}{2} + 1\right) P \tag{4}$$

Where π is the inflation rate $(\Delta P/P)$. But in the long run, the form of the aggregate demand is: $P.y = OM.V$, where OM is the money supply in the equilibrium and V is the income velocity of circulation. Substituting this in the last equation, we obtain:

$$\frac{\Delta(W + CT)}{\Delta y} = OM(\pi + 2)\frac{V/2}{y} \tag{5}$$

Moreover, following the Baumol (1952) and Tobin (1956) model of money demand for transactions, the term V/2 can be substituted by the number of journeys (N) per capita made in a country during a year for transferring bonds by money. This number of journeys is very related with the total journeys made by an agent during a year in a country, following Barreiro-Pereira (1998). As a result, substituting in the last formulation $V/2 = N/PO$, where PO is the total population of a country, we will have:

$$\frac{N/PO}{y/PO} = \frac{V/2}{y/PO} = \frac{PO(\Delta W + \Delta CT)}{OM(\pi + 2)\Delta y} \tag{6}$$

Where y/PO is the real income per capita (Y). The term N/y reflects the weight of the transportation in the real income of each agent, which is related to variations in the transport costs (ΔCT). If the tariffs in transport costs are efficient (tariffs coincide with the marginal cost), then the net social payoff (W) will be a maximum and ΔW will tend toward zero. Thus, assuming for the sake of simplicity, a constant level of prices, we can write finally:

$$\frac{V}{Y} = \left(\frac{PO}{\left(\frac{OM}{\bar{P}}\right)}\right) \frac{\Delta CT}{\Delta \Psi} \tag{7}$$

This demonstrates that the coefficient V/Y is directly related to variations in transport costs; we have taken this ratio (V/Y) as a proxy of the variation of transport costs relative to the variations in monetary income (Ψ). Table 20.1 shows the values of this ratio for fifty-eight countries in 1978 (column 1) and in 1990 (column 2). The effect of globalisation produced the falling of the ratio V/Y between 1978 and 1990 in some countries, showing that for these, unitary transport costs decreased in this period. In column 3 of Table 20.1 we collect the trends followed by transportation costs through time, as a result of the fifty-eight regressions corresponding to the fifty-eight countries. These regressions were made by OLS method of estimation with autocorrelation corrected by means of a first order auto-regressive process. The coefficients contained in column 3 are the estimators of the regression between V/Y and time, and denote the trend of the relative transport costs in this period. In the countries submitted to globalisation forces the transport costs fall continuously and as shown by the negative coefficients that appear in Table 20.1, column 3.

Table 20.1   Stylised facts and degree of globalisation in 1980s

Countries	Transport cost ratio 1978	Transport cost ratio 1990	Trend Tran. cost/ t 1978–90	Share of trade 1978	Share of trade 1990	Commodity prices STD 1983–86	Commodity prices STD 1987–90	β-absolute convergence 1978–90	Globalisation degree 1978–90
Algeria	0.93	1.19	0.01	60.2	29.8	0.027	0.079	-0.008	0
Cameroon	6.88	7.07	0.05	63.4	35.6	0.057	0.059	-0.006	0
Egypt	5.16	4.40	-0.06	39.5	38.6	0.011	0.037	0.003	2
Kenya	14.73	20.00	0.64	66.8	56.7	0.019	0.016	-0.007	1
Madagascar	13.83	29.12	1.41	46.9	41.5	0.023	0.039	-0.010	0
Malawi	30.73	40.71	0.51	62.5	57.2	0.023	0.038	-0.009	0
Morocco	3.07	2.48	-0.04	45.7	55.3	0.023	0.008	-0.005	3
Tanzania	42.90	51.08	1.28	44.2	77.8	0.010	0.027	-0.007	1
Tunisia	2.44	2.69	0.00	63.7	89.8	0.015	0.018	-0.013	1
Zaire	24.45	35.75	0.46	50.6	54.3	0.010	0.166	-0.011	1
Zambia	8.05	17.11	0.66	70.1	60.8	0.015	0.164	-0.018	0
Argentina	1.73	3.61	0.15	18.9	15.0	0.001	0.339	-0.081	0
Bolivia	8.27	23.54	1.65	43.9	37.3	0.090	0.032	-0.022	1
Brazil	2.62	3.84	0.07	15.0	12.9	0.001	0.290	-0.028	0
Canada	0.45	0.32	-0.01	50.1	51.0	0.008	0.004	0.008	4
Chile	8.04	7.15	-0.01	42.6	70.4	0.043	0.059	-0.002	2
Colombia	6.52	7.83	0.09	31.5	38.5	0.025	0.060	-0.006	1
Ecuador	5.74	9.70	0.35	50.6	52.6	0.013	0.094	-0.013	1
USA	0.31	0.29	-0.01	17.0	20.4	0.001	0.001	0.014	3
Mexico	3.29	5.10	0.26	21.5	32.6	0.020	0.100	-0.018	1
Paraguay	7.63	6.26	-0.08	37.6	75.5	0.030	0.094	-0.007	2
Peru	2.70	5.30	0.15	41.7	24.3	0.001	0.337	-0.034	0
Uruguay	3.53	4.75	0.09	36.9	45.9	0.018	0.161	-0.016	1
Venezuela	1.33	3.36	0.14	63.4	58.2	0.014	0.099	-0.046	0
South Korea	3.48	1.90	-0.16	68.6	61.7	0.015	0.023	-0.011	2
Philippines	14.26	16.08	0.29	42.1	57.5	0.048	0.019	0.051	2
India	25.04	16.95	-0.79	13.4	17.2	0.009	0.013	0.001	3
Indonesia	23.80	13.87	-0.74	42.8	53.1	0.006	0.014	0.003	3
Iran	0.96	1.52	0.04	56.8	7.4	0.067	0.046	-0.095	1
Israel	1.15	1.27	0.01	106.2	70.2	0.244	0.145	-0.006	1

Table 20.1 cont'd

Countries	Transport cost ratio 1978	Transport cost ratio 1990	Trend Tran. cost/t 1978–90	Share of trade 1978	Share of trade 1990	Commodity prices STD 1983–86	Commodity prices STD 1987–90	β-absolute convergence 1978–90	Globalisation degree 1978–90
Japan	**0.19**	**0.14**	**-0.01**	**20.6**	**21.2**	**0.033**	**0.029**	-0.007	3
Jordan	**2.02**	**1.90**	**-0.02**	**113.8**	**154.1**	**0.016**	**0.015**	-0.007	3
Malaysia	**3.30**	**1.87**	**-0.11**	**92.5**	**154.9**	0.007	0.016	**0.005**	3
Myanmar	**45.39**	**36.61**	**-0.36**	17.8	5.2	0.003	0.018	-0.002	1
Pakistan	**12.82**	**8.05**	**-0.37**	**31.6**	**42.7**	0.010	0.011	**0.001**	3
Sri Lanka	**18.08**	**17.40**	**-0.09**	74.3	65.4	0.010	0.014	-0.004	1
Syria	**1.14**	**1.08**	**-0.58**	49.7	33.3	0.022	0.054	-0.020	1
Thailand	**11.2**	**6.90**	**-0.36**	**44.8**	**81.0**	0.001	**0.008**	**0.012**	3
Turkey	2.08	3.26	0.76	14.1	42.3	0.019	0.121	-0.006	1
W. Germany	**0.30**	**0.21**	**-0.01**	**48.1**	**57.3**	0.014	0.022	**0.006**	3
Austria	**0.38**	**0.35**	**-0.01**	**66.4**	**79.1**	0.016	0.024	**0.006**	3
Belgium	0.25	0.27	0.01	**101.5**	**139.1**	**0.024**	**0.016**	**0.007**	3
Czechoslovakia	**1.27**	**0.95**	**-0.02**	75.4	65.9	0.004	0.006	-0.007	1
Denmark	**0.23**	**0.12**	**-0.01**	**60.9**	**69.3**	**0.022**	**0.018**	**0.007**	4
Spain	**0.34**	**0.27**	**-0.01**	**28.9**	**37.2**	**0.066**	**0.025**	**0.014**	4
Finland	**0.65**	**0.42**	**-0.01**	55.6	46.3	**0.056**	**0.036**	-0.003	2
France	**0.19**	**0.18**	**-0.11**	**41.3**	**47.3**	**0.038**	**0.004**	**0.009**	4
Greece	**0.87**	**0.86**	**-0.01**	41.9	49.0	0.071	0.091	-0.070	2
Netherlands	**0.30**	**0.21**	**-0.01**	**85.1**	**104.2**	0.008	0.031	**0.015**	3
Ireland	0.55	0.60	0.01	**109.6**	**117.8**	**0.042**	**0.023**	-0.007	2
Italy	**0.15**	**0.14**	**-0.01**	43.9	40.7	**0.067**	**0.040**	**0.004**	3
Norway	**0.28**	**0.11**	**-0.01**	82.3	81.3	**0.057**	**0.026**	**0.002**	2
Poland	**4.65**	**3.65**	**-0.08**	59.7	53.4	0.001	0.147	**0.027**	3
Portugal	0.58	0.57	0.00	**52.8**	**81.2**	**0.082**	**0.047**	**0.006**	2
UK	**0.45**	**0.14**	**-0.02**	54.6	50.8	0.022	0.028	**0.010**	3
Sweden	0.36	0.36	0.00	**55.5**	**61.4**	0.045	0.063	**0.006**	2
Switzerland	0.08	0.11	0.01	**81.1**	**83.6**	**0.015**	**0.009**	**0.006**	3
Yugoslavia	0.91	1.26	0.03	38.7	41.6	0.001	0.280	-0.024	1

Note: Bold numbers mean globalisation criteria fulfilled, accounted in the last column (degree).
Sources: United Nations Statistical Yearbooks.

The Rise in the Share of Trade

Because a good indicator of globalisation in an economy is the continuous rise in the share of trade (understanding share of trade as a ratio between total exports plus imports divided all by GDP) it can be used as a well proxy for globalisation. Facts such as a rise in trade and the falling of transport costs and trade barriers imply that we are immersed in a globalisation process. In columns 4 and 5 of Table 20.1, we show the values of those ratios for the fifty-eight countries in 1978 and 1990 respectively. Countries where this ratio increases between 1978 and 1990 are interpreted as being in a process of globalisation during this period.

Commodity Prices Convergence

However, the volume of trade is not a totally satisfactory indication of commodity market integration because it is the cost of moving goods between markets and relative commodity prices that count. As O'Rourke and Williamson (2000) emphasise, the convergence in commodity prices is the most significant stylised fact in a globalisation process because the trade forces will change the domestic commodity prices before anything else can happen. In this sense, important evidence that globalisation is taking place is the continuous decline in the international dispersion of commodity prices, or put in a different way, commodity prices convergence, something that is statistically verified during all waves of globalisation. In order to check this convergence, Froot, Kim and Rogoff (1995), amongst others, obtained data on prices in England and Holland since 1273 for a series of commodities and observed how their price dispersion decreased through time. The identification of international price differentials is more evident in the case of specific goods than in the case of aggregate price indices and, due to the variability of the exchange rate, price differentials are far larger across national borders than within countries. Williamson (2000) indicates that the ratios between the price indices of agricultural and manufactured goods, or export and import goods are generally smaller for land-scarce regions. If there is a larger degree of aggregation when the comparison between countries a good alternative is to use aggregate price indices, such as the prices measured by means of the purchasing power parity. In this case we can find only weak, but significant, evidence on international price differentials. In our case we will take this aggregate price index measured as power parity purchasing, calculating its dispersion sequence between 1983 and 1990. The measure of dispersion used in this paper is the comparison of the standard deviations in the periods 1983–1986 (column 6 in Table 20.1) and 1987–1990 (column 7), applied to the fifty-eight countries mentioned above. If the dispersion coefficient for a country is bigger in the 1983–1986 period than in the 1987–1990 period, then there exists σ convergence in prices in that country. In our sample of fifty-eight countries there are 19 that fulfil this criteria and can be considered to have experienced the process of globalisation. In these cases, the coefficient of column 7 is smaller than in column 6, which implies that there is σ-convergence in prices. Considering the nineteen pre-globalised countries in overall terms, the average standard deviation of purchasing power parity prices (calculated from the data of columns 6 and 7 of Table 20.1) falls from $\sigma = 0.520$ for the 1983–1986 period to $\sigma = 0.495$ for the 1987–1990 period.

This suggests the existence of commodity price convergence in the period between 1983 and 1990.

The β-absolute Divergence-convergence Process in Real Income Per Capita

With regard to the last two waves of globalisation several authors have analysed the effects of globalisation on income per capita distribution and they have studied some types of resulting disparities. The second wave of globalisation (1820–1914) resulted in the industrialisation of the North (Europe and the North-American continents) and the de-industrialisation of the South, a pattern that was not changed during the period between the second and third waves (1914–1970). In the present wave of globalisation some income divergence between groups of countries that were not initially disparate has been generated and this amounts to the most important implication of the Industrial Revolution in Europe. The second wave is also influenced by high transport costs and the fact that there was little trade and primitive industry. In the second stage of the process the cost of exchanging goods fell faster than the cost of exchanging ideas and innovations and, once transport costs were sufficiently diminished, the distribution of the industry was achieved by means of agglomeration forces. The third wave of globalisation (from 1970 to the present day) began with the consequences of the second wave. In specific terms, it resulted from a very large income gap and a consequential de-industrialisation of the North and industrialisation of the South, largely caused by the significant fall in the transports costs of technological innovations. In the South, industrial investment rose and income grew whereas the North experienced some de-industrialisation and tended to specialise in services. It is in this way that globalisation forces first generated a huge divergence of real incomes and later tended to cause an increase in the development and likelihood of income convergence.

The convergence-divergence process is related with economic growth; the convergence concept refers to what should be the value of the real income per capita growth rate as a country moves with time towards the steady-state. In an economic growth process, the speed at which the economy converges during the dynamic transition toward the steady-state is the speed of convergence (known as β), and it denotes, following Barro (1997), the time taken to arrive at the real per capita income which represents the mid point between the initial and steady state real per capita, provided that its real income per capita grows at a constant rate. In this paper we try to analyse if there was any possibility of convergence among fifty-eight countries at the beginning of the third wave of globalisation, from 1978 to 1990. To analyse this question, we suppose for each economy a neoclassical Cobb-Douglas growth process such as: $y = (AL)^{1-\alpha}K^{\alpha}$, with a technical progress neutral in Harrod and labour augmenting, where y is the output, L is labour and K is physical capital and α is a constant exponent minor than one. Rearranging this production function and operating within it, we can write it in terms of initial (Y_0) and final (Y_T) real per capita incomes with T denoting the number of time periods:

$$Y_T = B \ (Y_0)^b \tag{8}$$

This expression approaches in discrete time the growth process of the real per capita income with respect to average real per capita incomes, where b is a coefficient depending on time t. The growth rate of real per capita income with respect to the average per capita income accumulated during the period $(0,T)$ will be $\sum_{t=0}^{t=T} \frac{\Delta Y_t}{Y_t}$; and taking the limit we have:

$$\int_0^t \frac{dY}{Y} = \ln Y_T - \ln Y_0 = \frac{Y_T}{Y_0} \tag{9}$$

Taking logarithms in expression 8 and rearranging, we obtain the growth rate of per capita real income in relation to the average in the period $(0,T)$ as:

$$\ln \frac{Y_T}{Y_0} = \ln B - (1 - b)\ln Y_0 \tag{10}$$

where $b = e^{-\beta T}$, and β is, in the dynamic transition toward the steady-state, the coefficient that indicates the speed of convergence of the real per capita income towards steady state. Then, the average rate of per capita real income in relative terms will be:

$$\frac{1}{T} \cdot \ln \frac{Y_T}{Y_0} = a - \left[\frac{1 = e^{-\beta \cdot T}}{T} \right] \cdot \ln Y_0 \tag{11}$$

where a is $(ln\ B)/T$. This expression denotes how the growth rate of relative real per capita income is related negatively with the logarithm of the initial level of relative real per capita income (lnY_0). Alternatively explained, for a determined level of the interaction term (a) related with each steady state, the higher the per capita income in a country the lower the growth rate will tend to be. If the value of b is positive, and a is the same in all countries of the sample, then there will exist absolute convergence; if b is zero or negative it means that there is divergence. The coefficient β represents the speed of convergence, and if $\beta \geq 0$ and the interaction term (a) is the same for all countries, then the poor economies grow more quickly than the richer ones, and in such cases absolute convergence is said to exist. In our case, we take the data base for the real per capita income from the International Financial Statistics Yearbook in order to obtain the logarithm of the initial and final real per capita income. With this data we can estimate equation 11 for the sample of the fifty-eight countries collected in Table 20.1, between (1978–1990). The estimation of equation 11 has been carried out by means of the maximum likelihood (LIML) method applied to this panel data. The result for the value of this coefficient β of absolute convergence is: –0.003. This is the coefficient of the logarithm of the initial real per capita income. Due to the fact that some of these countries do not have the same steady-state condition, the negative value of this coefficient shows that the fifty-eight countries (considered from an overall perspective for the period concerned) are characterised by real per capita income divergence. The absolute convergence concept cannot be utilised amongst economies, which have different steady state conditions. This is the most common situation and as a result the conditional convergence concept must be utilised. However, assuming one common steady-state condition that is defined by means of the unique interaction term (*a*), coming from the estimation of equation 11, and then substituting it in the same equation 11, particularised for each country, we will obtain the particular speed of convergence for each country with respect to this hypothetical common steady-state related to *a*. The results of the estimation indicate that the value of *a* is: 0.009. Depending on whether the sign of β is positive or negative, one country could converge or not with this common steady-state condition.

Stylised Facts of Globalisation in the 1990s

The third wave of economic globalisation shows some specific stylised events. In basic terms these are the fact that trade, investment in research and development (R&D), direct foreign investment and technology links are increasing on a worldwide basis. Other factors include the liberalisation of the telecommunications system and the rise of the internet which creates a truly global marketplace that has given rise to new opportunities for the international exchange of information. The economic analysis of the impact of informational barriers to trade, following Rauch and Cassella (1998), is different to that of conventional barriers because the impact of trade on relative wages across countries causes changes in relative labour supplies. However, conventional trade theory argues that the impact of trade on relative wages operates through price competition. In this sense, the liberalisation of trade with countries whose initial volume of trade is high will have a greater impact on wages, as can be seen in the work of Rauch and Trindade (2000). In addition, new telecommunication systems are creating a great service sector that does not depend on the locations of technology production sites but does require advanced technological solutions. This structural change is also accompanied by an increasing proportion of highly qualified employees and an associated increase in wages. These changes are also related to a migration process of skilled labour. Apart from the symptoms of informational globalisation in labour markets, capital flow volumes are in themselves an important indicator of globalisation. Following Baldwin and Martin (1999), the most spectacular indications of financial globalisation in the 1990s are the two consecutive financial crisis around 1994 in Latin-America and 1997 in the Pacific Rim countries.

The Role of High Technology

Product and process innovations are crucial for productivity increases and economic growth, but the rapid diffusion of new technologies is also important. The major contribution of new growth theory has been to endogenise technological change that is related to investment in research and development (R&D) and also to the consideration of human capital as a production factor. Following Grossman and Helpman (1994), the attributes of technological change become endogenous in the new growth theory. The higher values of these attributes lead in turn to higher growth rates, and there will be increasing returns derived from technological change and endogenous growth as argued by Romer (1990). As Arrow (1962) points out, the theoretical justification for high technology comes from the fact that economic activity based on new knowledge produces some market failures that emanate from the tendency of new knowledge to be traded in a monopolistic market with uncertainty. The implications for government policy of high technology under endogenous growth are different to those under the neoclassical growth theory. This is due to the fact that in the new growth models there are some reasons for governments to undertake an active policy in shaping high technology due to the existence of knowledge externalities in the form of knowledge spillovers. High technology involves the production and commercialisation of new economic knowledge which is inherently different from the more traditional factors of production like land, labour, and physical capital. However, it is necessary to consider the distinction between knowledge and information because in conventional economic thought the marginal costs of transmitting information may be invariant to distance. However, we have to admit that the marginal costs of transmitting knowledge rise with distance, country, language, and culture. The telecom networks is a crucial element in the diffusion of technological knowledge for linking firms and households in a way that allows fast communication and data transmission. While traditional telephone networks establish a dedicated connection between the two parties of a telephone conversation, the internet uses flexible routing for digitalised packages of communication data.

Across a sample of 46 OECD and non-OECD countries, Table 20.2 of this chapter supplies some information on Internet users and addresses in 1999 (columns 2 and 3) and on the production of information technology in 1997 (column 1). In this year the most important countries in the production of information technology were the USA (30 per cent of the world production), Japan (24.5 per cent), South Korea (5.4 per cent), Singapore (4.8 per cent), United Kingdom (4.2 per cent), Germany (3.9 per cent) and Taiwan (3.6 per cent).

Multinational Companies

The gradual increase in the R&D-GDP ratios in OECD countries and non-industrialised countries (NICs) has encouraged an increasing number of firms from an ever increasing number of countries to become multinational companies. R&D, the international location strategies of transnational cooperation, and international trends in innovation in terms of technical preferences are changing substantially. Multinational companies following these structural changes in technology can combine their priority decision with a location decision and pursue some parts of their R&D in one country and other parts in another country. In other words, an MNC can produce a good in a foreign market or else establish a foreign affiliate to import the good from the national market where MNCs' headquarters are located. As regarding individual industries one may note that international relocation of production and other company activities is rather easy except for some exceptions in immobile Schumpeterian industries. Schumpeter industries require the continuous cooperation of R&D and production, such as in the aerospace industry, which implies very limited options for dislocating production activities to low income and wage countries. One can observe different strategies for internationalisation about MNCs in two different ways: The first group of high-tech corporations has a global orientation investing a large amount of R&D. Taking Spain as a reference (see Table 20.3), companies like ABB, IBM, Philips, and chemical-pharmaceutical companies like Ciba-Geigy, Hoechst, Roche and Sandoz belong to this group. The second cluster consists of a group of enterprises active in the area of medium to high technology. They have divisions classified as high-tech but their overall R&D intensity is lower than for the first group; this group does not transfer more than half of their R&D function to countries outside those in which they have their headquarters.

The Investment in R&D

An important contribution to the linkage between research and industry is the existence of spillover effects because knowledge created within an institution spills over for use by other institutions. This is the case with enterprises and academic institutions but also between the research and the industrial sectors. Following Audretsch and Stephan (1996), the empirical evidence clearly suggests that R&D and other sources of knowledge not only generate these externalities. However, some other analysis also suggests that such linkages tend to be geographically bound within the region where the new economic knowledge was created. For the technologically leading countries, increasing high technology competition will mean that investment in human capital and software needs. However, firms from high technology countries will also face specific risks in the sense that higher R&D and software investment increase the sunk costs. The rise of the dynamics of international technology implicates the creation of new fields of technology and the reduction of sunk costs which can create new and improved opportunities for firms and newcomers from other sectors.

In column 4 of Table 20.2 we show the expenses in R&D in US$ per capita for each country. The biggest R&D expenses per capita during 1998 were seen in the USA ($774), Sweden ($734), Switzerland ($710), Japan ($681), Finland ($559), Germany ($527), Denmark ($515), France ($481), Netherlands ($463), Luxemburg ($435), Norway ($418), South Korea ($418), Israel ($399), and United Kingdom ($397).

Foreign Direct Investment

The rapid growth of foreign direct investment (FDI) coming from the activity of MNCs, together with the privatisation, the deregulation of sectors and the removal of barriers to investments, for many countries, creates favourable prospects for higher trade growth and accelerated technology transfer. The ability of a country to accommodate foreign multinational companies is crucial for economic growth and full access to the international trade network, part of which is intra-company trade. In the same sense there is considerable evidence, as in Fujita (1995), that the transnational activities of small enterprises (SMEs) have been increasing over time according to two features that have been shaping the trends in foreign direct investment engaged in by SMEs. The first of these trends is that the share of total foreign direct investment activity accounted for by SMEs remains small in value but large in terms of the number of affiliates. The second trend exhibited in the foreign direct investment activities of SMEs is that they have a greater propensity to choose a host county among the developed countries than do large enterprises. As we can see in Table 20.2 column 6, the top seven net FDI source countries in 1998 were the US with $193.3b, followed by the UK ($63.1b), the Popular Republic of China ($45.4b), The Netherlands ($31.8b), Brazil ($28.7b), France ($28.0b), and Belgium ($20.8b).

Table 20.2   Main indicators of the globalisation in 1990s and disparities

Countries	Production information technology 1997	Internet users thousands 1999	Internet address %/00 inhabitants 1999	R&D(US$) per capita expenditure 1998	Share of trade 1998	Net-direct foreign inv. US$m 1998	Spanish direct inv. in world % 1988-94	Per capita ppp income US$ 1998	Unemployment rate 1998	Pop. millions inhabitant 1999
OECD										
Australia	0.4	3944	42.50	369	42.2	6568	0.0	21949	8.0	18.532
Austria	0.3	779	21.20	351	91.5	5915	0.0	23077	4.8	8.072
Belgium	0.6	1000	20.80	370	141.3	20889	2.2	23242	9.3	10.181
Canada	1.0	5137	36.90	390	79.7	16500	0.0	23761	8.3	30.563
Denmark	0.2	1353	56.30	515	68.6	6623	0.0	25514	5.4	5.284
Finland	0.6	2475	106.00	559	70.8	11115	0.0	20488	14.4	5.140
France	3.5	9959	8.57	481	49.3	28039	5.4	21293	12.3	58.683
Germany	3.9	12727	17.60	527	52.1	6623	1.3	22049	9.8	82.133
Greece	0.0	232	4.85	67	39.7	700	0.1	13912	11.7	10.498
Hungary	0.0	478	9.41	73	102.2	1935	0.0	9875	8.0	10.155
Iceland	0.0	116	89.80	385	72.2	112	0.0	24836	2.7	0.282
Ireland	1.2	403	24.20	287	141.6	6820	0.4	20634	10.3	3.661
Italy	1.8	4038	6.71	223	50.3	2611	5.1	21265	12.3	57.563
Japan	24.5	11768	13.30	681	21.0	3192	0.1	24574	4.9	126.281
Luxemburg	0.0	36	18.30	435	186.4	870	3.6	33119	2.8	0.424
Mexico	0.0	553	1.18	28	64.4	10238	1.7	8454	3.0	93.561
Netherlands	0.9	2766	39.80	463	104.9	31859	10.9	22142	4.0	15.277
New Zealand	0.0	616	35.90	173	57.1	1160	0.0	17846	7.5	3.761
Norway	0.1	1438	71.90	418	75.5	3597	0.0	26771	3.3	4.393
Portugal	0.0	254	5.60	84	71.5	1711	0.0	14562	7.5	9.950
S. Korea	5.4	1099	4.03	418	84.5	5143	15.9	14477	2.6	46.109
Spain	0.8	3600	7.79	156	55.6	11307	–	16502	15.4	39.628
Sweden	1.1	4000	48.5	734	80.6	19358	0.0	20439	8.9	8.848
Switzerland	0.6	1113	34.5	710	75.4	3707	0.0	25902	4.2	7.087
Turkey	0.0	212	0.73	28	53.0	807	0.0	6463	6.6	63.745

Table 20.2 cont'd

Countries	Production information technology 1997	Internet users thousands 1999	Internet address %/00 inhabitants 1999	R&D(US$) per capita expenditure 1998	Share of trade 1998	Net-direct foreign inv. US$m 1998	Spanish direct inv. in world % 1988–94	Per capita ppp income US$ 1998	Unemployment rate 1998	Pop. millions inhabitant 1999
UK	4.2	9311	24.5	397	57.9	63124	6.3	20483	7.1	58.105
USA	30.0	75721	117.00	774	25.6	193375	7.0	29326	4.6	274.028
NO OECD										
Argentina	0.0	333	1.84	48	23.3	5697	5.7	10300	16.3	36.123
Brazil	2.2	1078	1.30	39	17.5	28718	0.9	6480	6.9	165.851
Chile	0.0	151	2.03	59	56.4	4792	1.6	12700	5.3	14.824
China P.R	0.0	780	0.14	16	86.7	45460	0.1	3130	3.0	1255.200
India	0.5	626	0.14	14	24.8	2258	0.0	1670	4.4	982.223
Indonesia	0.7	73	0.07	4	105.6	356	0.0	3490	4.1	206.338
Iran	0.0	14	0.04	28	28.0	300	0.0	5460	4.7	65.758
Israel	0.5	575	19.20	399	75.0	1839	0.0	18150	7.7	5.984
Malasia	3.3	238	2.21	38	207.0	3727	0.0	8140	2.5	21.410
Morocco	0.0	25	0.20	15	44.1	258	0.1	3310	17.8	27.377
Pakistan	0.0	156	0.21	27	36.0	497	0.0	5460	5.4	148.166
Peru	0.0	21	0.19	22	28.7	1930	7.8	4680	7.7	24.797
Russia	0.0	1005	1.24	31	58.5	2183	0.0	4370	13.3	147.434
Singapore	4.8	370	21.20	374	287.2	7218	0.0	28460	2.4	3.476
S. Africa	0.1	717	3.64	52	50.3	371	0.0	7380	5.1	39.357
Taiwan	3.6	1534	14.00	261	49.3	5311	0.0	19870	4.1	21.908
Thailand	1.4	111	0.34	7	101.3	6969	0.0	6690	0.9	60.300
Uruguay	0.0	77	4.68	43	44.4	164	0.3	9200	10.2	3.289
Venezuela	0.0	44	0.37	41	40.1	3737	0.9	8860	10.2	23.242

Sources: International Monetary Fund and United Nations Development Programme.

Table 20.3 Main MNCs by Spanish autonomous community and R&D intensities (1997)

Autonomous communities	Siemens	IBM	ABB	Philips	Hoechst	Sony	Ciba-Geigy	Bosch	Roche	BASF	Sandoz	Sharp	Other MNCs
Andalusia	1												9
Aragon													9
Asturias													6
Balearic Islands													1
Canary Islands													0
Cantabria													7
Castilia-Mancha													3
Castilia-Leon													9
Catalonia	1			1	1	1				1			34
Extremadura													1
Galician Country													4
Madrid	2	1						1	1			1	31
Murcia													1
Navarre							1						6
Basque Country			1										15
Rioja											1		2
Valencia Country													11
R&D Intensities %	9.2	7.1	8.0	6.2	6.2	5.8	10.6	6.7	15.4	4.5	10.4	7.0	
Foreign R&D %	28	55	90	55	42	6	54	9	60	20	50	6	–

Source: Meyer-Krahmer and Reger (2000).

The Rise of the Share of Trade

Studies of national economies as in Engelbrecht (1997) and Helpman (1999) have provided estimates of the extent to which R&D contributes to the total factor productivity of the performing countries. There are two ways in which trade and investment contribute to total factor productivity, firstly, by making available products and services that embody foreign knowledge and secondly, by providing foreign technologies and other types of knowledge that would otherwise be unavailable. One of the most common measures of a globalisation process is the share of trade. Comparing column 5 of Tables 20.1 and 20.2, it can be see that the share of trade rose during the period 1990–1998 in the following countries: Austria, Belgium, Canada, Finland, France, Ireland, Italy, Mexico, Netherlands, South Korea, Spain, Sweden, Turkey, United Kingdom, USA, Argentina, Brazil, India, Indonesia, Iran, Israel, Malaysia, Peru and Thailand.

Experience of Europe

The pre-globalisation period of the third wave began in Europe after World War II. As a response to the economic and military power of North-America and Soviet Union, six European countries initiated the first attempt to build an European integrated market in 1957. This was done by means of the Rome treatise which created the European Common Market (ECM). In the subsequent years the ECM tried to obtain total monetary union and proposed a single currency: the EURO. The Maastricht treatise (1992) which changed the name of the ECM to the European Union (EU) was formed by the following fifteen countries (France, Italy, Belgium, The Netherlands, Luxemburg, Germany, Ireland, Spain, Austria, Portugal, Finland, Greece, United Kingdom, Denmark and Sweden). The same treatise also created European Monetary Union (EMU), which is formed by the first twelve countries of the fifteen members mentioned above. In May 2004 the European Union was extended to twenty-five members. The ten new countries are: Czech Republic, Hungary, Poland, Estonia, Latvia, Lithuania, Slovakia, Slovenia, and two little countries such as Malta and Cyprus. Currently there are advanced negotiations with three other European countries to became full members of the EU in 2007. Those countries are: Rumania, Bulgaria and Croatia.

Although the development of the EU is still not totally finished, the third wave of globalisation is producing very important effects across all European countries even in those that are not included in the system of monetary union. Today the EU continues trying to carry forward the unification process with the aim of creating an integrated market that would, without doubt, amplify the magnitude of the globalisation process.

Facts such as the renaissance of sciences and arts, the creation of the modern concept of state and the discovery of America gave rise to the first wave of globalisation in the modern era which generated a series of small bordering states in the European zone that had similar cultures, technologies and were of a similar size. From this perspective, one can say that Europe was the focus of globalisation in its first wave and although not the focus continues to have an important role. The second wave of globalisation that coincided with the Industrial Revolution, was slowly being felt in other regions, besides Europe, especially in North America with the USA as a leading country. The current wave of globalisation is also generating a new focus of globalisation in the Pacific Rim zone. This is characterised by a careful management of financial markets and production of new technologies controlled by MNCs, which established in regions/zones with high levels of human capital, population density and very low levels of labour costs. In this zone, Japan was the initial leading country with Hong Kong and the rest of China, Singapore, Taiwan, and Malaysia following.

Experience of Spain

The current wave of globalisation is having some effects in Spain which are augmented by the arrival of democracy to the country, its entering of the EU and its system of monetary union which all occurred in a very short period of time. The second wave of globalisation developed the north of the country industrially in detriment to the south with remained un-industrialised. However, the last wave is having an effect on development in the Mediterranean east cost of Spain from Andalusia to Catalonia, and also on the zone of the Ebro river valley. At the moment, this last wave is not generating substantial development in the western regions. As in the rest of the world, the impact in Spain of the last wave of globalisation is basically related to the development of new technologies in the Information Technology sector, the de-centralisation of industry (resulting from the increased role of MNCs), the rise in R&D investment, the increase in foreign direct investment, the rise in capital flow and an increase in the share of trade.

In Spain the most important part of the high technology industries is the sector of information technologies and telecommunications, which, at the beginning of 2000 generated 5.8 per cent of GDP. The privatisation and de-regulation of this sector resulted in spectacular developments in Spanish telecommunications. With respect to the production of information technology, Spain is now one of the fifteen most important countries worldwide (Table 20.2, column 1). A great part of this information technology is produced by firms situated in technology parks.

The pioneer Spanish technological parks were established around the main Universities and include: Zamudio (Bilbao), El Valles (Barcelona) and Tres Cantos (Madrid). In subsequent years many other technology parks have been created. The main technological initiatives in Spain correspond to the sectors of telecommunications, microelectronics, and computers, followed by the air transportation and navigation industries, chemical, electrical machinery and motor vehicle sectors. These last two sectors have been central to the remarkable high-tech advances made in the modernisation of the Spanish railway system, especially the construction of the high speed lines between Madrid and Seville (1992) and in 2004 between Madrid and Lleida (near Barcelona). Spain is now one of the seven countries in the world which have high speed trains that travel at up to 150 miles per hour.

In the last twenty years many foreign multinational companies have been established in Spain and in the last ten years several Spanish MNCs have broken into international markets, especially in Latin America. The internationalisation of Spanish companies happened at the same time as many processes of absorption, fusion and acquisition amongst different enterprises. Although the weight of MNCs in Spanish industry is very important, generally they have still not reached leadership positions in all sectors.

In 1998, Spain was situated in the twenty-fifth position in the ranking of countries for annual R&D investment per capita with US$156, as can be seen in Table 20.2 column 4. From this point of view, Spain can be considered to be a country that has been positively affected by the last wave of globalisation. According to column 1 of Table 20.4, the autonomous community with the largest expenses in this field was Madrid (US$376 annual per capita) followed by the Basque Country ($253) and Catalonia ($234).

The Spanish industrial sector, which receives the biggest amount of foreign direct investment through international technological alliances is the telecommunications sector, followed by the air transport industries, the microelectronic and the biotechnology sector. The seventeen autonomous communities receive different quantities of foreign investment. From 1986 to 1990, the largest percentage of foreign direct investment in Spanish industry (Table 20.4, column 2) was received by Catalonia, followed by Madrid and Andalusia, the Basque Country and Aragon. The communities that receive the biggest percentage of foreign direct investment in the service sector Table 20.4, column 3) are Madrid, followed by Catalonia and Andalusia.

On the other hand the volume invested by Spain in other countries appears in Table 20.2, column 7. We also know that the biggest percentage of Spanish investment going to EU countries between 1988 and 1994 was to: Portugal (15 per cent), The Netherlands (10.9 per cent), United Kingdom (6.3 per cent), France (5.4 per cent), Italy (5.1 per cent) and Belgium (2.2 per cent). The second economic area, which receives Spanish investment, is Latin America.

Concluding Remarks

The last wave of globalisation has affected Spain through two processes, firstly, the worldwide process of globalisation and secondly, the particular process that stems from the European Union. In terms of these twin processes Spain, along with Denmark and France, is among the four countries that fulfil the four globalisation criteria analysed in this chapter. If we consider the main stylised facts of globalisation in the 1990s, at the end of this decade, Spain is among the most affected countries by the globalisation process. It is the sixteenth country in the production of information technology, the twenty-fifth in R&D investment per capita, and the twenty-third in the real income per capita ranking, although its unemployment rate is around the highest. This level of unemployment is due to the hysteresis caused in the labour market by structural change stemming from the pre-globalisation period. In addition to the positive effects of globalisation seen in Spain, it is also necessary to consider several disparities amongst regions that result from this process. In this context it is necessary to remark upon the unequal distribution of the real per capita income, R&D per capita investment, foreign direct investment, and the unemployment rate among the different regions. It is also relevant to note a non-uniform distribution of high-tech sectors among the different regions as a result of which, a small number

Table 20.4   Globalisation and disparities among the Spanish autonomous communities

Autonomous communities	R&D (US$) per capita expenditure 1998	% foreign investment in industry 1986–90	% foreign investment in services 1986–90	Ppp capita income (US$) 1998	GDP growth rate 1987–96	Migration attraction/ expulsion A–1987–E	Nominal wage growth rate 1980–96	Unemployment rate % 1975-87-98	Population millions inhabitants 1999
Andalusia	87	10.3	8.0	12261	8.5	0.08/0.02	8.99	13–30–26	6.87
Aragon	128	4.3	0.3	18779	8.1	0.02/0.04	9.65	2–14–7	1.21
Asturias	80	0.2	0.1	15066	7.0	0.01/0.03	8.68	2–20–17	1.11
Balearic Islands	60	0.2	3.1	22575	8.8	0.00/0.04	9.63	2–14–6	0.75
Canary Islands	85	0.4	1.8	15314	8.9	0.03/0.03	8.16	9–24–15	1.61
Cantabria	137	0.3	0.6	16040	8.4	0.00/0.03	9.73	2–18–15	0.52
Castilia-Mancha	71	0.7	0.1	13565	8.9	0.03/0.05	9.35	8–15–13	1.66
Castilia-Leon	79	2.8	0.3	15000	7.8	0.06/0.05	9.24	3–17–14	2.60
Catalonia	234	37.7	18.2	20561	9.2	0.06/0.04	9.26	2–20–9	5.97
Extremadura	46	0.2	0.0	11518	8.5	0.02/0.04	9.06	7–26–22	1.08
Galician Country	72	1.5	0.4	12822	8.2	0.02/0.01	8.82	4–18–15	2.78
Madrid	376	18.9	57.1	20462	9.1	0.11/0.04	9.38	4–17–12	5.03
Murcia	89	0.4	0.2	14654	8.1	0.01/0.03	8.73	7–19–14	1.01
Navarre	195	1.0	0.7	19951	8.4	0.02/0.04	8.94	5–16–7	0.51
Basque Country	253	4.8	1.4	19489	7.5	0.05/0.05	9.64	2–23–14	2.13
Rioja	100	1.9	0.3	18878	8.5	0.01/0.05	9.82	1–13–8	0.26
Valencia Country	108	3.2	1.5	16320	8.2	0.06/0.06	8.89	3–19–15	3.77

Sources: OECD Economic Surveys on Spain, and Villaverde (1992).

of specific areas of the country can be considered to be almost outside the process of globalisation. Faced with globalisation forces the optimal redistributive policy of the central government should be a balance between international and intranational redistributions, a fact that Asian nations must bear in mind.

References

Arrow, K.J. (1962), 'The Economic Implications of Learning by Doing', *Review of Economic Studies*, Vol. 24, pp. 155–73.

Audretsch, D.B. and P.E. Stephan (1996), 'Company-scientist Locational Links: The Case of Biotechnology', *American Economic Review*, Vol. 86, No. 3, pp. 641–52.

Baldwin, R.E. and P. Martin (1999), 'Two Waves of Globalisation: Superficial Similarities, Fundamental Differences', NBER Working Paper No. 7784, National Bureau of Economic Research.

Barreiro-Pereira, F. (1998), 'Spatial Effects on Economic Equilibrium', *Regional Science Review*, Vol. 18, pp. 13–30.

Barro, R. (1997), *Determinants of Economic Growth: A Cross-country Empirical Study*, The MIT Press, Cambridge, MA.

Baumol, W.J. (1952), 'The Transactions Demand for Cash: An Inventory Theoretic Approach', *Quarterly Journal of Economics*, Vol. 66, pp. 545–56.

Engelbrecht, H.J. (1997), 'International R&D Spillovers, Human Capital, and Productivity in OECD Economies: An Empirical Investigation', *European Economic Review*, Vol. 41, pp. 1479–88.

Froot, K., M. Kim and K. Rogoff (1995), 'The Law of One Price over 700 Years', NBER Working Paper No. 5132, National Bureau of Economic Research, Cambridge, MA.

Fujita, M. (1995), 'Small and Medium-size Transnational Corporations: Trends and Patterns of Foreign Direct Investment', *Small Business Economics*, Vol. 7, No. 3, pp. 183–204.

Grossman, G. and E. Helpman (1994), 'Endogenous Innovation in the Theory of Growth', *Journal of Economic Perspectives*, Vol. 8, pp. 23–44.

Helpman, E. (1999), 'R&D and Productivity: The International Connection', in Assaf Razin and Efraim Sadka (eds), *The Economics of Globalisation*, Cambridge University Press, Cambridge, MA, pp. 17–30.

International Monetary Fund (1999), *International Financial Statistics Yearbook 1999*, IMFS, Washington, DC.

Meyer-Kramer, F. and G. Reger (2000), 'European Technology Policy and Internationalization', in J. Molero (ed.), *Competencia Global y Cambio Tecnológico*, Pirámide, Madrid, pp. 31–70.

OECD (2000), *Spain 1999–2000*, OECD Economic Surveys.

O'Rourke, K. and G. Williamson (2000), 'When Did Globalisation Begin?', NBER Working Paper No. 7632, National Bureau of Economic Research, Cambridge, MA.

Rauch, J.E. and A. Casella (1998), 'Overcoming Informational Barriers to International Resource Allocation: Prices and Group Ties', NBER Working Paper No. 6627, Cambridge, MA.

Rauch, J.E. and V. Trindade (2000), 'Information and Globalisation: Wage Co-movements, Labor Demand Elasticity, and Conventional Trade Liberalization', NBER Working Paper No. 7671.

Romer, P. (1990), 'Endogenous Technological Change', *Journal of Political Economy*, Vol. 98, pp. 71–102.

Samuelson, P. (1952), 'Spatial Price Equilibrium and Linear Programming', *American Economic Review*, Vol. 42, pp. 283–303.

Small, K. and C. Winston (1999), 'The Demand for Transportation', in J.G.-Ibañez, W.B. Tye and C. Winston (eds), *Essays in Transportation Economics and Policy*, Brooking Institute Press, New York, pp. 11–56.

Tobin, J. (1956), 'The Interest Elasticity of Transactions Demand for Cash', *Review of Economic Studies*, Vol. 25, pp. 241–7.

United Nations (1999), *Statistical Yearbook 43 Issue*, United Nations, New York.

United Nations (2000), *United Nations Development Programme 2000*, Communications Development Incorporated, New York.

Villaverde, J. (1992), *Los desequilibrios regionales en España*, Instituto de Estudios Economicos, Madrid.

Williamson, J.G. (2000), 'Land, Labor and Globalisation in the Pre-industrial Third World', NBER Working Paper No. 7784, National Bureau of Economic Research, Cambridge, MA.

Postscript

Economics of Globalisation:

Partha Gangopadhyay and Manas Chatterji

The preceding chapters have examined diverse themes associated with the notion of globalisation. Yet, we see a string of unifying ideas that have emerged to bind these diverse issues into a cohesive form. We will now analyse these ideas to conclude the edited volume on the economics of globalisation.

Issues Concerning Global Trade

We begin with one of the greatest trade theorists, Murray Kemp, who examines the conventional wisdom that development and economic progress proceed at a higher rate in open economies than in closed economies. Does free trade enhance the welfare of a nation? His chapter addresses this issue in the light of the gains-from-trade propositions. He re-examines his comprehensive proof of gains-from-trade propositions under the assumptions of complete markets, coexistence of all agents, convexity of preferences and production sets, barter system, and also in the absence of market distortions. Earlier, this line of research faced serious challenges from Hart (1975) and Newbery and Stiglitz (1984) among others: Hart shows that competitive equilibrium may be constrained to sub-optimal levels if markets are incomplete. Newbury and Stiglitz evince the possibility of Pareto-inferior free trade in the context of incomplete markets. These findings cast a shadow on the merits of free trade in achieving a Pareto efficient post-trade equilibrium. Kemp highlights how Kemp and Wong (1995), and Kemp and Wolik (1995) demonstrate that the conclusions of gains-from-trade, in the presence of incomplete markets, are still valid. He also stresses his work and other work that show Parato's possibility of harmful free trade. More interestingly, he argues that conclusions about the gains from free trade are valid if international borrowing and lending are unhindered. The upshot is that considerable progress has been made in broadening the context in which international trade is potentially beneficial.

The chapter by Arijit Mukherjee, Sugata Margit and Sarbajit Sengupta examines foreign trade policy when markets are non-competitive and firms are partially foreign-owned. The interesting result is that a larger foreign ownership in exporting firms is likely to enhance welfare of the exporting country. Similarly, a larger foreign ownership in the import-competing firm reduces the welfare of the importing country. In the presence of industrial and trade policies; trade patterns and firm values are shown to depend on the shareholding patterns between competing countries.

The chapter by Prabal Ray Chaudhuri and Uday Sinha generalises the 'cross-hauling' model of Brander (1981). They establish that cross-hauling and reciprocal dumping are very likely if the monopoly mark-up exceeds the per unit transport cost. They further relate the level of cross-hauling to movement in international incomes. This result sheds light on cross-hauling trade during global booms and recessions. Specific conditions are derived to establish that cross-hauling trade will run counter to the business cycle.

Trans-border trade is typically propelled by large oligopolistic firms. These firms are often unionised. A serious concern in this context is to understand the role of profit sharing between the union and the firm on market share rivalry. Subhayu Bandyopadhyay and Sudeshna Bandyopadhyay look at the welfare implications of unionisation in a trade model with market imperfections. They argue that the magnitude of the effect of foreign subsidisation on the domestic wage (so called 'wage effect') will determine the direction of the domestic welfare effect. If a unionisation parameter raises the absolute value of the wage effect, then domestic welfare is positively associated with the unionisation parameter. They show that while profit sharing raises domestic welfare under free trade, it paradoxically reduces welfare in a policy equilibrium.

Globalisation and a New Era of Global Interdependence

As one of the leading thinkers Paul Krugman raises a poignant question about the inevitability of financial crises as a by-product of the increased integration of the global economy through trade and investment. He provides a compelling story about the gradual evolution of the global economy that culminates in the 1990s as a global system. He argues that this global system is characterised by a serious fragility that can cascade into deep financial crises in the event of adverse real shocks. He also considers various policy measures to attenuate and eliminate financial crises.

The vulnerability of a nation to financial crises, Krugman argues, is typically evaluated in the 1980s as a function of its openness to trade. It is widely held that a nation's openness to trade reduces the likelihood of financial crises. The conventional wisdom is that countries with a given GDP/debt ratio are less likely to get caught up in the crises, the higher the ratio of exports to GDP. The implicit model is that an open economy has greater credibility in repaying debts. International lending agencies pay heed to this credibility and lend funds to these countries to tide them over during financial crises. Thus, by opening to trade, a country commits to a greater cost of trade disruption and thereby signals its high credibility to the financial markets. Such high credibility acts as protection against crises. The Asian crisis of 1997 has caused a major change in this kind of reasoning: high ratios of exports to GDP fail to deter crises. What went wrong in Asia? An answer to this question leads to the latest modelling of the Asian crisis.

Economists tend to entertain two distinct lines of reasoning to explain the Asian crises. It is widely viewed as an inevitable and predictable endgame in a process of excessive borrowing and investment. On the other hand, it is also viewed as a product of a temporary lapse into a bad equilibrium in an inherently fragile system. There is an increased trust in the explanation of some kind of self-fulfilling panic. The vulnerability of an economy to such panic is typically viewed as a result of two types of mismatches – debt maturity mismatch and currency mismatch.

The story subsumes that crises are generated by a self-fulfilling process of capital flight, and by sudden balance-sheet collapse. The key ingredients for the crises are threefold. The first, vulnerability of countries to capital flight, exists because there is a large pool of potentially mobile funds. Secondly, firms are vulnerable to balance-sheet calamity, because they have large debts in foreign currency. Finally, one may highlight the psychology of investors who can get caught up in the individually rational – but collectively disastrous – panic. He also provides a detailed list of policy prescriptions to fight financial crises.

The most important insight of his analysis is the rationale behind the increased vulnerability of globalised nations. With increased globalisation, nations have liberalised their exchange market along with many other parts of their economy, and are successful in achieving high growth through increased productivity and expansion of non-traditional exports. This success attracts considerable foreign investment. Some of this investment is direct, but there have also been huge financial inflows, mainly loans to domestic firms in foreign denominations. A considerable proportion of domestic lending is also denominated in foreign currency. The result is that an economy – that is doing much better in good times – gets more vulnerable to sudden crises. Bad news and rumours can have disastrous consequences.

The most poignant question is, 'why does a nation get caught up with such vulnerability?' The fact of the matter is that these economies now have significant potential gains from trade in the global economy due to increased integration and foreign investment. These gains are not fully exploited by control mechanisms. Thus, the cost of maintaining control, which can deter crises, is too expensive since such control interferes with trade flow and discourages multinational enterprise. By removing such control, these nations attempt to gain a bigger share of the global market. But by doing so, they make themselves vulnerable to financial crises.

Jeffrey Sachs, one of the most accomplished modern economists, looks into the causes of the Asian crises in the preface. His fundamental point is that what we see in Asia is not the result of the 'sins' of the Asian economies, but has a lot more to do with the structure and operation of the current global economic system as a whole.

These economies were highly regarded by the international community almost until the moment of collapse. They were not pariahs, shunned for their corruption and cronyism and national mismanagement. Their economic success attracted widespread attention from overseas investors – the five worst hit countries attracted $527b of cross-border lending up to the point of the crisis. The key point is that two-thirds of the loans were short-term loans, typically maturing in less than a year. This made the system extremely volatile, since the system is prone to sharp reversals when lenders' expectations change.

At the same time, many of these nations were pegging their exchange rates for the US dollar. As a result, their exchange rates were getting overvalued and investors began to gradually withdraw money from these countries. Central banks started lowering reserves to maintain the parity. This is where the crises unfolded, with self-fulfilling panic by lenders. The IMF also fuelled this self-fulfilling prophecy of doom, as the IMF's rhetoric was quite dramatic: '[the] situation is much worse than you think, this is crony capitalism of the worst form'. The recommended measures by IMF also added fuel to the panic. The downturn is believed to be temporary, because it is caused by a gamut of events leading to a panic and not due to fundamental weaknesses of these economies.

Iwan Azis looks at the Asian crisis to understand the appropriateness of policy responses to a crisis. On the advice and insistence of the IMF, these affected nations adopted a policy mix of credit tightening and fiscal restraints. This policy prescription seems to have derived from the IMF's successful experience of handling the Latin American crisis. But the pre-crisis situation was very different in Asia from that of Latin America, mainly in terms of inflation, budget deficit and the balance of payments and nature of debts.

Beyond the standard policy, the IMF also insisted on rather drastic and fundamental changes in economic and institutional structures. The IMF experience with policy adjustments in Eastern Europe and the former Soviet block had inspired the IMF to initiate the same policy package for East Asian nations. Azis used a particular method to measure the effectiveness of the IMF's policies.

The finding is enormously interesting: the initial analysis, before the events took place, suggests that the IMF policies were meant to be effective. The post-factual analysis, however, suggests the opposite. The upshot is that, in a relatively short time, it is difficult for the IMF to carefully design and systematically prescribe a set of policies for the countries affected by this severe crisis. In light of this inability, Azis looks for a set of optimal policy measures.

Diffusion of Economic Cultures, Models, Ideas and Institutions and their Homogenisation and Convergence

Globalisation is viewed as a process involving the spread of market, investment and technology. As David Colander aptly puts it: 'the dynamics of trade and specialisation lie at the foundation of globalisation'. Thus the process of globalisation cannot be understood by the syntactic concept of equilibrium that is the dominant tool of analysis in deductive economic reasoning. The end state of the dynamic process, or *escatology*, will fail to shed any light since the dynamic path of the global economy entails a significant amount of complexity. The perspective of viewing globalisation as a dynamic process will have far-reaching ramifications. Colander sets the perspective of viewing globalisation as a process of dynamic growth that is subject to thermodynamic turbulence.

Colander provides a robust foundation for this perspective. He argues that this perspective of globalisation will have a positive impact on economic science, as the profession will have to analyse the dynamics of growth as opposed to their focus on static efficiency. The upshot is that the dynamic of growth is capable of generating all sorts of complexities, and what are most likely to emerge from globalisation are uneven paths of development and growth for nations. Path-dependency, geo-specific virtuous and vicious cycles of growth and economic progress will surface in the global economy. Colander provides a compelling story of the impact of dynamic growth on prospects for the US economy, the economics profession, and economics' geographic centre of gravity.

A key aspect of globalisation is the gradual convergence of ideologies and beliefs mainly in the value of a market economy and free trade system. The direct consequence of this convergence has created an insatiable demand for the privatisation of state-owned enterprises and the liberalisation of prices. There is little analysis of the role of the government in the transition to the market economy. Mike Intriligator effectively argues that globalisation is an important aspect of the new world system and will shape the future of our planet. He highlights three salient aspects of globalisation. Firstly, he calls forth the need to clarify the notion of globalisation as it is generally applied to the world economy. Secondly, he evaluates the potential benefits and costs of globalisation. Finally, he examines the mechanism of international cooperation and new global institutions that are necessary to mitigate the costs, or damages, stemming from globalisation.

David Andersson and Åke Andersson expound that globalisation cannot be simply viewed as a process of increasing reliance on cross-border trade. Such a one-dimensional approach is incorrect because it fails to capture the spatial integration of the global production structure and trade flows. In a model that captures quantitative as well as spatial degree of expansion of global production and trade, they argue that the process of globalisation depends on scale economies of globalised production with decreasing transport and other spatial transaction costs.

In the global economy, they show that the long-run prices of goods and factors tend to be established at the minimum of the sum of average production, transport and transaction costs. An improvement in network capacity and a corresponding decrease of transport and transaction costs will therefore lead to a further exploitation of increasing returns to scale by globalisation. Thus, the future path of globalisation will hinge on the transition phase of networks modelled in the chapter.

Globalisation and Labour Market

Peter Nijkamp, van Delft, van veen-Groot argue that globalisation and mobility are interconnected phenomena. Globalisation would have remained a cherished goal unless the mobility of people and goods became feasible at a reasonable cost. Modern transport networks have created conditions for unprecedented local and global mobility. However, the greater freight movement and personal mobility have caused strains on the capacity of transport infrastructure.

In previous eras, public authorities have responded to such increases in demand by adjusting the supply of infrastructure. But such an option has a diminished scope, due to ecological and economic reasons. The success of future globalisation will depend on a successful utilisation of advanced means of communication by the new information technology sector as well as through the integration of disjointed transport systems.

In a two-sector model involving the North and the South, Amitava K. Dutt examines the impact of labour flows on growth and inequality in the global economy. If globalisation is a process of growth and change, it is inevitable that the complex path of the global economy will be intimately bound with geographically uneven growth, prosperity, and cascading crises.

Dutt emphasises the flow of labour in the globalisation process. He argues that the process of globalisation has only triggered transborder flows of goods and investment while labour flows between countries, and especially between the North and the South, are insignificant. The migration has been restricted primarily to skilled labour.

He provides a compelling model to examine labour flows from the South to the North – both for skilled and unskilled labour – to understand the effect of such labour flows on economic growth and income distribution in the North and the South. The finding is two-fold and crucial for understanding the process of globalisation. Firstly, increased skill labour flows from the South to the North will increase the wage of unskilled workers in the North and reduce it for the South. It will increase inequality in the South and reduce inequality in the North. The impact of such migration on wages of skilled labour in the North and the South is unclear. Secondly, such migration will exacerbate inequality between the North and the South, as per capita income will fall in the South while rising in the North.

Keith Lehrer analyses the extent to which non-economic forces need to be addressed in order to explain the duress of low-paid workers in low-technology industries worldwide. His argument turns on the pivot that market forces, free trade, and globalisation do not operate in a vacuum. Economists tend to blame these forces as responsible for the below-poverty level of pay and inhuman conditions of millions of vulnerable workers.

He recommends that we must identify the roles of international organisations and institutions within a global framework in order to redress the global inequity and poverty. The failure to achieve equity must be examined in light of the dynamics of power among international actors and the behaviour of organisations and institutions.

Globalisation and Governance

Riccardo Cappellin examines the process of international integration by multinational firms. His main question is, 'what is the ideal approach to the governance of the globalisation process?' Cappellin highlights economic development in a model of territorial networks and examines the role of institutions in a bottom-up approach to integration. He explores the structural evolution in the organisation of multinational firms and stresses the importance of the concept of network evolution, as opposed to the traditional concept of market competition. He further explores the role of local institutions in the development of the firm. He considers a model of territorial networks and the multidimensional nature of the process of integration. Finally he examines international integration in the light of the proposed model. He recommends the adoption of a federalist, or a regionalist approach in the governance of the globalisation to tackle the problem from the bottom up, rather than wait for the un-probable establishment of supranational institutions. The major obstacle to the regional, or federal, approach remains in the old-fashioned nationalistic ideologies.

To prevent crises, collapses, and over-exploitation associated with the dynamic growth path of the global economy, it is necessary to introduce appropriate regulatory mechanisms. Richard Damania argues that regulatory policies require government agencies to monitor the degree of compliance. The problem here is that these tasks are normally delegated to bureaucrats who are driven by self-seeking motives that result in corruption.

He sketches a strategy that can prevent corrupt behaviour by generating sufficient uncertainty about returns from corruption. Damania argues that regulatory policies call forth an enforcement mechanism that requires government agencies to monitor the degree of compliance. Since these tasks are typically delegated to bureaucrats who are actuated by self-love, it is likely that the delegation can lead to corrupt behaviour among law enforcers. The problem worsens when governments (the principal) are imperfectly informed about the degree of compliance while the bureaucrats (agents) are fully informed. Damania etches out a strategy on behalf of the regulator that can successfully thwart such principal-agent problems if there is sufficient uncertainty about returns from corruption.

Globalisation and Implications for Financial Markets

Debasis Bandyopadhyay argues that the received doctrine in financial development is that a lower share of government ownership in the domestic financial induces greater efficiency and promotes a higher growth rate. His study does not find any strong support for this conclusion in the economies of APEC. Bandyopadhyay shows that a greater degree of privatisation with a high interest rate, under the philosophy of financial repression, has not improved overall efficiency. However, the growth has been stimulated when interest rates declined with an increased access of a country to international markets. Thus, the growth in the Asia-Pacific economies can be sustained so long as the region has access to international credit markets. Thus, the key to sustained economic growth and progress lies in the access of a country to international credit markets.

The internationalisation of production operations and increased flows of foreign direct investment have meant that companies are increasingly subject to risks associated with exchange rate movements. Robert Grant and Luc Soenen posit that the most important component of global business is the exposure to exchange risk. They identify three components of foreign exchange exposure: direct operating exposure, the market demand effect, and the competitive effect. The size and relative importance of these components depend upon international market structures and firm strategies. This work unravels a very important link between the market structure and exchange rate risks, and highlights that the conventional financial instruments for hedging foreign exchange risks are ineffective in managing operating exposures. As a result, the policy prescription for firms operating in global industries is to emulate the currency cost structure of the competitor.

Problems and Prospects of Globalisation

Peter Forsyth argues that globalisation breaks down barriers between nations and brings previously distant countries together. The driving force behind globalisation is the steady decline in transaction costs of conducting business between nations. One can see that costs of communications, costs of capital flows, and transport costs have fallen over time.

He focuses on the falling transport costs over the centuries that resulted in the increased scope for and intensification of trade between nations. The major catalyst is the post war development of air transport whilst the role of air transport is to facilitate globalisation. It is also imperative to appreciate that aviation has emerged as a global industry. Cheap and reliable air transport has led to the creation and consolidation of the movement of people and the international tourism industry.

Forsyth discusses the economic ramifications of aviation as a globalising force for a small open economy like Australia. The crux of his argument turns on the important observation that the aviation industry has failed to be global due to rampant regulations and state-owned airlines. Until recently, it was next to impossible for foreign interests to invest in an international airline of another country.

In recent years, there is a wind of change as economic forces are gently pushing airlines to be more global while governments have been deregulating the industry. Airline regulation, flight regulation and home country policies prevent them from becoming global. A consequence of these regulations is that limited competition results in low productivity and high prices. The aviation industry, however, is becoming more integrated as airlines around the world are strategising their alliances to form global union.

At the same time, governments are more amenable to liberalise, due to a gradual consolidation of market ethos in the global economy and also to look after consumer interests. The result has been the widespread and meaningful liberalisation of the industry over the past decade, which can significantly lower the costs of air transport and thereby facilitate the process of globalisation.

Neil Warren examines ramifications of the Internet revolution for national governments, international agencies and international businesses. He argues that the Internet will provide the catalyst for a significant change in the role of international agencies such as the WTO, OECD, IMF, World Bank and the ILO. He persuasively argues that new international agencies will need to be developed for tax cooperation, consumer protection and for monitoring environmental degradation. His final message is that the Internet is a force with which nations must learn to live while nations have yet to reach a consensus about how to respond to the fundamental challenges posed by the Internet.

Tapani Köppä argues that the revival of cooperation in the 1990s can be seen as a solution to recent shortcomings of the market mechanism and public sector institutions. In Finland, cooperation has gained a significant momentum among its people for addressing the challenges of globalisation and liberalisation in Finland. The necessity of collective action at the grassroot level is fast becoming a powerful weapon, but cooperation is a precarious enterprise in the absence of a commitment device.

Fernando Barreiro-Pereira and Francisco Mochón argue that the growth in international interdependence due to globalisation could be highly asymmetric, causing some disparities, which would explain why small countries are generally less exposed to the international economy than large countries. They offer a picture of such asymmetries in the context of Spanish experiences of globalisation.

Additional References

Hart, O.D. (1975), 'On the Optimality of Equilibrium when the Market Structure is Incomplete', *Journal of Economic Theory*, Vol. 11, pp. 418–43.

Newbery, D.M.G and J.E. Stiglitz (1984), 'Pareto Inferior Trade', *Review of Economic Studies*, Vol. 51, pp. 1–12.

Index